SECRETS
OF
HEAVEN

SECRETS

OF

HEAVEN

The Portable New Century Edition

EMANUEL SWEDENBORG

Volume 8

Translated from the Latin by Lisa Hyatt Cooper

SWEDENBORG FOUNDATION

Royersford, Pennsylvania

Originally published in Latin as *Arcana Coelestia,* London, 1749–1756. The volume contents of this and the original Latin edition, along with ISBNs of the annotated version, are as follows:

Volume number in this edition	Text treated	Volume number in the Latin first edition	Section numbers	ISBN (hardcover)
1	Genesis 1–8	1	§§1–946	978-0-87785-486-9
2	Genesis 9–15	1	§§947–1885	978-0-87785-487-6
3	Genesis 16–21	2 (in 6 fascicles)	§§1886–2759	978-0-87785-488-3
4	Genesis 22–26	3	§§2760–3485	978-0-87785-489-0
5	Genesis 27–30	3	§§3486–4055	978-0-87785-490-6
6	Genesis 31–35	4	§§4056–4634	978-0-87785-491-3
7	Genesis 36–40	4	§§4635–5190	978-0-87785-492-0
8	Genesis 41–44	5	§§5191–5866	978-0-87785-493-7
9	Genesis 45–50	5	§§5867–6626	978-0-87785-494-4
10	Exodus 1–8	6	§§6627–7487	978-0-87785-495-1
11	Exodus 9–15	6	§§7488–8386	978-0-87785-496-8
12	Exodus 16–21	7	§§8387–9111	978-0-87785-497-5
13	Exodus 22–24	7	§§9112–9442	978-0-87785-498-2
14	Exodus 25–29	8	§§9443–10166	978-0-87785-499-9
15	Exodus 30–40	8	§§10167–10837	978-0-87785-500-2

ISBN of e-book of library edition, vol. 8: 978-0-87785-735-8

ISBN of Portable Edition, vol. 8, containing translation only: 978-0-87785-435-7

ISBN of e-book of Portable Edition, vol. 8: 978-0-87785-730-3

(The ISBN in the Library of Congress data shown below is that of volume 1.)

Library of Congress Cataloging-in-Publication Data

Swedenborg, Emanuel, 1688–1772.
  [Arcana coelestia. English]
  Secrets of heaven / Emanuel Swedenborg ; translated from the Latin by
Lisa Hyatt Cooper. — Portable New Century ed.
    p. cm.
  Includes bibliographical references and indexes.
  ISBN 978-0-87785-408-1 (alk. paper)
  1. New Jerusalem Church—Doctrines. 2. Bible. O.T. Genesis—Commentaries—Early works to 1800. 3. Bible. O.T. Exodus—Commentaries—Early works to 1800. I. Title.
  BX8712.A8 2010
  230'.94—dc22

2009054171

Ornaments from the first Latin edition, 1749–1756
Text designed by Joanna V. Hill
Senior copy editor, Alicia L. Dole
Typesetting by Mary M. Wachsmann and Sarah Dole
Cover design by Karen Connor
Cover photograph by Magda Indigo

Further information about the New Century Edition of the Works of Emanuel Swedenborg can be obtained directly from the Swedenborg Foundation, 70 Buckwalter Road, Suite 900 PMB 405, Royersford, PA 19468 U.S.A.
Telephone: (610) 430-3222 • Web: www.swedenborg.com • E-mail: info@swedenborg.com

Contents

Volume 8

Genesis Chapter 44

Conventions Used in This Work

MOST of the following conventions apply generally to the translations in the New Century Edition Portable series. For introductory material on the content and history of *Secrets of Heaven,* and for annotations on the subject matter, including obscure or problematic content, and extensive indexes, the reader is referred to the Deluxe New Century Edition volumes.

Volume designation *Secrets of Heaven* was originally published in eight volumes; in this edition all but the second original volume have been divided into two. Thus Swedenborg's eight volumes now fill fifteen volumes, of which this is the eighth. It corresponds to approximately the first half of Swedenborg's volume 5.

Section numbers Following a practice common in his time, Swedenborg divided his published theological works into sections numbered in sequence from beginning to end. His original section numbers have been preserved in this edition; they appear in boxes in the outside margins. Traditionally, these sections have been referred to as "numbers" and designated by the abbreviation "n." In this edition, however, the more common section symbol (§) is used to designate the section numbers, and the sections are referred to as such.

Subsection numbers Because many sections throughout Swedenborg's works are too long for precise cross-referencing, Swedenborgian scholar John Faulkner Potts (1838–1923) further divided them into subsections; these have since become standard, though minor variations occur from one edition to another. These subsections are indicated by bracketed numbers that appear in the text itself: [2], [3], and so on. Because the beginning of the first *subsection* always coincides with the beginning of the *section* proper, it is not labeled in the text.

Citations of Swedenborg's text As is common in Swedenborgian studies, text citations of Swedenborg's works refer not to page numbers but to section numbers, which unlike page numbers are uniform in most editions. In citations the section symbol (§) is generally omitted after the title of a work by Swedenborg. Thus "*Secrets of Heaven* 29" refers to section 29 (§29) of Swedenborg's *Secrets of Heaven,* not to page 29 of any edition.

Subsection numbers are given after a colon; a reference such as "29:2" indicates subsection 2 of section 29. The reference "29:1" would indicate the first subsection of section 29, though that subsection is not in fact labeled in the text. Where section numbers stand alone without titles, their function is indicated by the prefixed section symbol; for example, "§29:2".

Citations of Swedenborg's unnumbered sections Some material in *Secrets of Heaven* was not given a section number. Swedenborg assigns no section numbers to his quoting of a biblical chapter before he takes up each verse in turn. He also gives no section numbers to occasional prefatory material, such as his author's table of contents in *Secrets of Heaven* (before §1), his prefaces to Genesis 16 and 18 (before §§1886 and 2135, respectively), and his preface to Genesis 22 (before §2760). The biblical material needs no section number, as it is referred to simply by chapter and verse. In this edition, references to the author's unnumbered prefaces follow these models: "(preface to Genesis 22)"; "see the preface to Genesis 18."

Citations of the Bible Biblical citations in this edition follow the accepted standard: a semicolon is used between book references and between chapter references, and a comma between verse references. Therefore "Matthew 5:11, 12; 6:1; 10:41, 42; Luke 6:23, 35" would refer to Matthew chapter 5, verses 11 and 12; Matthew chapter 6, verse 1; Matthew chapter 10, verses 41 and 42; and Luke chapter 6, verses 23 and 35. Swedenborg often incorporated the numbers of verses not actually represented in his text when listing verse numbers for a passage he quoted; these apparently constitute a kind of "see also" reference to other material he felt was relevant. This edition includes these extra verses and also follows Swedenborg where he cites contiguous verses individually (for example, John 14:8, 9, 10, 11), rather than as a range (John 14:8–11). Occasionally this edition supplies a full, conventional Bible reference where Swedenborg omits one after a quotation.

Quotations in Swedenborg's works Some features of the original Latin text of *Secrets of Heaven* have been modernized in this edition. For example, Swedenborg's first edition generally relies on context or italics rather than on quotation marks to indicate passages taken from the Bible or from other works. The manner in which these conventions are used in the original suggests that Swedenborg did not belabor the distinction between direct quotation and paraphrase; but in this edition, directly quoted material is indicated by either block quotations or quotation marks, and paraphrased material is usually presented without such indicators. In passages of dialog as well, quotation marks have been introduced that were not present as such in the original. Furthermore, Swedenborg did not mark his omissions from or changes to material he quoted, a practice in which this edition generally follows him. One exception consists of those instances in which Swedenborg did not include a complete sentence at the beginning or end of a Bible quotation. The omission in such cases has been marked in this edition with added points of ellipsis.

Grammatical anomalies Swedenborg sometimes uses a singular verb with certain dual subjects such as love and wisdom, goodness and truth, and love and charity. The wider context of his works indicates that his reason for doing so is that he understands the two given subjects as forming a unity. This translation generally preserves such singular verbs.

Italicized terms Any words in indented scriptural extracts that are here set in italics reflect a similar emphasis in the first edition.

Special use of vertical rule The opening passages of the early chapters of *Secrets of Heaven,* as well as the ends of all chapters, contain material that derives in some way from Swedenborg's experiences in the spiritual world. Swedenborg specified that the text of these and similar passages be set in continuous italics to distinguish it from exegetical and other material. For this edition, the heavy use of italic text was felt to be antithetical to modern tastes, as well as difficult to read, and so such passages are instead marked by a vertical rule in the margin.

Changes to and insertions in the text This translation is based on the first Latin edition, published by Swedenborg himself (1749–1756); it also reflects emendations in the third Latin edition, edited by P. H. Johnson, John E. Elliott, and others, and published by the Swedenborg Society (1949–1973). It incorporates the silent correction of minor errors, not only in the text proper but in Bible verse references and in section references to this and other volumes of *Secrets of Heaven.* The text has usually been changed without notice where the verse numbering of the Latin Bible cited by Swedenborg differs from that of modern English Bibles. Throughout the translation, references or cross-references that were implied but not stated have been inserted in brackets; for example, [John 3:27]. In many cases, it is very difficult to determine what Swedenborg had in mind when he referred to other passages giving evidence for a statement or providing further discussion on a topic. Because of this difficulty, the missing references that are occasionally supplied in this edition should not be considered definitive or exhaustive. In contrast to such references in square brackets, references that occur in parentheses are those that appear in the first edition; for example, (1 Samuel 30:16), (see §42 above). Occasionally square brackets signal an insertion of other material that was not present in the first edition. These insertions fall into two classes: words likely to have been deleted through a copying or typesetting error, and words supplied by the translator as necessary for the understanding of the English text, though they have no direct parallel in the Latin. The latter device has been used sparingly, however, even at the risk of some inconsistency in its application. Unfortunately, no annotations concerning these insertions can be supplied in this Portable edition.

Biblical titles Swedenborg refers to the Hebrew Scriptures as the Old Testament and to the Greek Scriptures as the New Testament; his terminology has been adopted in this edition. As was the custom in his day, he refers to the Pentateuch (Genesis, Exodus, Leviticus, Numbers, and Deuteronomy) simply as "Moses"; for example, in §5335:2 he writes, "It is put this way in Moses," and then quotes a passage from Numbers. Similarly, in sentences or phrases introducing quotations he sometimes refers to the Psalms as "David," to Lamentations as "Jeremiah," and to the Gospel of John, the Epistles of John, and the Book of Revelation as simply "John." Conventional references supplied in parentheses after such quotations specify their sources more precisely.

Problematic content Occasionally Swedenborg makes statements that, although mild by the standards of eighteenth-century theological discourse, now read as harsh, dismissive, or insensitive. The most problematic are assertions about or criticisms of various religious traditions and their adherents—including Judaism, ancient or contemporary; Roman Catholicism; Islam; and the Protestantism in which Swedenborg himself grew up. These statements are far outweighed in size and importance by other passages in Swedenborg's works earnestly maintaining the value of every individual and of all religions. This wider context is discussed in the introductions and annotations of the Deluxe edition mentioned above. In the present format, however, problematic statements must be retained without comment. The other option—to omit them—would obscure some aspects of Swedenborg's presentation and in any case compromise its historicity.

Allusive References in Expositional Material

Swedenborg's use of pronouns that refer back to vague or distant antecedents may cause confusion for readers. Such allusive references occur in two situations in his expositions:

In mentions of Jesus If the pronoun *he* without a nearby antecedent appears in a proposition, the reader can assume that it refers to Jesus, the main topic of the exegesis as a whole.

In preview material Swedenborg's preview sections (see the Deluxe edition of *Secrets of Heaven,* vol. 1, pages 30–35) feature a series of propositions, each of which consists of a phrase of biblical text followed by a brief assertion of its inner meaning. These glimpses of the inner meaning quite often use pronouns that point back to other inner meanings mentioned earlier in the preview section. For instance, in *Secrets of Heaven* volume 7, §4962, a preview section, we read this:

> *And Joseph* symbolizes spiritual heavenliness drawing on rationality. *Was taken down to Egypt* means to religious learning. *And Potiphar, Pharaoh's chamberlain, bought him* means that **it** had a place among items of inner knowledge. *The chief of the bodyguards* means **that** were of primary importance in interpretation. *An Egyptian man* symbolizes earthly truth.

The words "it" and "that" (shown here in boldface) are confusing: *What* had a place among items of inner knowledge? *What things* were of primary importance in interpretation? The answers lie in the fragments of inner meaning given in propositions earlier in the preview section: The "it" refers back to the "spiritual heavenliness" mentioned in the first proposition. The referent of "that" is the "items of inner knowledge" mentioned at the end of the immediately preceding proposition. Thus Swedenborg has laid the propositions out in such a way that if put together, the five statements might read as follows:

> *And Joseph was taken down to Egypt, and Potiphar, Pharaoh's chamberlain, the chief of the bodyguards, an Egyptian man, bought him* means that spiritual heavenliness drawing on rationality was brought to religious learning and given a place among items of inner knowledge and earthly truth that were of primary importance in interpretation.

Secrets
of
Heaven

First seek God's kingdom and its justice
and you will gain all.

—Matthew 6:33

Genesis 41

1. And it happened at the end of two years of days that Pharaoh was dreaming, and look: he was standing by the river.

2. And look: from the river, seven cows coming up, of beautiful appearance and fat flesh, and they grazed in the reeds.

3. And look: seven other cows coming up after them from the river, of poor appearance and thin flesh, and they stood next to the cows on the bank of the river.

4. And the cows of poor appearance and thin flesh ate the seven cows of beautiful appearance and fat [flesh]. And Pharaoh woke up.

5. And he fell asleep and dreamed a second time, and look: seven ears of grain coming up on one stalk, fat and good.

6. And look: seven ears of grain thin and scorched by an east wind, sprouting after them.

7. And the thin ears swallowed up the seven ears fat and full. And Pharaoh woke up, and look: it was a dream.

8. And it happened in the morning that his spirit was shaken, and he sent and called all the magicians of Egypt and all its sages, and Pharaoh told them his dream, and there was no one interpreting the [dreams] for Pharaoh.

9. And the chief of the cupbearers spoke with Pharaoh, saying, "My sins I remember today.

10. Pharaoh was enraged over his servants and put me in jail in the house of the chief of the bodyguards—me and the chief of the bakers.

11. And we dreamed a dream one night, I and he; each according to the interpretation of his own dream we dreamed.

12. And there with us was a Hebrew youth, slave to the chief of the bodyguards, and we told him, and he interpreted our dreams for us; for each according to his own dream he interpreted.

13. And it happened that, as he interpreted for us, so it was; me he returned to my position, and him he hanged."

14. And Pharaoh sent and called Joseph, and they rushed him from the pit, and he cut his hair and changed his clothes and came to Pharaoh.

15. And Pharaoh said to Joseph, "A dream I dreamed, and there was no one interpreting it. And I heard [someone] saying about you that you can listen to a dream to interpret it."

16. And Joseph answered Pharaoh, saying, "Not of myself! God will answer peace, Pharaoh."

17. And Pharaoh spoke to Joseph: "In my dream, there I was, standing by the bank of the river.

18. And look: from the river, seven cows coming up, of fat flesh and beautiful form, and they grazed in the reeds.

19. And look: seven other cows coming up after them, of very skinny and poor form, and scrawny flesh; I have not seen [any] like them in all the land of Egypt for poorness.

20. And the cows scrawny and poor ate the seven earlier, fat cows.

21. And they came into their belly, and one could not tell that they had come into their belly, and their appearance was [as] poor as in the beginning, and I woke up.

22. And I saw in my dream, and look: seven ears of grain coming up on one stalk, full and good.

23. And look: seven ears of grain dried up, thin, and scorched by an east wind, sprouting after them.

24. And the thin ears swallowed up the seven good ears. And I told [the dreams] to the magicians, and there was no one pointing out [the meaning] to me."

25. And Joseph said to Pharaoh, "Pharaoh's dream is one; what God is doing he has told to Pharaoh.

26. The seven good cows are seven years, and the seven good ears are seven years; the dream is one.

27. And the seven cows thin and poor coming up after them are seven years, and the seven empty ears scorched by an east wind will be seven years of famine.

28. This word that I have spoken to Pharaoh, which God is doing, he has caused Pharaoh to see.

29. Watch: seven years are coming, a great abundance of grain provisions in all the land of Egypt.

30. And seven years of famine will rise after them, and the whole abundance of grain provisions in the land of Egypt will be forgotten, and the famine will consume the land.

31. And abundant grain provisions will not be known in the land afterward in view of this famine, because it will be very heavy.

32. And about the dream's being repeated to Pharaoh two times—[it is] because the word has been set by God and God is hurrying to do it.

33. And now let Pharaoh look for a man understanding and wise, and put him over the land of Egypt.

34. Let Pharaoh act and put officers in charge over the land and take one fifth from the land of Egypt in the seven years of abundant grain provisions.

35. And let them gather all the food of those coming good years, and pile up the grain under Pharaoh's hand—the food, in the cities—and guard it.

36. And let the food serve as a store for the land for the seven years of famine that will occur in the land of Egypt, and the land will not be cut off in the famine."

37. And the word was good in the eyes of Pharaoh and in the eyes of all his servants.

38. And Pharaoh said to his servants, "Shall we find another like this man, in whom there is the spirit of God?"

39. And Pharaoh said to Joseph, "Now that God has caused you to know all this, no one is understanding and wise like you.

40. You will be over my house, and with [the words of] your mouth all my people will comply; only in relation to the throne will I be greater than you."

41. And Pharaoh said to Joseph, "See? I have put you over all the land of Egypt."

42. And Pharaoh removed his ring from his hand and put it on Joseph's hand and dressed him in clothes of fine linen and put a gold necklace on his neck.

43. And he caused him to ride in the second chariot that was his—and they shouted "Abrech!" before him—putting him over the whole land of Egypt.

44. And Pharaoh said to Joseph, "I am Pharaoh; other than you, no man will lift his hand or his foot in all the land of Egypt."

45. And Pharaoh called Joseph's name Zaphenath-paneah and gave him Asenath, daughter of Potiphera (priest of On), as his woman. And Joseph went out over the land of Egypt.

46. And Joseph was a son of thirty years when he stood before Pharaoh, monarch of Egypt, and Joseph went out from before Pharaoh and crossed into all the land of Egypt.

47. And the earth made heaps in the seven years of abundant grain provisions.

48. And he gathered all the food of the seven years that they had in the land of Egypt and put the food in the cities; the food from the city's field that was all around it he put in the middle of it.

49. And Joseph piled up grain like the sand of the sea, very much of it, until he ceased to count, because there was no number for it.

50. And to Joseph were born two sons, before the year of the famine came, whom Asenath, daughter of Potiphera (priest of On), bore him.

51. And Joseph called the name of the firstborn Manasseh "because God has made me forget all my toil and all my father's house."

52. And the name of the second he called Ephraim "because God has made me fruitful in the land of my affliction."

53. And the seven years of abundant grain provisions that were in the land of Egypt were completed.

54. And the seven years of the famine started to come, as Joseph had said, and there was famine in all lands, but in all the land of Egypt there was bread.

55. And all the land of Egypt was starving, and the people shouted to Pharaoh for bread, and Pharaoh said to all Egypt, "Go to Joseph; what he says to you, you are to do."

56. And the famine was on the whole face of the earth, and Joseph opened everything in which [there was grain] and sold to Egypt, and the famine grew strong in the land of Egypt.

57. And all the earth came to Egypt to buy, to Joseph, because the famine grew strong in all the earth.

Summary

5191 THE inner meaning of this chapter has to do with a second stage for the spiritual heavenliness that is Joseph. In this stage it is elevated over the contents of the earthly, outer self and therefore over all the knowledge there (meant by Egypt).

Pharaoh means the earthly plane in general, which has now begun to  rest, leaving everything to the spiritual heavenliness that is Joseph. The seven years of abundant grain provisions in the land of Egypt mean types of information to which the goodness that grows out of spiritual heavenliness can be attached. The seven years of famine mean types of information belonging to a subsequent stage, when they are devoid of goodness, except for the goodness that grows out of divine spiritual heavenliness, which comes from the Lord's divine humanity. These ideas are discussed in detail below.

5192

Inner Meaning

G ENESIS 41:1, 2, 3, 4. *And it happened at the end of two years of days* **5193** *that Pharaoh was dreaming, and look: he was standing by the river. And look: from the river, seven cows coming up, of beautiful appearance and fat flesh, and they grazed in the reeds. And look: seven other cows coming up after them from the river, of poor appearance and thin flesh, and they stood next to the cows on the bank of the river. And the cows of poor appearance and thin flesh ate the seven cows of beautiful appearance and fat [flesh]. And Pharaoh woke up.*

And it happened at the end of two years of days means after a state of union. *That Pharaoh was dreaming* symbolizes what was provided for the earthly level. *And look: he was standing by the river* means from one boundary to the other. *And look: from the river* means on the boundary. *Seven cows coming up* symbolizes there was earthly-level truth. *Of beautiful appearance* symbolizes the kind of truth connected with faith. *And fat flesh* symbolizes the kind connected with neighborly love. *And they grazed in the reeds* symbolizes instruction. *And look: seven other cows coming up after them from the river* symbolizes falsity on the earthly plane, also on the boundary. *Of poor appearance* symbolizes the kind not connected with faith. *And thin flesh* means or with neighborly love. *And they stood next to the cows on the bank of the river* means that it stood on the outer bounds, where truth was. *And the cows of poor appearance and thin flesh ate* means that falsity unconnected with faith and charity would abolish . . . *The seven cows of beautiful appearance and fat [flesh]* symbolizes truth on the earthly plane connected with faith and charity. *And Pharaoh woke up* symbolizes an enlightened state.

5194   *And it happened at the end of two years of days* means after a state of union—union between sensations on the outer earthly level and sensations on the inner earthly level, which are discussed in the previous chapter [§5077]. This can be seen from the symbolism of *two years of days* or a two-year period as a state of union. *Two* symbolizes union (§§1686, 3519), and *years* and *days* symbolize states. (For this symbolism of years, see §§487, 488, 493, 893; and for that of days, §§23, 487, 488, 493, 2788, 3462, 3785, 4850.)

Two symbolizes union because absolutely everything in the spiritual world and consequently in the physical world relates to two things, goodness and truth. It relates to goodness as its active, inflowing element, and to truth as its passive, receptive element. Since everything relates to these two, and no fruit is ever produced unless the two become one through something akin to a marriage, two symbolizes union.

[2] Something akin to a marriage exists in every part of nature and its three kingdoms. Without it, nothing whatever comes into being. For something to emerge in the realm of nature, there must be warmth and light. Warmth in the physical world corresponds to love and its goodness in the spiritual world, while light corresponds to faith and its truth. These two, warmth and light, must act as one if they are to produce anything. If they fail to act as one, as happens in wintertime, nothing at all comes of them. The same holds true spiritually, as is plain from humankind. Human beings have two faculties, the will and the intellect. Our will is designed to take in spiritual warmth, or a loving, charitable goodness, and our intellect to receive spiritual light, or faith's truth. Unless these two form a single unit in us, they produce nothing. Love and its goodness without faith and its truth does not give shape or quality to anything, while faith and its truth without love and its goodness does not accomplish anything. In order for us to take part in the heavenly marriage, then, or to have the heavenly marriage in us, the two must be unified in us.

That is why the ancients used a simile of marriage in regard to each and every thing in the world, and each and every thing in a person (§§54, 55, 568, 718, 747, 917, 1432, 2173, 2516, 2731, 2739, 2758, 3132, 4434, 4835, 5138).

All this shows why two symbolizes union.

That Pharaoh was dreaming symbolizes what was provided for the **5195** earthly level, as the following shows: *Pharaoh* represents the earthly dimension, as discussed at §§5079, 5080, 5095, 5160. And *dreaming* symbolizes a prediction of the future and therefore, in the highest sense, foresight, as discussed at §§3698, 4682, 5091, 5092, 5104. Since it symbolizes foresight, or what is foreseen, it also symbolizes providence, or what is provided, since one cannot exist without the other. Providence looks to a succession of states to eternity; and it cannot provide for this if it does not foresee it. To provide for the present without foreseeing the future is to fail to provide for the future in the present, and this would be pointless, reckless, and therefore lacking in wisdom and understanding. So it would not come from the Divine.

However, providence applies to what is good, and foresight to what is not good (§5155). Foresight cannot apply to what is good, because goodness exists in the Divine; it comes into being from the Divine and in keeping with the Divine. No, foresight applies to what is not good and to evil, because this comes into being outside the Divine, from others who oppose the Divine. Consequently, since providence is associated with goodness, it is associated with the union between earthliness and spiritual heavenliness— the theme of the current chapter. In this case, then, dreaming symbolizes what was provided.

And look: he was standing by the river means from one boundary to **5196** the other. This can be seen from the symbolism of a *river*—here, the river of Egypt, or the Nile—as a boundary. A river means a boundary because major rivers (the Euphrates, the Jordan, and the Nile) and the sea were the outer bounds of the land of Canaan. Canaan itself represented the Lord's kingdom, so all locations in it represented features of that kingdom. The rivers accordingly represented its outermost parts, or boundaries; see §§1866, 4116, 4240.

The Nile, the river of Egypt, represented sensations under the control of the intellectual side of the mind and therefore pieces of information gleaned from those sensations because these are the outermost spiritual entities of the Lord's kingdom.

This phrase means from one boundary to the other because Pharaoh is the person said to be standing by the river, and he represents the earthly plane as a whole (§5160). To take a view of anything from its inner level to its outermost level is represented as standing by the outermost part.

That is what is done in the spiritual world. One then takes a view from border to border, so this is the symbolism of the clause in an inner sense.

5197   *And look: from the river* means on the boundary. This is established by the symbolism of a *river* as a boundary (discussed just above in §5196). *From the river* means on the boundary because that is where [the cows] appeared.

5198   *Seven cows coming up* symbolizes there was earthly-level truth. This can be seen from the symbolism of *cows* as truth on the earthly level (discussed below). There were *seven* because seven symbolizes holiness (§§395, 433, 716), and the number therefore adds a holy quality to the matter under discussion (§881). The subject discussed here is holy anyway, because it is the further rebirth of the earthly level through its union with spiritual heavenliness.

The symbolism of female cattle old or young as truth on the earthly plane can be seen from the symbolism of male cattle old and young as goodness on the earthly plane (§§2180, 2566, 2781, 2830). In the Word, wherever a male symbolizes goodness, the female symbolizes truth, and the reverse: where a male symbolizes truth, the female symbolizes goodness. So it is that a cow symbolizes truth on the earthly level, since a bull symbolizes goodness there.

[2] All animals named in the Word symbolize desires. Bad, useless animals symbolize negative desires, but gentle, useful ones symbolize positive desires; see §§45, 46, 142, 143, 246, 714, 715, 719, 776, 1823, 2179, 2180, 3218, 3519. This symbolism is due to representations in the world of spirits. When heaven's inhabitants talk about desires, animals are represented in the world of spirits, and the animals correspond to the kind of desires being talked about. This I have often been allowed to see. Sometimes I wondered why it was, but I perceived that the life force in an animal is nothing but desire. Animals are led by their desires instinctually, without the use of reason, and this leading directs them each to their role. No other bodily form matches these unreasoning desires than the kind animals have on earth. As a result, when the conversation is strictly about desires, the desires present themselves in an outermost form that resembles the form of body these animals have. Those desires can be clothed only in shapes that correspond to them.

I have also seen strange beasts that exist nowhere in the world. They were produced by unknown desires and mixed emotions.

[3] As a consequence, animals in the Word symbolize desires, but which specific desires can be seen only from the inner meaning. For the symbolism of bulls as goodness on the earthly plane, look in the sections

cited above. The symbolism of cows as truth on the earthly plane can be seen from passages mentioning them, such as Isaiah 11:7; Hosea 4:16; Amos 4:1. It can also be seen from the [sin] removal water used for cleansing people, made from a *red cow* burned to ash outside the camp, with cedar wood, hyssop, and double-dyed scarlet mixed in (Numbers 19:2–10). Using the inner meaning to unlock the mystery of this procedure shows that a red cow symbolizes unclean truth on the earthly plane that is cleansed by fire and by the qualities that cedar wood, hyssop, and double-dyed scarlet symbolize. The water therefore represented a means of purification.

Of beautiful appearance symbolizes the kind of truth connected with faith. This can be seen from the symbolism of *beauty* and *appearance.* Spiritual beauty is a desire for inner truth, and a spiritual appearance is faith, so *of beautiful appearance* symbolizes a desire for the truth connected with faith (see §§553, 3080, 3821, 4985).

The reason spiritual beauty is a desire for inner truth is that truth is the form of goodness. Goodness itself from the Divine in heaven is the source of life for angels, but the form of their life comes through truth rising out of that goodness. It is not faith's truth that creates beauty, though, but the desire within that truth, and desire stems from goodness. Beauty resulting merely from religious truth resembles the beauty of a face that has been drawn or carved, but beauty resulting from the kind of desire for truth that springs from goodness resembles the beauty of a living face animated by heavenly love. The nature of the love or desire beaming from the form of the face determines the nature of the beauty.

That is why angels look indescribably beautiful. From their faces shines love's goodness expressed through faith's truth. Not only do this goodness and truth present themselves before the eyes, they are also perceived from the auras the angels give off. The reason this is the source of their beauty is that the whole of heaven is a universal human and corresponds to each and every thing in a human being. Anyone with a loving goodness and consequently with religious truth, then, is in the form of heaven. Such a person possesses beauty, and the beauty contains heaven, where divine energy from the Lord is the all-in-all.

For the same reason, the inhabitants of hell are horribly ugly, since they oppose what is good and true. In heaven's light they look like monsters rather than people.

The reason spiritual appearance—the way something looks spiritually— is faith is that to look and see in an inner sense is to understand. In a still

5199

deeper sense it is to believe. See §§897, 2150, 2325, 2807, 3863, 3869, 4403–4421.

5200   *And fat flesh* symbolizes the kind [of truth] connected with neighborly love, as the following shows: *Fat* symbolizes something heavenly and applies to the goodness connected with love and charity, as discussed in §353. And *flesh* symbolizes a will brought to life by goodness from the Lord, as discussed in §§148, 149, 780, 999, 3812, 3813. So it too symbolizes the goodness connected with love and charity. It follows, then, that since "of beautiful appearance" symbolizes something connected with faith, *of fat flesh* symbolizes something connected with neighborly love. The two phrases describe truth on the earthly plane (symbolized by the cows) in terms of its form and its essence. Its form consists of elements relating to faith, and its essence, of elements relating to neighborly love. The literal meaning does not make it clear that this is so.

5201   *And they grazed in the reeds* symbolizes instruction. This can be seen from the symbolism of *grazing* as being taught (discussed below) and from that of *reeds*—relatively large grasses growing near rivers—as items of information for the earthly self. The meaning of grass as items of information is clear from the Word. Grazing in the reeds accordingly means being taught information and learning from it about truth and goodness. Items of information are a means and resemble a mirror that reflects something deeper. This reflection in turn acts as a mirror presenting and representing religious truth and goodness and therefore features of heaven, which are referred to as spiritual. However, this reflection, being interior, appears only to people who have faith because they have neighborly love. That is what *grazing in the reeds* symbolizes in its genuine sense.

[2] Passages in the Word mentioning grazing show that it means being taught. In Isaiah, for example:

> And he will give rain for the seed with which you sow the land, and bread from the produce of the land, and there will be fat and richness; your livestock will *graze* that day *in a broad meadow*. (Isaiah 30:23)

The livestock stand for people with goodness and truth. Grazing in a broad meadow stands for receiving abundant instruction. [3] In the same author:

> I gave you as a pact with the people, to restore the earth, to apportion devastated inheritances, to say to prisoners, "Go on out!"; to those in

darkness, "Show yourselves!" *On paths they will graze,* and on all the slopes will be their *pasture.* (Isaiah 49:8, 9)

This is about the Lord's Coming. Grazing on paths stands for being taught truth (paths meaning truth; see §§627, 2333). The pasture stands for the actual instruction. In Jeremiah:

> Doom to *shepherds* destroying and scattering the flock of *my pasture!* Therefore Jehovah, God of Israel, has said against the *shepherds shepherding my people,* . . . (Jeremiah 23:1, 2)

The shepherds stand for people who teach, and the flock, for people who are taught (§§343, 3795), so shepherding stands for teaching. It has become customary to refer to teachers as shepherds and to the people who learn from them as a flock. [4] As a result, when people talk about preaching or about instruction from doctrine or the Word, one standard word they use for it is *pastoring.* They use the term as a metaphor, though, not a symbol, as the Word does. Why is it used as a symbol in the Word? In the world of spirits, spiritual things appear in an earthly form, and when heaven's inhabitants talk about instruction and about doctrine from the Word, there appear in the world of spirits visual representations of meadows, green with grass and flowers and dotted with flocks. The image varies widely, depending on what is being said in heaven about instruction and doctrine. [5] In the same author:

> I will return Israel to its dwelling place to *graze* in Carmel and Bashan, and on the mountain of Ephraim and in Gilead their soul will receive its fill. (Jeremiah 50:19)

Grazing in Carmel and Bashan stands for learning about the goodness belonging to faith and charity. In the same author:

> From the daughter of Zion has departed all her honor. Her chieftains have become like deer; they have not found *pasture.* (Lamentations 1:6)

In Ezekiel:

> *In a good pasture I will pasture them,* and on the mountains of Israel's loftiness will be their *fold,* and they will lie in a *good fold,* and *rich pasture they will graze,* on Israel's mountains. (Ezekiel 34:14)

[6] In Hosea:

> Now Jehovah will *pasture* them like a sheep in a broad place. (Hosea 4:16)

Pasturing an animal in a broad place stands for teaching someone truth. For the meaning of breadth as truth, see §§1613, 3433, 3434, 4482. In Micah:

> You, Ephratean Bethlehem—from you one will emerge for me who will be a ruler in Israel; he will stand and *shepherd* in the strength of Jehovah. (Micah 5:2, 4)

In the same author:

> *Shepherd your people* with your rod, the flock of your inheritance living alone; let them *graze* in Bashan and Gilead as in the days of old. (Micah 7:14)

In Zephaniah:

> The survivors of Israel will *graze* and lie down, and none will terrify them. (Zephaniah 3:13)

[7] In David:

> Jehovah is *my shepherd.* He will make me lie down in *grassy pastures;* he will lead me to quiet waters. (Psalms 23:1, 2)

In the same author:

> He made us—his people and the *flock of his pasture*—and not we ourselves, so we are his, his people and the flock of his *pasture.* (Psalms 100:3)

In Revelation:

> The Lamb who is in the middle of the throne will *pasture them* and lead them to lively springs of water. (Revelation 7:17)

In John:

> I myself am the doorway; if any come in through me, they will be saved, and go in and out, and *find pasture.* (John 10:9)

In the same author:

> Jesus said to Peter, "*Pasture* my lambs." And a second time, "*Pasture* my sheep." And a third time, "*Pasture* my sheep." (John 21:15, 16, 17)

5202   *And look: seven other cows coming up after them from the river* symbolizes falsity on the earthly plane, also on the boundary, as the following shows: *Cows* symbolize truth on the earthly plane, as discussed just above at §5198, so in a negative sense they symbolize falsity. Most objects in the Word also have a negative meaning, which can be recognized from the positive meaning. Since cows in a positive sense mean truth on the earthly level, then, in a negative sense they mean falsity of the same kind and therefore falsity on the earthly level. And a *river* symbolizes a boundary, as also discussed above, at §§5196, 5197. The fact that the falsity was on the outer bounds can also be seen from the statement that the cows *came up* from the river, because "coming up" is an expression used for advancement from outer to inner levels (§§3084, 4539, 4969).

[2] As this idea is the theme of what follows, I should say something about it. The previous chapter spoke of the outer earthly plane and about the contents of that plane belonging to the category of the intellect and the contents belonging to the category of the will [§§5077–5078]. The first category was accepted; the second, rejected [§§5165, 5167]. The cupbearer represented what belonged to the category of the intellect, and the baker represented what belonged to the category of the will. What belonged to the intellect was accepted, so it also submitted to the inner earthly level. That is what the previous chapter was about, and this was the first stage in the rebirth of the earthly plane.

[3] The current chapter is about the inflow of spiritual heavenliness into the elements of the earthly plane that were kept—that is, into elements of the earthly plane's intellectual side. That is what the cows of beautiful appearance and fat flesh symbolize. The rebirth of the earthly plane cannot involve only intellectual traits, though. There have to be traits of will too. Everything has to contain something of the intellect and something of the will in order to be anything. And since the will in its previous form was rejected, a new will must flow in instead. The new will comes from spiritual heavenliness, and spiritual heavenliness and its inflow into the earthly dimension is the subject of the current chapter. The inner meaning describes the situation of the earthly dimension in this state, which is that the truth there was abolished by falsity, and the earthly dimension was therefore left to spiritual heavenliness. The symbolic imagery for this situation is the seven good cows eaten by the bad ones and the full ears of grain swallowed up by the empty ones, followed by Joseph's oversight of all Egypt. More will be said about all this below, with the Lord's divine mercy.

[4] These concepts are not readily accessible to the light of the human intellect. They are the secrets of rebirth, which are countless in any case,

and we know hardly any of them. A person with goodness is being reborn every second, from infancy to the end of life in the world and on to eternity. This rebirth involves not only the inner levels but the outer levels as well and is accomplished by astounding processes. Most of an angel's wisdom has to do with such processes, and everybody knows that angelic wisdom is ineffable, containing what ear has not heard and eye has not seen and what has never entered human thought. The Word's inner meaning deals with these subjects and is therefore suited to angelic wisdom. When it flows down into the literal meaning, it becomes suited to human wisdom and secretly touches the hearts of people who sincerely long to know truth from the Word.

5203   *Of poor appearance* symbolizes the kind not connected with faith, which can be seen from the symbolism of the phrase "of beautiful appearance" as the kind connected with faith (discussed above in §5199). *Of poor appearance* therefore symbolizes something unconnected with faith.

5204   *And thin flesh* means or with neighborly love. This can be seen from the symbolism of the phrase "of fat flesh" as the kind connected with neighborly love (also discussed above, in §5200). *Of thin flesh,* then, means the kind unconnected with neighborly love, since they are opposites.

5205   *And they stood next to the cows on the bank of the river* means that it stood on the outer bounds, where truth was. This can be seen from the symbolism of *standing next to something on the bank of the river* as being on the boundary, a river meaning a boundary (see §§5196, 5197), and from that of *cows* as truth on the earthly plane (discussed above at §5198).

What does it mean to say that falsity stood on the outer bounds, where truth was? This will become clear later—specifically, when it comes time to explain what is symbolized on an inner level by the famine of seven years in the land of Egypt, predicted and symbolized by the seven cows of poor appearance and thin flesh and by the seven ears of grain thin and scorched by an east wind [§§5207, 5270, 5280, 5376].

5206   *And the cows of poor appearance and thin flesh ate* means that falsity unconnected with faith and charity would abolish . . . , as the following shows: *Eating* means destroying, as mentioned in §§5149, 5157. Here it means abolishing, though, because until truth on the earthly level has been brought to life by spiritual heavenliness and therefore been reborn, falsity in effect abolishes or banishes it. *Cows of poor appearance* symbolize what is unconnected with faith, as mentioned just above in §5203. And *of thin flesh* symbolizes what is unconnected with neighborly love, as also mentioned above, in §5204.

The seven cows of beautiful appearance and fat [flesh] symbolizes truth on the earthly plane connected with faith and charity. This is established by the symbolism of *cows* as truth on the earthly level (discussed above at §5198), by that of the phrase *of beautiful appearance* as something connected with faith (discussed at §5199), and by that of *fat* as something connected with neighborly love (discussed at §5200).

To take up the actual subject of truth abolished from the earthly level by falsity on the border: Be aware that this always happens at the start of rebirth. The truth we first absorb is inherently true, admittedly, but it is not true in us until goodness is connected with it. The goodness connected to it is what makes truth true. Goodness is the essence, and truth is its form. Consequently truth has falsity near it to begin with, which is to say that falsity is also present on the border, where truth is. As goodness unites with truth, though, falsity flees. This is what actually happens in the other world, too, where a cloud of falsity foists itself on truth, depending on how strongly goodness influences truth. When goodness has little influence, the cloud of falsity hovers close by. As goodness exerts more influence, the cloud moves farther off, and when goodness forms a solid bond with truth, the cloud disappears entirely. When a cloud of falsity hovers close—which it does in the beginning, as just mentioned— truth seems to be abolished, but meantime it is hiding deep inside, where it becomes filled with goodness and is gradually sent back out. That is what is symbolized by the seven cows and seven ears of grain, and later on by the seven years of abundant grain provisions and seven years of famine.

However, readers who know nothing about regeneration and readers who know nothing about a person's inner state will not grasp these things.

And Pharaoh woke up symbolizes an enlightened state. This is established by the symbolism of *waking up* as being enlightened (mentioned at §3715) and by the representation of *Pharaoh* as the earthly plane (dealt with before). Clearly, then, *Pharaoh woke up* symbolizes a state of enlightenment on the earthly plane.

Enlightenment here means general enlightenment coming from spiritual heavenliness and therefore from within. Enlightenment that originates or flows from inside is vague and general when shed on a lower level. Yet it gradually becomes less general and eventually specific as truth based on goodness is instilled on the lower level. Every bit of truth based on goodness shines and illuminates. That is why I said just above in §5206

5207

5208

that truth is abolished from the earthly level. It is abolished in order for the earthly level to be enlightened in a general way from within. Then, under the glow of this general enlightenment, or broad light, truth can be restored there in its proper pattern, enlightening the earthly level in a detailed way.

[2] Our spiritual and earthly levels, or our inner and outer levels, are brought into correspondence in just this way. First we acquire truth. Then that truth is banished, so to speak, although it is not really banished but only hidden. Next our lower levels are enlightened in a general way by our higher levels, or our outer levels by our inner levels. Under that illumination, truth is restored in its proper pattern. As a result, all individual truths on that level become an image of their general truth and correspond to it.

What is more, in each and every thing that exists, in the physical world as well as the spiritual, the general form comes first. Afterward less general forms are gradually inserted into it and, finally, particular ones. If everything were not inserted or integrated this way, none of it would stick. Whatever is not part of a larger whole and does not depend on a larger whole vanishes; see §§917, 3057, 4269, 4325 at the end, 4329 in the middle, 4345, 4383.

5209   Genesis 41:5, 6, 7. *And he fell asleep and dreamed a second time, and look: seven ears of grain coming up on one stalk, fat and good. And look: seven ears of grain thin and scorched by an east wind, sprouting after them. And the thin ears swallowed up the seven ears fat and full. And Pharaoh woke up, and look: it was a dream.*

And he fell asleep symbolizes a dim state. *And dreamed a second time* symbolizes what is provided. *And look: seven ears of grain coming up on one stalk* symbolizes items of knowledge on the earthly level, bound together. *Fat and good* means that qualities of faith and charity could be incorporated into them. *And look: seven ears of grain thin* symbolizes useless knowledge. *And scorched by an east wind* means full of corrupt cravings. *Sprouting after them* means coming into view nearby. *And the thin ears swallowed up the seven ears fat and full* means that useless knowledge would abolish good knowledge. *And Pharaoh woke up* symbolizes a general state of enlightenment. *And look: it was a dream* means in the dimness.

5210   *And he fell asleep* symbolizes a dim state. This can be seen from the symbolism of *sleeping* as a dim state. In fact, sleep in a spiritual sense is nothing else, just as wakefulness is nothing but a clear state. Spiritual sleep occurs when truth is dim, and spiritual wakefulness, when truth is clear. The state of truth among spirits actually determines how awake or asleep they are. Plainly, then, *falling asleep* means a dim state.

And dreamed a second time symbolizes what is provided. This can be seen from the discussion in §5195 of the symbolism of *dreaming* as what is provided.

5211

And look: seven ears of grain coming up on one stalk symbolizes items of knowledge on the earthly level, bound together. This can be seen from the symbolism of *ears of grain* as items of knowledge on the earthly level (discussed below) and from that of *on one stalk* as bound together. After all, things that are on one stalk are bound together at their source.

5212

Ears of grain symbolize items of knowledge because grain itself symbolizes goodness on the earthly level (§3580). Items of knowledge hold earthly goodness just as ears of grain hold the grain. All truth in general is a container for goodness, so items of knowledge are too, since they are truth at its lowliest. Truth on its lowest level, the outer earthly level, is called knowledge, because it is stored in a person's earthly or outer memory and partakes mostly of the world's light. It can therefore be presented and represented to others in words, or through ideas formed into words dealing with matters of the world and its light.

What the inner memory holds is not called knowledge but truth, so far as it partakes of heaven's light. It can be understood only in heaven's light and expressed only in words or through ideas formed into words dealing with matters of heaven and its light.

The items of knowledge symbolized by these ears of grain are things that are known to the church. To learn about them, see §§4749, 4844, 4964, 4965.

[2] The reason there were two dreams, one about the seven cows and one about the seven ears, is that the inner meaning is dealing with both earthly levels, the inner and outer, and later on, with the rebirth of both. The seven cows symbolize the contents of the inner earthly level, which are called truth on the earthly level (§5198). The seven ears symbolize truth on the outer earthly level, which is called knowledge.

[3] Items of inner and outer knowledge are symbolized by the ears of grain of the river Euphrates to the river of Egypt in Isaiah:

> Again, it will happen on that day that Jehovah will thresh *from the ear of grain of the river [Euphrates] to the river of Egypt,* and you will be gathered one to the other, children of Israel. Again, it will happen on that day that a large horn will be blown, and people perishing in the land of

> Assyria and outcasts in the land of Egypt will come and bow down to
> Jehovah on the holy mountain, in Jerusalem. (Isaiah 27:12, 13)

People perishing in the land of Assyria stand for inner truth, and outcasts
in the land of Egypt, for outer truth, or knowledge.

[4] The simile in Mark of the blade, ear, and grain also has to do with
the rebirth of a human through knowledge, religious truth, and neighborly kindness:

> Jesus said, "This is how it is with God's kingdom: as when you toss seed
> onto the earth, then sleep, and rise night and day, but the seed sprouts
> and grows while you yourself are unaware. For the earth bears fruit on
> its own—first a *blade,* then an *ear,* then the *grain in the ear.* But when
> the fruit is produced, immediately you will send in the sickle, because
> the harvest looms." (Mark 4:26, 27, 28, 29)

God's kingdom, which is compared to a blade, ear, and grain, is the heaven
we have in us through regeneration. People who have been reborn have
God's kingdom in them and turn into an image of God's kingdom, or
heaven. The blade means initial knowledge, the ear means resulting knowledge about truth, and the grain means resulting goodness.

The types of things symbolized by ears of grain were also represented
in the laws laid down *about gleanings* (Leviticus 19:9; 23:22), about the
license people had to *pluck ears* from their companion's crop (Deuteronomy 23:25), and about the ban on eating bread or a *toasted ear* or a *green
one* before they had brought God's offering (Leviticus 23:14).

5213 *Fat and good* means that qualities of faith and charity could be incorporated into them, as the following shows: When the term *fat* applies
to the items of knowledge symbolized by ears of grain, it means that
they are open to faith's goodness and therefore that something of faith
can be incorporated into them. Items of knowledge are containers, and
to describe them as fat is to symbolize their capacity for holding what
comes of a faith based on charity. And when the term *good* applies to the
items of knowledge symbolized by the ears, it means that they are open to
charity's goodness and therefore that something of charity can be incorporated into them.

The association of "fat" with aspects of faith and of "good" with aspects
of charity is due to a custom throughout the Word. Where two adjectives
describe a single object, one involves matters of faith, and the other, matters of charity. This is because of the marriage of truth and goodness in
every part of the Word (§§683, 793, 801, 2173, 2516, 2712, 4137 at the end,

5138). The symbolism of "fat" as aspects of faith and of "good" as aspects of charity is also evident from the earlier parallel regarding the cows (§§5199, 5200).

There are many items of knowledge that can have qualities of faith and charity incorporated into them. One example is all that is known to the church, as symbolized by Egypt in its good sense (discussed at §§4749, 4844, 4964, 4966). Also included, then, are all items of knowledge constituting the truth about correspondence, representation, symbolism, spiritual inflow, the divine design, understanding and wisdom, and desires. The category even includes all truth about nature in its inner and outer dimensions, both visible and invisible, since this truth corresponds to spiritual truth.

And look: seven ears of grain thin symbolizes useless knowledge. This is established by the symbolism of *ears of grain* as items of knowledge (discussed above at §5212) and by that of *thin* as useless. "Thin" is opposite to "full," and something is called full when it has a use—in other words, when it contains goodness. All goodness is useful. "Thin" consequently means useless. **5214**

Items of useless knowledge are ones that have no goal except to bring us glory and sensual pleasure. These goals are useless because they are no help to our neighbor.

And scorched by an east wind means full of corrupt cravings. This can be seen from the symbolism of being *scorched by an east wind* as being consumed by the fire of corrupt cravings. In a positive sense, an east wind and the east itself mean love for the Lord and love for our neighbor (§§101, 1250, 3249, 3708, 3762). In a negative sense, then, they mean love for ourselves and love for worldly advantages, so they mean corrupt passions and cravings, because these are products of such love. Fire is mentioned in connection with them for the reason discussed in §5071, and consequently scorching is also associated with them. **5215**

[2] There are two sources of heat, just as there are two sources of light. One source of heat is the world's sun, and the other is heaven's sun, which is the Lord. Everyone knows that the world's sun sheds warmth on its realm and everything its realm contains. It is not as well known that heaven's sun sheds warmth on all of heaven, but it *can* be known. All that is needed is to reflect on the inner warmth we have within us that shares nothing with the world's warmth—that is, on what is called vital heat. This reflection can lead to the realization that vital heat is something different from the world's heat. Vital heat is alive, and the world's heat is

not a bit alive. Since vital heat is alive, it kindles our inner reaches, or our will and intellect, and enables us to form desires, to love, and to be moved. Longings, loves, and desires are therefore different kinds of spiritual warmth and are referred to as such. It is obvious that they are forms of warmth, because living bodies radiate heat from every pore, even in the coldest weather. In addition, the more the heart swells with longing and desire—that is, with love—the warmer one's body grows.

This warmth is what the Word means by heat, fire, and flame. In a positive sense the warmth is heavenly and spiritual love, and in a negative sense it is body-centered and materialistic love. Clearly, then, being scorched by an east wind means being consumed by the fire of corrupt cravings. When applied to the items of knowledge meant by the thin ears, it just as clearly means that they are full of such cravings.

[3] The symbolism of an *east wind* as gusts of craving and of consequent delusions can be seen from Scripture passages mentioning this wind. In David, for instance:

> He caused an *east wind* to set out in the heavens, and in his strength led a south wind out, and rained flesh on them like dust, the bird with its wing like the sand of the sea. (Psalms 78:26, 27)

The flesh that this wind brought symbolizes cravings, and the bird with its wing symbolizes the delusions that cravings lead to. Moses makes this plain in Numbers 11:31–35, saying that the name of the place where the people suffered a plague for eating flesh "was called the Graves of *Craving*, because there they buried the people who had *felt a craving*." [4] In Ezekiel:

> Look: will the transplanted grapevine prosper? When the *east wind* touches it, won't it *utterly wither*? On the beds of its sprouting it will *wither*. (Ezekiel 17:10)

And in the same author:

> The grapevine was torn out in anger, was tossed onto the earth, and the *east wind dried up* its fruit. All its strong stalks were torn off and *withered*. *Fire* ate up each one, because *fire* issued from a stalk of its branches; it ate up the [vine's] fruit, so that there will not be on it a strong stalk, a scepter for ruling. (Ezekiel 19:12, 14)

This east wind stands for gusts of craving. [5] In Isaiah:

> He meditated on *his hard gale* on the day of an *east wind*. (Isaiah 27:8)

In Hosea:

> An *east wind,* Jehovah's gale, will come rising from the desert, and his fount will *dry up,* and his spring will *evaporate;* he will plunder the treasury of every desirable vessel. (Hosea 13:15)

Again the eastern gale or east wind stands for gusts of craving. Likewise in Jeremiah:

> Like an *east wind* I will scatter them before their enemy. (Jeremiah 18:17)

[6] In David:

> With an *east wind* you will shatter the ships of Tarshish. (Psalms 48:7)

In Isaiah:

> You abandoned your people, the house of Jacob, because they were filled with an *east wind* and are diviners like the Philistines. (Isaiah 2:6)

In Hosea:

> Ephraim is grazing on a breeze and pursues an *east wind;* every day he multiplies lies and devastation. (Hosea 12:1)

The breeze here stands for delusions, and the east wind, for cravings.

The same thing is also meant in an inner sense by the *east wind* that brought out the locusts and then hurled them into the sea (Exodus 10:13, 19) and the one that parted the water of the Suph Sea (Exodus 14:21).

Sprouting after them means coming into view nearby. This can be seen from the symbolism here of *sprouting* as coming into view, and from the meaning of *after them* as nearby, on the border. The same thing is symbolized by the cows poor and thin that came up *after them*—after the cows beautiful and fat (§5202). "After them" means nearby because *after* is next in time. The spiritual world and therefore the spiritual sense lacks any notion of time; time is replaced by a corresponding notion of state.

5216

And the thin ears swallowed up the seven ears fat and full means that useless knowledge would abolish good knowledge, as the following shows: *Thin ears* symbolize useless knowledge, as discussed above in §5214. *Ears fat and full* symbolize items of knowledge that could have qualities of faith and charity incorporated into them, as discussed in §5213, and therefore good knowledge. And *swallowing up* means abolishing, just as "eating" does where it is attributed to the cows, above in §5206. See §5207 for the idea that good knowledge is abolished by useless knowledge, or that truth

5217

is abolished by falsity. That is actually how matters stand in the spiritual world, too. Where there is falsity, truth cannot survive, and in turn where there is truth, falsity cannot survive. The one banishes the other, because they are opposites. The reason is that falsity comes from hell, and truth from heaven.

Sometimes it looks as though one and the same person adopts both truths and falsities, but the falsities in this case are not ones that oppose the truths that person knows. Instead they are associated with those truths through the way they are applied. A person in whom truths coexist with falsities that are opposed to them is called lukewarm. One in whom falsities and truths are mixed together is called profane.

5218   *And Pharaoh woke up* symbolizes a general state of enlightenment, as shown by the explanation above in §5208, where the same words occur.

5219   *And look: it was a dream* means in the dimness. This can be seen from the symbolism of a *dream* as a dim state (discussed at §§1838, 2514, 2528, 5210).

I am using the word "dim" because truth had been banished, and where truth is absent, things are dim. The light of heaven flows only into truth, because heaven's light is divine truth from the Lord. Consequently, truths as they exist with angels, spirits, and people on earth are merely reflectors, but they take their light from divine truth, owing to the goodness in them. Unless truth comes from what is good—that is, unless truth has goodness in it—it cannot receive any light from the Divine. It receives light through what is good. Goodness is like a fire or flame, and truth is like the light radiating from it.

Even truth devoid of goodness glows in the other world, but it glows with a wintry light that turns dark on the approach of heavenly light.

All this shows what is meant here by dimness. It refers to conditions on the earthly plane when good forms of knowledge have been abolished by useless ones. This dimness is a kind that can be lit with a general light (§§5208, 5218), but dimness resulting from falsity cannot be lit at all. Falsities are so many shadows quenching heaven's light and spreading a darkness that cannot be relieved until the falsities have been removed.

5220   Genesis 41:8. *And it happened in the morning that his spirit was shaken, and he sent and called all the magicians of Egypt and all its sages, and Pharaoh told them his dream, and there was no one interpreting the [dreams] for Pharaoh.*

And it happened in the morning means in that new state. *That his spirit was shaken* symbolizes turmoil. *And he sent and called all the magicians of*

Egypt and [all] its sages means in consulting inner and outer knowledge. *And Pharaoh told them [his] dream* means about the future. *And there was no one interpreting the [dreams] for Pharaoh* means that it was not known what would happen.

And it happened in the morning means in that new state. This can be seen from the meaning of *it happened*, which involves something new (as discussed in §§4979, 4987), and from the symbolism of *morning* as an enlightened state (discussed in §§3458, 3723). This state is the new one meant; see the remark about it just above at §5218. The text is talking about this state of enlightenment and its nature, which was turbulent because future events were dim. Hardly anyone can know anything about the nature of this state, though, without being in spiritual surroundings and noticing what goes on deep inside. Otherwise one cannot even know what it is to be enlightened in a general way or in a particular way. In fact, one cannot know what it is to be enlightened at all, let alone that a general state of enlightenment starts with turmoil and that calm does not arrive till truth based on goodness has been restored in its proper pattern.

Angels and even good spirits sense clearly how these matters stand, because they are in an atmosphere that is spiritual. Their wisdom and thoughts on the subject bring them pleasure, but the topic is boring to people in an atmosphere that is earthly. It is even more boring to those immersed in the realm of sense impressions, and more boring still to those immersed in the grossly sensory realm of the flesh and of physical matter.

That his spirit was shaken symbolizes turmoil, which can be seen from the symbolism of being *shaken in spirit* as being in turmoil.

Here as in several other Scripture passages, *spirit* means inner feeling and thought, which are indeed activities of the human spirit. The ancients called these "spirit," but more narrowly by *spirit* they meant the inner self that will live on after the body's death. When the term is used in this sense today, it simply means cogitation, without anything to do the thinking besides the body in which it occurs. This is the modern definition because people no longer believe that the inner self is the actual person. They consider the inner self (which is usually called the soul or spirit) to be pure thought, without any medium adapted to thought. Since they consider the inner self to be thought, without any medium for thought to occur in, they think it will evaporate after bodily death, like a wisp of ether or flame. That is the modern view of the spirit when it is referred to in such phrases as *troubled in spirit, sad in spirit, glad in spirit,*

5221

5222

or *jubilant in spirit.* In reality it is the inner self itself (called the spirit) that is troubled, sad, glad, or jubilant, and this is the self—in a form that is entirely human, even though it is invisible to physical eyes—that does the thinking.

5223 *And he sent and called all the magicians of Egypt and [all] its sages* means in consulting inner and outer knowledge. This can be seen from the symbolism of *magicians* in a positive sense as inner knowledge (discussed below) and from that of *sages* as outer knowledge (also discussed below).

Egypt's magicians and sages symbolize types of knowledge because Egypt was among the kingdoms where the ancient, representative church existed (§§1238, 2385). Egypt specialized in developing the knowledge of that church, which had to do with correspondence, representation, and symbolism. Such knowledge explained what was written in the ancient church's books and what was practiced in its sacred worship (§§4749, 4964, 4966). That is how Egypt ended up symbolizing knowledge in general (§§1164, 1165, 1186, 1462), as did Pharaoh, its monarch.

The leading experts in and teachers of that knowledge were called magicians and sages. Magicians were expert in mystical knowledge, and sages were expert in knowledge that was not mystical, so magicians were expert in inner knowledge, and sages in outer knowledge. That is why such knowledge is symbolized by them in the Word.

However, after they started to misuse the church's inner knowledge and turn it into magic, Egypt started to symbolize the knowledge it had perverted. The magicians of Egypt and its sages had the same symbolism.

[2] The magicians of that era knew about the spiritual world, having learned about it from correspondences and representations known to the church. Many of them therefore communicated with spirits, from whom they learned the deceptive arts they used in performing magic miracles. The ones called *sages,* however, had no interest in such things but solved hard questions and taught about the causes of physical phenomena. These were the main elements of wisdom in that day, and to have an ability with them was called wisdom. What 1 Kings reports about Solomon shows that this is so:

> *Solomon's wisdom* multiplied beyond the *wisdom* of all the children of the east and beyond all the *wisdom of the Egyptians,* so that he was *wise* beyond all people—beyond Ethan the Ezrahite, and Heman and Calcol and Darda, the children of Mahol. He spoke three thousand *proverbs* and his songs were one thousand five. Moreover, he spoke of woods,

from the cedars that are in Lebanon to the hyssop that is growing out of the wall. He also spoke of the animal and of the bird and of the creeping thing and of the fishes. So they came from all the peoples to hear Solomon's *wisdom,* from the side of all the monarchs of the earth who had heard of *his wisdom.* (1 Kings 4:30–34)

The mention of Sheba's queen in the same book also demonstrates it:

She came to test him with *hard questions,* and Solomon told her all she asked; there was nothing hidden from the king, nothing he did not tell her. (1 Kings 10:1 and following verses)

[3] This clarifies how wisdom was defined at the time and who was called a sage, not only in Egypt but also in other places, such as Syria, Arabia, and Babylon. In the inner meaning, though, Egyptian wisdom actually symbolizes the study of earthly matters, and magic symbolizes the study of spiritual matters. Sages accordingly symbolize outer knowledge, magicians symbolize inner knowledge, and Egypt symbolizes knowledge in general (§§1164, 1165, 1186, 1462, 4749, 4964, 4966). That is exactly what Egypt and its sages meant in Isaiah:

Stupid are the chieftains of Zoan; the advice of *Pharaoh's sage advisors* has turned brutish. How can it be said to Pharaoh, "*I am the offspring of sages,* the offspring of the monarchs of old"? Where are your *sages* now? (Isaiah 19:11, 12)

[4] The fact that people adept at spiritual studies and therefore at receiving revelation were called *magi* can be seen from the magi who came from eastern parts to Jerusalem asking where the one born as king of the Jews was and saying they had seen his star in the east and had come to worship him (Matthew 2:1, 2). It can also be seen from Daniel, who is called the *chief of the magi* (Daniel 4:9). And in another place:

The queen said to King Belshazzar, "There is a man in your kingdom in whom is the spirit of the holy gods; and in your father's days, light and understanding and wisdom like the wisdom of the gods was found in him. So King Nebuchadnezzar, your father, set him up as *chief of the magi,* diviners, Chaldeans, and determiners." (Daniel 5:11)

And again:

Of them all there was not found [one] like Daniel, Hananiah, Mishael, and Azariah, for when they stood before the king, in every word of wisdom [and] understanding that the king asked them, he found them ten times *above all the magi,* the diviners, who were in his kingdom. (Daniel 1:19, 20)

[5] In a negative sense magicians mean people who perverted spiritual knowledge and used it to perform magic, as is known. Examples are the people mentioned in Exodus 7:9, 10, 11, 12; 8:7, [18,] 19; 9:11.

Magic was actually a corruption and misapplication of laws governing the spiritual world; that is where magic originated. Nowadays, though, this magic is called physical magic, because no one acknowledges anything above or beyond nature anymore. People deny a spiritual dimension, unless it is defined as a deeper physical dimension.

5224   *And Pharaoh told them [his] dream* means about the future. This can be seen from the symbolism of a *dream* as foresight, a prediction, and the outcome (discussed at §§5091, 5092, 5104), and therefore as the future.

Context shows what is going on here in the inner meaning. The verse is talking about a new state for the earthly level at a point when it is in the dark because truth has been banished from it. The state is one of turmoil for the earthly level in consulting knowledge to learn the future. After all, when we fall into that darkness, we immediately start to wonder what will happen. The experience is common to every dim state we undergo while being reborn, which is why the inner meaning describes the state here.

[2] People do not know about such states these days, though, partly because few regenerate and partly because those who do regenerate do not reflect on the subject. People today do not care what is going on inside them, because superficialities win their undivided attention. When superficialities monopolize our attention—when we make them the goal of our life—deeper matters have no value. Concerning mental darkness, we would say, "What do I care about all that? There's no wealth or prestige in it. Why should I consider whether my soul or inner self enters a dim state when truth is abolished, and whether it enters a clear state when truth is restored to it? What good does it do me to know that? I'm not sure whether there's an inner self, or whether the soul has a different state of existence than the body. I'm not even sure there is such a thing as a soul that survives death. Who has come back from the dead to say?" That is what religious people say to themselves in modern times. That is what they think when they hear or read anything about the state of the inner self. This shows why the things that go on inside a human being now go on in secret and are totally unknown.

[3] The minds of the ancients were never in such darkness. Their wisdom consisted in cultivating their inner depths and perfecting their two faculties of intellect and will as a means of caring for their soul. Their writings that are still extant today make it clear that these were matters of concern to them. Another piece of evidence was the universal desire to hear Solomon:

> *So they came from all the peoples to hear Solomon's wisdom, from the side of all the monarchs of the earth who had heard of his wisdom.* (1 Kings 4:34)

The queen of Sheba came for the same reason, and out of the sense of blessing that Solomon's wisdom brought her she said:

> *Fortunate are your men, fortunate these servants of yours who stand before you always and hear your wisdom!* (1 Kings 10:8)

Who these days would call themselves fortunate on that account?

And there was no one interpreting the [dreams] for Pharaoh means that it was not known what would happen, as the following shows: To *interpret* means to know what will happen, as noted at §5141, so *no one interpreting* means not to know. *No one* negates whatever the inner meaning is talking about, so it means *not.* The concept of person changes into the concept of some attribute in the inner meaning. For instance, the idea of a man, husband, woman, wife, son, daughter, young man, or young woman turns into the idea of something true or good; and as above in §5223, the idea of a magician and sage turns into the idea of inner and outer knowledge. The reason for the change is that in the spiritual world, or heaven, the inhabitants focus on attributes rather than people. Thinking of individual people narrows and limits the mind to something finite; but attributes, rather than narrowing and limiting the mind, widen it to the infinite and therefore to the Lord.

It is for the same reason that when the Word mentions a person, heaven never perceives the person but rather the attribute the person represents. Heaven also never perceives a people or nation but the character of it. In fact, heaven knows nothing whatever of any narrative detail in the Word about a person, nation, or people. Its inhabitants accordingly do not know who Abraham, Isaac, Jacob, the Israelite people, or the Jewish nation were. Instead they perceive *what* Abraham is, what Isaac is, what Jacob is, what the Israelite people are, what the Jewish nation is, and so on. Angels' language as a result is unlimited and almost universal.

5226   Genesis 41:9, 10, 11, 12, 13. *And the chief of the cupbearers spoke with Pharaoh, saying, "My sins I remember today. Pharaoh was enraged over his servants and put me in jail in the house of the chief of the bodyguards—me and the chief of the bakers. And we dreamed a dream one night, I and he; each according to the interpretation of his own dream we dreamed. And there with us was a Hebrew youth, slave of the chief of the bodyguards, and we told him, and he interpreted our dreams for us; for each according to his own dream he interpreted. And it happened that, as he interpreted for us, so it was; me he returned to my position, and him he hanged."*

And the chief of the cupbearers spoke with Pharaoh symbolizes a thought coming from the senses under the control of the intellectual side. *Saying* symbolizes a resulting perception. *My sins I remember today* means concerning a state of disconnection. *Pharaoh was enraged over his servants* means when the earthly part turned away. *And put me in jail in the house of the chief of the bodyguards* symbolizes rejection by [knowledge] of primary importance in interpretation. *Me and the chief of the bakers* symbolizes both kinds of senses. *And we dreamed a dream one night* symbolizes what was foreseen in the dimness. *I and he* means concerning both types of senses. *Each according to the interpretation of his own dream we dreamed* symbolizes the outcome for both. *And there with us was a Hebrew youth* means that the church's guiltlessness was cast there so it could be put to the test. *Slave of the chief of the bodyguards* means it contained truth that served primarily for interpretation. *And we told him* means that it resulted in a perception. *And he interpreted our dreams for us* symbolizes the inner content of what was foreseen in the dimness. *For each according to his own dream he interpreted* means truthfully. *And it happened that, as he interpreted for us, so it was* means that this was how it turned out. *Me he returned to my position* means that sense impressions on the intellectual side were accepted. *And him he hanged* means that sense impressions on the will side were rejected.

5227   *And the chief of the cupbearers spoke with Pharaoh* symbolizes a thought coming from the senses under the control of the intellectual side. This is established by the symbolism of *speaking* as thinking (discussed in §§2271, 2287, 2619) and by the representation of the *chief of the cupbearers* as the senses under the control of the intellectual side (discussed in §§5077, 5082).

For what a thought coming from the senses is, see §5141.

5228   *Saying* symbolizes a resulting perception. This is established by the symbolism of *saying* as perceiving (discussed in §§1791, 1815, 1819, 1822, 1898, 1919, 2080, 2619, 2862, 3395, 3509).

I cannot explain what a perception resulting from thought is in a way that readers will grasp. No one knows what spiritual perception is anymore, and what is unknown does not make sense, no matter how it is described.

Perception is actually the words or thoughts of the angels present with us. When their speech or thought flows into us, it becomes a perception that a thing is either so or not so. The only people it flows into, though, are the ones with a loving, charitable goodness, because it flows in through goodness. In them such perception produces thoughts—perception being the common wellspring of all their thoughts.

However, there is no such thing as perception from thought in actuality, only in appearance.

Nothing more can be said about this secret, though, since (again) no one today knows what perception is.

My sins I remember today means concerning a state of disconnection. This can be seen from the symbolism of *sins* as disorder (discussed at §5076) and from that of *remembering* as uniting (discussed at §5169). *Remembering sins,* then, means uniting with something disorderly and therefore disconnecting from the earthly element that Pharaoh represents. Anything united with what is disorderly disconnects from what is in proper order.

5229

Remembering means uniting because in the next world the remembrance of another person creates a bond. As soon as one spirit recalls another, the other spirit stands present—so directly present that they can talk together. That is why angels and spirits can meet all the people they knew or had heard of, can see them in person, and can talk to them, if the Lord allows them to remember those others (§1114).

Pharaoh was enraged over his servants means when the earthly part turned away, as can be seen from earlier explanations at §§5080, 5081, where similar words occur.

5230

And put me in jail in the house of the chief of the bodyguards symbolizes rejection by [knowledge] of primary importance in interpretation. This too can be seen from earlier explanations, at §§5083, 5084, where similar words occur.

5231

Me and the chief of the bakers symbolizes both kinds of senses. This is established by the representation of the chief of the cupbearers—*me*—as the senses subject to the intellectual side in general (discussed at §§5077, 5082) and by that of the *chief of the bakers* as the senses subject to the will side in general (discussed at §§5078, 5082). *Me and the chief of the bakers,* then, symbolizes both kinds of senses.

5232

I speak of "both kinds" of senses because there are two faculties in us that constitute our life: the will and the intellect. Everything in us relates to them.

The reason there are two faculties in us that constitute our life is that there are two components to the life force in heaven: goodness and truth. Goodness relates to the will, and truth, to the intellect. Plainly, then, there are two elements that make a person spiritual and therefore bless a person in the other life: charity and faith. Charity is goodness, and faith is truth. Charity relates to the will, and faith to the intellect.

[2] What is more, absolutely everything in the material world relates to these two, goodness and truth. That is what everything emerges from and is sustained by. The fact that everything relates to these two is obvious from warmth and light. Warmth relates to goodness, and light to truth, so spiritual warmth is a loving goodness, and spiritual light is faith's truth.

Since everything in the whole material world relates to these two, goodness and truth, and goodness is represented in warmth, while faith is represented in light, you may judge for yourself what we are like as a result of faith alone without charity—in other words, from simply understanding truth without forming any good intent. Surely we resemble wintry conditions, in which light shines but everything languishes because it lacks warmth. That is the state we are in when we have faith alone and lack a loving goodness. We are in the cold and the dark—in the cold, because we oppose goodness, and in the dark, because we consequently oppose truth. After all, when we oppose goodness, we also oppose truth, however much it may seem to us that we do not. The one drags the other over to its side. Such is our state after death.

5233   *And we dreamed a dream one night* symbolizes what was foreseen in the dimness. This can be seen from the symbolism of a *dream* as what was foreseen (dealt with at §§3698, 5091) and from that of *night* as a state of shadow (dealt with in §1712) and therefore as dimness.

5234   *I and he* means concerning both types of senses. This can be seen from the representation of the cupbearer—*I*—as one type and from that of the baker—*he*—as the other, both discussed just above at §5232.

5235   *Each according to the interpretation of his own dream we dreamed* symbolizes the outcome for both. This is established by the symbolism of *interpretation* as the content and what would happen (noted at §§5093, 5105, 5107, 5141) and therefore as the outcome—an outcome based on foresight, which is what the *dream* symbolizes (§5233).

And there with us was a Hebrew youth means that the church's guilt-   **5236**
lessness was cast there so it could be put to the test. This can be seen from
the symbolism of a *youth* as guiltlessness (discussed below) and from that
of a *Hebrew* as someone in the church (discussed at §5136) and therefore
as a quality of the church. Joseph was cast there in order to be tested, and
this is symbolized by his being *there,* in jail. The jail to which he was sent
symbolizes a state of trial (§§5036, 5037, 5039, 5044, 5045); this was the
subject of Genesis 39 and 40.

[2] A *youth* means guiltlessness because in the inner meaning a little
child means innocence. The Word mentions babies, children, and youths,
who symbolize three levels of innocence. A baby symbolizes the first level; a
child, the second; and a youth, the third. Since youths are starting to shed
innocence, though, they symbolize the innocence that is called guiltlessness.

As they symbolize three levels of innocence, they also symbolize three
levels of love and charity, because heavenly and spiritual love—love for
the Lord and charity for one's neighbor—can exist only within innocence.

It is important to know, though, that the innocence of babies, children, and youths is shallow. We cannot have deep innocence until we
have been born anew, or become babies, children, and youths all over
again. This second childhood is what youngsters in the Word symbolize. In the Word's inner sense, only what is spiritual is meant and therefore only spiritual birth, which is called rebirth or regeneration.

[3] The symbolism of a youth, [or child,] as the innocence called guiltlessness can be seen in Luke:

Jesus said, "Whoever does not accept the kingdom of God like a *child*
will not enter it." (Luke 18:17)

Accepting God's kingdom as a *child* means accepting neighborly love and
faith with innocence. In Mark:

Jesus took a *child,* stood him in their midst, and hugged him. He said
to them, "Whoever accepts one of these *children* in my name accepts
me." (Mark 9:36, 37; Luke 9:47, 48)

The child represented innocence, and whoever accepts innocence accepts
the Lord, because he is the source of all innocence. Anyone can see that
accepting a child in the Lord's name does not mean accepting a child, and
consequently that it represented something of heaven. [4] In Matthew:

The *children* in the Temple shouted, "Hosanna to the child of David!"
[The chief priests and scribes] were indignant, so Jesus said to them,

"Haven't you read that 'Out of the mouth of *toddlers* and *nursing babies* you have perfected praise'?" (Matthew 21:15, 16; Psalms 8:2)

The children shouted "Hosanna to the child of David!" to represent the fact that only innocence acknowledges and accepts the Lord. That is, only people with innocence do so. "Out of the mouth of toddlers and nursing babies you have perfected praise" means that praise cannot reach the Lord by any other route than innocence. Innocence alone is the conduit for all communication, all inflow, and consequently access. That is why the Lord in the same author says:

> Unless you have been turned around and become like *children,* you will not enter the kingdom of the heavens. (Matthew 18:3)

[5] A child symbolizes innocence in the following places as well. In Zechariah:

> The streets of the city were filled with *boys* and *girls* playing in its streets. (Zechariah 8:5)

This is about a new Jerusalem, or the Lord's kingdom. In David:

> Praise Jehovah, young men and also young women, elders along with *children!* (Psalms 148:[7,] 12)

In the same author:

> Jehovah renews your life from the pit; he satisfies your mouth with something good, so that you are renewed like the eagle by *your youth.* (Psalms 103:4, 5)

In Joel:

> Over my people they cast lots, because they traded a *boy* for a whore, and a *girl* they sold for wine, which they drank. (Joel 3:3)

In Jeremiah:

> Through you [as my instrument] I will scatter man and woman, and through you I will scatter elder and *child,* and through you I will scatter young man and young woman. (Jeremiah 51:22)

In Isaiah:

> *A child has been born for us,* a son has been given to us, on whose shoulder will be sovereignty, and they will call his name Miraculous, Counselor, God, Hero, Eternal Father, Prince of Peace. (Isaiah 9:6)

Slave of the chief of the bodyguards means it contained truth that served ▮5237▮ primarily for interpretation. This is established by the association of the word *slave* with truth (discussed at §§2567, 3409) and by the symbolism of the *chief of the bodyguards* as a primary means of interpretation (discussed at §§4790, 4966, 5084). Besides, truth serves for interpretation—that is, interpretation of the Word. A slave of the chief of the bodyguards here symbolizes truth that serves.

And we told him means that it resulted in a perception, which is estab- ▮5238▮ lished by the symbolism of *telling* as perception (discussed in §3209).

And he interpreted our dreams for us symbolizes the inner content of ▮5239▮ what was foreseen in the dimness. This is established by the symbolism of *interpreting* as the inner content (discussed at §§5093, 5105, 5107) and from that of *dreams* as what was foreseen in the dimness (mentioned above at §5233).

For each according to his own dream he interpreted means truthfully. ▮5240▮ *And it happened that, as he interpreted for us, so it was* means that this was how it turned out. This can be seen from the fact that the phrases are talking about the outcome of the episode, which truly was such as Joseph had predicted.

Me he returned to my position means that sense impressions on the ▮5241▮ intellectual side were accepted, as the following shows: The cupbearer, *me,* symbolizes sense impressions on the intellectual side, as noted above [§§5227, 5232]. And *returning one to one's position* means reducing something to order and subordinating it, as discussed in §§5125, 5165, so it also means accepting it.

And him he hanged means that sense impressions on the will side were ▮5242▮ rejected. This can be seen from the symbolism of the baker, *him,* as sense impressions on the will side (noted above [§5232]) and from that of *hanging* as rejecting (discussed in §§5156, 5167).

There is no need to explain these details further, as they have already been explained. The text repeats them as part of the story line.

Genesis 41:14. *And Pharaoh sent and called Joseph, and they rushed* ▮5243▮ *him from the pit, and he cut his hair and changed his clothes and came to Pharaoh.*

And Pharaoh sent symbolizes eagerness in the new earthly level. *And called Joseph* means for accepting spiritual heavenliness. *And they rushed him from the pit* symbolizes a swift rejection of hindrances left over from a state of trial, and a consequent change. *And he cut his hair* symbolizes rejection and change in regard to elements on the outer earthly plane. *And changed his clothes* means in regard to elements on the inner earthly plane, by putting on something more suitable. *And came to Pharaoh* symbolizes resulting communication with the new earthly plane.

5244   *And Pharaoh sent* symbolizes eagerness in the new earthly level. This can be seen from the representation of *Pharaoh* as a new earthly self (discussed in §§5079, 5080). An eagerness for accepting spiritual heavenliness is symbolized by his *sending* and calling Joseph. The enthusiasm itself is plain from what comes later—that he put Joseph over his house and over all the land of Egypt and said that with [the words of] Joseph's mouth all his people would comply (verses 40, 41, 42, 43).

The situation is that when conditions are ripe—when everything on the earthly level is ready to accept inflow from within, or above, and apply it to itself—it also finds itself eager. In other words, it actually wants to accept it. The one level therefore adapts to the other when the Lord renews us.

5245   *And called Joseph* means for accepting spiritual heavenliness. This can be seen from the representation of *Joseph* as spiritual heavenliness (discussed in §§4286, 4585, 4592, 4594, 4963). See just above at §5244 for the fact that *he called* means for accepting it.

5246   *And they rushed him from the pit* symbolizes a swift rejection of hindrances left over from a state of trial, and a consequent change. This is established by the symbolism of a *pit* as a place of devastation and of trial (discussed at §§4728, 4744, 5038) and by that of *rushing him from* it as a swift rejection of anything left over from a state of trial. When a pit means a trying state, rushing someone from it means removing what came from that state and rejecting it. The same thing can also be seen from what follows next, because Joseph rejected what he brought from the pit by cutting his hair and changing his clothes.

[2] Compared to conditions afterward, conditions during times of trial are like those in a pit or dungeon: squalid and dirty. When we are being tested, unclean spirits come close, circle around, and stir up the evil and falsity in us. They keep us in the grip of evil and falsity, piling more on until we reach a point of despair. That is why we then find ourselves in dirt and squalor.

In addition, when the state is made visible in the other world (all spiritual states can be displayed visually there), it looks like a haze seeping from a foul environment; and it gives off a stench, too. Such is the appearance of the atmosphere that surrounds a person undergoing trials, and also a person being devastated—that is, a person in a pit in the underground realm, as described in §4728.

[3] When the state of trial ends, the haze evaporates and the air clears. This is because trials expose and remove the falsities and evils in us. On their exposure, the haze appears, and on their removal, clear air appears. The same change of state is also symbolized by Joseph's cutting his hair and changing his clothes.

[4] A state of trial can also be compared to the state of people who fall among thieves. When they come away from the encounter, their hair is a mess, their face is grim, and their clothes are ripped. If they fail in their trials, they stay in that condition. If they win, then after they compose their face again, comb their hair, and change their clothes, they enter a cheerful, sunny state. In the former state there are hellish spirits and demons who actually surround them like thieves, attack, and subject them to trials.

This discussion now shows that *they rushed him from the pit* symbolizes swift rejection of hindrances left over from a state of trial, and a consequent change.

And he cut his hair symbolizes rejection and change in regard to elements on the outer earthly plane. This can be seen from the symbolism of *cutting the hair* of one's head and beard as rejecting what belongs to the outer earthly plane. The hair that was cut symbolizes this outer earthliness (see §3301).

5247

What is more, head hair and beard hair correspond to outer earthliness in the universal human. There are some people who are absorbed in their senses, which means they had believed in nothing but the earthly dimension [during their physical life], refusing to understand that there was anything deeper or purer than what they could grasp with their senses. Because of the correspondence of hair in the universal human, they look shaggy in the other world, in heaven's light—so shaggy that their faces are hardly anything but beard hair. I have seen these furry faces many times.

There are others who had been rational beings, though—in other words, spiritual beings whose earthly level was properly subordinated. They appear with hair that is well cared for. In fact, in the other life you can tell from people's hair what they are like in regard to their earthly level. Spirits have hair because spirits in the other life look exactly like people on earth. That is also why the Word occasionally describes the hair of the angels people saw.

[2] These remarks show what *cutting hair* symbolizes, as in Ezekiel:

The priest-Levites, sons of Zadok, shall strip off *their garments* in which they are ministering and lay them aside in the holy rooms and *put on other garments* and not consecrate the people *while wearing their own garments*. And *their head they shall not shave,* and their *locks they shall not clip off; they shall surely trim the hair on their heads.* (Ezekiel 44:19, 20)

This is about a new temple and a new priesthood—that is, a new religion. Putting on other garments means putting on sacred truth. Not shaving their head or clipping off their locks but making sure to trim the hair on their heads means not rejecting the earthly dimension but adapting it to harmonize and therefore subordinating it. Anyone who regards the Word as holy can see that what the prophet says here and elsewhere about the new land, new city, new temple, and new priesthood will certainly not come true as literally described. The priest-Levites, sons of Zadok, will not minister there, stripping off the garments of their ministry and putting on others, or trim the hair on their heads. No, each and every detail there symbolizes something [spiritual] to be found in the new religion.

[3] There are also Moses' decrees for the high priest, the sons of Aaron, and the Levites:

The high priest from [among] his brothers, on whose head has been poured the anointing oil, and [who] has filled his own hand *so that he can put on the clothes, shall not shave his head* and *shall not rip his clothes.* (Leviticus 21:10)

The sons of Aaron shall *not make their head bald nor shave the corner of their beard.* They shall be holy to their God and not profane the name of their God. (Leviticus 21:5, 6)

You are to purify the Levites this way: spatter on them the atonement water, *and they shall pass a razor over their flesh* and wash *their clothes* and be pure. (Numbers 8:7)

These steps would never have been commanded if they had not contained something holy. The warning that the high priest should not shave his head or rip his clothes, that Aaron's sons should not make their head bald nor shave the corner of their beard, that when being purified the Levites should be shaved with a razor over their flesh—what is there of holiness or religion in any of this? To subject our outer, earthly self to our inner, spiritual self and to subject both to the Divine is what is holy and is what angels perceive when people on earth read these things in the Word.

[4] It is the same with Nazirites, who were holy to Jehovah:

If [someone] dies beside them by chance, suddenly, and they defile the head of their Naziriteship, they shall *cut the hair on their head* on the day of their cleansing; on the seventh day they shall *cut it.* (Numbers 6:9)

And Nazirites, on the day on which the days of their Naziriteship are fulfilled, shall *cut the hair on the head of their Naziriteship* at the doorway of the meeting tent and take the *hair of their head* and put it onto the fire that is under the sacrifice of peace offerings. (Numbers 6:13, 18)

For what Nazirites were and what holy quality they represented, see §3301. It is impossible to comprehend how holiness could have been present in their hair without knowing what hair is by correspondence and therefore what holy quality a Nazirite's hair corresponds to.

It is equally impossible to comprehend how Samson's hair gave him strength. As he himself said to Delilah:

"A razor has not gone up onto my head, because God's Nazirite I have been from my mother's womb. *If I am shaved,* my strength will withdraw from me and I will become weak and be like any person." And Delilah called in a man *who shaved the seven locks of his head,* and his strength withdrew from him. And then, *when the hair of his head began to grow (as it had been shaved off),* his strength returned. (Judges 16:17, 19, 22)

Surely a knowledge of correspondence is necessary if one is to recognize that a Nazirite represented the Lord's divine earthliness. That is precisely what Naziriteship was, and Samson's strength came from the representation.

[5] One who does not know—and particularly one who does not believe—that the Word has an inner meaning, and that the literal meaning serves to represent the ideas of the inner meaning, will acknowledge hardly any sanctity in these texts. Yet they contain the greatest holiness. One who does not know—and particularly one who does not believe—that the Word has an inner meaning that is holy will also be unable to see what the following passages embrace. In Jeremiah, for instance:

Truth has perished and been cut off from their mouth; *chop off the hair of your Naziriteship* and throw it away. (Jeremiah 7:28, 29)

In Isaiah:

On that day the Lord, *by a hired razor* in the fords of the river—by Assyria's monarch—will *cut the hair on the head* and the *hair of the feet,* and the *beard* he will also devour. (Isaiah 7:20)

In Micah:

> *Make yourself bald* and *shave yourself* because of the children of your pleasures; *broaden your baldness* like the eagle because they have moved away from you. (Micah 1:16)

Such people will also be unable to see how it involves anything holy to describe Elijah as a *hairy man* girded at his hips with a belt of hide (2 Kings 1:8) or why the youths who called Elisha *baldhead* were mauled by bears from the forest (2 Kings 2:23, 24). [6] Elijah and Elisha represented the Lord as the Word, so they represented the Word, particularly the prophetic part; see the preface to Genesis 18 and §2762. Hairiness and a belt of hide symbolized the Word's literal meaning—"a hairy man," truth in the literal meaning, and "a belt of hide at his hips," the goodness there. The Word's literal meaning is its earthly meaning, because the contents come from the world. The inner meaning is a spiritual meaning, because its contents come from heaven. These two meanings resemble a person's inner and outer levels. There is no inner part without the outer part, because the outer part is the outermost level of the divine design on which the inner part depends for existence. It was insulting to the Word, then, to call Elisha baldhead, as if there were no outer part—as if the Word had no level of meaning adapted to human grasp.

[7] From this it can be seen that every word of Scripture is holy. However, the holiness in Scripture is not visible to the intellect except in one who knows its inner meaning. Nonetheless, the holiness can be sensed through an inflow from heaven into one who believes the Word is sacred. The inflow comes by way of the inner meaning—the meaning angels are alive to. Although people on earth do not understand this meaning, it still affects them, since the angels alive to it share the emotion it inspires in them. This in turn shows that the Word was given to people on earth to grant them contact with heaven and to let the divine truth in heaven touch them with its inflow.

5248 *And changed clothes* means [rejection and change] in regard to elements on the inner earthly plane, by putting on something more suitable. This can be seen from the symbolism of *changing* as removing and rejecting, and from that of *clothes* as elements on the inner earthly plane (discussed below). The idea that [spiritual heavenliness] put on something more suitable, symbolized by the new clothes, follows as a consequence.

The Word mentions clothing frequently, and by it is meant anything lower or outward that envelops what is higher or inward. So clothes symbolize our outer dimension and consequently our earthly dimension, because this envelops our inner, spiritual part. Specifically, clothes symbolize the truth taught by faith, because this envelops the goodness urged by neighborly love.

The symbolism has its source in the clothes that spirits and angels are seen wearing. Spirits appear in clothing that does not shine, but angels appear in clothing that shines, that is almost made of light, because the glow surrounding them appears like a garment. Their clothes resemble those the Lord wore when he was transfigured, which were like the light (Matthew 17:2) and dazzling white (Luke 9:29). In addition, clothes indicate what spirits and angels are like in respect to their religious truth, because clothes represent that truth, but only as it exists on the earthly plane. Religious truth as it exists on the rational plane reveals itself in the face and its beauty. The radiance of their clothes comes from their loving, charitable goodness, whose translucence imparts brilliance. These remarks show what clothes represent in the spiritual world and therefore what they mean in a spiritual sense.

[2] The clothes Joseph changed—the ones he took off—were clothes from the pit, or prison clothes, which symbolize the illusions and falsities that evil demons and spirits stir up during a state of trial. *He changed clothes,* then, symbolizes the rejection and change of elements on the inner earthly level, and the clothes he put on were the type of elements that were suitable. That is why the clause also means putting on something more suitable.

See earlier statements and evidence concerning clothes: What is heavenly is not clothed, but what is spiritual and earthly is: 297. Clothes mean relatively lowly truth: 1073, 2576. Changing clothes was representative of putting on sacred truth, which was the origin of "clothes for changing," or ceremonial clothing: 4545. The tearing of clothes was a representation of mourning over lost truth: 4763. The symbolism of the one who came in not wearing wedding clothes: 2132.

And came to Pharaoh symbolizes communication with the new earthly plane. This can be seen from the symbolism of *coming* as communication— in the form of an inflow, in this case—and from the representation of *Pharaoh* as the new earthly plane (discussed in §§5079, 5080, 5244).

5249

What the words of this verse enfold can be seen from the preceding explanations. You see, the verse describes how Joseph was delivered from the pit and came to Pharaoh. Joseph in an inner sense represents the Lord's spiritual heavenliness. Pharaoh represents his earthly, outer self. The pit

Joseph was in represents a state of trial for the Lord's spiritual heavenliness. Pharaoh's calling him from the pit symbolizes a state of deliverance from his trials followed by a state of inflow into and communication with his new earthly level. Clearly, then, the inner meaning describes how the Lord made his earthly level into something new and eventually made it divine.

[2] These are the thoughts heavenly angels think when people read the story. To think this way is their highest pleasure, because they are within the Lord's divine atmosphere and are therefore in the Lord, so to speak. They feel their deepest joy when they think about the Lord and the way he saved the human race by making the human nature in himself divine. They like to stay in this heavenliest joy and wisdom, and for that purpose the Word's inner meaning describes the divine process in detail. At the same time it describes the process of human rebirth, because a person's rebirth is an image of the Lord's glorification (§§3138, 3212, 3296, 3490, 4402).

Many will wonder, perhaps, what angels talk to each other about and therefore what people after death who become angels talk about. The answer is that they talk about the kinds of topics the Word contains in its inner meaning: the Lord's glorification, his kingdom, the church, and the way we are reborn through the goodness that comes of love and the truth belonging to faith. The substance of their conversation, though, consists of deep secrets that are mostly inexpressible.

5250 Genesis 41:15, 16. *And Pharaoh said to Joseph, "A dream I dreamed, and there was no one interpreting it. And I heard [someone] saying about you that you can listen to a dream to interpret it." And Joseph answered Pharaoh, saying, "Not of myself! God will answer peace, Pharaoh."*

And Pharaoh said to Joseph symbolizes a perception by spiritual heavenliness on the earthly plane. *A dream I dreamed* symbolizes a prediction. *And there was no one interpreting it* symbolizes not knowing the implications. *And I heard [someone] saying about you* symbolizes the ability spiritual heavenliness had. *That you can listen to a dream to interpret it* means for perceiving the implications of foreseen events. *And Joseph answered Pharaoh* symbolizes knowledge. *Saying, "Not of myself!"* means not from his human side alone. *God will answer peace, Pharaoh,* means from divine humanity, through union.

5251 *And Pharaoh said to Joseph* symbolizes a perception by spiritual heavenliness on the earthly plane, as the following shows: *Saying* in the Word's narratives means perceiving, as mentioned many times before. *Pharaoh* represents the earthly plane, as discussed in §§5079, 5080, 5095, 5160. And *Joseph* represents spiritual heavenliness, as discussed at §§4286, 4592, 4594, 4963, 5086, 5087, 5106, 5249.

The reason these words symbolize a perception by spiritual heavenliness on the earthly plane is that both Joseph and Pharaoh represent the Lord. Joseph represents his spiritual heavenliness, and Pharaoh, his earthly plane. So "Pharaoh said to Joseph" symbolizes a perception the Lord had from spiritual heavenliness on his earthly plane.

The identity and nature of that perception cannot be explained intelligibly, though, except to people who have first formed some notion of spiritual perception, spiritual heavenliness, and ways in which the earthly plane differs from the spiritual. I have already discussed these subjects to some extent, of course, but they would have had to be reiterated.

A dream I dreamed symbolizes a prediction. This is established by the symbolism of a *dream* as foresight and therefore a prediction (discussed at §§3698, 5091, 5092, 5104, 5233). What follows also makes it clear that this dream is a prediction, because it predicted the seven years of abundant grain provisions and seven years of famine.

5252

And there was no one interpreting it symbolizes not knowing the implications. This can be seen from the symbolism of *interpreting* as the inner content (discussed at §§5093, 5105, 5107, 5141). *No one interpreting,* then, symbolizes not knowing the implications.

5253

In an inner sense, *no one* does not mean no one, or nobody, but is simply a negation. In this verse, therefore, it means *not*—that is, that the thing is not known, or is unrecognized. The reason this is so is that the inner meaning does not focus on any individual or even on anything limited to individuals (see §5225), and "no one" or "nobody" involves the vague concept of an individual.

There are three categories of ideas that disappear from the Word's literal meaning when it becomes an inner meaning: those relating to time, to space, and to an individual. This is because there is no time or space in the spiritual world. Both qualities are proper to the physical world. People who are dying, then, are said to be passing beyond time and leaving temporal things behind. The reason the spiritual world does not focus on anything limited to individuals is that talk centering on individuals narrows and limits the mind rather than broadening it and removing the limitations. Broadening one's speech and removing limitations from it makes it universal, bringing countless ideas within its embrace and enabling it to express even the inexpressible. That is what angels' speech is like as a result—especially the speech of heavenly angels, which is comparatively free of limits. So they always end up talking about infinity and eternity and therefore the Lord's divinity.

5254   *And I heard [someone] saying about you* symbolizes the ability spiritual heavenliness had. *That you can listen to a dream to interpret it* means for perceiving the implications of foreseen events. This can be seen from the following: *Hearing about you* means perceiving and knowing that he was like this and consequently that the ability was there. *Joseph,* the one these words are addressed to, represents spiritual heavenliness, as discussed in §§4286, 4592, 4594, 4963, 5086, 5087, 5106. *Listening* means perceiving, as discussed in §5017. A *dream* symbolizes what is foreseen, as noted just above in §5252. And *interpreting* symbolizes the implications, as also noted just above, in §5253. These meanings show that *I heard [someone] saying about you that you can listen to a dream to interpret it* symbolizes the ability of spiritual heavenliness to perceive the implications of foreseen events.

5255   *And Joseph answered Pharaoh* symbolizes knowledge. This can be seen from the symbolism of *answering* a question, when asked, as informing someone how the matter stands and therefore as knowledge.

5256   *Saying, "Not of myself!"* means not from his human side alone. This can be seen from the meaning of *not of myself,* or not in his own capacity—when it applies to the Lord, being represented by Joseph—as not from his human side alone but from his divine side. The Divine has foresight and knows what is involved.

The Lord possessed foresight and providence when he was in the world, even in his human nature, but he possessed it from his divinity. Since that time, having been glorified, he possesses it from his divinity alone, because his glorified humanity is divine. Humanity viewed in itself is nothing but a form designed to receive life from the Divine, but the Lord's glorified humanity, or his divine humanity, is not a form designed to receive life from the Divine. Rather, it is the very essence of life, and what radiates from it is life. That is how angels think of the Lord; but almost all who go to the other world from the Christian religion these days think of the Lord the same way they think of any other person. They picture the Lord as being not only separate from the Divine (although they tack divinity on to him) but also separate from Jehovah and in addition separate from his holy influence. They do talk of one God but they think three and actually divide the Divine in three. They split the Divine into persons, calling each one God and assigning a distinct role to each. As a result, Christians are said in the other world to worship three gods, because they think three, even if they say one.

People who formerly were outside the church and converted to Christianity, on the other hand, worship only the Lord in the other life. This is because they believed that the highest God had to have revealed himself on earth as a person and that the highest God is a divine person. They felt that if they did not picture the supreme God as a person they could not picture him at all, and this being so, they could not think about God or consequently know him, let alone love him.

God will answer peace, Pharaoh, means from divine humanity, through union. This can be seen from the remarks just above in §5256 and from the *peace* that *God will answer,* which means from the Lord's divine humanity. That *God* means what is divine is self-evident. See §§3780, 4681 for the idea that *peace* in its highest sense means the Lord. "Through union" is part of the meaning—union with spiritual heavenliness and through this with the earthly plane—because such union is the subject here.

5257

Genesis 41:17, 18, 19, 20, 21, 22, 23, 24. And Pharaoh spoke to Joseph: *"In my dream, there I was, standing by the bank of the river. And look: from the river, seven cows coming up, of fat flesh and beautiful form, and they grazed in the reeds. And look: seven other cows coming up after them, of very skinny and poor form, and scrawny flesh; I have not seen [any] like them in all the land of Egypt for poorness. And the cows scrawny and poor ate the seven earlier, fat cows. And they came into their belly, and one could not tell that they had come into their belly, and their appearance was [as] poor as in the beginning, and I woke up. And I saw in my dream, and look: seven ears of grain coming up on one stalk, full and good. And look: seven ears of grain dried up, thin, and scorched by an east wind, sprouting after them. And the thin ears swallowed up the seven good ears. And I told [the dreams] to the magicians, and there was no one pointing out [the meaning] to me."*

5258

And Pharaoh spoke to Joseph symbolizes a thought by spiritual heavenliness on the earthly plane. *In my dream* symbolizes what was foreseen in the dimness. *There I was, standing by the bank of the river,* means from one boundary to the other. *And look: from the river* means on the boundary. *Seven cows coming up* symbolizes there was earthly-level truth. *Of fat flesh* symbolizes the kind connected with neighborly love. *And beautiful form* symbolizes the kind connected with the resulting faith. *And they grazed in the reeds* symbolizes instruction. *And look: seven other cows coming up after them* symbolizes falsity on the earthly plane, nearby. *Of very skinny and poor form* symbolizes the kind that is worthless and not connected at all with faith. *And scrawny flesh* means or with neighborly love. *I have not seen [any] like them in all the land of Egypt for poorness* means such that there would be no way of uniting them with truth and goodness. *And the cows scrawny and poor ate* means that falsity unconnected with charity and faith would abolish . . . *The seven earlier, fat cows* symbolizes truth connected with the faith that results from charity. *And they came into their belly* symbolizes being inwardly abolished. *And one could not tell that they had come into their belly* means that truth-from-goodness was not to be found any longer. *And their appearance was [as] poor as in the beginning* means that there would be no communication or union. *And I woke up* symbolizes an enlightened state. *And I saw in my dream* symbolizes something else foreseen in the dimness. *And look: seven ears of grain coming up on one stalk* symbolizes items of knowledge on the earthly level, bound together. *Full and good* means that qualities of faith and charity could be incorporated into them. *And look: seven ears of grain dried up, thin, and scorched by an east wind* symbolizes useless knowledge full of corrupt passions. *Sprouting after them* means coming into view nearby. *And the thin ears swallowed up the seven good ears* means that useless knowledge would abolish useful knowledge. *And I told [the dreams] to the magicians* symbolizes consulting inner knowledge. *And there was no one pointing out [the meaning] to me* means not gaining any perception from it.

5259   *And Pharaoh spoke to Joseph* symbolizes a thought by spiritual heavenliness on the earthly plane. This can be seen from the discussion above at §5251, where the same words appear, except that the text there says Pharaoh *said* to Joseph, whereas here it says he *spoke* to him. "Said" symbolizes perception; *spoke* symbolizes thought (§§2271, 2287, 2619).

"Pharaoh spoke to Joseph" symbolizes a thought by spiritual heavenliness on the earthly plane rather than the other way around because the outer parts of the mind never think under their own power but under the power of something within. To put the same thing another way, the lower parts think only under the power of something higher— even though outer, lowlier parts appear to think on their own when that is the level on which inner, higher parts do their thinking. It is an illusion. The case is like that of a person who sees an object in a mirror but does not know the mirror is there. The person thinks the object is where it appears even though it is not. [2] Now since spiritual heavenliness is inner, or higher, and the earthly plane is outer, or lower, "Pharaoh spoke to Joseph" in an inner sense symbolizes a thought by spiritual heavenliness on the earthly plane.

In short, nothing at the bottom can do anything on its own. Any ability it has comes from higher up. This being so, the obvious consequence is that everything comes from the highest level—that is, from the Divine. What we think with our intellect and do from our will, then, comes to us from the top, or from the Divine. When we think falsely and behave evilly, it is because of the form we have molded ourselves into, but when we think truly and behave well, it is because of the form we have received from the Lord beforehand. People recognize that one and the same power and force produces different kinds of motion, depending on the intermediate and outermost structures involved. So life from the Divine in human beings produces different kinds of thought and action, depending on the form.

The remaining points in this sequence are almost the same as those explained earlier in the chapter, at §§5195–5217, so there is no need to explain them further.   **5260**

Genesis 41:25, 26, 27. *And Joseph said to Pharaoh, "Pharaoh's dream is one; what God is doing he has told to Pharaoh. The seven good cows are seven years, and the seven good ears are seven years; the dream is one. And the seven cows thin and poor coming up after them are seven years, and the seven empty ears scorched by an east wind will be seven years of famine."*   **5261**

And Joseph said to Pharaoh symbolizes a perception by the earthly level from spiritual heavenliness. *Pharaoh's dream is one* means that the same outcome was foreseen for both. *What God is doing he has told to Pharaoh* means that the earthly level was allowed to perceive what was being provided. *The seven good cows are seven years* symbolizes states in which truth multiplies on the inner earthly plane. *And the seven good ears are seven years* symbolizes states in which truth multiplies on the outer earthly plane. *The dream is one* means that both will happen through union. *And the seven cows thin and poor coming up after them are seven years* symbolizes states in which falsity infesting the inner earthly plane multiplies. *And the seven empty ears scorched by an east wind* symbolizes states in which falsity infesting the outer earthly plane multiplies. *Will be seven years of famine* symbolizes an apparent lack and loss of truth as a result.

Joseph said to Pharaoh symbolizes a perception by the earthly level from spiritual heavenliness. This can be seen from the symbolism of *saying* in scriptural narrative as perceiving, from the representation of *Joseph*   **5262** as spiritual heavenliness, and from the representation of *Pharaoh* as the earthly level. Each of these has been discussed many times before.

5263 *Pharaoh's dream is one* means that the same outcome was foreseen for both, as the following shows: A *dream* symbolizes something foreseen, as dealt with in §§3698, 5091, 5092, 5104, 5233. *Pharaoh* represents the earthly level, as dealt with in §§5079, 5080, 5095, 5160. And *is one* means the same for both—both parts of the earthly level, inner and outer. Concerning the twofold nature of the earthly level, see §§5118, 5126. What Pharaoh dreamed about the cows was foreseen for the inner earthly level, and what he dreamed about the ears of grain was foreseen for the outer. Since the two parts come together as a single unit, the clause means that things were the same for both.

5264 *What God is doing he has told to Pharaoh* means that the earthly level was allowed to perceive what was being provided, as the following shows: *What God is doing* symbolizes what was provided, as discussed below. *Telling* means communicating and allowing to perceive, as discussed at §§3608, 4856. And *Pharaoh* represents the earthly level, as noted above in §5263. This shows that *what God is doing he has told to Pharaoh* means that the earthly level was allowed to perceive what was being provided.

The reason *what God is doing* means what was provided is that everything God (the Lord) does is providence. Since providence comes from the Divine, it contains what is eternal and infinite. It contains what is eternal because it pays no regard to any starting or stopping point. It contains what is infinite because it regards the whole in every detail and every detail in the whole. This is called providence. Since this trait is present in absolutely everything the Lord does, what he does can only be expressed by the word *providence.*

The fact that absolutely everything the Lord does contains what is infinite and eternal will be illustrated with examples elsewhere, the Lord in his divine mercy willing.

5265 *The seven good cows are seven years* symbolizes states in which truth multiplies on the inner earthly plane. This can be seen from the symbolism of *cows* in a positive sense as truth on the inner earthly plane (discussed at §5198) and from that of *years* as states (discussed at §§482, 487, 488, 493, 893).

The reason there were seven is that *seven* symbolizes something holy and therefore adds a holy quality to the matter being discussed (§§395, 433, 716, 881). It also involves an entire period from beginning to end (§728). That is why seven cows and seven ears of grain appeared in the dream, and why seven years of abundant grain provisions and seven years of famine then occurred. It is also why the seventh day was consecrated, why the seventh year was a Sabbath year in the representative religion, and why the jubilee came after seven times seven years.

[2] Seven symbolizes something holy because of the meaning numbers have in the world of spirits. In that world every number has significance. On several occasions, numbers appeared before my eyes. I saw both simple numbers and their products, and one time there was a long train of them. Wondering about the meaning, I learned that they rose out of angels' conversations and that it is not unheard of for ideas to be expressed in numbers. The numbers appear in the world of spirits, where such things are presented visually, rather than in heaven.

This was known to the earliest people, who were heavenly and talked with angels, so they created a mathematics for the church, in which the numbers were used to give generalized expression to ideas they stated more specifically in words. The meaning of the individual numbers did not survive among their descendants, only the symbolism of the simple ones: two, three, six, seven, eight, and twelve, and consequently twenty-four, seventy-two, and seventy-seven. The main symbolism to survive was that of seven as something very holy—specifically, on the highest level, as divinity itself, and on a representative level, as the heavenly quality of love. That is why the seventh day symbolized the state of a heavenly person (§§84, 85, 86, 87).

The symbolic role of numbers is obvious from many numbers in the Word, such as this one in John:

> Let one who has understanding calculate the number of the beast, since it is the number of a human. To be specific, its number is six hundred sixty-six. (Revelation 13:18)

And in another place in the same author:

> The angel measured the wall of the holy Jerusalem at one hundred forty-four cubits, which is the measure of a human, that is, of an angel. (Revelation 21:17)

One hundred forty-four is the product of twelve times twelve or of two times seventy-two.

And the seven good ears are seven years symbolizes states in which truth multiplies on the outer earthly plane, as the following shows: In a positive sense, *ears* of grain symbolize items of knowledge, as discussed in §5212,

5266

and therefore truth on the outer earthly plane, since this truth is called knowledge. And *years* symbolize states, as noted just above in §5265. For the symbolism of *seven,* see the same section.

5267   *The dream is one* means that both will happen through union. This can be seen from the discussion above in §5263.

5268   *And the seven cows thin and poor coming up after them are seven years* symbolizes states in which falsity infesting the inner earthly plane multiplies, as the following shows: In a positive sense, *cows* symbolize truth on the inner earthly plane, as discussed in §§198, 5265. In a negative sense they symbolize falsity there, as mentioned in §5202. The previous cows, then, are called good ones, and these are called thin and poor. *Coming up* symbolizes an advance toward inner levels, as mentioned in §5202. And *years* symbolize states, as mentioned just above in §5265.

Just as *seven* symbolizes something holy, in a negative sense it also symbolizes something profane. Most objects in the Word have a negative meaning too, the reason being that when something arising in heaven filters down toward hell, it turns into its opposite and becomes actually opposed. The holy attributes symbolized by the number seven, then, become profane there.

[2] Let me use instances of seven just in the Book of Revelation to confirm that it symbolizes both what is holy and what is profane. The following passages show that it symbolizes something holy there:

> John to the *seven churches:* Grace and peace from him who is and who was and who is to come, and from the *seven spirits* who are before his throne. (Revelation 1:4)

> These words says he who has the *seven spirits* and the *seven stars.* (Revelation 3:1)

> From the throne issued *seven* fiery *lamps,* burning before the throne, which are God's *seven spirits.* (Revelation 4:5)

> I saw on the right hand of the one sitting on the throne a book written inside and on the back, sealed with *seven seals.* (Revelation 5:1)

> I looked, when there! In the middle of the throne, a Lamb, standing as if slaughtered, having *seven horns* and *seven eyes,* which are the *seven spirits of God* sent out into the whole earth. (Revelation 5:6)

> To the *seven angels* were given *seven trumpets.* (Revelation 8:2)

In the days of the *seventh angel's* voice, the mystery of God was to come to an end. (Revelation 10:7)

The *seven angels* having the *seven plagues* went out from the temple, dressed in white and shining linen and encircled around their chests with golden sashes. Then one of the four living creatures gave the *seven angels seven golden bowls.* (Revelation 15:6, 7)

[3] The symbolism of seven in a negative sense as something profane is clear from these passages in the Book of Revelation:

Look: a big red *dragon* having *seven heads* and ten horns, and on its heads, seven crowns! (Revelation 12:3)

I saw a beast coming up out of the sea, and it had *seven heads* and ten horns, and on its ten horns, crowns, but on its heads was the name of blasphemy. (Revelation 13:1)

I saw a woman, sitting on a scarlet beast, full of the names of blasphemy, and it had *seven heads* and ten horns. Here is understanding, if anyone has wisdom: The *seven heads* are *seven mountains,* on which the woman sits, and they are *seven monarchs.* The beast that was and [now] is not— he is the eighth king and is *from the seven* and goes to destruction. (Revelation 17:3, 7, 9, [10,] 11)

And the seven empty ears scorched by an east wind symbolizes states in which falsity infesting the outer earthly plane multiplies. This can be seen from the symbolism of *ears* of grain as items of knowledge, or truth on the outer earthly plane (mentioned above at §5266), and so in a negative sense as falsity there (§§5202, 5203, 5204). For the meaning of *empty* and *scorched by an east wind,* see above [§§5214, 5215].

Will be seven years of famine symbolizes an apparent lack and loss of truth. This can be seen from the symbolism of *famine* as a lack of knowledge (dealt with at §§1460, 3364) and so as a loss of truth. Falsity was going to abolish truth, so that it would look as though it no longer existed. This is symbolized by "The cows scrawny and poor ate the seven fat cows, and they came into their belly, and one could not tell that they had come into their belly," and by "The thin ears swallowed up the seven good ears" (verses 4, 7, 20, 21, 24; §§5206, 5207, 5217).

The situation in all this—that truth will at first multiply on both earthly planes but afterward dwindle to the point where hardly any shows—is a secret that can be known only by people who have had the opportunity to learn how human reformation and rebirth works.

Since the rest of the chapter deals with this secret in its inner meaning, I should discuss it briefly here at the outset. [2] When we are reforming, we first learn truth from the Word or from our theology and store it in our memory. If we cannot be reformed, we believe we have done enough once we learn the truth and lay it up in our memory, but we are sadly mistaken. The truth we have learned needs to be introduced to goodness and unite with it, which cannot happen as long as the evils of love for ourselves and love for worldly advantages remain in our earthly self. It was these two kinds of love that first introduced the truth, but it can never unite with them. If there is to be union, then, the truth introduced and retained by these kinds of love needs to be banished first. It is not really banished but is drawn within, where it is no longer visible. That is why it is called an apparent loss of truth. After this happens, our earthly level is enlightened from within, and the evils of self-love and materialism then give way. To the extent that they give way, truth is restored and unites with goodness.

The state in which we seem to be deprived of truth is called desolation in the Word and is compared to evening, which we undergo before we reach the morning. As a result, the day began at evening in the representative church.

5271   Genesis 41:28, 29, 30, 31, 32. *"This word that I have spoken to Pharaoh, which God is doing, he has caused Pharaoh to see. Watch: seven years are coming, a great abundance of grain provisions in all the land of Egypt. And seven years of famine will rise after them, and the whole abundance of grain provisions in the land of Egypt will be forgotten, and the famine will consume the land. And abundant grain provisions will not be known in the land afterward in view of this famine, because it will be very heavy. And about the dream's being repeated to Pharaoh two times—[it is] because the word has been set by God and God is hurrying to do it."*

This word that I have spoken to Pharaoh symbolizes what the earthly dimension thought about from spiritual heavenliness. *Which God is doing* means about what was being provided. *He has caused Pharaoh to see* symbolizes a perception the earthly level had. *Watch: seven years are coming* symbolizes providential states. *A great abundance of grain provisions in all the land of Egypt* symbolizes a multiplying of truth on both earthly levels. *And seven years of famine will rise after them* symbolizes later states, when there is a lack of truth. *And the whole abundance of grain provisions in the land of Egypt will be forgotten* symbolizes the removal of truth and an apparent loss of it on both earthly levels. *And the famine will consume the land* means to the point of despair. *And abundant grain provisions will not be known in the land* means that none of the previous truth will be perceptible there. *Afterward in view of this famine, because it will be very heavy* means on account of the lack. *And about the dream's being repeated to Pharaoh two times* means because it was foreseen for both earthly levels. *[It is] because the word has been set by God* means that it is divine. *And God is hurrying to do it* means along with the whole outcome.

This word that I have spoken to Pharaoh symbolizes what the earthly dimension thought about from spiritual heavenliness, as the following shows: A *word* means a thing, as discussed below. *Speaking* means thinking, as discussed at §§2271, 2287, 2619, 5259. Joseph, the one speaking here, represents spiritual heavenliness, and *Pharaoh* represents the earthly dimension, as discussed above. Plainly, then, *This word that I have spoken to Pharaoh* symbolizes the thing the earthly dimension thought about from spiritual heavenliness. See also §5262.

5272

About the term *word:* In the original language a thing is called a word, which is why divine revelation is called the Word, and why in its highest sense it also refers to the Lord. Since "the Word" refers to the Lord and divine revelation from him, in the next highest sense it means divine truth, from which everything there is comes into existence.

[2] Everything there is, past and present, has been brought into existence through divine truth from the Lord and accordingly through the Word. This is a secret not previously revealed. Most people think it means that everything was created by God's saying and commanding so, like a monarch in her or his realm. However, this is not what it means to say that everything was made and created through the Word. Divine truth coming from divine goodness—that is, from the Lord—is what everything emerged from in the past and emerges from now. Divine truth coming from divine goodness is the most real and most essential thing there is in the universe. It is what makes and creates things. Hardly anyone has any other picture of divine truth than one of words pouring from a speaker's mouth and disappearing in the air, and this image of divine truth has produced the opinion that "the Word" just means what has been commanded. As a consequence we think everything was made simply by command, not out of anything real that emanated from the Lord's divinity. Again, though, divine truth coming from the Lord is essential reality itself and the source of everything. Forms of goodness and truth come from

it. More about this secret later, however, with the Lord's divine mercy [§§6880, 7678, 8200].

5273 *Which God is doing* means about what was being provided. This can be seen from the symbolism of *which God is doing* as what was provided (discussed above at §5264).

5274 *He has caused Pharaoh to see* symbolizes a perception the earthly level had. This can be seen from the symbolism of *seeing* as understanding and perceiving (discussed at §§2150, 2325, 2807, 3764, 4567, 4723) and from the representation of *Pharaoh* as the earthly level (discussed before).

5275 *Watch: seven years are coming* symbolizes providential states. This can be seen from the symbolism of *years* as states (discussed in §§487, 488, 493, 893) and from that of *coming* as being providential. Coming, and happening, when ascribed to the Divine, or to something God does, means the outcome of providence and consequently something providential. To see that what God does is providence, look back at §§5264, 5273.

The next few verses talk about the seven years of abundant grain provisions and seven years of famine, and the years mentioned there symbolize states. The years of abundant grain provisions symbolize states in which truth multiplies on the earthly plane, and the years of famine symbolize states in which there is a lack and loss of truth on the earthly plane. Overall, in their inner meaning, the seven years of abundant grain provisions and seven years of famine in the land of Egypt depict states of human reformation and rebirth, and in the highest sense, states of glorification of the Lord's human nature. The abundance and famine occurred in Egypt precisely in order to represent these processes. They occurred there because Egypt and Pharaoh in an inner sense mean the earthly dimension, and the glorification of that dimension in the Lord is the subject of those verses.

[2] Be aware that what took place in those days and was recorded in the Word served to represent the Lord himself and the glorification of his human nature. In a representative sense it portrayed his kingdom and consequently the church generally and individually and therefore a person's rebirth—rebirth being the means by which a person becomes an individual church. The main reason the events of that period had such a representation was so that the Word could be written down and thus contain images representing divine, heavenly, and spiritual information in an unbroken series. As result the Word would serve angels in heaven as well as people in the church. After all, angels perceive divine content in the Word, which fills them with awe, and this is communicated to people who read the Word willingly, so that they too feel awe.

That is why the abundance and famine occurred in the land of Egypt. *A great abundance of grain provisions in all the land of Egypt* symbolizes a multiplying of truth on both earthly levels. This can be seen from the symbolism of a *great abundance of grain provisions* as multiplication of truth (discussed below) and from that of the *land of Egypt* as both earthly levels. Egypt symbolizes knowledge (see §§1164, 1165, 1186, 1462, 4749, 4964, 4966), and since it symbolizes knowledge it also symbolizes the earthly plane, because what exists on the earthly plane is called knowledge. The land of Egypt therefore means the earthly mind, which holds knowledge. *All* the land of Egypt, then, symbolizes both earthly levels, inner and outer (since the earthly plane consists of inner and outer levels; see §§5118, 5126).

5276

An abundance of grain provisions symbolizes multiplication of truth because it is the opposite of famine, which symbolizes a lack of truth. The word in the original language for the abundant grain provisions is the opposite of the word for famine and on an inner level symbolizes a full supply of knowledge, or plenty of it, because famine symbolizes a lack of knowledge.

Knowledge is simply truth for the earthly self, but truth that we have not yet adopted as our own, and the multiplication of such truth is the meaning here. Knowledge does not become truth for us till we acknowledge it with our intellect, which happens when we confirm it. And we do not adopt this truth as our own till we live according to it, because we adopt only what becomes part of our life. Such truth has a bit of our life in it, so it has a bit of ourselves.

And seven years of famine will rise after them symbolizes later states, when there is a lack of truth. This is established by the symbolism of *years* as states (discussed in §§482, 487, 488, 493, 893), by that of *famine* as a lack of knowledge (discussed in §§1460, 3364), and by that of *after them* as later.

5277

And the whole abundance of grain provisions in the land of Egypt will be forgotten symbolizes the removal of truth and an apparent loss of it on both earthly levels, as the following shows: Forgetting, or *being forgotten,* symbolizes removal and therefore an apparent loss. The *abundance of grain provisions* symbolizes multiplication of truth, or truth that has multiplied, as discussed just above in §5276. And the *land of Egypt* symbolizes the earthly mind, or a person's earthly level. In this case it means both earthly levels, as also above in §5276.

5278

The reason forgetting or *being forgotten* symbolizes removal and an apparent loss is that they are equivalent, as far as memory and consequently thought are concerned. What we are thinking about is directly under our gaze, and related matters arrange themselves around it in order, all the way out to unrelated matters at the furthest remove, which become forgotten. Anything that opposes the central point is separated from it, drops down, and stations itself underneath, where it balances what lies above it. This arrangement is brought about by inflowing goodness. Such is the case with all our thinking, and the fact that it is so is apparent from thought as it exists in the other life. There, in heaven's light, it is not unusual for thoughts to be presented visually, and when they are, this is the pattern in which they are arranged.

In an inner sense, then, forgetting actually means removal and an apparent loss.

5279   *And the famine will consume the land* means to the point of despair. This can be seen from the symbolism of *famine* as a lack of knowledge and therefore a loss of truth (discussed above at §§5277, 5278) and from that of the *land*—the land of Egypt—as the earthly mind (also discussed above, at §§5276, 5278). The reason it means to a point of despair is that the text says the famine *will consume* the land. Since the land symbolizes the earthly mind and famine symbolizes a loss of truth, despair is necessarily meant, because despair consumes us spiritually.

The words depict a state of desolation created by a loss of truth, and the final phase of such a state is despair. Despair is the final phase of that state because it removes any pleasure in a love for ourselves and worldly advantages, replacing it with pleasure in a love for what is good and true. People being reborn despair over their spiritual life and consequently over their loss of truth and goodness, because when they are deprived of truth and goodness, they despair of spiritual life. When they emerge from despair, they feel elation and bliss.

5280   *And abundant grain provisions will not be known in the land* means that none of the previous truth will be perceptible there. This can be seen from the symbolism of *being known* as being perceived, from that of *abundant grain provisions* as truth that has multiplied (discussed above in §§5276, 5278), and from that of the *land*—the land of Egypt—as the earthly mind (also discussed above, in §§5276, 5278, 5279). *Abundant grain provisions will not be known in the land,* then, clearly means that none of the previous truth will be perceptible on the earthly level.

[2] This verse is about the final phase of desolation, when despair sets in, right before we are reborn. Because this experience is the focus, it needs to be explained. Everyone has to reform and be born again, or

regenerate, in order to go to heaven, because *no one, unless born anew, can see the kingdom of God* (John 3:3, 5, 6). We are born into sin, which is accumulated in a long series by our great-grandparents, grandparents, and parents and becomes hereditary, so that it passes on to the next generation. Every human born is born into all the inherited evil that has steadily grown this way. That is why we are nothing but sin. Unless we are reborn, then, we remain totally immersed in sin.

If we are to be reborn, we first have to reform, and the means to reformation is religious truth. We need to learn about goodness from the Word or from teachings based on the Word, and this knowledge of goodness from the Word or from teachings based on it is called religious truth. All religious truth wells up out of goodness and flows toward goodness, because it considers goodness to be the ultimate goal. [3] This is the first state and is called a state of reformation. Most people in the church are being introduced to this state from childhood to early adulthood, but few are reborn. After all, most people in the church learn religious truth (or knowledge about goodness) with a view to reputation and status and to monetary gain. So although these drives introduce us to religious truth, we cannot be born anew or regenerate until they have been removed.

For the sake of their removal, then, we are brought into a state of trial, which is done this way: Hell's crew, which likes to wallow in such passions, stirs them to life. At the same time, though, angels stir up a desire for truth and goodness, which is instilled into us in states of innocence from childhood on and is then stored up inside us, preserved for this purpose. A fight ensues between the evil spirits and the angels, and we experience it as a time of trial. Since the issue is over truth and goodness, the truth that was instilled earlier is seemingly banished by falsity that evil spirits inject, with the result that it is no longer visible. (This is discussed above at §§5268, 5269, 5270.) Afterward, as we allow ourselves to be reborn, the Lord instills into our earthly dimension the light shed by truth based on goodness, sending it along an inner path. In that light, truth returns, arranged in its proper pattern.

[4] That is what happens with people who are regenerating, but few today are let into this state. Of course so far as we allow it, we all start to be reformed by learning about the true concepts and good desires of spiritual life, but as soon as we reach adulthood we let the world carry us away. We defect to the side of the hellish spirits, who gradually wean us away from heaven, until we barely believe anymore that heaven exists. As a consequence, we also cannot be tested spiritually, because if we were,

we would succumb immediately. Then our later condition would be worse than our earlier (Matthew 12:45).

These remarks show how matters stand with the contents of the inner meaning here—that is, with the states of reformation and regeneration. The current verse depicts the final stage of trial, which is a state of despair (discussed just above at §5279).

5281   *Afterward in view of this famine, because it will be very heavy* means on account of the lack, as the following shows: *Famine* symbolizes a lack of knowledge about goodness, which means a lack of truth (as discussed above in §§5277, 5278), so it symbolizes despair at the end on account of the lack (§5279). And *very heavy* means huge.

This verse continues to speak of desolation's final stage—despair—and its increasing severity (discussed above in §5279).

5282   *And about the dream's being repeated to Pharaoh two times* means because it was foreseen for both earthly levels, as the following shows: The *dream* symbolizes what was foreseen, as discussed at §§3698, 5091, 5092, 5104. *Pharaoh* represents the earthly level, as discussed at §§5079, 5080, 5095, 5160. And *being repeated two times* means that it has to do with both earthly levels, inner and outer. For there being two earthly levels, inner and outer, see §§5118, 5126. A vision for the inner earthly level was foreseen in the first dream, about the cows (§§5198, 5202), and one for the outer earthly level was foreseen in the second dream, about the ears of grain (§5212). That is why *being repeated two times* means that it has to do with both.

5283   *[It is] because the word has been set by God* means that it is divine. This can be seen without explanation, because when a *word* is attributed to *God,* it means divine truth, and when divine truth is said to be *set by God,* it means that the thing will absolutely come to pass.

5284   *And God is hurrying to do it* means along with the whole outcome, as the following shows: *Doing,* when attributed to *God,* symbolizes providence, as discussed at §5264, so it also symbolizes an outcome. What is in divine providence results without fail. And *hurrying* to do something symbolizes the whole outcome. In an inner sense, hurrying or a hurry does not mean speed but certainty and also completeness, so it means along with the whole outcome. Hurry involves time, and there is no time in the spiritual world, but state instead. A rush in time, then, relates to the corresponding aspect of a state there, and the corresponding aspect of a state is that many forces combine to bring something about—which makes the outcome certain and complete.

Genesis 41:33, 34, 35, 36. *"And now let Pharaoh look for a man under-* **5285**
standing and wise, and put him over the land of Egypt. Let Pharaoh act
and put officers in charge over the land and take one fifth from the land of
Egypt in the seven years of abundant grain provisions. And let them gather
all the food of those coming good years, and pile up the grain under Pharaoh's
hand—the food, in the cities—and guard it. And let the food serve as a store
for the land for the seven years of famine that will occur in the land of Egypt,
and the land will not be cut off in the famine."

And now let Pharaoh look symbolizes a provision by the earthly plane.
For a man understanding and wise means for an inflow of truth and goodness. *And put him over the land of Egypt* means which will organize everything in the earthly mind. *Let Pharaoh act* symbolizes another provision.
And put officers in charge over the land symbolizes the organized arrangement of general ideas in the earthly mind. *And take one fifth from the land*
of Egypt means which were to be preserved and then stored away. *In the*
seven years of abundant grain provisions means which had been instilled
during the time when truth multiplied, along with goodness. *And let them*
gather all the food symbolizes everything useful. *Of those coming good years*
means which was to be learned about during that time. *And pile up the*
grain symbolizes the goodness to which truth leads, all in one place. *Under*
Pharaoh's hand means as needed and therefore arranged on the earthly
plane. *The food, in the cities* symbolizes these attributes in the earthly mind's
inner depths. *And guard it* means which were to be stored up there. *And let*
the food serve as a store for the land means that it would always be there for
the earthly mind's use. *For the seven years of famine* means as needed when
there was a lack. *That will occur in the land of Egypt* means on the earthly
level. *And the land will not be cut off in the famine* means to prevent the person from perishing.

And now let Pharaoh look symbolizes a provision by the earthly plane. **5286**
This can be seen from the symbolism of *looking* as making a provision.
In this case looking is an action Pharaoh is being asked to take, but when
looking does not involve the need to act, the meaning is to understand
and perceive, as shown in §§2150, 2325, 2807, 3764, 3863, 4403–4421,
4567, 4723, 5114.

A word about this provision by the earthly plane: Our earthly plane,
or earthly mind, which lies below our rational mind, does not provide
anything on its own. It does seem to, but its provision is from an inner
dimension, which provides for the outer dimension. It is almost the same
as looking at oneself in a mirror, since the reflection seems to be right

there in the mirror. The situation is presented in the inner meaning by the fact that Joseph spoke this word to Pharaoh. Joseph represents spiritual heavenliness, which is inside, and Pharaoh represents the earthly plane, which is outside; and the man understanding and wise that Joseph mentioned was seen by Pharaoh to be Joseph himself.

5287   *For a man understanding and wise* means for an inflow of truth and goodness. This can be seen from the symbolism of an *understanding man* as truth and of a *wise man* as the goodness that goes with it. It is important to know that in an inner sense, a man understanding and wise does not mean some man like this but the quality of an understanding, wise person abstracted from the person. So it means truth and goodness. In the other life, particularly in the heavens, everything the inhabitants think and therefore everything they say is in terms abstracted from individuals. Consequently thought and speech there is universal and relatively unlimited. The more one's thought and speech focuses on individuals and their particular qualities, and the more it focuses on names and words, the less universal it grows. It grinds to a halt in the subject at hand and stays put there. However, the more it focuses on subject matter abstracted from individuals and words instead, the more it uses that matter as a starting point and reaches outside itself. It becomes a higher and therefore more universal point of view.

[2] This is obvious from the way our minds work. The more we concentrate on the words a person says, the less we concentrate on the meaning. Inside our own selves, the more we concentrate on trivial information in our memory and get bogged down in it, the less we perceive the true nature of things. Above all, the more we concentrate on ourselves at every turn, the more we constrict our thinking and deny ourselves a broad overview of a given matter. As a result, the more we love ourselves at the expense of others, the less wise we are.

These considerations now show why anything that applies narrowly to individuals in the literal sense symbolizes something abstracted from individuals in an inner sense. See also §5225.

The Word in places distinguishes among wisdom, understanding, and knowledge. Wisdom means what comes of goodness, understanding means what comes of truth, and knowledge means both of these on our earthly level. In Moses, for instance:

> I have filled Bezalel with the spirit of God as to *wisdom* and as to *understanding* and as to *knowledge* and as to every kind of work. (Exodus 31:2, 3; 35:30, 31)

And in the same author:

> Give yourselves *men wise* and *understanding* and *knowledgeable,* according to your tribes, so that I may make them your heads. (Deuteronomy 1:13)

And put him over the land of Egypt means which will organize every- **5288** thing in the earthly mind, as the following shows: *Putting someone over something* means putting someone in charge of organizing it, so it means the organizing itself. And the *land of Egypt* symbolizes the earthly mind, as above in §§5276, 5278, 5279. *Him* refers to the man understanding and wise, who symbolizes truth and goodness. This shows the meaning of the clause to be that truth and goodness will organize everything in the earthly mind.

It really is goodness and truth that organize each and every thing in the earthly mind. Goodness and truth flow in from within, which enables them to arrange it all in order.

The uninformed will find nothing to marvel at in this. They do not know how our intellectual faculty works—how we are able to examine a situation, grasp it, analyze it, form conclusions, and finally refer the matter to our will and thereby to action. They imagine it all happens naturally in this order. They have no idea that everything results from an inflow from the Lord through heaven. Without this inflow we cannot think a single thought, and when it is cut off, all our thinking is cut off too, as they also fail to realize. So they are unaware that goodness flowing in through heaven from the Lord organizes everything and shapes everything to resemble heaven, so far as we allow. Our thoughts therefore conform to the pattern of heaven in their flow. The pattern of heaven is the pattern in which heavenly communities are arranged, and heavenly communities are arranged in the pattern imposed on them by goodness and truth radiating from the Lord.

Let Pharaoh act symbolizes another provision. This can be seen from **5289** the explanation above in §5286.

And put officers in charge over the land symbolizes the organized arrange- **5290** ment of general ideas in the earthly mind. This can be seen from the symbolism of *putting someone in charge* as organizing, from that of *officers* as something general (dealt with below), and from that of the *land*—the land of Egypt—as the earthly mind (as just above in §5288).

Officers symbolize something general because particulars are contained within general categories and come under them; see §§920, 4269, 4325 at the end, 4329, 4345, 4383, 5208. Chiefs, though, symbolize something of primary importance (§§1482, 2089, 5044).

5291   *And take one fifth from the land* means which were to be preserved and then stored away. This can be seen from the symbolism of *taking one fifth,* which involves the same thing here as tithing, [or taking one tenth]. Tithing in the Word means creating a remnant, and creating a remnant means gathering truth and goodness and then storing them away. See §§468, 530, 560, 561, 661, 1050, 1906, 2284, 5135 for the idea that a remnant consists of goodness and truth hidden away in our inner self by the Lord; and see §§576, 1738, 2280 for the idea that tenths in the Word symbolize a remnant. Ten symbolizes the same thing (§§1906, 2284), so five does as well, being half of ten. Half or double a number in the Word carries the same meaning [as the number itself]. For instance, twenty means the same as ten, four means the same as two, six means the same as three, twenty-four means the same as twelve, and so on. A number's larger multiples also have the same meaning: a hundred and a thousand mean the same as ten, and seventy-two and one hundred forty-four mean the same as twelve. The significance of multiples, then, can be seen from the simple numbers that are their factors and multipliers. The significance of the simpler numbers, on the other hand, can be seen from their wholes. The meaning of five, for example, can be seen from ten; the meaning of two and a half can be seen from five; and so on. You should be aware that in general a number means the same thing but fuller when multiplied, and the same thing but less full when divided.

[2] Regarding five specifically, it has a double meaning: as a small amount and therefore "some," and as a remnant. It symbolizes a small amount in relation to numbers symbolizing a large amount—that is, in relation to a thousand and a hundred, and consequently in relation to ten. A thousand and a hundred symbolize a large amount (see §§2575, 2636), so ten does too (§§3107, 4638). That is why five symbolizes a small amount and "some" (§§649, 4638). Five symbolizes a remnant when it relates to ten and ten means a remnant, as noted above.

To see that all numbers in the Word have symbolic meaning, see §§575, 647, 648, 755, 813, 1963, 1988, 2075, 2252, 3252, 4264, 4495, 4670, 5265.

[3] People who do not realize the Word has any inner meaning—a meaning not visible in the literal text—will be dumbfounded to hear that numbers in the Word also have symbolic meaning, particularly because they cannot form any spiritual idea from numbers. Numbers do arise

from a spiritual idea in the minds of angels, though; see §5265. It is possible to learn what idea or quality a number corresponds to, but the source of the correspondence still lies hidden. Why, for example, does twelve correspond to faith and all that composes it? Why does seven correspond to something holy? Why do ten and five correspond to goodness and truth stored up by the Lord in the inner self? And so on. However, it is enough to know that the correspondence exists, that it causes all numbers in the Word to symbolize something in the spiritual world, and that divine inspiration therefore lies hidden even in them.

Take for instance the following passages that mention the number five: [4] There is the Lord's parable about the man who went abroad and handed over his resources to his servants—*five talents* to one, *two* to another, and *one* to a third. And the one who received *five talents* did business with them and made another *five talents*. Likewise the one who received *two* made *another two*. But the one who received *one* hid his master's silver in the earth (Matthew 25:14 and following verses). If you do not look beyond the literal meaning you cannot help thinking that these numbers—five, two, and one—were chosen merely for the literary composition of the parable and that they lack any further significance. In reality, though, these very numbers hide a secret. The servant who received five talents symbolizes people who have let in goodness and truth from the Lord, which means that they have received a remnant. The one who received two talents symbolizes people who have added neighborly love to faith in their later years. The one who received one talent symbolizes people who have adopted faith alone without neighborly love. The text says this servant hid his master's silver in the earth, and on an inner level the silver assigned to him symbolizes religious truth (§§1551, 2954). Faith without charity is of no advantage; it bears no fruit. That is the kind of meaning the numbers hold.

[5] It is similar in other parables. Take the one about the man traveling to a far territory to receive a kingdom for himself:

> He gave his servants *ten minas* and told them to do business with them until he came. When he returned, the first said, "Master, your mina made *ten minas* more," and to him [the master] said, "Well done, you good servant! Since you were faithful over a very little, be over *ten cities*." The second said, "Master, your mina made *five minas*," and to him [the master] also said, "You too be over *five cities*." The third had laid his mina aside in a handkerchief, but the master said, "Take the mina

from him and give it to the one who has *ten minas.*" (Luke 19:12 and following verses)

Here too ten and five symbolize a remnant. The ten symbolizes a larger remnant; the five, a smaller one. The servant who laid the mina aside in a handkerchief stands for people who amass religious truth but do not unite it with neighborly kindness. It brings them no advantage, no fruit.

[6] The case is the same with other parables in which the Lord uses these numbers, as for instance in the one about the man who was called to a supper and said, "*Five yokes of oxen* I bought, and I am going off to try them out" (Luke 14:19). There was the rich man who said to Abraham, "I have *five brothers;* [I ask you] to send someone to tell them not to come into this place of torment" (Luke 16:[27,] 28). There were the *ten* young women, of whom *five* were prudent and *five* stupid (Matthew 25:1–13). The case is the same with these words of the Lord's:

> Do you think that I came to give peace on earth? No, I say to you, but division. For from now on there will be *five* in one house, divided *three* against *two,* and *two* against *three.* (Luke 12:51, 52)

It is even the same with the following historical details: The Lord fed *five thousand people* with *five loaves* and *two fish,* ordering the people to recline *by hundreds* and *by fifties,* and after they had eaten, they gathered *twelve* large baskets of scraps (Matthew 14:15–21; Mark 6:38 and following verses; Luke 9:12–17; John 6:5–13). [7] Because these are historical facts, it is hard to believe there is significance to the numbers—the five thousand people, the five loaves, the two fish, the hundreds and fifties of eaters reclining, the twelve large baskets of scraps—but each holds a secret. Each came about in providence, to represent something divine.

[8] In the following passages, five again symbolizes the same things it corresponds to in the spiritual world, in both senses, positive and negative. In Isaiah:

> Gleanings will be left in it, as in the shaking of an olive tree—*two, three* fruits at the crown of the branch; *four, five* on the branches of a productive tree. (Isaiah 17:6, 7)

In the same author:

> On that day there will be *five cities* in the land of Egypt speaking the tongues of Canaan and swearing to Jehovah Sabaoth. (Isaiah 19:18)

In the same author:

> *One thousand* flee at the reproach of one; at the reproach of *five* [you] are fleeing, until you alone survive as a standing pole at the head of the mountain and as a banner on the hill. (Isaiah 30:17)

In John:

> The *fifth* angel trumpeted; then I saw a star from the sky fallen to the earth, which was given the key to the pit of the abyss. The locusts that issued from it were told not to kill the people who did not have God's seal on their foreheads but to torment them *five months.* (Revelation 9:1, 5, 10)

In the same author:

> Here is understanding, if anyone has wisdom: The *seven* heads are *seven* mountains, on which the woman sits, and there are *seven* monarchs. The *five* fell, and the *one* is [alive]; the other did not yet come, and when he comes, he has to stay briefly. (Revelation 17:9, 10)

[9] The number five held a similar representation in the following regulations: A man or woman's monetary value was determined by his or her age, from a month to *five years,* and *from five years to twenty* (Leviticus 27:1–8). If a field was redeemed, a *fifth* of the value was to be added (Leviticus 27:19), and if tithes were redeemed, a *fifth* was again to be added (Leviticus 27:31). The firstborns who outnumbered [the Levites] were to be redeemed with *five shekels* (Numbers 3:46–end), and the firstborn of an unclean animal was to be redeemed with an *added fifth* (Leviticus 27:27). In certain transgressions a *fifth* was to be added as a fine (Leviticus 22:14; 27:13, 15; Numbers 5:6, 7, 8). Anyone who stole an ox or a sheep and slaughtered or sold it was to restore *five oxen* for an ox, and *four sheep* for a sheep (Exodus 22:1).

[10] The fact that a secret of heaven lies within the number five and also within ten, is plain from the guardian beings described in 1 Kings:

> Solomon made two guardian beings of olive wood in the inner sanctum, *ten cubits* the height of each; *five cubits* the wing of one being, and *five cubits* the wing of the other being; *ten cubits* from the tips of its wings to the tips of its wings; so *ten cubits* a guardian being, one measure and one proportion for both beings. (1 Kings 6:23–27)

The same fact is plain from the washbowls around the Temple and from the lampstands, also described in 1 Kings:

> *Five* stands that were for washbowls were put along the shoulder of the House to the right and *five* along the shoulder of the House to the left. *Five* lampstands were put on the right and *five* on the left in front of the inner sanctum. (1 Kings 7:39, 49)

The bronze sea was *ten cubits* from rim to rim and *five cubits* in height and *thirty cubits* around (1 Kings 7:23) so that not only would ten and five be able to symbolize something holy but thirty would as well. A circumference of thirty does not match the diameter geometrically, but its spiritual significance is the same as the symbolism of that vessel's edge.

[11] The fact that all numbers symbolize something in the spiritual world is obvious from the numbers mentioned by Ezekiel where he is describing the new land, new city, and new temple, measured by the angel in all their detail; see Ezekiel 40, 41, 42, 43, 45, 46, 47, 48. Almost all the sacred ideas depicted in those chapters are displayed as numbers, so anyone who does not know what the numbers involve can learn hardly any of the secrets there. The numbers ten and five come up (Ezekiel 40:7, 11, 48; 41:2, 9, 11, 12; 42:4; 45:11, 14), not to mention the multiples twenty-five, fifty, five hundred, and five thousand. The new land, new city, and new temple symbolize the Lord's kingdom in the heavens and therefore his church on earth, as every item there shows.

[12] I have brought together these examples of the number five because this verse and later ones [Genesis 47:24, 26] say that during the seven years of abundance in the land of Egypt a fifth of the grain was to be collected and saved for use in the years of famine to come. That is why I have shown that a fifth symbolizes goodness and truth that the Lord stores away in us and reserves for use in times of future famine, or when we have a lack and loss of goodness and truth. Unless the Lord stored them away inside us, we would have nothing to lift us up in a state of trial or devastation. Consequently we would have no way of being reborn, and in the other world we would be without means of salvation.

5292   *In the seven years of abundant grain provisions* means which had been instilled during the time when truth multiplied, along with goodness. This can be seen from the symbolism of *years* as states and therefore as some span of time (discussed below) and from that of *abundant grain* *provisions* as a multiplying of truth, or truth that has multiplied (discussed above at §§5276, 5278, 5280). In this case, then, it symbolizes truth that has multiplied, along with goodness, because truth is nothing without goodness. No truth is stored up in our inner self (as described just above in §5291) except that which is united with goodness.

Years symbolize some span of time as well as states because on an inner level a year symbolizes a whole state, or the whole span of a state from beginning to end. The span of a state can only be expressed as a span of time, and that is the only way it can be grasped by time-bound beings. For the meaning of years and days as both states and spans of time, see §§23, 487, 488, 493, 893, 2906.

And let them gather all the food symbolizes everything useful. This is indicated by the symbolism of *gathering* as bringing together and storing, and by that of *food* as something useful.

5293

Properly speaking, *food* on an inner level symbolizes what nourishes our soul, or what nourishes us when bodily life ends, since we then live as a soul, or spirit. We no longer need physical food, as we did in the world, but spiritual food. Spiritual food is everything useful and everything that leads to something useful. What leads to usefulness is knowing what is good and true, and usefulness itself is to will and do what is good and true. These are what nourish angels and are therefore called spiritual and heavenly food.

Even while we are living in our body, this is the only food nourishing the part of our mind that holds our deeper intellect and deeper will, or our purposes and aims. Physical food does not penetrate that far. It reaches only as far as our bodily parts, which it sustains with the goal of enabling this level of our mind to relish its food while our body relishes its. In other words, the goal is a sound inner mind in a sound body.

[2] The reason food in a spiritual sense means everything useful is that whatever we know, whatever we understand or have wisdom in, and whatever we accordingly intend needs to have usefulness as its goal. The quality of the use it serves determines the quality of our life.

The meaning of food in an inner sense as everything useful is plain from these words of the Lord's:

> Jesus said to the disciples, "I have *food to eat* that you do not know of." The disciples said to each other, "Has someone brought him something to eat?" Jesus said to them, "*My food is to do the will of him who sent me, and I will finish his work.*" (John 4:32, 33, 34)

And in another place:

> Work, *not for the food that perishes,* but for the *food* that lasts to eternal
> life, which the Son of Humankind will give you; on him the Father,
> God, set a seal. (John 6:27)

5294   *Of those coming good years* means which was to be learned about during that time. This can be seen from the symbolism of *years* as states and
also as spans of time (discussed just above at §5292). *Coming good years,*
then, mean times in which truth multiplies, along with goodness, as symbolized by the seven years of abundant grain provisions.

5295   *And pile up the grain* symbolizes the goodness to which truth leads, all
in one place. This can be seen from the symbolism of *piling up* as collect-
ing into one place and preserving, and from that of *grain* as goodness on
the earthly level (discussed at §3580)—here, the goodness to which truth
leads on the earthly level. The goodness to which truth leads is truth in
our will and our actions.

Grain means goodness because a field in a spiritual sense means religion. So objects and activities associated with a field—seed, sowing, har-
vest, a crop, grain, and a spike or ear of grain, not to mention particular
grains such as wheat, barley, and so on—mean features of religion; and all
features of religion relate to goodness and truth.

5296   *Under Pharaoh's hand* symbolizes a need and resulting arrangements
on the earthly plane, as the following shows: A *hand* symbolizes power,
as discussed in §§878, 3387, 4931–4937, so *under someone's hand* means
as arranged in every case of need. What is in someone's power is at the
person's disposal, after all. And *Pharaoh* represents the earthly plane, as
discussed before.

5297   *The food, in the cities* symbolizes these attributes in the earthly mind's
inner depths. This can be seen from the symbolism of *food* as everything
useful and therefore as truth and goodness (discussed just above at §5293)
and from that of *cities* as the earthly mind's inner depths. In the broadest
sense cities symbolize the church's doctrinal teachings (see §§402, 2268,
2449, 2451, 2712, 2943, 3216, 4492, 4493), but in particular they symbolize
a person's inner depths, where doctrinal teachings reside, or rather where
truth united with goodness resides. Truth and goodness in us form a kind
of city; see §3584. As a result, we ourselves are called the city of God if we
have the church inside us.

The symbolism of a city resembles that of a house. A house in the
broadest sense symbolizes goodness, but in particular a person (§3128),

and specifically a person's mind as regards the united goodness and truth there (§§3538, 4973, 5023). What is more, a house with its rooms, outbuildings, and courtyards is a miniature city.

[2] The inner reaches of the earthly mind are symbolized by cities in Isaiah:

> On that day there will be *five cities in the land of Egypt* speaking the tongues of Canaan and swearing to Jehovah Sabaoth. (Isaiah 19:18)

And goodness and truth in those inner reaches are symbolized by cities in the Lord's parable in Luke:

> He said to the one who with his mina had made ten more minas, "Well done, you good servant! Since you were faithful over a very little, *be over ten cities.*" And he said to the second one, who had made five more minas, "You too *be over five cities.*" (Luke 19:12 and following verses)

In the current verse, then, "Let them pile up food in the cities and guard it" means that truth united to goodness was to be stored up in the earthly mind's inner reaches. Once stored away there, this truth and goodness is called a remnant. Our spiritual life itself consists in this remnant, which feeds us spiritually whenever we stand in need and want—in other words, whenever we face spiritual famine.

And guard it means which were to be stored up there. This can be seen from the symbolism of *guarding* as storing up—storing up in the earthly mind's inner depths, symbolized by the cities, as discussed just above in §5297.　**5298**

Let the food serve as a store for the land means that it would always be there for the earthly mind's use, as the following shows: *Food* symbolizes goodness and truth, as discussed above in §5293. *As a store* means that the hidden supply would always be there for use—seeing that it was for use in the years of famine to come. And the *land*—the land of Egypt—symbolizes the earthly mind, as also discussed above, in §§5276, 5278, 5279, 5288.　**5299**

For the seven years of famine means as needed when there was a lack. This is indicated by the symbolism of *famine* as a lack of truth (discussed above in §§5277, 5278). Clearly it was to be there as needed, since *years* in an inner sense mean states, as shown many times above, and *for those years* consequently means for states in which there would be need.　**5300**

That will occur in the land of Egypt means on the earthly level. This can be seen from the symbolism of the *land of Egypt* as the earthly mind (discussed at §§5276, 5278, 5279, 5288).　**5301**

Here and elsewhere I speak of the earthly level, by which I mean the earthly mind. We have two minds, a rational one and an earthly one. The rational mind belongs to our inner self, and the earthly mind, to our outer self. The latter mind or self is what I mean by the earthly level.

The mind is the actual person, as the next section will show.

5302 *And the land will not be cut off in the famine* means to prevent the person from perishing, specifically through a lack of truth. This can be seen from the symbolism of being *cut off* as perishing, and from that of the *land*—the land of Egypt—as the earthly mind (discussed just above at §5301). Because the land symbolizes the earthly mind, it symbolizes the actual person, since it is our mind that makes us human. Our mind is actually who we are, and its quality determines our nature. The mind means a person's intellect and will, so it means a person's very life.

Fools imagine that we are human because of our outward form—in other words, because we have a human face. Lesser fools say that being able to speak makes us human, and those who are still less foolish say that being able to think does. None of these is what makes us human, however. No, what makes us human is the fact that we can think what is true and will what is good, and that when we do so we can catch sight of what is divine and consciously receive it. This distinguishes us from brute animals. [2] Looking human and being able to speak and think does not otherwise make us human. If we think what is false and will what is evil, we make ourselves brute animals and worse, because we use these capacities themselves to destroy the humanity in us and make ourselves wild beasts.

This fact is especially clear to see from spirits of this kind in the other life. When they appear in heaven's light, and angels look at them, at that moment they look like monsters, and some look like wild animals. Deceivers look like snakes, and other spirits, like other creatures. Removed from that light, though, and returned to the twilight they have in hell, they look human to each other.

The situation, then, is that we are doomed when truth is lacking if we do not have a store of goodness and truth laid up by the Lord in our inner depths, which is symbolized by the food serving as a store for the land for the seven years of famine, to keep the land from being cut off in the famine. This situation will be discussed later in the chapter [§§5357–5376].

5303 Genesis 41:37, 38, 39, 40. *And the word was good in the eyes of Pharaoh and in the eyes of all his servants. And Pharaoh said to his servants, "Shall we find another like this man, in whom there is the spirit of God?" And Pharaoh* *said to Joseph, "Now that God has caused you to know all this, no one is understanding and wise like you. You will be over my house, and with [the words of] your mouth all my people will comply; only in relation to the throne will I be greater than you."*

And the word was good in the eyes of Pharaoh symbolizes satisfaction on the earthly plane. *In the eyes of all his servants* symbolizes satisfaction for every part of the earthly plane. *And Pharaoh said to his servants* symbolizes a perception by the earthly plane with all its component parts. *Shall we find another like this man, in whom there is the spirit of God?* means concerning the inflow of truth containing goodness that comes from within and therefore containing spiritual heavenliness. *And Pharaoh said to Joseph* symbolizes a perception received by the earthly level from spiritual heavenliness. *Now that God has caused you to know all this* means because the latter possessed foresight and providence. *No one is understanding and wise like you* means that it was the only source of truth and goodness. *You will be over my house* means that the earthly mind will be under its command and control. *And with [the words of] your mouth all my people will comply* means that every part of that plane will be obedient to it. *Only in relation to the throne will I be greater than you* means that the earthly level will seem to be the source because it will be the conduit, but spiritual heavenliness will be the actual source.

And the word was good in the eyes of Pharaoh symbolizes satisfaction on the earthly plane, as the following shows: *The word was good* means to give satisfaction. The stock phrase *in the eyes of* is used because an eye symbolizes inner sight. Consequently it symbolizes intellect, perception, awareness, and other functions of inner sight (§§2701, 2789, 2829, 3198, 3202, 3820, 4083, 4086, 4339, 4403–4421, 4523–4534). *The word was good in his eyes,* then, symbolizes satisfaction. And *Pharaoh* represents the earthly plane, as noted many times before. **5304**

And in the eyes of all his servants symbolizes satisfaction for every part of the earthly plane. This can be seen from the symbolism of "the word was good in their eyes" as satisfaction (discussed just above in §5304) and from that of *servants* as the contents of the earthly plane, particularly the outer earthly plane. **5305**

The Word often speaks of a "servant," which in an inner sense means something that serves something else. In general it means anything low down in relation to something up high. The orderly way is for what is lower to serve what is higher, and to the extent that it does so it is called a servant.

In this verse, though, "servants" refers to the contents of the earthly plane. Pharaoh represents the earthly dimension as a whole, and the general whole is what individual parts have to serve, just as the common good is served in kingdoms. For the identification of Pharaoh with the earthly dimension as a whole, see §5160.

5306 *And Pharaoh said to his servants* symbolizes a perception by the earthly plane with all its component parts. This can be seen from the symbolism of *saying* in scriptural narrative as perceiving (discussed in §§1791, 1815, 1819, 1822, 1898, 1919, 2061, 2080, 2238, 2619, 2862, 3395, 3509), from the representation of *Pharaoh* as the earthly plane, (discussed in §§5079, 5080, 5095, 5160), and from the symbolism of *his servants* as all the contents of the earthly plane (discussed just above in §5305).

5307 *Shall we find another like this man, in whom there is the spirit of God?* means concerning the inflow of truth containing goodness that comes from within and therefore containing spiritual heavenliness. This can be seen from the symbolism of a *man* as truth (discussed at §§3134, 3309, 3459) and from that of the *spirit of God* as goodness from within and therefore from the Divine. The spirit of God is what radiates from the Divine and consequently from goodness itself (since the Divine is goodness itself). What radiates is truth containing goodness, and this is what the spirit of God symbolizes in the Word. It is not his spirit itself that radiates but the truth that has goodness inside it, or sacred truth. His spirit is the means for producing it.

This "truth containing goodness" is the spiritual heavenliness that Joseph represents.

[2] The church recognizes that Joseph in a spiritual sense is the Lord, so it calls the Lord the heavenly Joseph, but no one knows what it is about the Lord that Joseph represents. The Lord is represented by Abraham, Isaac, and Jacob, Moses and Elijah, Aaron, David, and many other Bible figures, but each represents him in a different way. Abraham represents divinity itself in the Lord; Isaac, his divine rationality; Jacob, his divine earthliness; Moses, the Lord as the law, or as the narrative part of the Word; Elijah, the Lord as the prophetic part; Aaron, the Lord's priestly role; and David, his kingly role. For Joseph's representation, see §§3969, 4286, 4585, 4592, 4594, 4669, 4723, 4727, 4963, 5249. What he represents is called spiritual heavenliness on the earthly level; it cannot be expressed in any other terms. The heavenly element is goodness from the Divine, and the spiritual element is truth growing out of that goodness, or truth-from-goodness from the Lord's divine humanity. This truth is what the

Lord embodied when he lived in the world. Once he glorified himself, though, he rose above it and became divine goodness itself, or Jehovah, right down to his human nature. [3] There is nothing more that can be told in any detail about this secret.

All that can be told is the purpose in Joseph's going to Egypt, serving at first in the household of Potiphar, the chief of the bodyguards, then being held in jail, and later becoming ruler over Egypt. The purpose was for this history to represent the way the Lord made the humanity in himself more and more divine, and for the process to be written up in the Word. The Word would then contain a divine message in its inner sense, which would be mainly for the use of angels, whose wisdom—incomprehensible and inexpressible, compared to human wisdom—deals in such concepts. It would also be for the use of people on earth, who love the stories better than any other part [of the Word] and who when reading them mull over the kinds of thoughts in which angels, through an inflow from the Lord, perceive divine ideas.

And Pharaoh said to Joseph symbolizes a perception received by the earthly level from spiritual heavenliness. This can be seen from the symbolism of *saying* in the Word's narratives as a perception (noted just above in §5306) and from the representation of *Pharaoh* as the earthly level and of *Joseph* as spiritual heavenliness (mentioned many times before). **5308**

Now that God has caused you to know all this means because the latter possessed foresight and providence. This can be seen from the symbolism of *knowing,* when associated with *God,* as foresight and providence. God cannot be said to be caused to know anything, because he already knows everything on his own, and humankind's ability to know anything comes from him. In God, then, knowing means foreseeing and providing. To foresee means to know everything from the eternal past into the eternal future, and to provide means to act on that knowledge. **5309**

Foresight and providence are ascribed to it—to spiritual heavenliness— because the inner meaning here has to do with the Lord, who is the spiritual heavenliness represented by Joseph.

No one is understanding and wise like you means that [spiritual heavenliness] was the only source of truth and goodness. This can be seen from the symbolism of a person with *understanding* as truth and of a person who is *wise* as goodness (discussed above at §5287). The fact that these came from no other source than [spiritual heavenliness] alone is symbolized by *no one.* In an inner sense, no one or nobody is a negation, so it excludes everyone else; see §§5225, 5253. **5310**

5311   *You will be over my house* means that the earthly mind will be under its command and control. This can be seen from the symbolism of a *house* as the mind (discussed at §§3538, 4973, 5023), and in this case as the earthly mind, since Pharaoh, representing the earthly plane, calls it *my* house. The fact that it will be under the command and control [of spiritual heavenliness] is symbolized by [Joseph's] *being over* it. A person who is over another's house is really in charge of it, and everyone in the house is under that person's command and control, even if the owner remains nominally in charge and higher in apparent rank.

5312   *And with [the words of] your mouth all my people will comply* means that every part of that plane will be obedient to it. This can be seen from the symbolism of *complying with [the words of your] mouth* as acknowledging and following orders and therefore as obeying, and from that of *all my people* as everything on the earthly plane. *People* symbolize truth (see §§1259, 1260, 3581, 4619), so on the earthly plane they symbolize concepts of goodness and truth, and items of knowledge, because these are the earthly form of truth (§5276).

5313   *Only in relation to the throne will I be greater than you* means that the earthly level will seem to be the source because it will be the conduit, but spiritual heavenliness will be the actual source. This can be seen from the symbolism of *being greater than another* as being more important— apparently or superficially so, in this case—and from the symbolism of the *throne* here as the earthly level. A *throne* means the earthly level when the person sitting on it means spiritual heavenliness. Earthliness resembles a throne for spirituality, or in this case, for spiritual heavenliness. Generally speaking, what is lower is like a throne for what is higher. The higher element lies within the lower and acts through it, and because the activity comes through the lower element it seems to come from it. This is the idea behind Pharaoh's saying to Joseph, *Only in relation to the throne will I be greater than you.*

[2] The Word mentions thrones in many passages treating of divine truth and judgment based on that truth. In the inner meaning of these passages the throne symbolizes the exercise of divine kingship, and the throne's occupant symbolizes the Lord himself as king or judge. However, the symbolism of a throne, like that of many other objects, is relative. When the occupant stands for divinity itself and the Lord's divine humanity, a throne means divine truth radiating from him. When the occupant stands for divine truth radiating from the Lord, a throne means

the entirety of heaven, which is filled with divine truth. When the occupant means the Lord as divine truth in the higher heavens, a throne means divine truth in the lowest heaven and in the church. The symbolism of a throne, then, is relative.

A throne symbolizes something connected with divine truth because a king in the Word symbolizes truth, as does a kingdom. For this symbolism of a king, [or monarch,] see §§1672, 1728, 2015, 2069, 3009, 3670, 4581, 4966, 5044, 5068. For this symbolism of a kingdom, §§1672, 2547, 4691.

[3] The exact meaning of a throne in the Word becomes clear from the context, as in Matthew:

> I myself say to you, you shall not swear at all—neither by *heaven,* since it is *God's throne,* nor by earth, since it is *his footstool,* nor by Jerusalem, since it is the city of the great monarch. (Matthew 5:34, 35)

And in another place in the same author:

> One who swears by *heaven* swears by *God's throne* and by him who sits on it. (Matthew 23:22)

These passages explicitly say that heaven is God's throne. The earth, which is called his footstool, symbolizes what lies below heaven, which is the church. For the equating of the earth, [or land,] with the church, see §§566, 662, 1066, 1068, 1262, 1413, 1607, 1733, 1850, 2117, 2118, 2928, 3355, 4447, 4535. Likewise in Isaiah:

> This is what Jehovah has said: "*The heavens are my throne;* and the earth, my footstool." (Isaiah 66:1)

In David:

> Jehovah in the *heavens* has established *his throne.* (Psalms 103:19)

In Matthew:

> When the Son of Humankind comes in his glory, and all the holy angels with him, then he will sit *on his glorious throne.* (Matthew 25:31)

This is talking about the Last Judgment, and the one sitting on the throne is called a king in verses 34, 40 of that chapter. The glorious throne in an inner sense means divine truth in heaven springing from divine goodness.

The one sitting on the throne is the Lord, who is called a king because divine truth makes him a judge. [4] In Luke:

> He will be great and will be called the Child of the Highest One, and the Lord God will give him the *throne of David,* his father. (Luke 1:32)

This is what the angel said to Mary. Anyone can see that the throne of David is not the kingdom David had—a kingdom on earth—but a kingdom in heaven. David therefore does not mean David but the Lord's divine royalty. The throne symbolizes divine truth radiating [from him], which makes his kingdom. In John:

> I was in the spirit, when, here now, *a throne placed in heaven,* and *one sitting on the throne!* And the one sitting was similar in appearance to jasper and sard stone. But a rainbow *around the throne* was similar in appearance to emerald. *Around the throne* were *twenty-four thrones,* and *on the thrones* I saw twenty-four elders sitting. From the *throne* issued lightning bolts and thunder claps and voices, and also seven fiery lamps, burning *before the throne,* which are God's seven spirits. Moreover, *before the throne* was a sea of glass like crystal. Lastly, in the *middle of the throne* and *around the throne* were four living creatures full of eyes in front and behind. But when the living creatures give glory and honor and thanks to the *one sitting on the throne,* living forever and ever, the twenty-four elders will fall down *before the one sitting on the throne,* and worship the one living forever and ever, and cast their crowns *before the throne.* (Revelation 4:2–end)

[5] This describes the Lord's glorious throne, which portrays divine truth emanating from him. It uses representation, however, and one who does not know what the representations mean can have hardly any idea what the prophecy holds within it. Such a person will have to consider it all literally true and devoid of anything more profoundly divine. People who do not know any better cannot help picturing a heavenly kingdom that resembles a worldly one.

In reality, though, the throne placed in heaven symbolizes divine truth there, and consequently heaven in regard to divine truth. The one sitting on the throne means the Lord. He looked similar in appearance to jasper and sard stone because those stones, like all precious stones in the Word, symbolize divine truth (§§114, 3858, 3862), and stones in general symbolize religious truth (§§643, 1298, 3720, 3769, 3771, 3773, 3789, 3798). [6] The rainbow around the throne symbolizes truth transparent with goodness, because colors in the other world come from the light of heaven, and heaven's light is divine truth. (Concerning rainbows in the other world, see §§1042, 1043, 1053, 1623, 1624, 1625. Concerning colors there, §§1053, 1624, 3993, 4530, 4677, 4741, 4742, 4922.) The twenty-four thrones around the throne symbolize all truth taken as a whole—the same symbolism as twelve. (To see that twelve means all truth taken as a whole, see §§577, 2089, 2129, 2130, 3272, 3858, 3913.) The lightning bolts, thunderclaps, and voices that were issuing from the throne symbolize the terror that divine truth strikes in people who lack goodness. The seven fiery, burning lamps mean desires for truth based on goodness, which actually inflict harm on people lacking goodness, and that is why they are called God's seven spirits. The fact that they inflicted harm is plain from what follows there. [7] The glassy sea before the throne means all truth on the earthly level, so it means sacred and secular knowledge. (For this meaning of the sea, consult §§28, 2850.) The four living creatures in the middle of the throne and around the throne, full of eyes in front and behind, mean intellectual gifts in the heavens bestowed by the Divine. Four symbolizes the union of them with matters of the will—truth being on our intellectual side and goodness on our will side. That is why the passage says the creatures were full of eyes in front and behind, because eyes symbolize the contents of the intellect and, on an even higher level, matters of faith (§§2701, 3820, 4403–4421, 4523–4534; for the idea that four means union, as two does, see §§1686, 3519, 5194). The holiness of divine truth as it emanates from the Lord will be described below.

[8] Since the twenty-four thrones and twenty-four elders symbolize all truth or all matters of faith as a whole, and twelve has the same symbolism, as just mentioned, in an inner sense the twelve thrones on which the twelve apostles would sit plainly mean all truth as the source and standard of judgment. They are described this way in Matthew:

> Jesus said to the disciples, "Truly, I say to you that you who have followed me—in the rebirth, when the Son of Humankind sits *on his glorious throne,* you too will sit *on twelve thrones* judging the twelve tribes of Israel." (Matthew 19:28)

And in Luke:

> I myself am arranging for you—as my Father arranged for me—a kingdom, so that you may eat and drink at my table in my kingdom and *sit on thrones* judging the twelve tribes of Israel. (Luke 22:29, 30)

The twelve apostles mean all truth (see §§2129, 2553, 3354, 3488, 3858), as do Jacob's twelve sons and therefore Israel's twelve tribes (§§3858, 3921, 3926, 3939, 4060, 4603). Besides, the apostles cannot judge even one person (§§2129, 2553). [9] Likewise in John:

> I saw *thrones,* and people sat on them, and the power of judgment was given to them. (Revelation 20:4)

These thrones also symbolize the entirety of truth as a source and standard of judgment. The same thing is meant by the angels the Lord was to bring when he arrived for judgment (Matthew 25:31). Angels in the Word symbolize some trait of the Lord's (see §§1705, 1925, 2319, 2821, 3039, 4085), which in this verse is truth from the Divine. In the Word, such truth is called judgment (§2235).

[10] Many other passages too ascribe a throne to Jehovah or the Lord, and that is because there is something representative of his kingdom in thrones. When the inhabitants of a higher heaven converse on divine truth and judgment, a throne appears in the lowest heaven. That is why thrones are representative, as noted, and why the prophetic part of the Word mentions them so often. It is also the reason that a throne became the token of a monarch, starting in ancient times, and that as a token it symbolizes the exercise of royal power—as it does in the following places. In Moses:

> Moses built an altar and called its name Jehovah-nissi. Moreover he said, "Since their hand is on *Jah's throne,* Jehovah will be at war against Amalek from generation to generation." (Exodus 17:15, 16)

What is the hand on Jah's throne, or Jehovah's war against Amalek from generation to generation? No one can know except from the inner meaning, or by learning what a throne and Amalek mean. In the Word, Amalek symbolizes falsity that battles with truth (§1679), and a throne symbolizes divine truth itself, the target of the attack. [11] In David:

> Jehovah, you have taken up *my judgment* and my cause; *you have sat on a throne, a just judge.* Jehovah will remain forever; he has prepared *his throne* for *judgment.* (Psalms 9:4, 7)

In the same author:

> *Your throne,* God, is forever and ever; the scepter of uprightness is the scepter of your kingdom. (Psalms 45:6)

In the same author:

> Cloud and darkness are around him; justice and judgment are the *underpinning of his throne.* (Psalms 97:2)

In Jeremiah:

> In that time they will call Jerusalem *Jehovah's throne,* and all the nations will be gathered to it. (Jeremiah 3:17)

[12] Jerusalem stands for the Lord's spiritual kingdom, which is also meant by the new Jerusalem in Ezekiel and the holy Jerusalem coming down out of heaven in the Book of Revelation. The Lord's spiritual kingdom is the kingdom whose main focus is on divine truth that contains divine goodness, while his heavenly kingdom is the one whose main focus is on divine goodness that gives rise to divine truth. This shows why Jerusalem is called Jehovah's throne. And David says:

> In Jerusalem there sit *thrones for judgment.* (Psalms 122:5)

Zion, though, is called Jehovah's glorious throne in Jeremiah:

> Have you utterly spurned Judah? Has your soul grown disgusted with Zion? Do not despise it, for your name's sake! May you not degrade *your glorious throne!* (Jeremiah 14:19, 21)

Zion means the Lord's heavenly kingdom.

[13] Visual sights appear in heaven that are mentioned in various places in the Prophets, and the way the Lord's role as judge is represented there can be seen in Daniel:

> I was looking, *until thrones were overturned,* and the Ancient One sat. His clothing was like white snow, and the hair of his head was like clean wool; *his throne* was a fiery flame, its wheels a burning fire. A river of fire was pouring forth and going out before him; thousands upon thousands were waiting on him, and myriads upon myriads were standing before him. He sat [in] judgment, and books were opened. (Daniel 7:9, 10)

Scenes like these never stop appearing in heaven, and they are all representative. They result from angels' conversation in the higher heavens, which generates these sights as it descends. Angelic spirits, who receive perception from the Lord, know what they symbolize. For instance, they know what is symbolized by the Ancient One, clothing like white snow, hair of the head like clean wool, a throne like a fiery flame, wheels that are a burning fire, and a river of fire pouring forth from him. The fiery flame and river of fire represent the goodness that is inherent in divine love (§§934, 4906, 5071, 5215). [14] A similar passage in Ezekiel:

> Above the expanse that was over the head of the guardian beings was a seeming appearance of sapphire stone, *like a throne*. And on the *likeness of a throne* was what looked like the appearance of a person on it, high above. (Ezekiel 1:26; 10:1)

Another in 1 Kings:

> "I saw"—said Micaiah the prophet—"*Jehovah sitting on his throne,* and the entire army of the heavens standing next to him, on his right and on his left." (1 Kings 22:19)

Anyone who does not know what each detail represents and therefore symbolizes can only believe that the Lord, like monarchs on earth, has a throne and the other items mentioned. But there are no such things in the heavens. They are simply displayed for viewing by the lowest heaven's inhabitants, who study them as pictures and see divine secrets in them.

[15] The Lord's role as monarch, which symbolizes divine truth radiating from him, was also represented by the throne Solomon built, described this way in 1 Kings:

> Solomon made a *large throne of ivory* and laminated it with refined gold. There were six steps *up to the throne* and a round cap *to the throne* on its back. There were arms on this side and on that side attached to the seat, and two lions standing next to the arms, and twelve lions standing there on the six steps on this side and on that side. (1 Kings 10:18, 19, 20)

This is how the glorious throne was represented. The lions mean divine truth fighting and winning. The twelve lions mean all such truth taken as a whole.

[16] Since almost everything in the Word also has a negative meaning, a throne does too, and in that sense it symbolizes the reign of falsity, as in John:

> [To] the angel of the church in Pergamum: "I know your works and where you live, where *Satan's throne* is." (Revelation 2:13)

In the same author:

> The dragon gave the beast coming up out of the sea its strength and *its throne* and great authority. (Revelation 13:2)

In the same author:

> The fifth angel poured out his bowl *on the beast's throne,* and its kingdom became darkened. (Revelation 16:10)

In Isaiah:

> You have said in your heart, "I will climb into the heavens; I will raise *my throne* above the stars there." (Isaiah 14:13)

This is about Babylon.

Genesis 41:41, 42, 43, 44. *And Pharaoh said to Joseph, "See? I have put* **5314** *you over all the land of Egypt." And Pharaoh removed his ring from his hand and put it on Joseph's hand and dressed him in clothes of fine linen and put a gold necklace on his neck. And he caused him to ride in the second chariot that was his—and they shouted "Abrech!" before him—putting him over the whole land of Egypt. And Pharaoh said to Joseph, "I am Pharaoh, and other than you, no man will lift his hand or his foot in all the land of Egypt."*

And Pharaoh said to Joseph symbolizes a further perception received by the earthly level from spiritual heavenliness. *See? I have put you over all the land of Egypt* symbolizes dominion over both earthly levels. *And Pharaoh removed his ring from his hand* means a sign confirming the power that used to be his. *And put it on Joseph's hand* means that he yielded all that power to spiritual heavenliness. *And dressed him in clothes of fine linen* means an outward sign symbolizing spiritual heavenliness—*clothes of fine linen* being truth from the Divine. *And put a gold necklace on his neck* means a sign symbolizing the union of inner planes with outer ones, brought about by goodness. *And he caused him to ride in the second chariot* means a sign symbolizing that all teachings about goodness and truth come from him. *That was his* means that they come by way of the earthly dimension. *And they shouted "Abrech!" before him* means acknowledging in faith and adoring. *Putting him over the whole land of Egypt* means that this is the nature of his authority. *And Pharaoh said to Joseph* symbolizes yet another perception. *I am Pharaoh* means that this is where the earthly plane originates. *And other than you, no man will lift his hand* means that every bit of power on the spiritual plane comes from spiritual heavenliness. *Or his foot* means that every bit of power on the earthly plane also does. *In all the land of Egypt* means on both earthly planes.

5315   *And Pharaoh said to Joseph* symbolizes a perception received by the earthly level from spiritual heavenliness. This is established by the symbolism of *saying* in the narratives of the Word as perceiving (discussed many times before) and from the representation of Pharaoh as the earthly level and of Joseph as spiritual heavenliness (also discussed before). The reason the clause symbolizes a perception received by the earthly level from spiritual heavenliness is that the earthly dimension receives all its perception from something higher than itself. In this case it receives its perception from spiritual heavenliness, which is higher.

5316   *See? I have put you over all the land of Egypt* symbolizes dominion over both earthly levels. This is established by the symbolism of *putting someone over something* as dominion, and from that of *all the land of Egypt* as both earthly levels (mentioned above at §5276).

The text is talking at still further length about the dominion over the land of Egypt that Pharaoh transferred to Joseph, stripping himself of his own authority and placing all Egypt under Joseph. This event took place in divine providence, so that Joseph could take on the representation of the spiritual heavenliness that the Lord had when he was in the world. Through spiritual heavenliness the Lord reorganized his earthly level and even his physical senses to gradually make them divine. This was done so that the part of the Word telling Joseph's story would contain a divine message, a message that has the utmost holiness for the heavens and suits the angels there. Heaven's angels are in the Lord because they are in the aura of divine truth emanating from the Lord. As a result, the divine message of the Word's inner meaning, which is about the Lord and the glorification of his human nature, touches their hearts. In fact, as they are wise and understanding, it is in this message that they find all their bliss.

5317   *And Pharaoh removed his ring from his hand* means a sign confirming the power that used to be his. This can be seen from the representation of *Pharaoh* as the earthly level (discussed before), from the symbolism of a *ring* as a sign of confirmation (discussed below), and from that of a *hand* as power (discussed in §§878, 3091, 3387, 4931–4937, 5296). Plainly, then, "He removed the ring from his hand" means that he gave up the power he used to have, and "He put it on Joseph's hand" (which comes next) means that he yielded it all to spiritual heavenliness.

It is not very clear from parallel passages in the Word that a ring on the hand is a sign confirming power, because the only other place that mentions one is in Luke, where the father of the son who had squandered everything said to his slaves:

> Bring out the best robe and dress him and put a *ring on his hand* and shoes on his feet. (Luke 15:22)

(Here too the ring means a sign confirming his power within the household—the power he once had as a son.) Nonetheless, the symbolism is evident in rituals from ancient times still present among us, such as betrothals, weddings, and ordinations, in which rings are put on people's hands. These rings too symbolize a confirmation of power.

In addition, signets, which were also worn on the hand (Jeremiah 22:24), symbolize consent and confirmation; see §4874.

And put it on Joseph's hand means that he yielded all that power to spiritual heavenliness. This can be seen from the symbolism of *putting a ring on another's hand* as a sign confirming that one is yielding to the other the power one used to have (§5317) and from the representation of *Joseph* as spiritual heavenliness (mentioned many times before). **5318**

And dressed him in clothes of fine linen means an outward sign symbolizing spiritual heavenliness, and *clothes of fine linen* mean truth from the Divine. This can be seen from the symbolism of *clothes* as truth (discussed in §§1073, 2576, 4545, 4763, 5248). Clothes *of fine linen* mean truth from the Divine because clothing of fine linen was bright white and shiny, and truth from the Divine is represented by clothes with this kind of brilliance and sheen. The reason for the representation is that light from the Lord gives heaven a brilliance and gleam, and light from the Lord is divine truth itself (§§1053, 1521–1533, 1619–1632, 2776, 3195, 3222, 3339, 3485, 3636, 3643, 3862, 4415, 4419, 4526, 5219). When the Lord was transfigured before Peter, James, and John, then, *his clothes* looked *like the light* (Matthew 17:2), *radiant, very white, like snow, such as a fuller on earth could not whiten them* (Mark 9:3), and *dazzling* (Luke 9:29). Divine truth itself from the Lord's divine humanity was what was represented in this way. **5319**

However, bright white clothes in the heavens represent outer truth. Inner truth is represented by a bright, shining face. That is why being dressed in clothes of fine linen is an outward sign here—a sign of truth flowing from spiritual heavenliness, since the Lord's divinity then consisted in that truth.

[2] Fine linen and clothes of fine linen symbolize truth from the Divine in other places in the Word as well, such as Ezekiel:

> I clothed you with embroidery and gave you shoes of badger and *swathed you in fine linen* and covered you in silk. So you were adorned in gold and silver, and your clothes were *fine linen* and silk and embroidery. (Ezekiel 16:10, 13)

This is about Jerusalem, which in these verses means the ancient church. The truth known to that religion is depicted as clothes made of embroidery, fine linen, and silk and by adornment made of gold and silver. The embroidery symbolizes truth in the form of knowledge; the fine linen, earthly truth; and the silk, spiritual truth. [3] In the same author:

> *Fine linen with embroidery from Egypt was what you spread out* to serve you *as a banner.* Blue-violet and red-violet fabric from the islands of Elishah was your covering. (Ezekiel 27:7)

This is about Tyre, which also means the ancient church, but in regard to concepts of goodness and truth. The fine linen with embroidery from Egypt that it spread out symbolizes truth growing out of knowledge, as a "banner" or outward sign for that religion. [4] In John:

> The merchants of the earth will cry and mourn over Babylon, that their wares no one buys anymore—wares of gold and silver and precious stone and pearl and *fine linen* and red-violet fabric and silk, and every ivory vessel and every vessel of the most precious wood and of bronze and of iron and of marble. (Revelation 18:11, 12)

Each and every item in this passage symbolizes something about the church and therefore something having to do with truth and goodness, but since it is associated with Babylon, the meaning is a negative one. Anyone can see that the Word, which comes down from heaven, would never list such products if there were not something heavenly within each of them. For the meaning of this list of worldly wares, see the treatment of Babylon, which symbolizes a profane religion. Similarly in the same author:

> Alas, alas, you great city, *who were dressed in fine linen* and red-violet and scarlet [and were] gilded with gold and precious stone and pearls! (Revelation 18:16)

[5] The fact that each item symbolizes something divinely heavenly is obvious in the same author where he identifies fine linen as the righteous deeds of the godly:

> The time came for the Lamb's wedding, and his wife prepared herself. Then it was granted to her *to be dressed in fine linen clean and shining. The fine linen is the righteous deeds of the godly.* (Revelation 19:7, 8)

Fine linen is the righteous deeds of the godly because people who are devoted to truth from the Divine all clothe themselves in the Lord's righteousness. Light from the Lord makes their clothing white and shiny, so truth itself is represented in heaven by whiteness (§§3301, 3993, 4007). As a further result, [spirits] who are taken out of a state of devastation up into heaven appear in white, because they then strip off any shred of self-righteousness and put on the garment of the Lord's righteousness.

[6] In order for truth from the Divine to be represented in the Jewish religion, it was commanded that byssus or fine linen also be used in Aaron's garments and in the curtains around the ark. This is what Moses says about it:

> For Aaron you shall make a checkered *tunic of byssus* and make a *miter of byssus.* (Exodus 28:39)

> They made *the tunics of byssus,* the work of a weaver, for Aaron and his sons. (Exodus 39:27)

> The dwelling place you shall make of ten curtains—*interwoven byssus* and blue-violet and red-violet and double-dyed scarlet. (Exodus 26:1; 36:8)

> You shall make the courtyard of the dwelling place; there shall be hangings for the courtyard *of interwoven byssus.* (Exodus 27:9, 18; 38:9)

> There was a veil for the gate of the courtyard, the work of an embroiderer—blue-violet and red-violet and double-dyed scarlet and *interwoven linen.* (Exodus 38:18)

Byssus is fine linen, and its use was commanded because everything in and around the ark and everything about Aaron's garments represented spiritual and heavenly qualities. From this you can see how little of the Word people understand when they do not know what such items represent. In fact, they understand hardly any of it if they believe the Word has no holiness beyond the visible, literal message.

[7] Angels, who are devoted to truth from the Divine, seem to wear fine linen, or shining white, as is clear in John, where he talks about the white horse:

> The one sitting on the *white horse* was dressed in a garment dyed with blood, and his name is called the Word. His armies in heaven followed him *on white horses, dressed in fine linen, white and clean.* (Revelation 19:13, 14)

This passage makes it quite plain that fine linen is an outward symbol of truth from the Divine, since the one sitting on the white horse is the Lord as the Word. The text explicitly calls him the Word, and the Word is truth itself from the Divine. The white horse is the Word's inner meaning (see §§2760, 2761, 2762), so the multiple white horses are truths from the Divine, because the Word's inner meaning consists entirely in such truths. The rider's armies were accordingly seen on white horses, dressed in fine linen white and clean.

5320   *And put a gold necklace on his neck* means a sign symbolizing the union of inner planes with outer ones, brought about by goodness. This can be seen from the symbolism of a *neck* as inflow and communication between higher and lower planes—in other words, inner and outer ones (discussed at §3542). A *necklace,* then, since it circles the neck, is a symbol of union between them. A *gold* necklace symbolizes union through goodness, or union brought about by goodness, because gold means goodness (§§113, 1551, 1552).

In Ezekiel a necklace on the throat symbolizes a mark of union between inner and outer truth:

> I decked you in finery and put bracelets on your hands and a *necklace on your throat.* (Ezekiel 16:11)

5321   *And he caused him to ride in the second chariot* means a sign symbolizing that all teachings about goodness and truth come from him. This can be seen from the symbolism of a *chariot* as teachings about goodness and truth (discussed below). Because of this symbolism, *causing him to ride in a chariot* is a sign symbolizing that those teachings come from him.

This clause is related to Pharaoh's earlier words in verse 40: "You will be over my house, and with [the words of] your mouth all my people will comply; only in relation to the throne will I be greater than you."

The reason this symbolizes the fact that teachings about goodness and truth come from the Lord is that Joseph represents the Lord's divine spirituality (§§3971, 4669) and therefore the Lord as divine truth radiating from his divine humanity (§§4723, 4727). From this divine truth comes spiritual heavenliness.

All teachings about goodness and truth come from the Lord because he is that teaching. All teachings originate in him and have to do with him, because they have to do with the goodness that comes from love and the truth that leads to faith. This goodness and truth come from the Lord, so he not only is in them but *is* both of them. Clearly, then, teachings about goodness and truth are about the Lord alone and arise from his divinely human nature.

[2] No teachings can come from divinity itself; they can come only through divine humanity—that is, through the Word, which in its highest sense is divine truth from the Lord's divine humanity. Not even angels in the inmost heaven can grasp ideas coming directly from divinity itself, because such ideas are infinite. They transcend all understanding, including that of angels. Angels can, on the other hand, grasp teachings that come from the Lord's divine humanity, which treat of God as a divine human. Of this some idea can be formed on the basis of one's own humanity, and any conception of [the Lord's] humanity is accepted, no matter what it is like, as long as it grows out of innocent goodness and is accompanied by neighborly kindness. That is what the Lord's words in John mean:

> God has never been seen by anyone; the only-born Son, who is in the Father's embrace, is the one who has revealed him. (John 1:18)

And in the same author:

> You have never heard the Father's voice or seen his form. (John 5:37)

And in Matthew:

> No one knows the Father except the Son and those to whom the Son wishes to reveal him. (Matthew 11:27)

[3] The Word frequently mentions *chariots,* and hardly anyone knows that they symbolize teachings about goodness and truth and the items of knowledge that go to make up those teachings. People do not know this because nothing spiritual enters their minds when the Word mentions a chariot or the horses that draw it. All they think of is the earthly story line. Yet in reality, horses in the Word symbolize matters of the intellect (§§2760, 2761, 2762, 3217), so a chariot symbolizes teachings and the items of knowledge composing them.

[4] The meaning of chariots as religious teachings and items of knowledge has become clear to me from seeing chariots so many times in the other life. Furthermore, there is an area off to the right, surrounding the underground realm, where chariots and horses appear, and a line of stables too. People walk and talk together there who had been scholars in the world and whose goal in acquiring education had been to use it in their life. Sights like these come to them from angels in the higher heavens, whose conversations about intellectual matters and about teachings and items of knowledge present such sights to the spirits there.

[5] This symbolism of chariots and horses is plain enough from the following evidence: Elijah was seen being carried to heaven by a fiery chariot and fiery horses, and he and Elisha were called the chariot of Israel and its horsemen. This is what 2 Kings says about the events:

> Look! A *fiery chariot* and *fiery horses* intruded between them, and Elijah went up in a whirlwind into heaven, and Elisha was watching and shouting, "My father! My father! *The chariots of Israel, and its horsemen!*" (2 Kings 2:11, 12)

And concerning Elisha in the same book:

> When Elisha became sick with the illness of which he died, Joash king of Israel went down to him and wept before his face and said, "My father! My father! *The chariots of Israel, and its horsemen!*" (2 Kings 13:14)

The reason they were called this is that both Elijah and Elisha represented the Lord as the Word; see the preface to Genesis 18 and §§2762, 5247 at the end. The Word itself above all is the teaching of goodness and truth, because it is the source of all teachings. It was for the same reason that a *mountain full of horses and fiery chariots* was seen around Elisha by his boy, whose eyes Jehovah opened (2 Kings 6:17).

[6] Other Scripture passages also show that a chariot means a teaching, and a horse a matter of the intellect. In Ezekiel, for instance:

> You will be sated at my table on *horse* and on *chariot,* on mighty one and on every man of war. So will I give my glory to the nations. (Ezekiel 39:20, 21; Revelation 19:18)

This is talking about the Lord's Coming. Anyone can see that the horse and chariot do not mean a horse and chariot, because no one will ever be sated on these at the Lord's table. No, we will be sated on the kinds of things they symbolize, which are intellectual nourishment and teachings concerning goodness and truth.

[7] Horses and chariots symbolize the same things in the following places. In David:

> *God's chariots* are two myriads, thousands of the peaceful; the Lord is among them, as Sinai in his sanctuary. (Psalms 68:17)

In the same author:

> Jehovah covers himself with the light as clothing, stretches out the heavens like a tent curtain, laying beams for his dining rooms in the waters, *makes clouds his chariots,* walks on the wings of the wind. (Psalms 104:2, 3)

In Isaiah:

> An oracle of the wilderness beside the sea: This is what the Lord said to me: "Station a sentry to watch [and] tell." *So he saw a chariot, a pair of riders, a donkey chariot, a camel chariot,* and listened very closely, an extremely close listening. For he shouted, "I am always standing by day, Lord, as a lion on the watchtower, and I am set on my guard all the nights." But then, look: *a human-drawn chariot, a pair of riders!* And he said, "Babylon has fallen, fallen!" (Isaiah 21:6, 7, 8, 9)

[8] In the same author:

> Then they will bring all your kin in all the nations, a gift to Jehovah, *on horses,* and *in a chariot,* and *in coaches,* and *on mules,* and *on swift camels,* to my holy mountain, to Jerusalem. (Isaiah 66:20)

In the same author:

> Watch: Jehovah will come in fire, and *his chariots* will be like a windstorm. (Isaiah 66:15)

In Habakkuk:

> Did Jehovah rage in the rivers? Was your anger against the rivers? Was your wrath against the sea? *For you ride on your horses; your chariots are salvation.* (Habakkuk 3:8)

In Zechariah:

> I raised my eyes and looked, when there! *Four chariots* going out from between two mountains, and the mountains were bronze mountains.

For the first chariot, chestnut *horses; for the second chariot,* black *horses; for the third chariot,* white *horses; and for the fourth chariot,* hail-spotted *horses.* (Zechariah 6:1, 2, 3)

[9] And in Jeremiah:

Through the gates of this city will enter monarchs and chieftains, sitting on David's throne, *riding on a chariot and horses,* they and their chieftains, [each] a man of Judah, and residents of Jerusalem; and this city will be inhabited forever. (Jeremiah 17:25; 22:4)

The city that will be inhabited forever is not Jerusalem but the Lord's church, which is symbolized by Jerusalem (§§402, 2117, 3654). The monarchs who will enter through the gates of the city do not mean monarchs but truth known to the church (1672, 1728, 2015, 2069, 3009, 3670, 4575, 4581, 4966, 5044, 5068). Neither do the chieftains mean chieftains but the main, most important truths (1482, 2089, 5044). Those sitting on David's throne mean divine truth coming from the Lord (5313). Those riding on a chariot and horses mean resulting matters of the intellect and teachings.

Chariots also come up over and over in the Word's narrative parts. Since the narrative details of the Word all represent the kinds of things found in the Lord's kingdom and in the church, and the words symbolize those kinds of things, chariots have the same symbolism in the narratives.

[10] Most things in the Word also have a negative meaning, so chariots do as well. In a negative sense they symbolize evil and false teachings, and the items of knowledge supporting them, as in the following passages. In Isaiah:

Doom to those going down into Egypt for help! And *on horses they rely,* and they *trust in chariots* (that they are numerous) and *on riders* (that they are very strong), but they do not look to the Holy One of Israel. (Isaiah 31:1)

In the same author:

By the hand of your servants you blasphemed the Lord and said, "*Through the abundance of my chariots* I myself have climbed the height of the mountains, the flanks of Lebanon, where I will cut down the loftiness of its cedars, the choicest of its firs." (Isaiah 37:24)

This is the prophet's reply to the haughty speech of the Rabshakeh, commander to Assyria's king. In Jeremiah:

> Look! Water climbing from the north, which will become a flooding river and flood the earth and its abundance, the city and those living in it. And every resident of the land will wail at the *sound of the thud* of hooves of his mighty *horses, at the commotion of his chariot, the din of its wheels.* (Jeremiah 47:2, 3)

[11] In Ezekiel:

> *Because of the great number of his horses,* their dust will blanket you. *Because of the noise of rider and wheel and chariot,* your walls will shake when he comes into your gates, as one enters a breached city. *With the hooves of his horses* he will trample all your streets. (Ezekiel 26:10, 11)

In Haggai:

> I will overturn the throne of kingdoms and destroy the might of the kingdoms of the nations; I will also overturn the *chariot* and *those riding* in it, and *horses* and *their riders* will go down. (Haggai 2:22)

In Zechariah:

> "I will cut the *chariot* off from Ephraim and the *horse* from Jerusalem; I will cut off the war bow." On the other hand, he will speak peace to the nations. (Zechariah 9:10)

In Jeremiah:

> Egypt rises like a river, and like rivers its waters churn. For it has said, "I will go up; I will blanket the land; I will destroy the city and those living in it." *Go up, horses;* run mad, *chariots!* (Jeremiah 46:8, 9)

[12] In Exodus 14:6, 7, 9, 17, 23, 25, 26; 15:4, 19, the Egyptians pursue the children of Israel with *horses* and *chariots,* following Pharaoh into the Suph Sea, where the wheels of the chariots come off. These horses and chariots, and the frequent mention of them that makes up much of the event's description, symbolize matters of the intellect, teachings, and items of knowledge that are all false. So they symbolize reasonings that twist and extinguish the church's true ideas. The passage depicts the havoc and death inflicted by such falsities.

5322   *That was his* means that they come by way of the earthly dimension—
that is, teachings about goodness and truth do. This becomes clear from
the train of thought in the inner meaning and from the explanation above
in §5313.

5323   *And they shouted "Abrech!" before him* means acknowledging in faith
and adoring. This can be seen from the symbolism of *shouting* as acknowledging in faith (discussed below) and from that of *Abrech* as adoration.
In the original language, "Abrech!" means "Bend your knees!" and bending one's knees means adoration. All inward impulses of the will—and
therefore of love or desire and therefore of life—have outward gestures
corresponding to them. These acts or gestures stem from the real correspondence of outer levels with inner ones. The corresponding acts or
gestures for holy fear, for humility, and so for adoration are those of
bending one's knees, dropping down on them, and prostrating oneself
on the ground. In that state, if there is adoration from genuine humility, or humility from genuine holy fear, one's spirits fail, leading one's
joints to collapse at the borderline or midpoint where spirituality unites
with earthliness—that is, at the knees. The parts below the knees correspond with earthly attributes, and the parts above, with spiritual ones.
That is why the bending of one's knees is a symbol representing adoration. In heavenly people the act is spontaneous, but in the spiritual it is
deliberate.

[2] People once bent their knees before monarchs riding in a chariot because monarchs represented the Lord as divine truth and a chariot
symbolized the Word. This reverential custom started in a time when
everybody knew what it represented. Monarchs of that day considered
the object of adoration to be not themselves but royalty itself, which was
separate from but attached to them. In their view, monarchy was the
same as the law, and since the law came from divine truth, it was to be
adored in monarchs to the extent that they were guardians of it. The
monarchs themselves, then, attributed none of the royalty to themselves
except for their role as guardians of the law, and the more they abdicated
that role, the more they abdicated the monarchy. They realized that adoration based on anything but the law—adoration of anything but the law
in their person—was idolatry. For the equation of monarchy with divine
truth, see §§1672, 1728, 2015, 2069, 3009, 3670, 4581, 4966, 5044, 5068.
Monarchy therefore equates with law, which is essentially a kingdom's
truth—the truth by which its inhabitants are required to live. This shows
that "Abrech!" or "Bend your knees!" symbolizes adoration.

[3] Since a shout is another action that corresponds to professing something out loud, or acknowledging it in faith, the ancients also had the established custom of symbolizing such acknowledgment by shouting. For the same reason, the Word mentions shouting here and there when it deals with acclamation and acknowledgment inspired by faith. It says of John the Baptist, for instance, in John:

He testified of Jesus and *shouted,* saying, "This was the one of whom I said, 'The one coming later than I existed before me, because he was earlier than I.' I am the *voice of one shouting* in the wilderness, 'Straighten the Lord's path!'" (John 1:15, 23)

In the same author:

They took branches of palm trees and went to meet Jesus and *shouted,* "Hosanna! A blessing on the one who comes in the Lord's name, the King of Israel!" (John 12:13)

In Luke:

Jesus said to the Pharisees that if they kept silent, the stones would *shout.* (Luke 19:40)

Since shouting symbolized acknowledgment inspired by faith, and therefore acceptance as a result of that acknowledgment, we occasionally read that the Lord shouted. Examples are John 7:28, 37; 12:44, 45. And in Isaiah, too:

Jehovah will go forth as a hero; as a man of wars he will stir up his zeal. He will *shout,* even *bellow.* (Isaiah 42:13)

In a negative sense, shouting means refusal to acknowledge and therefore aversion (see §§5016, 5018, 5027) and is connected with falsity (§2240).

Putting him over the whole land of Egypt means that this is the nature of his authority. This can be seen from the symbolism of *putting him over the whole land of Egypt* as dominion over both earthly levels (discussed above at §5316). In this case, though, it means that the nature of his dominion is as described just above [§5323] and consequently that the nature of his authority is such.   **5324**

And Pharaoh said to Joseph symbolizes yet another perception. This is established by the symbolism of *saying,* the representation of *Pharaoh,* and the representation of *Joseph* as a perception received by the earthly level   **5325** from spiritual heavenliness (dealt with at §5315). Here it means another perception, because the words are repeated.

5326   *I am Pharaoh* means that this is where the earthly plane originates, which can be seen from the representation of *Pharaoh* as the earthly plane (discussed in §§5079, 5080, 5095, 5160). The symbolism of *I am Pharaoh* as the fact that this is where the earthly plane originates is clear from the next words, "Other than you, no man will lift his hand or his foot in all the land of Egypt," which mean that every bit of power on both earthly planes originates there. Because the contents of the earthly level are meant by these next words, the text first says, "I am Pharaoh."

"This is where the earthly plane originates" means that the earthly plane comes from spiritual heavenliness. Here is the situation: The earthly plane is completely different in people being created anew, or being reborn, than in people not being reborn. In nonregenerating people, the earthly plane is everything. Their thoughts come from there and their longings come from there, not from the rational plane, let alone the spiritual plane, since these two levels are closed and largely dead. [2] In regenerating people, though, the spiritual plane becomes everything. It not only oversees the thinking and longings of the earthly plane but actually becomes the earthly plane, just as a cause becomes an effect. The only active element in any effect is the cause. As a result, the earthly plane comes to resemble the spiritual. The contents of the earthly level (such as any type of concept that is somewhat worldly) do nothing on their own. They only agree to let the spiritual level act on and through the earthly level, which is to say that they let it act in an earthly way. The same with an effect. An effect contains elements that its cause does not, but those elements merely enable the cause to generate the effect itself in the effect and to bring itself (the cause) into concrete reality on that level.

This brief discussion shows how matters stand with the earthly level in a person who has been created anew, or reborn, and it is what is meant by saying that this is where the earthly plane originates, as symbolized by "I am Pharaoh."

5327   *And other than you, no man will lift his hand* means that every bit of power on the spiritual plane comes from spiritual heavenliness. This can be seen from the symbolism of a *hand* as power (discussed at §§878, 3387, 4931–4937, 5296). *No man other than you lifting his hand* consequently means no power for them except from that source alone, so it means that all power belongs to it—in other words, to spiritual heavenliness.

The fact that the hand symbolizes power *on the spiritual plane* will be seen in the next section.

Or his foot means that every bit of power on the earthly plane also does. This can be seen from the symbolism of a *foot* as the earthly plane (discussed at §§2162, 3147, 3761, 3986, 4280, 4938–4952). Here it symbolizes power on the earthly plane, because lifting a foot, like lifting a hand, symbolizes power. Lifting a hand symbolizes power on the spiritual level, and lifting a foot symbolizes power on the earthly level, since the parts of the body above the lower legs relate to spiritual qualities.

This is made especially clear by the universal human, or the three heavens. When the whole of heaven is presented to view as one person, the third or inmost heaven resembles the head, the second or middle heaven resembles the body, and the first or outermost heaven resembles the lower legs. The third or inmost heaven resembles the head because it is heavenly. The middle or second heaven resembles the body because it is spiritual. The first or outermost heaven resembles the lower legs because it is earthly. The neck, being an in-between part, accordingly symbolizes inflow and communication between heavenly and spiritual areas, and the knees, also being intermediate parts, symbolize inflow and communication between spiritual and earthly areas.

This shows that lifting a hand symbolizes power on the spiritual plane, and lifting a foot, power on the earthly plane. The power symbolized by a hand therefore relates to what is spiritual, or to truth rising out of goodness (§§3091, 3563, 4932).

"Spiritual" means what belongs to heaven's light on the earthly plane, and "earthly" means what belongs to the world's light on the earthly plane, because everything in the first category is called spiritual, and everything in the second, earthly.

In all the land of Egypt means on both earthly planes, which can be seen from the discussion in §5276 of the symbolism of *all the land of Egypt* as both earthly planes.

These are the kinds of concepts angels perceive when people on earth read that Pharaoh removed his ring from his hand and put it on Joseph's hand and dressed him in clothes of fine linen and put a gold necklace on his neck and caused him to ride in the second chariot that was his—and they shouted "Abrech!" before him—putting him over the whole land of Egypt. An angel has no way of perceiving the actual incidents in the story, because they are the kind of thing that belongs to the world, not heaven. What belongs to the world is not visible to them. Since everything in the world corresponds with something in heaven, though, angels perceive heavenly ideas where we perceive worldly ones. Otherwise no angel from heaven could possibly be present with us. To make it possible, a Word was given in which angels would perceive a sacred divine quality that they could share with the person on earth they are near to.

5330   Genesis 41:45. *And Pharaoh called Joseph's name Zaphenath-paneah and gave him Asenath, daughter of Potiphera (priest of On), as his woman. And Joseph went out over the land of Egypt.*

And Pharaoh called Joseph's name Zaphenath-paneah symbolizes the quality of spiritual heavenliness at that point. *And gave him Asenath, daughter of Potiphera (priest of On), as his woman* symbolizes the quality of the marriage between truth and goodness and between goodness and truth. *And Joseph went out over the land of Egypt* means when both earthly levels were the Lord's.

5331   *And Pharaoh called Joseph's name Zaphenath-paneah* symbolizes the quality of spiritual heavenliness at that point. This can be seen from the symbolism of a name and *calling a name* as the quality of something (discussed in §§144, 145, 1754, 1896, 2009, 2628, 2724, 3006, 3237, 3421).

Zaphenath-paneah in its original language means one who reveals mysteries and opens the future, and in a heavenly sense these two roles symbolize something divine in him, because revealing mysteries and opening the future belongs to God alone. This is the quality involved in the name. It is also the quality of spiritual heavenliness, because spiritual heavenliness is goodness that grows out of truth and that contains divinity, or stems directly from divinity.

Spiritual heavenliness containing divinity belonged exclusively to the Lord when he lived in the world and was the humanity that could hold divinity itself. It was also capable of being sloughed off when the Lord made everything human in himself divine.

5332   *And gave him Asenath, daughter of Potiphera (priest of On), as his woman* symbolizes the quality of the marriage between truth and goodness and between goodness and truth. This can be seen from the symbolism of *giving her to him as his woman,* which means marriage. It means the marriage of goodness with truth and of truth with goodness because that is precisely what marriage implies in a spiritual sense. So that is exactly what marriage implies in the Word.

The *daughter of the priest of On* symbolizes truth that grows out of goodness because a *daughter* means a desire for truth and a *priest* means goodness. Joseph, on the other hand, stands for goodness that grows out of truth and contains divinity, which is the same as spiritual heavenliness. This clarifies that what is being symbolized is the marriage of truth with goodness and of goodness with truth.

The quality of this marriage is what is being symbolized, but it cannot be explained any further because the quality the Lord had in the world cannot be comprehended, not even by angels. We can only form a sketchy picture of it from the kinds of things found in heaven, as for instance from the universal human and from the spiritual heavenliness existing there under the Lord's divine influence. Such a picture is like a thick shadow compared to light itself, though, because it is extremely vague and therefore almost worthless by comparison.

And Joseph went out over the land of Egypt means when both earthly levels were the Lord's. This is established by the symbolism here of *going out* as an inflow, and from that of the *land of Egypt* as the earthly mind (discussed many times before) and consequently as both earthly levels. Since going out symbolizes flowing in, and the land of Egypt symbolizes both earthly levels, this clause combined with the preceding ones symbolizes the quality of spiritual heavenliness and the quality of the marriage between goodness and truth and between truth and goodness, when spiritual heavenliness used an inflow to make both earthly levels its own. For what making the earthly level its own means, see §5326 just above.

5333

Genesis 41:46, 47, 48, 49. *And Joseph was a son of thirty years when he stood before Pharaoh, monarch of Egypt, and Joseph went out from before Pharaoh and crossed into all the land of Egypt. And the earth made heaps in the seven years of abundant grain provisions. And he gathered all the food of the seven years that they had in the land of Egypt and put the food in the cities; the food from the city's field that was all around it he put in the middle of it. And Joseph piled up grain like the sand of the sea, very much of it, until he ceased to count, because there was no number for it.*

5334

And Joseph was a son of thirty years symbolizes a state marked by a full remnant. *When he stood before Pharaoh, monarch of Egypt,* means together with its presence on the earthly plane. *And Joseph went out from before Pharaoh* means when the earthly dimension as a whole was the Lord's. *And crossed into all the land of Egypt* means when he brought everything that was there under his command and control. *And the earth made heaps in the seven years of abundant grain provisions* symbolizes early states, in which truth multiplied in series. *And he gathered all the food of the seven years* symbolizes preservation of truth connected with goodness, which multiplied in the early stages. *That they had in the land of Egypt* means which existed on the earthly level. *And put the food in the cities* means that he stored it away in the inner depths. *The food from the city's field* means fitting and proper for those depths. *That was all around it he put in the middle of it* means which had previously existed on the outer earthly level—he laid it up in the inner depths of the inner earthly level. *And Joseph piled up grain like the sand of the sea, very much of it,* symbolizes the multiplication of truth that comes out of goodness. *Until he ceased to count, because there was no number for it* symbolizes the kind that contains a heavenly quality from the Divine.

5335   *And Joseph was a son of thirty years* symbolizes a state marked by a full remnant. This can be seen from the symbolism of *thirty* as a full remnant (discussed below) and from that of *years* as states (discussed at §§482, 487, 488, 493, 893). Thirty in the Word symbolizes a certain amount of struggle, and it also symbolizes a full remnant. The reason it has two meanings is that it is the product both of five times six and of three times ten. Having five and six as its factors means that it symbolizes a certain amount of struggle (2276), because five symbolizes a certain amount (649, 4638, 5291) and six symbolizes struggle (720, 737, 900, 1709). Having three and ten as its factors, though, means that it symbolizes a full remnant, because three means full (2788, 4495) and ten symbolizes a remnant (576, 1906, 2284). A multiple has the same significance as the simple numbers that go into it (5291).

A remnant consists of truth joined with goodness, stored up by the Lord in a person's inner reaches; see §§468, 530, 560, 561, 576, 660, 1050, 1738, 1906, 2284, 5135.

[2] A full remnant is also symbolized by thirty, sixty, and one hundred in Mark:

> The seed that fell onto good earth yielded fruit shooting up and growing, and one bore *thirty,* and another *sixty,* and another *one hundred.* (Mark 4:8, 20)

All three of these numbers are multiples of ten and therefore symbolize a full remnant.

We cannot be reborn—that is, we cannot be let into the spiritual struggles by which we are reborn—until we have been given a full remnant. For this reason, it was decreed that the Levites not do the work in the meeting tent until they had reached thirty years old. Their work and duties are also called military service. It is put this way in Moses:

> Take a total of Kohath's sons from the midst of Levi's sons, from a *son of thirty years* and up, to a son of fifty years, *every one coming for military service,* to do the work in the meeting tent. (Numbers 4:2, 3)

The same thing is said about Gershon's sons and about Merari's in verses 22, 23, 29, 30 and again in verses 35, 39, 43 of that chapter. There is similar meaning in the fact that David was a *son of thirty years* when he started to reign (2 Samuel 5:4).

[3] From these considerations it is now clear why the Lord did not reveal himself until he was *thirty years old* (Luke 3:23); he then had a full remnant. However, the remnant the Lord had was one he had acquired for himself, and it was divine. He used it to unite his human essence with his divine essence and make his human essence divine (§1906). It is because of him, then, that thirty years symbolizes a state marked by a full remnant; that the priest-Levites entered on their duties when they were thirty years old; and that David, since he was to represent the Lord's royal aspect, did not start to reign until then. All representation traces its origin to the Lord, you see, so all representation relates to the Lord.

When he stood before Pharaoh, monarch of Egypt, means together with its presence on the earthly plane. This can be seen from the symbolism of *standing before someone* as presence and from the representation of *Pharaoh, monarch of Egypt,* as the new state of the earthly level, or the new earthly self (discussed at §§5079, 5080). Because Pharaoh represents this, he represents an earthly plane which now had spiritual heavenliness inside it and which spiritual heavenliness had now made its own. This is what is symbolized by the next words: "And Joseph went out from before Pharaoh." **5336**

And Joseph went out from before Pharaoh means when the earthly dimension as a whole was the Lord's. This can be seen from the symbolism of *going out,* which means being the Lord's (discussed below), and from the representation of *Joseph* as spiritual heavenliness and of *Pharaoh* as the earthly dimension (both discussed above). The fact that *going out* means being the Lord's, or being his own, is plain from the text before and after. It is also plain from the spiritual meaning of the expression, because in a spiritual sense, going out or issuing means making oneself present to another in a form adapted to that other. It therefore means presenting one's same self but in another form. This is the sense in which John says the Lord went out: **5337**

Jesus said of himself, "*I went out* and have come *from God.*" (John 8:42)

"The Father loves you because you have loved me and believed *that I went out from God. I went out from the Father* and have come into the world. Again I leave the world and go to the Father." The disciples said, "We believe *that you went out from God.*" (John 16:27, 28, 30)

"They recognized truly *that I went out from God.*" (John 17:8)

[2] Let the following examples illustrate what going out or issuing means:

Truth is said to go out or issue from goodness when truth is the form of goodness, or when truth is goodness in a form that the intellect can grasp.

The intellect too can be said to go out or issue from the will when the intellect is the will given form, or the will in a form discernible to the inner eye.

A thought in the intellect can likewise be said to go out or issue when it turns into speech, and the will can be said to go out when it turns into action. Thought adopts a different form when it becomes speech, but thought is still what is going out or issuing. The words or sounds clothing the thought are nothing but an addition or adaptation that makes the thought perceptible. The will is likewise given another shape when it turns into action, but the will is still what is manifesting itself in this shape. The gestures and motions clothing it are nothing but an addition or adaptation that makes it visible and effective.

Our outer self can also be said to go out or issue from our inner self, and in fact to go out in the shape of physical matter. The outer self is nothing but the inner self given a form that suits it for acting in the world in which it lives.

All this shows what going out or issuing means in a spiritual sense, when applied to the Lord. It means divinity in the form of a human and therefore divinity adapted to the perceptive ability of believers. Nonetheless, the divinity and humanity are one.

5338 *And crossed into all the land of Egypt* means when he brought everything that was there, in the earthly dimension, under his command and control. This is established by the symbolism of *all the land of Egypt* as both earthly planes (discussed in §§5276, 5278, 5280, 5288, 5301). The idea that *crossing* that land means bringing everything in the earthly dimension under his command and control follows from the preceding discussion.

5339 *And the earth made heaps in the seven years of abundant grain provisions* symbolizes early states, in which truth multiplied in series, as the following shows: The *seven years* symbolize early states, because first came seven years in which there were abundant grain provisions, and the seven years in which there was famine came afterward. *Years* mean states; see §§482, 487, 488, 493, 893. The *abundant grain provisions* symbolize multiplication of truth, as discussed in §§5276, 5280, 5292. The *earth made* means that this multiplication happened on the earthly level, since the earth, [or land,] here means the earthly level, as it does just above in §5338. And *heaps* symbolize series.

About the series symbolized by the heaps: A person who is reforming absorbs broad truths first, then the particular truths making up the broad ones, and finally the details making up the particulars. Particular truths are arranged under broad ones, and details are arranged under particular ones (§§2384, 3057, 4269, 4325 at the end, 4329 in the middle, 4345, 4383, 5208). These patterns or arrangements are symbolized in the Word by bundles and in the current case by heaps that are sheaves. They are actually the series in which multiplied truths are arranged or organized.

In people who have been reborn, these series match the arrangement of communities in the heavens. In people who have not been and cannot be reborn, they match the arrangement of communities in the hells. A person who indulges in evil and consequently in falsity, then, is a miniature hell, while a person who is devoted to goodness and therefore to truth is a miniature heaven.

However, more will be said about these series elsewhere, the Lord in his divine mercy willing [§§5343, 5530, 5881, 7408, 9394, 10303].

And he gathered all the food of the seven years symbolizes preservation **5340** of truth connected with goodness, which multiplied in the early stages, as the following shows: *Gathering* here symbolizes preserving. Joseph gathered the food and put it in the cities, in the middle of each, which symbolizes storing something up in the inner depths and therefore preserving it, because what was stored could be used in the years of famine. *Food* symbolizes everything that nourishes the inner self. What nourishes the inner self is goodness and truth, as is plain from the correspondence between earthly food, which feeds the outer self, and spiritual food, which feeds the inner self. Here it accordingly means truth connected with goodness, because this is what is preserved and stored up in the inner depths. The *seven years* symbolizes early states, in which truth multiplied (§5339). So *he gathered all the food of the seven years* plainly symbolizes preservation of truth connected with goodness, which multiplied in the early stages.

I speak about the preservation of truth connected with goodness, but few know what truth connected with goodness is, let alone how they connect and when, so I need to explain. Truth unites with goodness when we feel pleasure in helping our neighbor for the sake of truth and goodness, not for our own sake or the world's. When that is our frame of mind, the truth we hear or read or think unites with goodness. The union is usually sensed as a desire for truth for the sake of being helpful.

5341   *That they had in the land of Egypt* means which existed on the earthly level. This can be seen from the symbolism of the *land of Egypt* as the earthly mind (discussed in §§5276, 5278, 5280, 5288, 5301) and therefore as the earthly level.

5342   *And put the food in the cities* means that he stored it away in the inner depths—that is, he stored away truth connected with goodness. This can be seen from the symbolism of *putting* as storing away, from that of *food* as truth connected with goodness (discussed just above in §5340), and from that of *cities* as the earthly mind's inner depths (discussed above in §5297).

It is a secret known to few today that truth connected with goodness is stored away in the inner reaches of the earthly mind, where it is preserved for use later in life, especially for use in the trials we face when being reborn. The situation consequently needs to be explained. The seven years of abundant grain provisions symbolize truth that multiplies at first. The storing of grain in the cities and in the middle there symbolizes the storing of that truth in our inner reaches, once it is connected with goodness. The sustenance provided by the heaps during the seven years of famine symbolizes states in which we are regenerated by means of the truth connected with goodness that has been stored away in our interiors.

[2] Here is the secret: From infancy up to early adolescence, the Lord is introducing us into heaven, among the heavenly angels there. They hold us in a state of innocence, which we stay in from the time we are babies until we become adolescent, as everyone knows. When adolescence starts, we gradually shed the state of innocence but are still kept in a state of neighborly love through the feeling of love we share with our peers. In many of us this state lasts till adulthood, and during it we are among spiritual angels. Afterward, we start to think for ourselves and to act on such thoughts, with the result that we can no longer be kept in neighborly love as before. We then summon our inherited evil and allow it to lead

us. When this state arrives, the good states of neighborly love and innocence that we had previously welcomed are abolished by degrees, as we contemplate evil and solidify it with action. They are not really abolished, though. Instead, the Lord draws them up toward our inner depths and stores them away there.

[3] At that point we do not yet know truth, so the innocent and charitable goodness we had adopted in the first two stages has not yet developed a character. After all, truth gives goodness its quality (and goodness gives truth its being). From that age on, the instruction we receive and more especially our own thinking and resultant convictions instill truth in us. The more we then desire goodness, the more the Lord unites truth with goodness in us (§5340) and stores it up for our use. This state is the one symbolized by seven years of abundant grain provisions. Such truth connected with goodness is what is properly called a remnant.

Consequently, the more we allow ourselves to be reborn, the more our remnant serves its purpose, because to that extent the Lord brings some of the remnant out of storage and reintroduces it into our earthly level to create a correspondence between our outer and inner planes, or earthly and spiritual planes. This happens in the state symbolized by the seven years of famine. That is the secret.

[4] These days, people in the church believe that no matter how we have lived we can still be received into heaven out of pure mercy and enjoy eternal bliss there. They imagine it is just a matter of getting in, but they are badly mistaken. No one can be accepted and welcomed into heaven without receiving spiritual life, no one can receive spiritual life without being regenerated, and no one can be regenerated except through goodness in life united with truth in teachings. That is how we obtain spiritual life. The Lord explicitly says in John that no one can go to heaven without receiving spiritual life through rebirth:

> *Truly, truly, I say to you: unless one is born anew, one cannot see the kingdom of God.* (John 3:3)

And right afterward:

> *Truly, truly, I say to you: unless one has been born of water and spirit one cannot enter the kingdom of God.* (John 3:5)

The water is truth in our teachings (§§2702, 3058, 3424, 4976), and the spirit is goodness in our life.

No one enters by being baptized, but baptism is a symbol of the rebirth that religious people ought to keep in mind.

5343   *The food from the city's field* means truth connected with goodness in the inner depths that is fitting and proper for those depths. This can be seen from the symbolism of *food* as truth connected with goodness (discussed at §§5340, 5342).

The *food from the city's field* symbolizes truth that is fitting and proper for the inner depths because a field was customarily attached to a city and surrounded it. On an inner level, surroundings symbolize what is fitting and proper. That is why the text soon says, "that was all around it he put in the middle of it."

The reason surroundings symbolize what is fitting and proper is that all truth joined to goodness is arranged in series, and the series are set up this way: In the middle or at the core of each series lies truth joined with goodness. Around the middle or core lies truth that is fitting and proper for it, and so on in order, all the way to the periphery, where it vanishes. The series themselves are also arranged this way in relation to each other, but they change as a person's state alters.

The fact that truth joined with goodness is arranged this way is commonly presented to the inhabitants' very eyes in the other world. Such phenomena are capable of being displayed visually in heaven's light, which contains understanding and wisdom, but not in the world's light. They also cannot be displayed in heaven's light to a person on earth whose inner dimensions have not opened up, but she or he can still acknowledge them from reason's insight and can therefore see them from heaven's light in a rational way.

The pattern traces its origin to the arrangement of angelic communities in heaven, because the way communities there are arranged determines the way series of truth joined with goodness are arranged in regenerate people. The latter arrangement corresponds to the former.

5344   *That was all around it he put in the middle of it* means which had previously existed on the outer earthly level—he laid it up in the inner depths of the inner earthly level. This can be seen from the symbolism of *all around* as what is outside and therefore what is on the outer earthly level, and from that of the *middle* as what is inside (discussed at §§1074, 2940, 2973) and therefore what is on the inner earthly level. In the middle *of it*—the city—means in the inner depths of the inner earthly level because a city symbolizes inner depths (§§5297, 5342).

The inner reaches of the inner earthly level are the elements there that are called spiritual, and the spiritual elements there are the products of heaven's light. Heaven's light illuminates the elements there that come from the world's light, which are properly called earthly elements. The spiritual elements hold the store of truth connected with goodness.

The spiritual elements are ones that correspond to angelic communities in the second heaven. Our remnant puts us in touch with this heaven. The second heaven is the one that opens when we are being reborn, and it is the one that closes when we refuse to be reborn. The true ideas and good feelings laid up in our inner depths—our remnant—are actually qualities corresponding with the communities of that heaven.

And Joseph piled up grain like the sand of the sea, very much of it, symbolizes the multiplication of truth that comes out of goodness, as the following shows: The *piling up* here symbolizes multiplication. The *grain* symbolizes truth in our will and our actions, as discussed at §5295. When the multiplication of this truth is compared to the *sand of the sea,* it means that it results from goodness. In this case, it results from the goodness characterizing spiritual heavenliness, through an inflow of this. Truth in one's inner depths never multiplies except as a result of something good. The multiplication of truth that does not come from goodness is not the multiplication of truth, because that truth is not true, no matter how true it seems in outward form. It is more or less an imitation of truth, devoid of life. Being dead, it comes nowhere near the truth, because if truth is to be true for a person, it has to be alive with goodness. That is, goodness from the Lord has to bring it alive. When it is alive with goodness, then in a spiritual sense it can be said to multiply.

You can see that the multiplication of truth results only from goodness if you consider that nothing can multiply except in consequence of something that resembles a marriage. Truth cannot marry anything but goodness. If it marries something else, the liaison is not marriage but adultery. What marriage produces by multiplication is legitimate and therefore true, but what adultery produces is spurious rather than legitimate and is therefore not true.

Until he ceased to count, because there was no number for it symbolizes the kind of truth that contains a heavenly quality from the Divine. This can be seen from the fact that truth containing a heavenly quality from the Divine is limitless and therefore without *number.* Such truth existed for the sake of the Lord alone when he was in the world—the Lord being

5345

5346

represented by Joseph here, and the glorification of his earthly plane being the theme at the highest level of meaning.

5347   Genesis 41:50, 51, 52. *And to Joseph were born two sons, before the year of the famine came, whom Asenath, daughter of Potiphera (priest of On), bore him. And Joseph called the name of the firstborn Manasseh "because God has made me forget all my toil and all my father's house." And the name of the second he called Ephraim "because God has made me fruitful in the land of my affliction."*

And to Joseph were born two sons symbolizes goodness and truth from it. *Before the year of the famine came* means by way of the earthly plane. *Whom Asenath, daughter of Potiphera (priest of On), bore him* means as a result of the marriage. *And Joseph called the name of the firstborn Manasseh* symbolizes a new will on the earthly level, and its nature. *Because God has made me forget all my toil* symbolizes a removal after trials. *And all my father's house* symbolizes a removal of inherited evil. *And the name of the second he called Ephraim* symbolizes a new intellect on the earthly level, and its nature. *Because God has made me fruitful* symbolizes a consequent multiplication of truth springing from goodness. *In the land of my affliction* means where he had suffered spiritual trials.

5348   *And to Joseph were born two sons* symbolizes goodness and truth from it—from the inflow of spiritual heavenliness into the earthly plane—as the following shows: *Being born* symbolizes being reborn, so it symbolizes truth's birth from goodness, or faith's birth from neighborly love, as discussed at §§4070, 4668, 5160. For the births mentioned in the Word being spiritual births, see §§1145, 1255, 1330, 3263, 3279, 3860, 3868. And the *sons,* Manasseh and Ephraim, symbolize goodness and truth, as discussed just below [§§5351, 5354]. Manasseh symbolizes the will side of the new earthly level, and Ephraim, the intellectual side. To say the same thing another way, Manasseh symbolizes goodness on the new earthly level (since goodness is a feature of the will), and Ephraim symbolizes truth there (since truth is a feature of the intellect).

In other passages as well where we read that two sons were born, one of them symbolizes goodness, and the other, truth. Take Esau and Jacob: Esau symbolizes goodness (see §§3302, 3322, 3494, 3504, 3576, 3599) and Jacob truth (§§3305, 3509, 3525, 3546, 3576). Likewise the two sons Judah had by Tamar—Perez and Zerah (§§4927, 4928, 4929). The same here with Manasseh and Ephraim. Their birth comes up now because the last several verses have dealt with the inflow of spiritual heavenliness into the earthly plane and therefore with the earthly plane's rebirth, which is accomplished only through goodness and truth.

Before the year of the famine came means by way of the earthly plane. **5349** This can be seen from the symbolism of *before the year of the famine came*, which means while the state lasted in which truth that was based on goodness multiplied—a state symbolized by the years of abundant grain provisions. So it means before the state of desolation symbolized by the years of famine. In this prior state, truth based on goodness multiplied on the earthly plane, with the consequence that goodness and truth were born to spiritual heavenliness by way of the earthly plane. The clause therefore symbolizes this consequence.

Whom Asenath, daughter of Potiphera (priest of On), bore him means **5350** as a result of the marriage. This can be seen from the discussion above at §5332.

And Joseph called the name of the firstborn Manasseh symbolizes a new **5351** will on the earthly level, and its nature. This can be seen from the representation of *Manasseh* in the Word as spiritual goodness on the earthly plane and accordingly as a new will (discussed below). The name also involves the actual quality of this goodness, or of this new will. The fact that the name involves this quality can be seen from names given to other figures along with an explanation of the quality, just as Manasseh's name is explained in these words: "because God has made me forget all my toil and all my father's house." This describes the quality Manasseh symbolizes. Furthermore, when the text says someone "called the name," this too means that the name contains the quality, because a name and *calling a name* symbolize the quality of a thing; see §§144, 145, 1754, 1896, 2009, 2724, 3006, 3421.

[2] The reason the *firstborn*, called Manasseh, symbolizes spiritual goodness on the earthly plane, or a new will there, is that goodness really is firstborn in the church, or in a person becoming a church. Truth is not firstborn, although it appears to be so (see §§352, 367, 2435, 3325, 3494, 4925, 4926, 4928, 4930). This can be seen from the fact that in human beings, the will comes first. The human will is the beginning of human life. The human intellect comes after, and applies itself under the guidance of a person's will. What grows out of the will is called goodness in people who have received a new will from the Lord through regeneration. It is called evil in people who have refused to accept a new will. What comes from the intellect is called truth in the regenerate, but falsity in the unregenerate.

However, the human will is not perceptible to the senses except through the intellect. The intellect is the will given form, or the will in a perceptible form. Consequently, people suppose that truth emanating from the intellect is firstborn, when in reality this is just an appearance resulting from the cause just now mentioned.

[3] That is why people once debated which was firstborn, the truth that leads to faith or the goodness that comes from charity. People who decided on the basis of appearances said it was truth, but those who did not rely on appearances acknowledged that it was goodness. That is also why modern people make faith the first and most essential ingredient of religion, while they make charity secondary and nonessential. They have blundered into a much more sweeping error than the ancients, though, by presuming that faith alone saves us. In the church, "faith" means all doctrinal truth, and "charity" means all goodness in life. People do call charity and charitable deeds the fruits of faith, but who believes that the fruits contribute one whit to salvation? Consider the belief that we are saved by faith in the last hour of our life, no matter how we lived before. In fact, consider how people use doctrine to drive a wedge between the deeds constituting charity, and faith, saying that faith alone saves us without good deeds, or that deeds, which are a matter of life, contribute nothing to salvation. Oh, what a faith! Oh, what a religion! People revere a dead faith and reject a living faith, even though faith without charity is like a body without a soul. As everyone knows, bodies that have no soul are removed from sight and discarded, because they stink. The same for faith without charity in the other world. People who dedicated themselves to so-called faith devoid of charity are all in hell, but people who dedicated themselves to charity are all in heaven. Our life awaits each of us, not our theology, or at least no more of it than partakes of our life.

[4] The symbolism of Manasseh (a new will on the earthly plane—in other words, spiritual goodness there) is not as clear from other passages in the Word as the symbolism of Ephraim (a new intellect on the earthly plane, or spiritual truth there). Still, a conclusion about Manasseh can be drawn from Ephraim. Where the Word mentions this kind of pair, one symbolizes goodness, and the other, truth. Consequently, to see that Manasseh symbolizes spiritual goodness on the earthly plane, which belongs to the new will, read the section about Ephraim just below [§5354].

5352   *Because God has made me forget all my toil* symbolizes a removal after trials. This can be seen from the symbolism of *forgetting* as removal, [or distance] (discussed in §§5170, 5278), and from that of *toil* as combat and therefore as trials. So it is that *God has made me forget all my toil* symbolizes a removal after trials—that is, a removal of evil that has caused suffering. The symbolism is also plain from the story of Joseph in Canaan among his brothers and afterward in Egypt. In Canaan, he was thrown into a pit and sold. In Egypt, he served as a slave and stayed in prison several years. It has already been shown that these incidents symbolize trials, and they are clearly what the toil refers to.

And all my father's house symbolizes a removal of inherited evil. This can be seen from the symbolism of the *father's house* as inherited evil. On an inner level, a house symbolizes a person and in fact either the rational or the earthly mind of a person. In particular it symbolizes the will there, so it symbolizes good or evil, since these are traits of the will (see §§710, 2233, 3128, 4973, 4982, 5023). This being so, the father's house here symbolizes inherited evil. **5353**

The quality symbolized by Manasseh is present in this clause and the previous one. In the original language, Manasseh means forgetfulness and therefore, on an inner level, the removal of evil, both applied and inherited. When this evil has been removed, a new will arises. The inflow of goodness from the Lord brings a new will into being, and this inflow is constant in us, but applied and inherited evil hinder and block it from being received, so when these have been removed, the new will emerges.

That a new will then emerges is obvious from people subjected to misfortune, misery, and sickness. Under such circumstances, self-love and materialism are removed, and since they are the fount of all evil, the sufferer then thinks well of God and of fellow human beings, wishing them well. Likewise in trials, which are spiritual troubles, and therefore inner miseries and times of despair. These are the primary means of removing evil, and after it has been removed, heavenly goodness flows in from the Lord. This creates a new will on the earthly level, which is Manasseh in a representative sense.

And the name of the second he called Ephraim symbolizes a new intellect on the earthly level, and its nature. This can be seen from the symbolism of a *name* and *calling a name* as the quality of something (discussed in §§144, 145, 1754, 1896, 2009, 2724, 3006, 3421) and from the representation of *Ephraim* as the intellect on the earthly level, discussed below. **5354**

First I need to say what the new intellect and new will symbolized by Ephraim and Manasseh are. People in the church do know that we need to be born anew, or regenerated, if we are to enter the kingdom of

God. They know it because the Lord explicitly said so in John 3:3, 5. However, few know what being born anew is, because few know what good and evil are. People do not know what good and evil are because they do not know what charity for their neighbor is. If they knew this, they would also know what goodness is, and from that they would know what evil is, because everything that comes out of charity for one's neighbor is good.

[2] We cannot adopt this goodness on our own, because it is heavenliness itself flowing in from the Lord. The heavenliness flows in constantly, but evil and falsity block it from being received. In order to receive it, we have to remove any evil and, so far as we can, falsity too. That is how we position ourselves to accept the inflow. Once the evil has been removed and we are receiving the inflow, we are given a new will and a new intellect. Our new will enables us to feel pleasure in helping our fellow human for no selfish reason, and our new intellect makes us aware of pleasure in learning what is good and true for the sake of goodness and truth, and for the sake of life. Since this new intellect and new will come into existence through what flows in from the Lord, people who have been reborn acknowledge and believe that the goodness and truth affecting them come from the Lord, not from themselves. They also see that whatever comes from themselves on their own is nothing but evil. [3] These remarks show what being born anew is and what the new will and new intellect are.

The rebirth through which we acquire a new intellect and will does not happen in a moment. It takes place from infancy to the end of life and afterward in the other world forever, and is accomplished by divine means that are countless and indescribable. After all, we are nothing but evil on our own. This evil blasts continuously from a kind of furnace and constantly tries to stifle any goodness being born. To remove the evil and let goodness take root in its place—this cannot be done except throughout the course of life and by divine means that are countless and indescribable. Hardly any of the means are known today because people do not allow themselves to be reborn. They do not believe that rebirth is anything real because they do not believe in life after death. The process of regeneration, which contains much that cannot be described, constitutes the bulk of angelic wisdom and is such that no angel working to eternity can fully exhaust the subject. That is why it is the main subject of the Word's inner meaning.

[4] The fact that Ephraim is a new intellect on the earthly plane is clear from many places in the Word, especially in the prophet Hosea, who has a lot to say about Ephraim. Here is one passage:

> I know *Ephraim,* and it does not lie hidden from me, Israel, that you have committed utter whoredom, *Ephraim,* that Israel has been defiled. Israel and *Ephraim* will collapse because of their wickedness; Judah will also collapse with them. *Ephraim* will become a wasteland on the day of correction. And I am like a moth grub to *Ephraim,* and like a wood worm to the house of Judah. And *Ephraim* saw his own disease, and Judah his own wound, and *Ephraim went to Assyria* and sent to king Jareb, and he could not heal you. (Hosea 5:3, 5, 9, 11, 12, 13)

Again in the same author:

> When I healed Israel, then *Ephraim's* wickedness was revealed, as was Samaria's evil, because they practiced falsehood. And a thief came; a troop poured outside in all directions. And *Ephraim* was like a stupid pigeon: no heart. *They called Egypt; they left for Assyria.* When they go, I will spread my net out over them. (Hosea 7:1, 11, 12, and following verses)

[5] Other passages:

> Israel has been swallowed up; now they will exist among the nations like a vessel in which there is nothing desirable. When they went up to *Assyria,* they were a lone wild donkey. *Ephraim* procures itself lovers for a harlot's wages. (Hosea 8:8, 9)

> Israel will not live in Jehovah's land, and *Ephraim will return to Egypt,* and in *Assyria* they will eat what is unclean. (Hosea 9:3)

> *Ephraim* surrounded me with a lie, and the house of Israel [surrounded me] with deceit. And Judah still rules with God and with the holy ones of Israel. *Ephraim* is grazing on a breeze and pursues an east wind. Every day he multiplies lies and devastation; and with *Assyria* they strike a pact, and oil is carried off into *Egypt.* (Hosea 11:12; 12:1)

There are many other places in the same author that also mention Ephraim, such as 4:16, 17, 18; 5:3, 5, 9, 11, 12, 13; 7:8, 9; 9:8, 11, 13, 16; 10:6, 11; 11:3, 8, 9; 12:8, 14; 13:1, 12; 14:8. [6] In all these passages, Ephraim means the church's intellect, Israel means its spirituality, and Judah, its heavenliness.

Since Ephraim symbolizes the church's intellect, the text frequently describes Ephraim as going to Egypt and Assyria. Egypt symbolizes knowledge, and Assyria symbolizes reasoning based on knowledge. Both are attributes of the intellect. For the meaning of Egypt as knowledge, see §§1164, 1165, 1186, 1462, 2588, 3325, 4749, 4964, 4966; and for the meaning of Asshur or Assyria as the use and misuse of reason, see §§119, 1186.

[7] Ephraim also symbolizes the church's intellect in the following places. In Zechariah:

> Rejoice immensely, daughter of Zion; cheer aloud, daughter of Jerusalem! See: your king comes to you! *"I will cut the chariot off from Ephraim* and the horse from Jerusalem, and I will cut off the war bow." On the other hand, he will speak peace to the nations. And his rule will be from sea to sea, and from the river to the ends of the earth. I will stretch Judah out for myself; *I will fill Ephraim with the bow,* and I will stir up your sons, Zion, along with your sons, Javan. (Zechariah 9:9, 10, 13)

This is about the Lord's Coming and the church among non-Jewish nations. Cutting the chariot off from Ephraim, and the horse from Jerusalem, stands for cutting off the church's whole intellect. Filling Ephraim with a bow stands for giving the church a new intellect. A chariot means teachings (see §5321), a horse means the intellect (§§2760, 2761, 2762, 3217, 5321), and a bow also means teachings (§§2686, 2709). Teachings rely on our intellect, because when we understand teachings with our intellect, we believe them. Our understanding of teachings determines what our faith is like. [8] That is why Ephraim's sons are called archers in David:

> *Ephraim's* sons, who were armed and were *archers,* turned tail on the day of battle. (Psalms 78:9)

In Ezekiel:

> Son of humankind: take yourself one stick and write on it, "For Judah and for the children of Israel, his companions." Then take one stick and write on it, "To Joseph belongs the *stick of Ephraim* and of the whole house of Israel, his companions." Next, join them, one with the other for yourself, into one stick, so that they will both be one in my hand. Look: I myself shall take Joseph's stick, which is in the hands of *Ephraim* and of the tribes of Israel, his companions, and add those that are on top of him to Judah's stick, and make them into one stick, to be one in my hand. (Ezekiel 37:16, 17, 19)

Here too Judah means the church's heavenly side, Israel means its spiritual side, and Ephraim means its intellect. These will become one through the goodness that comes of neighborly love, which is symbolized by the idea that the two sticks would become one. A stick means the goodness that comes of neighborly love and therefore the goodness in good deeds; see §§1110, 2784, 2812, 3720, 4943. [9] In Jeremiah:

> There is a day that guards will shout *from the mountain of Ephraim,* "Rise! Go up Zion to Jehovah our God!" I will be as a father to Israel, and *Ephraim* is my firstborn. (Jeremiah 31:6, 9)

In the same author:

> I have clearly heard *Ephraim* lamenting, "You chastised me, and I am chastised; like a calf unaccustomed to it, turn me, so that I will be turned." Is *Ephraim* not a child precious to me? Was he not the offspring of my pleasures? For after I speak against him, I will certainly remember him again. (Jeremiah 31:18, 20)

In the same author:

> I will return Israel to its dwelling place to graze in Carmel and Bashan, and *on the mountain of Ephraim* and in Gilead their soul will receive its fill. (Jeremiah 50:19)

In Isaiah:

> Doom to the crown of pride, to *Ephraim's drunkards,* and to his drooping flower and glorious beauty, which lie at the head of the valley of rich things thrown into confusion by wine. (Isaiah 28:1)

[10] In these passages too Ephraim symbolizes the church's intellect. The church's intellect is what the people in the church understand of truth and goodness—that is, of the teachings about faith and charity—so it is a notion, concept, or idea of those topics. The truth itself is the spiritual element of the church, and the goodness is its heavenly element, but one individual understands truth and goodness in a different way than another. The way a person understands truth, then, determines the nature of truth for that person. The same for an understanding of goodness.

[11] What is the will of the church that Manasseh stands for? This can be seen from the intellect that Ephraim stands for. The church's will, like its intellect, varies from person to person.

Manasseh symbolizes the church's will in Isaiah:

> In the wrath of Jehovah Sabaoth, the earth has gone dark and the people
> have become like food for the fire; a man does not spare his brother. A
> man will eat the flesh of his own arm; *Manasseh* [will eat] *Ephraim,* and
> *Ephraim Manasseh.* Together they are against Judah. (Isaiah 9:19, 20, 21)

"A man will eat the flesh of his own arm; Manasseh [will eat] Ephraim,
and Ephraim Manasseh" means that what people in the church each want
will oppose what they understand, and what they understand will oppose
what they want. [12] In David:

> God has spoken in his holiness: "I will exult. I will split Shechem, and the
> valley of Succoth I will measure out. I own Gilead, and I own *Manasseh,*
> and *Ephraim* is the strength of my head." (Psalms 60:6, 7)

In the same author:

> Shepherd of Israel, turn an ear; you who lead Joseph like a flock, who
> sit upon the guardian beings, shine out *before Ephraim* and Benjamin
> and *Manasseh.* Arouse your might! (Psalms 80:1, 2)

Again Ephraim stands for the church's intellect, and Manasseh, for its will.

The same meaning is evident from the blessing Jacob gave Ephraim
and Manasseh before he died, as recorded in Genesis 48. It can also be
seen from the fact that Jacob replaced Reuben with Ephraim, and Simeon
with Manasseh (Genesis 48:3, 5). Reuben represented the church's intellect, or an intellectual, doctrinal faith (§§3861, 3866). Simeon represented
faith in action, or obedience and the intent to act on truth, which is the
source and means of neighborly love, so he represented truth in action,
which is the goodness of the new will (§§3869, 3870, 3871, 3872).

[13] Jacob, who by then was Israel, blessed Ephraim above Manasseh
by placing his right hand on Ephraim and his left on Manasseh (Genesis
48:13–20). This happened for the same reason that Jacob usurped Esau's
birthright. The same reason also operated in the case of Judah's sons
by Tamar—Perez and Zerah—when Zerah, although he was firstborn,
came out after Perez (Genesis 38:28, 29, 30). What was that reason? It
was that when a person is being reborn, religious truth (the province of
the intellect) seems to come first, and charitable goodness (the province
of the will) seems to come second, yet goodness is really first, and unmis-
takably so when the person has been reborn. On this subject, see §§3324,

3539, 3548, 3556, 3563, 3570, 3576, 3603, 3701, 4243, 4245, 4247, 4337, 4925, 4926, 4928, 4930, 4977.

Because God has made me fruitful symbolizes a consequent multiplica- **5355** tion of truth springing from goodness. This can be seen from the symbolism of *making fruitful* as multiplication—specifically, the multiplication of truth springing from goodness. Fruitfulness is mentioned in reference to goodness, and multiplication in reference to truth (§§43, 55, 913, 983, 1940, 2846, 2847). That is why Ephraim was named for fruitfulness, in the original language, and the character of the fruitfulness is contained in the words "because God has made me fruitful in the land of my affliction." The character of the fruitfulness is that after the trials [the Lord] suffered on his earthly plane, truth based on goodness multiplied there.

A few words describing the multiplication of truth that springs from goodness are called for: When we are intent on goodness—in other words, when we love our neighbor—we also love truth. The more intent we are on goodness, then, the more the truth affects us, because goodness lies within truth like a soul within its body. So when goodness causes truth to multiply, it propagates. If the goodness belongs to genuine love for our neighbor, it propagates in and by means of truth to an unlimited extent, because neither goodness nor truth has a stopping point. Infinity exists in everything, because everything comes from the Infinite. Nonetheless, this unlimited amount can never even begin to reach infinity, because there is no ratio between what is finite and what is infinite.

Truth rarely multiplies in the church today, because the goodness belonging to genuine love for one's neighbor is nonexistent. People believe it is enough to know the religious creed of the church they were born into and to confirm it in various ways. However, those possessing the goodness that comes of genuine charity and therefore a desire for truth are not content with this. No, they want light from the Word to show them what is true, and they wish to see it before they confirm it. Goodness also gives them light to see by, because goodness is what enables a person to discern truth. The Lord is present in what is good and supplies us with discernment. When we take our truth from these sources, it grows without limit. The situation resembles a tiny seed that grows into a tree and produces other tiny seeds that then create a garden; and so on.

In the land of my affliction means where he had suffered spiritual trials. **5356** This can be seen from the symbolism of the *land*—the land of Egypt—as the earthly level (discussed in §§5276, 5278, 5280, 5288, 5301) and from that of *affliction* as trial (discussed in §1846). *In the land of my affliction,* then, plainly means on the earthly level, where he suffered trials. So it means that truth springing from goodness multiplied there. This fruitfulness or multiplication of truth based on goodness is mainly accomplished through trials, which explains why the text says what it does.

The reason this fruitfulness is mainly accomplished through trials is that trials remove self-love and materialism, so they remove evil, and when evil has been removed, a desire for goodness and truth flows in from the Lord; see just above at §5354.

Trials also give quality to the perception of goodness and truth, through the opposites that evil spirits then pour in. When opposites are perceived, their relative value can be compared, and this relative value gives them all their quality. No one can know what is good without also knowing what is not good, and no one can know what is true without knowing what is not true.

Trials also reinforce goodness and truth, because during them we fight evil and falsity, and winning the fight brings us into stronger affirmation.

What is more, evil and falsity are so thoroughly subdued in times of trial that they no longer make the slightest attempt to rise up. As a result, evil is cast off to the sides along with falsity, and they are suspended there, face down and feeble. Goodness, in contrast, holds the center, along with truth. The more intense the desire for it, the more it rises up to heaven toward the Lord, the one who is raising it.

5357   Genesis 41:53, 54, 55, 56, 57. *And the seven years of abundant grain provisions that were in the land of Egypt were completed. And the seven years of the famine started to come, as Joseph had said, and there was famine in all lands, but in all the land of Egypt there was bread. And all the land of Egypt was starving, and the people shouted to Pharaoh for bread, and Pharaoh said to all Egypt, "Go to Joseph; what he says to you, you are to do." And the famine was on the whole face of the earth, and Joseph opened everything in which [there was grain] and sold to Egypt, and the famine grew strong in the land of Egypt. And all the earth came to Egypt to buy, to Joseph, because the famine grew strong in all the earth.*

And the seven years of abundant grain provisions were completed means after the states in which truth multiplied. *That were in the land of Egypt* means on the earthly level. *And the seven years of the famine started to come* symbolizes the desolate states that followed. *As Joseph had said* means as spiritual heavenliness foresaw. *And there was famine in all lands* symbolizes desolation throughout the earthly dimension. *But in all the land of Egypt there was bread* symbolizes a remnant of the truth-from-goodness that had multiplied. *And all the land of Egypt was starving* symbolizes desolation on both earthly levels. *And the people shouted to Pharaoh for bread* symbolizes the pressing need goodness had for truth. *And Pharaoh said to all Egypt* symbolizes a perception. *Go to Joseph* means that it came from spiritual heavenliness. *What he says to you, you are to do* means provided there is obedience. *And the famine was on the whole face of the earth* means that there was desolation to the point of despair. *And Joseph opened everything in which [there was grain]* symbolizes a communication from the remnant. *And sold to Egypt* symbolizes adoption. *And the famine grew strong in the land of Egypt* symbolizes increasing severity. *And all the earth came to Egypt* means that truth and goodness were inserted into the knowledge belonging to the church. *To buy* symbolizes their resulting adoption. *To Joseph* means where spiritual heavenliness existed. *Because the famine grew strong in all the earth* symbolizes desolation everywhere in the earthly dimension except there.

And the seven years of abundant grain provisions were completed means after the states in which truth multiplied, as can be seen from the explanation above at §§5276, 5292, 5339, where the same words occur. **5358**

That were in the land of Egypt means on the earthly level. This is established by the discussion in §§5080, 5095, 5276, 5278, 5280, 5288 of the symbolism of the *land of Egypt* as the earthly level. **5359**

And the seven years of the famine started to come symbolizes the desolate states that followed. This can be seen from the symbolism of *years* as states (discussed in §§482, 487, 488, 493, 893) and from that of *famine* as a lack of knowledge about truth and goodness (discussed in §§1460, 3364) and consequently as desolation. **5360**

The reason *famine* means this lack, or desolation, is that there is no heavenly or spiritual food except goodness and truth. These are what nourish angels and spirits; these are what they starve for when hungry and thirst for when thirsty. As a result, physical food corresponds to this food. Bread, for example, corresponds to heavenly love, wine corresponds to spiritual love, and so on for everything relating to bread or food and to wine or drink. When this heavenly and spiritual food runs out, there is famine, which the Word refers to as desolation and devastation—desolation when truth fails, and devastation when goodness fails.

[2] Many passages in the Word speak of this desolation and devastation, where it is depicted as ruination of the earth and of kingdoms, cities, nations, and peoples. Other expressions for it are an *emptying, a cutting off,* a *culmination,* a *wilderness,* and a *void.* The state itself is called

the great day of Jehovah, the day of his wrath and vengeance, a day of shadow and darkness, of cloud and dimness, a day of divine visitation, and the day when the earth will perish—that is, the last day, and the day of judgment. Since people have not understood the Word's inner meaning, they have so far been thinking that it is the day when the earth will be destroyed and that not until then will there be a resurrection and day of judgment. They fail to realize that the day there symbolizes a state, and the earth symbolizes the church. The day when the earth will be destroyed, then, is the state in which the church will die out. So when the Word talks about this death, it also talks about a new earth, which means a new religion. To learn about the new earth and new heaven, see §§1733, 1850, 2117, 2118 at the end, 3355 at the end, 4535. Strictly speaking, the devastation and desolation mentioned in the Word implies and depicts the church's final stage preceding the state of a new church.

Desolation and devastation in the Word also depict the state preceding a person's rebirth, and that state is symbolized here by the seven years of famine.

5361   *As Joseph had said* means as spiritual heavenliness foresaw, as the following shows: *Saying* in Scripture narrative means perceiving, as discussed many times in earlier sections. When it applies to the Lord, who is Joseph here, it means perceiving in himself and consequently foreseeing. And *Joseph* represents spiritual heavenliness, as discussed in §§5249, 5307, 5331, 5332.

5362   *And there was famine in all lands* symbolizes desolation throughout the earthly dimension. This is established by the symbolism of *famine* as desolation (discussed above at §5360) and from that of *all lands* as throughout the earthly dimension. For the symbolism of a land as the earthly mind and therefore the earthly level, see §§5276, 5278, 5280, 5288, 5301.

5363   *But in all the land of Egypt there was bread* symbolizes a remnant of the truth-from-goodness that had multiplied. This can be seen from the fact that *bread in all the land of Egypt* means the grain that was heaped up in the seven years of abundant grain provisions and stored in the cities. This grain symbolized a remnant stored away in the inner depths of the earthly mind, as was said and shown in several places above [§§5291–5299, 5339–5342]. *Bread in all the land of Egypt,* then, symbolizes a remnant of the truth-from-goodness that had multiplied.

Another piece of evidence that the bread in the land of Egypt means a remnant is this: In the seven years of famine, Egypt suffered as much as any other land, except that it had caches the other lands did not; and those years had already started. That is why the text now goes on to say, "And all the land of Egypt was starving."

And all the land of Egypt was starving symbolizes desolation on both earthly levels. This can be seen from the symbolism of *starvation*, [or famine,] as desolation (discussed above at §§5360, 5362) and from that of *all the land* as both earthly levels (discussed at §5276).

5364

And the people shouted to Pharaoh for bread symbolizes the pressing need truth had for goodness, as the following shows: *Shouting* is a sign of one grieving and mourning and therefore of one in dire need. *People* symbolize truth, as discussed in §§1259, 1260, 3295, 3581. *Pharaoh* represents the earthly plane, as discussed in §§5079, 5080, 5095, 5160. And *bread* symbolizes the heavenly quality of love, and therefore goodness, as discussed in §§276, 680, 2165, 2177, 3464, 3478, 3735, 3813, 4211, 4217, 4735, 4976. From this it follows that *the people shouted to Pharaoh for bread* symbolizes the pressing need truth had for goodness on the earthly plane.

5365

Admittedly this meaning seems remote from the literal, narrative one, but people focused on the inner meaning understand the shouting, the people, Pharaoh, and the bread in exactly the sense given here, so this overall meaning results.

[2] A word about the pressing need truth had for goodness: Truth needs goodness, and goodness needs truth. When truth feels a need for goodness, it unites with goodness, and when goodness feels a need for truth, it unites with truth. The reciprocal union of goodness and truth—the union of truth with goodness and of goodness with truth—is the heavenly marriage.

In the beginning stages of our rebirth there is a multiplication of truth but little multiplication of goodness. Because truth then does not have goodness to unite with, it is drawn up and stored away in our earthly plane's inner depths, to be brought back out as goodness grows. In this state, truth has a pressing need for goodness and even unites with goodness so far as goodness flows into our earthly level. This union does not produce any fruit, though. Once rebirth is complete, on the other hand, goodness grows, and as it grows it develops a pressing need for truth. It also goes about acquiring truth with which it can unite. The result is a union of goodness with truth, and when they unite, truth based on goodness and goodness based on truth do produce fruit.

[3] The world is deeply ignorant about this process, but heaven is very familiar with it. If the world knew (not merely as a piece of information but also by perception) what heavenly love or love to the Lord

was, and what spiritual love or charity for one's neighbor was, it would also know what goodness is, because all goodness belongs to those two kinds of love. The world would also know that goodness longs for truth, and truth for goodness, and that the two unite according to the strength and nature of the longing. Their connection with each other would be evident from the fact that when a true thought enters our mind, the goodness connected with it also makes an appearance, and when a good impulse stirs us, the truth connected with it also makes an appearance. Both come accompanied by a desire, longing, delight, or sacred yearning. This experience would reveal the nature of the connection. But the world has no hunch or perception to tell it what goodness is, so ideas like these cannot come to its awareness. What we do not know we do not understand, even when we stumble across it.

[4] Since it is generally unknown that spiritual goodness is charity for one's neighbor, the world and especially the scholars in it dispute what the highest good is. Hardly anyone has said that the highest good is the sensation of delight, good fortune, bliss, and happiness imparted by a mutual love that lacks any selfish or worldly goal. Rarely is it said that this sensation actually constitutes heaven. Plainly, then, today's world has no idea at all what spiritual goodness is. Still less does it know several other facts: that goodness and truth form a marriage between them, that heaven is to be found in this marriage, that people engaged in the marriage of goodness and truth have wisdom and understanding, and that they also experience good fortune and happiness in unbounded variety beyond words. The world does not know even one type of this happiness, so it does not acknowledge or believe in it. Yet such happiness is heaven itself—in other words, the heavenly joy that the church talks so much about.

5366   *And Pharaoh said to all Egypt* symbolizes a perception. This is established by the symbolism of *saying* in the Word's narratives as perceiving (discussed in §§1791, 1815, 1819, 1822, 1898, 1919, 2061, 2080, 2862, 3395, 3509), by the representation of *Pharaoh* as the earthly plane in general (discussed in §5160), and by the symbolism of *all Egypt* as both earthly planes (discussed in §§5276, 5364). This shows that *Pharaoh said to all Egypt* symbolizes a perception on both earthly planes, in general and in particular.

5367   *Go to Joseph* means that it came from spiritual heavenliness. This can be seen from the representation of *Joseph* as spiritual heavenliness (discussed many times before). *Going to* him means coming from him and specifically describes the goodness needed by truth, as symbolized by the bread for which the people shouted to Pharaoh (§5365).

What he says to you, you are to do means provided there is obedience. **5368** This can be seen from the meaning of *doing what someone says* as obeying. The symbolism is that goodness is connected to truth on the earthly plane as long as the earthly plane adapts and obeys.

A word also needs to be said about adaptation and obedience on the part of the earthly plane. People with a worldly focus and particularly a bodily focus and even more particularly a merely physical focus cannot grasp what it means to say that the earthly plane ought to adapt and obey. They think there is only one entity operating inside us, which means there cannot be one part commanding and another obeying. In reality, though, the inner self is what ought to command, and the outer self, to obey. The outer self obeys when we take heaven rather than the world—our neighbor rather than ourselves—as our goal, and therefore when we regard bodily and worldly advantages as a means rather than an end. And we regard these as a means rather than an end when we love our neighbor more than ourselves, and heavenly benefits more than worldly ones. When this is the case, the earthly level obeys. (The earthly level is the same as the outer self.)

And the famine was on the whole face of the earth means when there **5369** was desolation to the point of despair. This can be seen from the symbolism of *famine* as desolation (discussed above at §§5360, 5362, 5364) and from that of the *earth* as the earthly level. When famine is said to be *on its whole face,* despair is being symbolized, because desolation is then universal. The furthest point and final stage of desolation is despair (§§5279, 5280).

And Joseph opened everything in which [there was grain] symbolizes a **5370** communication from the remnant. This can be seen from the current symbolism of *opening* as communicating. *Everything in which* means the stores of grain, which symbolized the remnant, as noted several times before. (The remnant consists of goodness and truth stored up by the Lord in our inner reaches; see §§468, 530, 560, 561, 660, 661, 798, 1050, 1738, 1906, 2284, 5135, 5342, 5344.)

And sold to Egypt symbolizes adoption. This can be seen from the **5371** symbolism of *selling* as giving something to someone for adoption. After all, what is sold becomes the property of the buyer. The meaning of selling and buying as adoption will be seen below at §5374.

And the famine grew strong in the land of Egypt symbolizes increasing severity—the increasing severity of the desolation. This can be seen **5372** from the symbolism of *famine* and the *land of Egypt* as desolation on the earthly level. Its increasing severity is symbolized by *grew strong*.

5373   *And all the earth came to Egypt* means that goodness and truth were inserted into the knowledge belonging to the church, as can be seen from the symbolism of the *earth*. In the Word, the symbolism of the earth, [or land,] is varied. In general it symbolizes the church, so it also symbolizes properties of the church, or goodness and truth. Since it symbolizes the church, it also symbolizes a person in the church, because an individual is the church in particular. Since it symbolizes a person in the church, it symbolizes what is human in the person, which is the mind. That is why the land of Egypt symbolized the earthly mind several times above. In this case, though, the term is not referring to the land of Egypt but to the earth in general and consequently to properties of the church, or goodness and truth. For the symbolism of the earth, [or land,] being varied, see §§620, 636, 2571. On the point that in general the earth, [or land,] symbolizes the church, see §§566, 662, 1066, 1262, 1413, 1607, 1733, 1850, 2117, 2118 at the end, 2928, 3355, 4447, 4535.

[2] The meaning of *all the earth came to Egypt* as the idea that goodness and truth were inserted into knowledge can be seen from the symbolism of *Egypt*. In its proper sense Egypt symbolizes learning and therefore items of knowledge (see §§1164, 1165, 1186, 1462), and the knowledge it symbolizes in a positive sense is knowledge belonging to the church (§§4749, 4964, 4966).

It is not only the symbolism of the words—of [the term meaning] the earth rather than the land of Egypt, and of Egypt in its proper sense— that shows this to be the inner meaning of the clause, and not only the fact that the verb is plural in *all the earth came*. It is also the very sequence of events in the inner meaning, since the next event in sequence is that remaining traces of truth and goodness are inserted into knowledge.

[3] Here is the situation: When our earthly dimension is being reborn, absolutely all our good impulses and true ideas are instilled into our knowledge. Anything that does not lodge within knowledge on the earthly level is not present in that dimension, because the part of the earthly mind under the intellect's control consists exclusively of knowledge. Knowledge, which belongs to the earthly dimension, is on the outermost level of the divine design. Prior levels have to take up residence on outermost levels in order to emerge and make themselves visible in the earthly realm. Besides which, prior levels all extend as far as outermost levels (their boundaries or borders) and coexist there, just as causes coexist in their effects, or as higher levels coexist on lower levels, which are their containers. Knowledge, being part of the earthly dimension, is this kind of outermost element. That is

why the spiritual world rests on the earthly plane in a human being, where knowledge resides. What exists in the spiritual world is presented in a representational way. If spiritual qualities were not displayed on the earthly plane in a representational way, by means of things that exist in the world, we would not comprehend them at all.

This information shows that when our earthly dimension is being reborn, all inner truth and goodness coming from the spiritual world are inserted into our knowledge, so that they will become visible.

To buy symbolizes their adoption. This can be seen from the symbolism of *buying* as acquiring something and therefore adopting it. Spiritual acquisition and appropriation requires the coin of goodness and truth, where the corresponding worldly acquisition and appropriation requires silver and gold. Silver is truth and gold is goodness, in a spiritual sense. So buying something symbolizes adopting it for our own, as in the following Scripture passages. In Isaiah:

5374

> Everyone who is thirsty, come to the water, and whoever does not have silver, come, *buy* and eat! And come, without silver and without the price *buy* wine and milk! (Isaiah 55:1)

See also Jeremiah 13:1, 2, 11. In Matthew:

> The kingdom of the heavens is like treasure hidden in a field, which, when someone discovered it, he hides, and because of his joy he goes and sells absolutely everything he has and *buys that field*. Again, the kingdom of the heavens is like a merchant person looking for beautiful pearls, [who, when he had found a precious pearl,] went and sold everything that he had and *bought it*. (Matthew 13:44, 45, 46)

And in the same author:

> The prudent young women said to the stupid ones, "Go *to the vendors* and *buy yourselves oil."* As they went *to buy,* the groom came. (Matthew 25:9, 10)

[2] Since buying symbolized adoption, the Word carefully distinguishes things bought with silver from things acquired another way. Slaves who were bought with silver were like part of the family, although of lower status than ones born in the house. That is why they are occasionally mentioned together, as in Genesis:

> Circumcision is absolutely required for *[the slave] born in your house* and *anyone purchased with your silver*. (Genesis 17:13)

And in Leviticus:

> If a priest buys a soul with a *purchase of silver,* [that soul] and *[the slave] born in his house* shall eat of his bread. (Leviticus 22:11)

This shows what is symbolized in the Word by those *redeemed by Jehovah*—namely, people who have taken in goodness and truth and therefore who have adopted what is the Lord's as their own.

5375   *To Joseph* means where spiritual heavenliness existed. This can be seen from the representation of *Joseph* as spiritual heavenliness (mentioned many times before). Spiritual heavenliness is truth-based goodness received from the Divine.

5376   *Because the famine grew strong in all the earth* symbolizes desolation everywhere in the earthly dimension except there. This can be seen from the symbolism of *famine* as desolation (discussed before [§§5279, 5372]) and from that of the *earth* as the earthly dimension (also discussed before). The idea that it existed everywhere but there, among items of knowledge, where spiritual heavenliness resided, follows from the discussion above [§§5372–5375].

I have already described the desolation of the earthly level, or the loss of truth on that level, but since I will be talking further about it in what follows, it would be good to mention it again.

Early in their youth, people born within the church start learning from the Word and from the church's teachings about the truth composing faith and the goodness composing neighborly love. As they mature, they begin either to confirm or to deny for themselves the religious truth they have learned. They look at it through their own eyes and by this means either make such truth their own or reject it. We cannot make anything our own unless we acknowledge it from our own insight, that is, [unless] we know for ourselves rather than from another that it is so.

The truth they have absorbed from youth onward, then, has been unable to reach any more deeply into their life than the front entrance. From there it can be welcomed deeper inside or else thrown out the door.

[2] In people who are being reborn—that is, people who the Lord foresees will let themselves be reborn—this truth multiplies profusely, because they have a desire to know truth. When they come close to actually going through rebirth, though, the truth they had learned seems to be taken from them, because it is drawn deep within. Then they appear desolate. When they are being reborn, however, the truth is gradually sent back out to their earthly level, where it unites with goodness.

In people who are not being reborn—that is, people who the Lord foresees will not let themselves be reborn—truth does usually multiply, because they have a desire to know truth for the sake of reputation, high position, and wealth. As they mature, though, and submit such truth to their own scrutiny, they disbelieve it, deny it, or turn it into falsity. As a result, truth is not drawn deeper within them but is thrown out the door, although it remains in their memory for worldly purposes, devoid of life. The Word refers to this state too as desolation or devastation, but it differs from the first kind. The desolation of the former state is merely apparent; the desolation of the latter state is absolute. In the former state truth is not taken away from us, but in the latter state every bit of it is removed.

The desolation of the former state has been the theme of the inner meaning in this chapter and is still the theme in the next. It is what the seven-year famine symbolizes. [3] The Word talks about this same desolation in many other places, as for instance in Isaiah:

> Wake up! Wake up, Jerusalem, who *drank from Jehovah's hand the cup of his anger.* Two things have come upon you—who is commiserating with you?—*devastation* and *shattering, famine* and *the sword.* Who [am I] to comfort you? Your sons fainted; they lay at the head of all the streets. So hear this, please, you who are afflicted and drunk, but not on wine: Here, now, I have taken out of your hand the *cup of trembling, the dregs of the cup* of my *wrath.* You shall not continue to drink it anymore, but I will put it in the hand of those saddening you. (Isaiah 51:17–end)

This depicts the state of desolation experienced by a person in the church who is becoming a church, or regenerating. The desolation is referred to as devastation, a shattering, famine, the sword, the cup of Jehovah's anger and wrath, and the cup of trembling. The truth such a person then loses is meant by the sons who faint and lie at the head of all the streets. For the meaning of sons as truth, see §§489, 491, 533, 1147, 2623, 2803, 2813, 3373. For the meaning of streets as places of truth, §2336. Lying at the head of all the streets therefore means that truth seems to have been dispersed. Clearly the desolation is merely apparent and, like times of trial, is a means to rebirth, because it says that the person will not drink the cup anymore but that [Jehovah] will put it in the hand of those saddening the person. [4] In Ezekiel:

> This is what the Lord Jehovih has said: "Because they *devastate* and *devour* you from all around, therefore, in order that you yourselves may

be an inheritance to the rest of the nations, you mountains of Israel, hear the word of the Lord Jehovih." This is what the Lord Jehovih has said to the mountains and to the hills, to the brooks and to the valleys, and to the *desolate wastelands* and to the *deserted cities,* which have become plunder and a laughingstock to the rest of the nations that are all around: "I myself in my zeal and in my wrath have spoken, because of the disgrace of the nations [that] you bore: if the nations that are all around you do not carry their disgrace, . . . ! But you, mountains of Israel, will extend your branch and bear your fruit for my people Israel. Because look: I am with you, and I will turn to face you so that you may be tilled and planted. And I will multiply humankind upon you, the whole house of Israel, and *cities will be populated,* and *wastelands will be rebuilt.* I will cause you to live as in your ancient times, and I will do good to you beyond that at your beginnings." (Ezekiel 36:3–12)

This passage too is about the desolation that precedes rebirth. The desolation is symbolized by the desolate wastelands and deserted cities that became plunder and a laughingstock. Rebirth is symbolized by extending a branch and bearing fruit, by turning to face them so that they could be tilled and planted, so that humankind could multiply, cities be populated, and wastelands be rebuilt, and by causing them to live as in their ancient times and doing good to them beyond that done at their beginnings.

[5] What a state of desolation is like can be seen from inhabitants of the other world in that state. The ones experiencing desolation there are tormented by evil spirits and demons, who flood them with so many persuasive arguments for evil and falsity that they almost drown. Truth then becomes invisible. As the period of desolation comes to an end, though, light from heaven starts to shine in their minds and the evil spirits and demons are driven away, each to his or her own hell, where they undergo punishments. That is what is symbolized by "the cities have become plunder and a laughingstock to the rest of the nations that are all around" and "the nations that are all around will carry their disgrace." It is what is symbolized above in Isaiah by "the cup will be put in the hand of those saddening you," in another place in Isaiah (33:1) by "the devastator will be devastated," and in Jeremiah 25:12 by "I will exact punishment on (various destroyers) and turn them into eternal desolations." In Isaiah:

> *Your destroyers* will bring your sons in a hurry, and *your devastators* will leave you. Lift your eyes all around and look: all are gathering; they are

coming to you. For in regard to *your devastations* and *your desolations* and the *land of your destruction,* you will be too narrow for the inhabitants; *those swallowing you up have gone far away.* (Isaiah 49:17, 18, 19)

[6] Here too and throughout that chapter the subject is the desolation of people being reborn, rebirth and fruitfulness after the desolation, and the punishment of oppressors (verse 26). In the same author:

> *Doom to the devastator* who has not been devastated! When you *stop devastating, you will be devastated.* (Isaiah 33:1)

This is saying that people who create devastation are punished, as above. In the same author:

> Let *my outcasts* stay in you; Moab, be a hiding place for them *in the face of the destroyer,* because the *oppressor* has ceased, *devastation* has ended. (Isaiah 16:4)

In the same author:

> The day of Jehovah is near; it will come like *devastation* from Shaddai. (Isaiah 13:6)

Devastation from Shaddai stands for devastation in times of trial. The ancients used the name Shaddai for God in relation to spiritual trials; see §§1992, 3667, 4572. [7] In the same author:

> Then they will not grow thirsty. *In wastelands* he will lead them; water from rock he will bring flowing out for them, and he will split rock so that water can gush out. (Isaiah 48:21)

This is about conditions after desolation. In the same author:

> Jehovah will comfort Zion, he will comfort *all its wastelands,* in order to make *its wilderness* like Eden and *its desert* like a garden of Jehovah. Gladness and joy will be found in it; acclamation and the voice of song. (Isaiah 51:3)

The same here, because as noted above, desolation happens for the sake of human regeneration. In other words, it happens in order that truth can unite with goodness, and goodness with truth, once evil and falsity have been detached. A person born anew in respect to goodness is the one being compared to an Eden, and a person born anew in respect to truth, to a garden of Jehovah. In David:

> Jehovah brought me up *out of the pit of devastation,* out of the muddy clay, and set my feet on a rock. (Psalms 40:2)

[8] The devastation and desolation of a person in the church—or of the church in a person—was represented by the captivity of the Judean people in Babylon. The revival of the church was represented by the return from that captivity, which Jeremiah talks about in places, especially 32:37–end. Desolation is captivity, because during it people are essentially held captive. So captives in a prison or in a pit symbolize people going through desolation; see §§4728, 4744, 5037, 5038, 5085, 5096.

[9] The Word also talks occasionally about a state of desolation and devastation experienced by people who are not being reborn. That is the state of people who totally deny truth or else turn it into falsity. It is also the state of the church around the time of its end, when there is no longer faith or neighborly love. In Isaiah:

> I will make known to you what I will do to my vineyard, removing its hedge so that it can be grazed bare, breaking open its fence so that it can be trampled. *Then I will make it a desolation;* it will not be pruned or hoed, so that bramble and bush can come up. In fact, I will command the clouds not to rain on it. (Isaiah 5:5, 6, 7)

In the same author:

> "Tell this people, 'Listen—listen!—but do not understand, and see— see!—but do not know.' Make the heart of this people fat and make their ears heavy and smear their eyes, to prevent them from seeing with their eyes and hearing with their ears and understanding in their heart and turning to be healed." And I said, "How long, Lord?" and he said, *"Until the cities are devastated* (so that they are without a resident) and the houses (so that there is nothing in them) and *the land is reduced to a desert."* He will take humankind away. And *deserted [territory]* will multiply in the middle of the land; hardly a tenth will remain there, yet they are destined for expulsion. (Isaiah 6:9–end)

[10] In the same author:

> The survivors will return, the survivors of Jacob, to the mighty God, for it is a *set culmination,* overflowing with justice, for the Lord Jehovih

Sabaoth is making a *culmination* and *final settlement* on all the earth. (Isaiah 10:21, 22, 23)

In the same author:

Jehovah is *emptying* the earth and *draining* it and will distort its face. The earth will be *emptied bare,* the habitable earth will mourn, will be confused, the world will droop and be confused. A *curse* will devour the land, the new wine will mourn, the grapevine will droop. What is left in the city will be a *wasteland;* the gate will be crushed *to devastation.* The earth was shattered utterly; the earth split wide open; the earth quaked violently; the earth staggers helplessly like a drunkard. (Isaiah 24:1–end)

In the same author:

The paths have been *devastated;* the traveler on the way has ceased; the land mourns, droops. Lebanon blushed, wilted; Sharon became like a desert. (Isaiah 33:8, 9)

In the same author:

I will both *desolate* and swallow up; I will *devastate* mountains and hills, and all their grass I will wither. (Isaiah 42:14, 15)

[11] In Jeremiah:

I will exterminate all the surrounding nations and *turn them into a desolation* and a mockery and *eternal wastelands,* and I will abolish from them the voice of joy and the voice of gladness, the voice of the bridegroom and the voice of the bride, the voice of millstones and the light of a lamp, so that the whole land becomes *a desolation* and *a waste.* It will happen, when the seventy years have been fulfilled, that I will inflict punishment on the king of Babylon and on this nation for their wickedness and on the land of the Chaldeans and turn it [all] *into eternal desolations.* (Jeremiah 25:9, 10, 11, 12, and following verses)

In the same author:

A desolation, a reproach, *a wasteland,* and a *curse* will Bozrah become, and all its cities will become *eternal wastelands.* Edom will become *a desolation;* everyone who passes through it will be dumbfounded and hiss over all its plagues. (Jeremiah 49:13–18)

In Ezekiel:

> This is what the Lord has said to the residents of Jerusalem concerning the land of Israel: "They will eat their bread with anxiety and drink their water in shock, *so that the land of [Jerusalem] may be stripped of its abundance,* because of the violence of all the residents in it; *the inhabited cities will be laid waste,* and the land will be *desolated.*" (Ezekiel 12:19, 20)

[12] In the same author:

> When I turn you into a *desolate city,* like cities that are not inhabited; when I bring up against you the abyss, [and] many waters cover you, and I make you go down with those going down into the pit, to an ancient people, and settle you in the underground realm, *into a place desolate* from eternity, with those going down into the pit, . . . (Ezekiel 26:18–21)

This is about Tyre. In Joel:

> A day of shadow and darkness, a day of cloud and haze. Before it, fire consumes all, and after it, a flame blazes; like the Garden of Eden is the land before it, but after it, a *wilderness of devastation.* (Joel 2:2, 3)

In Zephaniah:

> The day of Jehovah is near; a day of wrath is this day, a day of anguish and distress, *a day of waste and devastation,* a day of shadow and darkness, a day of cloud and gloom. By the fire of Jehovah's zeal the whole land will be consumed, because I will make a *culmination* and indeed a speedy one with all the inhabitants of the land. (Zephaniah 1:14–end)

In Matthew:

> When you see the *desolate abomination* (predicted by Daniel the prophet) standing in the Holy Place, then those in Judea should flee into the mountains. (Matthew 24:15, [16]; Mark 13:14; Daniel 9:27; 12:10, 11, 12)

This evidence shows that desolation is a loss of truth—an apparent loss in people who are regenerating and an absolute loss in people who are not.

Correspondence
with the Universal Human (Continued):
Correspondence of the Internal Organs

THE end of the previous chapter was about the correspondence of certain internal organs of the body—the liver, pancreas, stomach, and some others—with the universal human [§§5171–5190]. Here I will continue with the correspondence of the peritoneum, kidneys, ureters, bladder, and intestines. You see, everything in us, whether in our outer or inner self, corresponds with the universal human. Nothing ever comes into existence or remains in existence if it lacks correspondence with that human—that is, with heaven, or in other words, with the spiritual world—because it has no link with anything prior to itself. So it has no link with the first origin, which is the Lord. Anything unconnected and therefore independent cannot survive for even a moment. Its continued existence results from a connection with and dependence on that which brings everything into existence, because survival is perpetual emergence.

[2] As a consequence, not only does each and every thing in a person correspond, but each and every thing in the universe does too. The sun corresponds, as does the moon, because in heaven the Lord *is* the sun and the moon. The sun's fire and warmth and its light correspond, the fire and warmth corresponding to the Lord's love for the entire human race, and the light corresponding to divine truth. Even the stars correspond, and what they correspond to is heaven's various communities and the dwellings in them—not that they are located there but that they are arranged in a similar pattern. Everything under the sun corresponds, including absolutely every member of the animal kingdom and of the plant kingdom, each of which would instantly collapse and die if there were no inflow from the spiritual world.

A great deal of experience has enabled me to know this, since I have been shown the correspondences of many members of the animal kingdom, and even more members of the plant kingdom. I have also seen that they have no lasting existence at all without that inflow. When primary

5377

entities are taken away, secondary ones necessarily fall, and the same when primary entities are merely separated from secondary ones.

[3] People most of all have a correspondence with heaven and through heaven with the Lord. Consequently, the nature of our correspondence determines how we appear in heaven's light in the other life. Angels therefore look indescribably radiant and beautiful, while the hellish look unspeakably dark and ugly.

5378   Some spirits approached me in silence, but later they spoke, though all as one, not as individuals. I could tell from the way they talked that they wanted to know everything and sought to explain everything, in order to prove to themselves that it was so. They were modest, saying they did nothing on their own, only on behalf of others, although seeming to act on their own.

Then they were accosted by other spirits—the ones constituting the area of the kidneys, ureters, and bladder, it was said. The first group answered calmly, but the second group continued to harass and vex them. This is what renal spirits are like. Unable to make any headway against them by being modest, the original spirits resorted to measures better suited to the renal spirits' character, ballooning up and terrifying them. They seemed to turn huge, but formed only a single, solitary figure, whose body loomed so large that he seemed to reach the sky, like Atlas. A spear appeared in his hand, but he had no intention of doing them harm, only of terrifying them. The renal spirits ran away. Someone showed up to chase them as they fled, and someone else darted between the giant's legs from front to back. The giant appeared to have wooden shoes that he threw at the renal spirits.

[2] Angels told me that the temperate spirits who grew bigger were those relating to the *peritoneum*. The peritoneum is a general membrane that surrounds and enfolds all the abdominal organs, just as the pleura surrounds all the organs in the chest. It is extensive, relatively large, and capable of expanding. That is why these spirits when harassed are allowed to make themselves look so large and inflict terror, especially on the spirits making up the area of the kidneys, ureters, and bladder. These organs or vessels, after all, are enveloped by the peritoneum and restrained by it.

The wooden shoes represented the lowliest physical substances, the kind that the kidneys, ureters, and bladder swallow up and carry away. For the meaning of shoes as the lowliest elements of the earthly level, see §§259, 4938–4952. In saying that they did nothing on their own, only at the bidding of others, the spirits again resembled the peritoneum, which also does not act on its own.

I was shown in a representational way what happens when spirits who compose the colon make trouble for spirits in the area of the peritoneum. **5379** Those who compose the colon are puffed up, like a colon bloated with gas. When they wanted to assault the peritoneal spirits, a wall seemed to be put in the way, and when they tried to tear down the wall, a new one always sprang up. This kept them at bay.

It is known that fluids are secreted and eliminated and that this hap- **5380** pens in a series of stages from the kidneys to the bladder. The kidneys come first in the series, the ureters are in the middle, and the bladder is at the end. The spirits who constitute those areas in the universal human also form a series, and although they belong to the same general type, they differ from each other as subtypes.

They talk with a raspy, cracked voice and long to invade the body but make no more than an attempt to do so. Their position in relation to the human body is this: The ones who relate to the kidneys are on the left side, close by the body under the elbow. The ones relating to the ureters are farther off from the body to the left, and the ones relating to the bladder are even farther off. Together they form almost a parabola curving forward from the left side, since they push forward on the left in a fairly long line.

This path is one common path toward the hells. The other goes through the intestines. Both end in the hells. The inhabitants of the hells correspond to the kind of stuff excreted by the intestines and the bladder, because the falsities and evils they indulge in are actually urine and stool in a spiritual sense.

Spirits constituting the area of the kidneys, ureters, and bladder in the **5381** universal human have a disposition that likes nothing better than examining and probing the character of others. They are also the type that long to scold and punish, as long as there is some justifiable reason for it.

The job of the kidneys, ureters, and bladder is similar. They screen the blood drawn into them for any useless or harmful bodily fluid in it, which they separate from what is useful. Then they purge it, propelling it downward and roiling it in various ways as it goes. These are the functions of the spirits constituting the area of those body parts.

On the other hand, the spirits and communities of spirits to which the urine itself corresponds are hellish, especially if the urine is foul smelling. As soon as it is separated from the blood, it is no longer part of the body, even if it is still in the ducts of the kidneys or in the bladder. What has been separated no longer circulates through the body, so it no longer contributes to the existence or survival of its parts.

5382 Many times I have learned from experience that spirits who constitute the region of the kidneys and ureters are ready and willing to examine or investigate the character, the thoughts, and the intentions of others. They crave uncovering grounds for action and accusing people of faults, mainly so they can discipline them. I have talked with them about this obsession and aim of theirs.

Many of this type while they were alive in the world were judges who privately rejoiced when they found an excuse—a justifiable excuse, in their eyes—for penalizing, chastising, and punishing people.

The activity of spirits like this is felt in an area toward the back where the kidneys, ureters, and bladder are located.

The spirits belonging to the bladder spread out toward Gehenna, where some of them sit as if in judgment.

5383 These spirits have many methods for exploring or investigating the mindset of others, but let me recount just this one: They make another spirit talk—a step managed in the next life through a kind of inflow that cannot be described intelligibly. If that spirit finds it easy to say the words foisted on her or him, they conclude that the spirit's character matches the words. They also impose a particular emotion. However, the spirits who probe this way are relatively coarse. Others do it differently; they sense the thoughts, wishes, and deeds of another immediately on arrival. They also sense past deeds that pain the person, which they seize on and even condemn the person for, if they deem that they have just cause.

One surprising feature of the other life that hardly anyone in the world could believe is this: As soon as one spirit comes up to another (and especially to a person on earth), the one instantly knows the other's thoughts, feelings, and past deeds and therefore the other's whole current state, exactly as if the two of them had been together a long time. That is what communication there is like. There are differences in the perceptions, though. Some perceive inner levels, and some, only outer ones. If the latter are interested in knowing more, they too have various methods for examining the inner levels of others.

5384 The spirits who constitute the region of the kidneys, ureters, and bladder in the universal human also use a range of methods for castigating others. Mostly they remove anything pleasant and cheerful and introduce what is unpleasant and depressing. Their glee in doing so puts them in touch with the hells, but the fact that they have just cause—and they make sure of this beforehand—puts them in touch with heaven. That is why they are kept in this region.

This discussion shows what the Word means when it says that Jehovah tests and examines kidneys and heart and that the kidneys chastise, as in Jeremiah:

5385

> Jehovah, *testing kidneys* and heart. (Jeremiah 11:20)

In the same author:

> Jehovah, testing the upright, *looking at kidneys* and heart. (Jeremiah 20:12)

In David:

> You, a just God, *test* hearts and *kidneys*. (Psalms 7:9)

In the same author:

> Jehovah, *search my kidneys* and my heart. (Psalms 26:2)

In the same author:

> Jehovah, *you* yourself *possess my kidneys*. (Psalms 139:13)

In John:

> I myself am the one who has *examined kidneys* and heart. (Revelation 2:23)

In these passages the kidneys symbolize spiritual attributes, and the heart, heavenly ones. That is, kidneys symbolize matters of truth and the heart matters of goodness. The reason is that kidneys purify serum, and the heart purifies the actual blood. So testing, searching, and examining the kidneys symbolizes testing, searching, and examining the amount and type of truth we have, or the amount and type of faith.

The symbolism can also be seen in Jeremiah:

> Jehovah, you are nearby in their mouth but far *from their kidneys*. (Jeremiah 12:2)

And in David:

> Jehovah, indeed, you desire *truth in the kidneys*. (Psalms 51:6)

It is also clear in David that the kidneys are said to chastise:

> By night *my kidneys chastise me*. (Psalms 16:7)

5386   There are organs for secretion and elimination elsewhere in the body too. In the brain there are the ventricles and mammillary bodies, which carry off the phlegm there; and everywhere there are glands. There are mucous and saliva glands in the head, and many other kinds in the body. Just under the skin are myriads of glands that excrete sweat and finer kinds of waste products.

The inhabitants of the spiritual world who correspond to these organs generally are ones with entrenched opinions who also burden the conscience of others in matters of no importance.

Some of them appear at an intermediate distance overhead, and they are the types who raise gratuitous moral objections. Because they burden the consciences of ordinary people, they are called moralizers. They do not know what true conscience is, since no matter what happens, they assume conscience applies. Once an objection or doubt has been expressed to an anxious, obsessive mind, it finds no lack of arguments to support and therefore intensify its concern.

When these spirits are present, they create a palpable anxiety in the part of the abdomen right under the diaphragm. They are also present with us in times of trial.

I once spoke with them and sensed that they have no breadth of thought that would enable them to compromise when useful and necessary. They could not listen to reason, because they were clinging tenaciously to their opinion.

5387   Spirits who correspond to urine itself are hellish, because urine, as noted above [§5381], is no longer part of the body, having already been separated from the blood. In itself it is nothing but unclean waste fluid that is disposed of. Let me provide the following information on these spirits.

I perceived a spirit, first inside my body but then outside on the right, and when he stationed himself there, he was hard to see. He had the skill to make himself inconspicuous. When questioned, he made no reply. Others told me that he had engaged in piracy during his physical life. (Who and what we had been is clearly discerned in the other world from the aura of the feelings and thoughts constituting our life, because our life awaits each of us.)

[2] He kept changing position, appearing now on the right and now on the left. I could tell he did this out of fear that someone would recognize him and force him to confess to something. Other spirits told me that this kind is extremely timid at the least danger but very bold in the

absence of danger. They also told me that such spirits oppose those corresponding to urination, working as hard as they can to interfere with it. In case I should doubt this, it was demonstrated to me by experience. When the pirate was at hand and the spirits who correspond to urination stepped back a little, my urine completely stopped flowing and backed up in a dangerous way. When they were called back, though, then the output of urine accorded with their presence.

[3] The spirit eventually admitted he was a pirate, saying he was good at hiding, and clever and energetic at deceiving his pursuers. He added that he now loves foul, urinous liquids much more than pure water, and that the disgusting stench of urine is of utmost pleasure to him. In fact, he wanted to make his home in ponds or even vats of reeking urine.

[4] I was also shown what kind of face he had. He did not have a face but something with a black beard instead of a face.

Later some other, less energetic pirates were summoned. They also said little, and to my surprise they gnashed their teeth. They too said that they love urine more than any other liquid, and liquid with dregs in it more than other kinds. These spirits did not have something bearded instead of a face like the first one but a dreadful rack of teeth. Beards and teeth symbolize the very lowest elements on the earthly level. Their lack of a face means that they have no rational life, because the absence of a face is a sign that their inner reaches do not correspond with the universal human. The way everyone appears in the next life in heaven's light is determined by correspondence, so hellish spirits look horribly ugly.

Once there was a spirit present with me and talking to me who had been without religion during bodily life and had not believed in life after death. He too was one of the energetic ones. He had been able to captivate people's minds by taking their side and agreeing with them, so his lack of faith was not obvious from his conversation at first. Words rolled off his tongue in a stream, as they do with good spirits. I finally saw through him, though, when he balked at discussing anything involving faith and neighborly love. He could not follow my thinking then but became withdrawn. After that, all the signs indicated that he went along with people in order to deceive them.

One kind of agreeability differs from another by its goal. If the goal is friendship, pleasant conversation, or something like that—even legitimate financial gain—it is not very bad. On the other hand, if it is to extort secrets and blackmail someone into malfeasance, or in general if the goal is to do harm, it is evil. This was the kind of aim this spirit had.

5388

He also worked against the spirits in the area of the kidneys and ureters and said he liked the reek of urine above all other smells. Moreover, he inflicted a painful cramp or tightness on the lower part of my stomach.

5389   There are gangs of spirits who roam around and return to the same places from time to time. Evil spirits are quite fearful of them, because the wandering spirits have a certain way of torturing them. I was told that they correspond to the fundus or upper part of the bladder in general and to the muscular ligaments from there that converge on the sphincter, where the urine is excreted by torsion.

These spirits attach themselves to the back where the cauda equina is. Their method of proceeding involves a rapid back-and-forth motion that no one is able to interfere with. It is a procedure that consists in pressing and squeezing upward to a point, in the shape of a cone. Evil spirits who are thrust inside the cone, especially at the top, suffer wretchedly from being twisted to and fro.

5390   There are other spirits who correspond to unclean discharges—specifically, spirits who held grudges when they were in the world. I saw them out in front toward the left. The unclean discharges also have their counterpart in spirits who drag spiritual ideas through earthly muck.

Spirits of this kind visited me, bearing with them sordid thoughts, which gave them sordid things to say. They bent and twisted what was clean into what was unclean. Many of the type were from the lowest social strata, but some were among the world's more respectable citizens. Of course during bodily life they did not talk that way in company, but they did think that way. They kept themselves from saying what they really thought, so as to avoid gaining a bad reputation and losing allies, wealth, and position. Still, among people like themselves, when they could speak freely, they had talked the way the lower classes do. In fact, their language was even worse, since they had intellectual gifts that they misused to defile the sacred teachings of the Word and of doctrine.

5391   There are also organs that are called *succenturiate kidneys* or *renal capsules*. Their function is not so much to separate out serum as actual blood and to send the purified blood on a shortcut to the heart. In this way they prevent the spermatic vessels nearby from taking all the purified blood. This work they carry out primarily in fetuses and newborns.

Chaste young women are the ones who make up this area in the universal human. Easily distressed and loath to face disruption, they lie in a quiet state low on the left side of the torso. If thoughts arise about going to heaven and a change in conditions for them, they fret and sigh, as I have been allowed to sense plainly several times. Whenever my thoughts turned to babies, they felt great comfort and inward joy, as they openly confessed. When my thoughts contained something that was not heavenly, they were again distressed. Their worries come primarily from their tendency to think obsessively about a single subject rather than dispel their anxieties with a change of focus. They belong to this area because they likewise train the minds of others continuously on certain thoughts, rousing and revealing whole chains of ideas that need to be extricated, or cleansed away from the person. The practice also exposes a person's inner depths more clearly to angels, because removing obstructions and distractions yields them clearer insight and influence.

The spirits relating to the stomach give some clue to the identity of the spirits making up the area of the *intestines* in the universal human. This is because the intestines extend from the stomach and continue its work with increased vigor all the way to the final stretches of intestine, the colon and rectum. The spirits in the intestines are consequently near the hells referred to as feces-laden. **5392**

The area of the stomach and intestines contains spirits in the underground realm, who bring with them from the world something dirty clinging to their thoughts and emotions. As a result they are kept there awhile until what is dirty has been wiped away—in other words, thrust off to the side. Once it has been, they can be taken up to heaven.

Spirits there are not in the universal human yet. They are like food particles sent to the stomach that cannot be introduced into the blood or therefore into the body until the dregs have been removed. Anyone tainted with earthly dregs is down below the spirits in the area of the intestines, but the actual excrement being expelled corresponds to the hells that are referred to as feces-laden.

It is recognized that the colon extends quite far, so the spirits in that province do too. They form a curved line reaching forward to the left, ending in a hell. **5393**

The spirits in that hell had been ruthless. Devoid of conscience, they had wished to destroy the human race by killing and robbing indiscriminately, whether the victims resisted or not, male or female. That is the savage mindset of most soldiers and their officers. They attack fiercely not in battle but after battle, preying on the defeated and disarmed, murdering and plundering madly.

I have talked with angels about this type, which is what people left to themselves are like. "When allowed to act freely and lawlessly," I said, "they are much wilder than the worst wild animals. Animals don't rush to slaughter their own kind this way but merely defend themselves. They fill their bellies on the species assigned to them as food, but once full, they stop. Not so with humankind, which behaves cruelly and ferociously." The angels shuddered to think of the human race that way.

[2] These spirits do not rejoice at heart or gloat in their minds until they see troops mown down and blood streaming all over the battlefield. They have no joy in the deliverance of their native land, only in their own reputation as grand heroes. Yet they call themselves Christian and believe they will go to heaven, which holds nothing but peace, mercy, and neighborly love. These are the ones in the hell of the colon and rectum.

On the other hand, the ones in whom there had been a touch of humanity appear to the left in front, in a curving line, behind a certain wall. Still, they possess a great deal of self-love.

When respect for what is good exists in spirits, this is sometimes represented by little stars that are almost fiery red rather than white.

I saw a wall seemingly of plaster, with carvings, near my left elbow. It grew longer and taller, and at the top it was almost blue. I heard that it represented some of the better ones of this type.

5394 People who have been cruel and adulterous love nothing more in the other world than garbage and excrement. They find the stink of these things very sweet and pleasant and prefer it to all agreeable sensations, because it corresponds.

Those hells are partly under the buttocks, partly under the right foot, and partly way down low in front. They are at the end of the route leading through the rectum.

A spirit was once transferred there, where he talked with me, saying that all he could see there was latrines. The residents spoke with him and led him to various latrines, of which there were many.

Later he was taken to another place slightly off to the left, and when he arrived he said that a ghastly stench was emanating from some caves there. He added that he could not move a toe for fear of slipping into one of them. An odor of dead bodies also wafted from the caves. This was because the inhabitants were cruel and deceitful, and people like that find the smell of corpses extremely pleasant.

These things need to be discussed later, though, where the hells are described, and specifically the hells laden with feces and with dead bodies [§7161].

5395 There are some who live for themselves, not for any service to their country or its communities. They take no delight in responsibilities but only in being honored and worshiped—which does inspire them to seek responsibilities. They also enjoy eating, drinking, playing games, and mixing socially, purely with a view to pleasure. In the other life they cannot possibly be among groups of good spirits, let alone angels, because what angels and good spirits enjoy is being useful, and the use they serve determines the amount and kind of pleasure they have. The Lord's kingdom is nothing but a kingdom of service. If everyone in an earthly kingdom is esteemed and honored for being useful, what must it be like in the heavenly kingdom?

Those individuals who have lived only for themselves and their pleasure without any other useful aim are also located under the buttocks. Depending on the kind of pleasures and the aims they have, they spend their lives among filth.

Let me add the following as a postscript: There was a large crowd of **5396a** spirits around me that sounded like a sort of chaotic stream. The spirits complained that everything was now going to ruin, because everything seemed disconnected among them, which made them fearful that the end was coming. They thought there would be total destruction, as is usual in these situations.

In their midst, though, I picked up a sound that was gentle, angelic, and sweet, containing only what was orderly. Angelic choruses were on the inside, and the confused crowd of spirits was on the outside. The angelic flow lasted a long time. I was told that it represented the way the Lord works from what is peaceful within to control what is messy and uncontrolled on the outside. Through this core of peace he reduces the chaos on the outer bounds to order, rescuing each part from the error of its own nature.

Genesis 42

1. And Jacob saw that there were grain provisions in Egypt, and Jacob said to his sons, "Why are you looking at each other?"

2. And he said, "Look, I have heard that there are grain provisions in Egypt. Go down there and buy for us from there, and let us live and not die."

3. And Joseph's ten brothers went down to buy grain from Egypt.

4. And Benjamin, Joseph's brother, Jacob did not send with his brothers, because he said, "Maybe he would meet with harm."

5. And Israel's sons came to buy in the midst of those who came, because there was famine in the land of Canaan.

6. And Joseph was the ruler over the land and was selling to all the people of the land. And Joseph's brothers came and bowed down to him, face to the earth.

7. And Joseph saw his brothers and recognized them and acted as a stranger to them and spoke harsh words with them and said to them, "Where do you come from?" And they said, "From the land of Canaan, to buy food."

8. And Joseph recognized his brothers, but they did not recognize him.

9. And Joseph remembered the dreams that he had dreamed in regard to them and said to them, "You are spies; you have come to see the nakedness of the land."

10. And they said to him, "No, my Lord, and your servants come to buy food.

11. We are all of us sons of one man; we are upright. Your servants are not spies."

12. And he said to them, "No, because you have come to see the nakedness of the land."

13. And they said, "Your twelve servants are brothers, sons of one man in the land of Canaan, and here, the youngest is with our father today, and one does not exist."

14. And Joseph said to them, "It is what I spoke to you, saying, 'You are spies.'

15. In this you will be tested: As Pharaoh lives, if you go out from here and your youngest brother does not come here, . . . !

16. Send one of you, and let him take your brother, and you your-selves will be tied up, and your words will be tested, whether there is truth with you; and if not, as Pharaoh lives, . . . ! Because you are spies."

17. And he confined them to jail three days.

18. And Joseph said to them on the third day, "Do this and you will live; I fear God.

19. If you are upright, let one of your brothers be tied up in the house where you were jailed, and you yourselves go, take grain provisions for the famine of your houses.

20. And your youngest brother you are to bring to me, and your words will be shown true, and you are not to die." And they did so.

21. And they said, a man to his brother, "Without a doubt we ourselves are guilty over our brother, whose distress of soul we saw in his pleading to us, and we did not listen; therefore this distress has come to us."

22. And Reuben answered them, saying, "Didn't I say to you, saying, 'Don't sin against the boy,' and you didn't pay attention? And his blood, too—here, it is being sought."

23. And they did not know that Joseph was listening, because the interpreter was between them.

24. And he turned from them and wept and returned to them and spoke to them and took Simeon from them and tied him up before their eyes.

25. And Joseph commanded, and they filled their containers with grain, and [he said] to return their silver, each one's into his sack, and to give them provision for the way. And that is what he did with them.

26. And [the brothers] lifted their grain provisions onto their donkeys and went from there.

27. And one of them opened his sack to give fodder to his donkey in the inn and saw his silver, and here, it was in the mouth of his bag!

28. And he said to his brothers, "My silver is returned, and also look—it is in my bag!" And their heart gave way, and they trembled, a man to his brother, saying, "What is this God has done to us?"

29. And they came to Jacob their father, to the land of Canaan, and told him everything that had happened to them, saying,

30. "The man, the lord of the land, spoke harsh words with us and accused us of spying out the land.

31. And we said to him, 'We are upright, we are not spies.

32. We are twelve brothers, sons of our father. One does not exist, and the youngest today is with our father in the land of Canaan.'

33. And the man, the lord of the land, said to us, 'In this I will know that you are upright: leave one of your brothers with me and take [food for] the famine of your houses and go.

34. And bring your youngest brother to me and I will know that you are not spies, because you are upright. I will give you your brother, and you will travel the land on business.'"

35. And it happened that they were emptying their sacks, and here, each one had the packet of his silver in his sack! And they saw the packets of their silver, they and their father, and were afraid.

36. And Jacob their father said to them, "You have bereaved me; Joseph does not exist, and Simeon does not exist, and Benjamin you are taking. On me will all these things be."

37. And Reuben said to his father, saying, "My two sons you may put to death if I do not bring him to you; put him on my hands and I will return him to you."

38. And he said, "My son will not go down with you all, because his brother is dead and he, he alone is left, and he may meet with harm on the way on which you will go, and you will make my white hair go down in sorrow to the grave."

Summary

5396b THE latter part of the previous chapter was about the way spiritual heavenliness flowed into items of knowledge on the earthly plane and united with them. The current subject is the way it flowed into and united with earthly-level religious truth known to the church.

5397 At first the chapter talks about the [Lord's] attempt to adopt this truth by using things known to the church (the knowledge that Egypt stands for) but without any middle ground (Benjamin) connecting to truth received from [his] divine side (Joseph). The attempt was fruitless, so the truth was sent back and a little of the goodness belonging to earthly truth was given [to him] for free.

Inner Meaning

I N this chapter and those concerning Jacob's sons and Joseph that fol- **5398** low, the inner meaning has to do with the rebirth of the earthly plane— specifically, of the religious truth and goodness on that plane. The message is that this rebirth is accomplished not through knowledge but through an inflow from the Divine.

People in the church today know so little about rebirth that it hardly amounts to anything. They do not even know these things: In a person being reborn, regeneration lasts for the whole course of life and continues in the other life. There are so many secrets about rebirth that angels are barely capable of learning a millionth of them, yet what they know forms the substance of their understanding and wisdom.

The reason people in the church today know so little about rebirth is that they talk so much about forgiveness of sin and about justification. They believe sin is forgiven instantaneously, and some think it is wiped away, as dirt is washed from the body by water. They believe we are justi- fied by faith alone, which means by a single instant of trust. People in the church think this way because they do not know what sin, or evil, is. If they knew, they would realize that sin can never be thoroughly wiped away. Instead it is detached from us—in other words, cast aside—so that it will not rise up again. This happens when the Lord holds us in good- ness, which cannot happen unless evil is constantly being removed, by means that are beyond counting and mostly indescribable.

[2] Individuals who have carried with them to the other world the opinion that faith instantly justifies us and rinses us completely clean of sin are astounded when it dawns on them that rebirth takes place by means, countless indescribable means. They laugh at the ignorance they had in the world (they also call it insanity) about instantaneous forgiveness of sin and about justification. At times they are told that the Lord always forgives the sins of anyone who sincerely desires it. However, forgiveness is not enough to detach them from the Devil's crew, to which they are bound by the evil consequences of the way they lived, since they take their whole life with them. Then they learn from experience that to separate from the hells is to separate from one's sins. This can be accomplished only by thousands upon thousands of means known to the Lord alone, following one after another, and continuing (believe it or not) forever. Humankind is such an evil thing that we

cannot be fully delivered from a single sin to all eternity. By the Lord's mercy (should we accept it), we can be withheld from sin and maintained in what is good, and that is all.

[3] Consequently, the method by which we receive new life and are reborn is contained in the sanctuary of the Word—its inner meaning. This is mainly so that when we read the Word, angels can gain happiness and wisdom from it and also the pleasure of facilitating [our rebirth].

In this chapter and the following ones, which tell about Joseph's brothers, the highest inner meaning is about the glorification of the Lord's earthly level. The representative meaning is about the regeneration of a person's earthly level by the Lord. The current chapter is about the rebirth of earthly-level truth known to the church.

5399 Genesis 42:1, 2, 3, 4, 5. *And Jacob saw that there were grain provisions in Egypt, and Jacob said to his sons, "Why are you looking at each other?" And he said, "Look, I have heard that there are grain provisions in Egypt. Go down there and buy for us from there, and let us live and not die." And Joseph's ten brothers went down to buy grain from Egypt. And Benjamin, Joseph's brother, Jacob did not send with his brothers, because he said, "Maybe he would meet with harm." And Israel's sons came to buy in the midst of those who came, because there was famine in the land of Canaan.*

And saw symbolizes concepts of faith. *Jacob* symbolizes the earthly dimension as regards truth known to the church. *That there were grain provisions in Egypt* symbolizes an intent to acquire truth by means of knowledge, which is *Egypt. And Jacob said to his sons* symbolizes a perception about truths in general. *Why are you looking at each other?* means why were they just standing there? *And he said, "Look, I have heard that there are grain provisions in Egypt,"* means that truth can be acquired through knowledge. *Go down there and buy for us from there* symbolizes adopting [truth] by means of it. *And let us live and not die* symbolizes the resulting spiritual life. *And went down* symbolizes the active effort. *Joseph's ten brothers* symbolizes such truth known to the church as corresponded. *To buy grain from Egypt* means to use knowledge as a means of adopting the goodness that comes of truth. *And Benjamin, Joseph's brother,* symbolizes heavenly spirituality, which was a middle ground. *Jacob did not send with his brothers* means that [it was attempted] without that middle ground. *Because he said, "Maybe he would meet with harm,"* means that without spiritual heavenliness (Joseph), it would cease to exist. *And Israel's sons came to buy in the midst of those who came* means that [the Lord] wanted to acquire spiritual truth through knowledge, the same way as with other kinds of truth. *Because there was famine in the land of Canaan* symbolizes desolation in respect to religious attributes on the earthly level.

And saw symbolizes concepts of faith. This is established by the symbolism of *seeing* as aspects of faith (discussed in §§897, 2325, 2807, 3863, 3869, 4403–4421). Sight abstracted from what is worldly—spiritual sight— is actually a perception of truth. In other words, it is a perception of the ideas that go to make up faith. So that is exactly what seeing symbolizes on an inner level. The inner meaning reveals itself when everything worldly is removed, because the inner meaning consists of what is heavenly. The light in heaven, which makes it possible to see there, is divine truth from the Lord. This appears to angels' eyes as light, a thousand times brighter than noonday light in the world. Since this light contains life, it illuminates angels' intellectual sight at the same time it illuminates their eyesight. It gives them a perception of truth, according to the amount and kind of goodness they have.

Because the chapter's inner meaning is about concepts of faith, or truth known to the church, it says "he saw" at the very beginning, and "he saw" symbolizes concepts of faith.

Jacob symbolizes the earthly dimension as regards truth known to the church. This is established by the representation of *Jacob* as teachings about truth on the earthly level, and in the highest sense as the Lord's earthly dimension in regard to truth (discussed in §§3305, 3509, 3525, 3546, 3599, 4009, 4538).

That there were grain provisions in Egypt symbolizes an intent to acquire truth by means of knowledge—which is *Egypt*—as the following shows: *Grain provisions* symbolize truth known to the church, or the truth of which faith consists. (An abundance of grain provisions means multiplication of truth; see §§5276, 5280, 5292.) And *Egypt* symbolizes knowledge, as discussed in §§1164, 1165, 1186, 1462. In a positive sense it symbolizes things known to the church; see §§4749, 4964, 4966. As for its symbolizing an intent to acquire such truth, this is implied, as the next few sentences show.

By things known to the church, which Egypt stands for here, I mean all knowledge of truth and goodness before it is internalized by the inner self, that is, before it is united through the inner self with heaven and through heaven with the Lord. The church's doctrines and rituals, a knowledge of the spiritual qualities they represent and how they represent them, and so on—these are nothing but items of knowledge until we see from the Word whether they are true and in the process adopt them as our own.

[2] There are two ways of acquiring religious truth: from doctrine and from the Word. When we obtain truth only from doctrine, we are putting our trust in the people who have decided that this is what the Word teaches. We confirm to ourselves that it is true because others have said so. We believe on the basis of others' faith, not our own. When we obtain truth from the Word, though, and confirm to ourselves from the Word that it is true, we believe it because it comes from the Divine. We believe on the basis of faith received from the Divine.

Everyone within the church first gains religious truth from doctrine, and this is proper, because we do not yet have the judgment to see truth in the Word for ourselves. At that point it is nothing but a body of knowledge to us. Eventually, though, we develop the ability to look into truth with our own power of judgment. If we then fail to consult the Word in order to see whether it is true, it remains a body of knowledge for us. If on the contrary we then consult the Word with the desire and intent to know the truth, and if we succeed in discovering it, we are acquiring religious truth from its genuine source, and the Divine gives us ownership of it.

This and more is the current subject matter of the inner meaning. Egypt stands for this knowledge, and Joseph stands for truth from the Divine and therefore truth from the Word.

5403   *And Jacob said to his sons* symbolizes a perception about truths in general. This is clear from the symbolism of *saying* in the narratives of the Word as perception (discussed in §§1791, 1815, 1819, 1822, 1898, 1919, 2080, 2619, 2862, 3395, 3509) and from that of *sons* as religious truth (discussed in §§489, 491, 533, 1147, 2623, 3373, 4257). Being *Jacob's* sons, they symbolize truth in general, because Jacob's twelve sons, like the twelve tribes, symbolized all facets of faith and therefore truth in general. See §§2129, 2130, 3858, 3862, 3926, 3939, 4060.

5404   *Why are you looking at each other?* means why were they just standing there? This is self-evident.

5405   *And he said, "Look, I have heard that there are grain provisions in Egypt,"* means that truth can be acquired through knowledge. This is established by the explanation just above at §5402, where "there were grain provisions in Egypt" symbolizes an intent to acquire truth by means of knowledge, which is "Egypt." See the same section for a definition of the knowledge for which Egypt stands.

These *grain provisions* are expressed in the original language by a word that means "breakage." The same word is used for *buying* and *selling*, where the chapter says that Jacob's sons bought [grain] in Egypt and that Joseph sold it there. The reason is that in the ancient church people broke bread when they gave it to someone. This symbolized offering something personal to someone else and having it received in a personal way, so it symbolized the sharing of love. When one person breaks bread and gives it to another, the first is offering something personal; or when several people break bread together, the one loaf becomes shared. The result is a bond of neighborly love. Clearly, then, the breaking of bread was a symbol of mutual love. [2] This was standard, customary practice in the ancient church, so "breaking" itself came to mean the grain provisions that were made communal. For the meaning of bread as a loving goodness, see §§276, 680, 1798, 2165, 2177, 3464, 3478, 3735, 3813, 4211, 4217, 4735, 4976.

That is why the Lord broke bread when he gave it to people, as in Matthew:

> Jesus, taking the five loaves and the two fish, looking up to heaven, blessed them; and *breaking* it, he gave the disciples the *bread*. (Matthew 14:19; Mark 6:41; Luke 9:16)

In the same author:

> Jesus, taking the seven loaves and the fish, giving thanks, *broke* them and gave them to his disciples, and the disciples, to the crowd. (Matthew 15:36; Mark 8:6)

In the same author:

> Jesus, taking the bread, blessing it, *broke* it and gave it to the disciples and said, "Take it, eat; this is my body." (Matthew 26:26; Mark 14:22; Luke 22:19)

In Luke:

> It happened when the Lord reclined [at table] with them that, taking the *bread*, he blessed it, and *breaking* it he handed it to them. And their eyes were opened, and they recognized him. The disciples told how the Lord had been recognized by them in the *breaking of the bread*. (Luke 24:30, 31, 35)

In Isaiah:

> This fast is the one I choose: to *break* your *bread* for the hungry. (Isaiah 58:6, 7)

Go down there and buy for us from there symbolizes adopting [truth] by means of it. This can be seen from the symbolism of *going down*, a term used for going toward outer levels (discussed below), and from that of

5406

buying as adopting for one's own (discussed at §§4397, 5374). By means of it—by means of knowledge—is symbolized by *from there,* or from Egypt. Egypt means knowledge, as shown above [§5402].

The Word occasionally talks about going up or down when it speaks of going from one place to another. This is not because the one place was at a higher elevation than the other but because "going up" is used for going in an inward or loftier direction, and "going down" for going in an outward or lowlier direction. In other words, "going up" is used for going toward spiritual and heavenly levels, because they are deeper inside and are believed to be higher. "Going down" is used for going toward physical and earthly levels, because they are outer and seem lower. As a result, people are said to go down from Canaan to Egypt and to go up from Egypt to Canaan, not only here but everywhere else in the Word too. Canaan symbolizes what is heavenly, and Egypt, what is earthly. The land of Canaan in a representative sense means the heavenly kingdom and therefore heavenly and spiritual goodness and truth, which lie deep inside a person who is a kingdom of the Lord. Egypt in a representative sense means the earthly kingdom and therefore goodness and truth in the outer part of the church. By and large it means knowledge. For the idea that going up has to do with going in an inward direction, see §4539.

5407   *And let us live and not die* symbolizes spiritual life. This can be seen from the symbolism of *living and not dying* as spiritual life, because that is the one thing meant in an inner sense by living and not dying. In the other world, "life" means heaven in general and eternal happiness in particular, while "death" means hell in general, and eternal unhappiness there in particular. Many scriptural passages make this plain. Heaven in general and eternal happiness in particular are called life because the wisdom to see what is good and the insight to see what is true are found there, and these contain life from the Lord, the source of all life. Hell holds the opposite. It holds evil instead of goodness, and falsity instead of truth, and therefore spiritual life that has been snuffed out. As a consequence one finds comparative death there, because spiritual death is evil and falsity. In a human being, spiritual death is evil intent and the distorted thinking it leads to.

Evil demons and spirits do not like hearing anyone describe them as not alive, or dead. They claim they do have life because they can will and can think, but they are told that if goodness and truth hold life, evil and falsity cannot possibly hold it. The two pairs are opposites.

And went down symbolizes the active effort—namely, to acquire and adopt truth by means of knowledge. This is plain from the symbolism of *going down* to Egypt as the effort put into action.   **5408**

Joseph's ten brothers symbolizes such truth known to the church as corresponded. This can be seen from the symbolism of *brothers* as truth known to the church. These truths are called the brothers of *Joseph,* who stands for truth from the Divine, because they correspond to such truth. Correspondence creates a bond between them, like the bond of brother to brother.   **5409**

Jacob's sons symbolize all aspects of faith, or the church's truth as a whole (§5403). So do Joseph's brothers, but because of correspondence [with truth from the Divine]. The ten sons Jacob had by Leah symbolize truth known to the outer part of the church, and the two sons he had by Rachel symbolize truth known to the inner part. This is evident from the explanations about Leah and Rachel, showing that Leah means a desire for outer truth, and Rachel, a desire for inner truth, as discussed in §§3758, 3782, 3793, 3819. The inner and outer parts of the church are brothers; see §1222. As a result, the Lord himself uses the term *brothers* for such truth and consequent goodness as corresponds [with something deeper] by reason of neighborly love and faith. That is, he uses the term for people devoted to truth and to the goodness that comes of it. In Matthew:

> The king will say to them, "Truly, I say to you: so far as you did it for one *of these least consequential brothers of mine,* you did it for me." (Matthew 25:40)

And in another place:

> Jesus answered them, saying, "Who is my mother or *my brothers?*" And looking all around he said, "Look: my mother and *my brothers.* For whoever does the will of God is *my brother* and my sister and my mother." (Mark 3:33, 34, 35; Matthew 12:49, 50; Luke 8:21)

To buy grain from Egypt means to use knowledge as a means of adopting the goodness that comes of truth. This can be seen from the symbolism of *buying* as adopting (discussed at §§4397, 5374, 5406), from that of *grain* as the goodness to which truth leads (discussed at §5295), and from that of *Egypt* as knowledge (discussed above at §5402).   **5410**

And Benjamin, Joseph's brother, symbolizes heavenly spirituality, which was a middle ground. This can be seen from the representation of *Benjamin*   **5411** as heavenly spirituality, which is discussed at §4592. See the same section for the idea that heavenly spirituality is a middle ground.

It is important to know generally that the inner dimension cannot connect with the outer dimension or the reverse unless there is a middle ground. So truth from the Divine, which is Joseph, cannot connect with truth in general on the earthly plane, which is Jacob's sons, without the middle ground represented by Benjamin, which is called heavenly spirituality. In order for a middle ground to provide a connection, it has to partake of both the inner and the outer dimensions.

The reason there has to be a middle ground is that the inner and outer dimensions are quite distinct from one another. They are so distinct that they can separate, the way our outermost shell (our body) separates from our inner core (our spirit) when we die. The outer shell dies when the connection is broken, and it lives when the connection is in place. What is more, the extent and quality of life the outer level possesses depends on the extent and quality of the connection the middle ground provides.

Because Jacob's sons were without Benjamin—that is, without a middle ground—Joseph could not reveal himself to his brothers. For the same reason, he spoke harsh words with them, calling them spies and putting them in jail. For the same reason, they did not recognize Joseph.

[2] The nature of the middle ground represented by Benjamin, which is called heavenly spirituality, cannot be described intelligibly. After all, people lack any notion of the spiritual heavenliness that is Joseph, the religious truth that is Jacob's sons so far as it consists of mere knowledge, and accordingly the heavenly spirituality that is Benjamin. In heaven, though, the nature of the middle ground is visible clear as day. It is displayed in the form of representations that cannot be described. They are presented in heaven's light, which also contains perception.

Heavenly light actually consists of the ability to understand, which emanates from the Divine, so everything represented in that light carries perception with it. The same is not true of the world's light, because this light contains no insight. The intellectual ability brought about through worldly light comes from an inflow of heaven's light into it and from an inflow of the perceptive ability contained in heaven's light. The result is that we have as much of heaven's light as we have understanding, as much understanding as religious truth, and as much religious truth as loving goodness. Consequently we have as much of heaven's light as we have of a loving goodness.

Jacob did not send with his brothers means that [it was attempted] without that middle ground, as can be seen from the remarks just above.

5412

Because he said, "Maybe he would meet with harm," means that without spiritual heavenliness (Joseph), it would cease to exist. This can be seen from the symbolism of *meeting with harm* as ceasing to exist. These are the words of Benjamin's father, who loved him and was afraid he would meet his end among his brothers, as Joseph had. However, the words are quoted in Scripture and have been received as part of it because of their inner meaning, which is that in the presence only of what was outward and the absence of what was inward the connection would cease to exist. The connection or middle ground is Benjamin, the outward elements are Jacob's sons, and the inward element is Joseph.

5413

The middle ground does indeed cease to exist in the presence solely of what is outward and the absence of what is inward. That is how the case stands with the middle ground. It emerges from the inner core, so it also survives off the inner core. It emerges when the inner level looks on the outer level with the desire and intent of affiliating with it. What is in the middle is therefore united with the inner level and from the inner level with the outer. It is not united with the outer level apart from the inner.

You can see, then, that the middle ground necessarily ceases to exist in the presence of the outer shell alone apart from the inner core.

Besides, it is a universal law. In the workings of both the spiritual and the physical worlds, anything prior can survive as long as it is connected to something still more prior, but not if it is connected to something subsequent apart from what is prior. If it is connected to something subsequent alone, it necessarily ceases to exist. This is because anything lacking connection with something prior to itself lacks connection with the first origin, from which everything emerges and by which it survives.

And Israel's sons came to buy in the midst of those who came means that [the Lord] wanted to acquire spiritual truth through knowledge, the same way as with other kinds of truth, as the following shows: *Israel's sons* symbolize spiritual truth. *Sons* mean truth (see above at §5403), and *Israel* means a heavenly-spiritual person in terms of his or her earthly level (§§4286, 4570, 4598), so Israel's sons mean spiritual truth on the earthly level. *Buying* means being acquired. And *in the midst of those who came* means the same way as with other kinds—the kinds acquired through knowledge.

5414

5415　　*Because there was famine in the land of Canaan* symbolizes desolation in respect to religious attributes on the earthly level, as the following shows: *Famine* symbolizes a lack of knowledge and consequent desolation, as discussed in §§3364, 5277, 5279, 5281, 5300, 5360, 5376. The *land of Canaan* symbolizes the church, as discussed in §§3686, 3705, 4447, and since it symbolizes the church, it symbolizes religious attributes. That is why *there was famine in the land of Canaan* symbolizes desolation in respect to religious attributes. The reason it means on the earthly level is that the famine is being connected with Jacob's sons, who symbolize outward religious attributes (§5409) and therefore religious attributes on the earthly level.

5416　　Genesis 42:6, 7, 8. *And Joseph was the ruler over the land; he was selling to all the people of the land. And Joseph's brothers came and bowed down to him, face to the earth. And Joseph saw his brothers and recognized them and acted as a stranger to them and spoke harsh words with them and said to them, "Where do you come from?" And they said, "From the land of Canaan, to buy food." And Joseph recognized his brothers, but they did not recognize him.*

And Joseph was the ruler over the land means that spiritual heavenliness, or truth from the Divine, would govern the earthly plane, where knowledge resides. *He was selling to all the people of the land* means that it was the sole source of the ability to adopt anything. *And Joseph's brothers came* symbolizes general religious truth without the connection of a middle ground. *And bowed down to him, face to the earth* symbolizes humility. *And Joseph saw his brothers and recognized them* symbolizes perception and recognition by spiritual heavenliness. *And acted as a stranger to them* means no union, because the middle ground was lacking. *And spoke harsh words with them* means no correspondence either, as a result. *And said to them, "Where do you come from?"* symbolizes a probing. *And they said, "From the land of Canaan,"* means from the church. *To buy food* means in order to adopt truth marked by goodness. *And Joseph recognized his brothers* means that this religious truth was visible to spiritual heavenliness in the latter's light. *But they did not recognize him* means that truth from the Divine was not visible in earthly light unlit as yet by heavenly light.

5417　　*And Joseph was the ruler over the land* means that spiritual heavenliness, or truth from the Divine, would govern the earthly plane, where knowledge resides, as the following shows: *Joseph* represents spiritual heavenliness, as discussed at §§4286, 4963, 5249, 5307, 5331, 5332. Spiritual heavenliness is truth from the Divine as will be seen below. A *ruler* means someone who is to govern. And the *land*—the land of Egypt—symbolizes the earthly mind and therefore the earthly plane, as discussed at §§5276, 5278, 5280, 5288, 5301. On the point that spiritual heavenliness was to govern the earthly plane, where knowledge resides, see §5373. Egypt in an inner sense means knowledge; see §§1164, 1165, 1186, 1462, 4749, 4964, 4966.

Spiritual heavenliness is truth from the Divine because the Lord's inner human nature before it was fully glorified was a container for his divinity and therefore consisted in spiritual heavenliness. That is the only way to put it, because it cannot be expressed in other terms or other forms of thought. This container for divinity is the same as truth from the Divine, and Joseph means such truth; see §§4723, 4727.

He was selling to all the people of the land means that it was the sole 【5418】 source of the ability to adopt anything. This can be seen from the symbolism of *selling* as granting the ability to adopt something for one's own (discussed at §§5371, 5374) and from that of the *people of the land* as truth known to the church (discussed at §2928)—in this case, on the earthly plane (§5409).

And Joseph's brothers came symbolizes general religious truth without 【5419】 the connection of a middle ground. This can be seen from the symbolism of *Joseph's brothers* as general truth known to the church (discussed above at §5409). It was without the connection of a middle ground because they were without Benjamin, the middle ground. For the meaning of Benjamin as the middle ground, see above at §§5411, 5413.

And bowed down to him, face to the earth symbolizes humility. This 【5420】 can be seen from the symbolism of *bowing down* as humility (discussed in §2153) and of *face to the earth* as humble reverence (§1999).

"Humility" here does not mean the humility of self-knowledge and therefore inner humility but outer humility, because it was a traditional humility before the ruler of the land. It means outer rather than inner humility because there was no correspondence [with spiritual heavenliness] yet and no union through correspondence. When the earthly plane is in this state, it can humble and even abase itself completely but only as an acquired habit. The gesture has no genuine emotion behind it, so it is merely an expression of the body without its soul. Such is the humility meant here.

And Joseph saw his brothers and recognized them symbolizes percep- 【5421】 tion and recognition by spiritual heavenliness. This can be seen from the symbolism of *seeing* as perception (discussed at §§2150, 3764, 4567, 4723), from the representation of *Joseph* as spiritual heavenliness (discussed above at §5417), from the symbolism of *his brothers* as general religious truth (also discussed above, at §5419), and from the symbolism of *recognizing* as recognizing from perception.

See below at §§5422, 5427, 5428 for a discussion of this recognition on Joseph's part and lack of recognition on his brothers' part.

5422   *And acted as a stranger to them* means no union, because the middle ground was lacking. This can be seen from the symbolism of *acting as a stranger* as nonunion because of the lack of middle ground. Anyone who lacks a mutual bond with another because all middle ground is missing seems a stranger, which is exactly how inner truth, or truth directly from the Divine, seems to people with outer truth. That is why Joseph acted as a stranger to his brothers. It is not that he was estranged; after all, he loved them, since he turned from them and wept (verse 24). No, it is estrangement on their side due to the lack of a bond; and this is represented by his acting like a stranger himself.

Take, for instance, the meaning of passages in which the Word says that Jehovah (or the Lord) acts as a stranger with people, opposes them, turns them away, condemns them, sends them to hell, punishes them, and delights in these acts. In an inner sense it means that they themselves act as strangers to Jehovah (the Lord), oppose him, and revel in evils that turn them away from his face, condemn them, send them to hell, and punish them. It also means that such actions never proceed from Jehovah (the Lord). The Word speaks in such terms because of appearances; that is how matters appear to the uninformed.

The case is the same with inner truth when observed by outer truth without union through a middle ground. Under those circumstances, inner truth looks completely alienated from outer truth and sometimes even opposed to it. However, the opposition is not in the inner but the outer truth. If it is not united with inner truth through a middle ground, outer truth cannot help viewing inner truth in the world's light apart from heaven's light. It consequently cannot help viewing inner truth as estranged from itself.

More on this in what follows, though.

5423   *And spoke harsh words with them* means no correspondence either, as a result. This can be seen from the explanation above about acting as a stranger. Acting as a stranger has to do with emotions in the will. Speaking harsh words has to do with thoughts in the intellect, because in an inner sense, *speaking* means thinking (§§2271, 2287, 2619). Superficiality sees inner depths as a stranger when it has no emotional attachment to them, and as speaking harsh words when it has no correspondence with them.

Correspondence is the manifestation of inner depth on the outer surface and the representation of it there. Where no correspondence exists, then, there is no manifestation of inner depth on the outer surface and accordingly no representation of it there. The result is a *harsh word*.

And said to them, "Where do you come from?" symbolizes a probing, as is self-evident.   **5424**

And they said, "From the land of Canaan," means from the church. This is evident from the discussion in §§3686, 3705, 4447 of the symbolism of the *land of Canaan* as the church.   **5425**

To buy food means in order to adopt truth marked by goodness. This is evident from the symbolism of *buying* as adopting for one's own (discussed in §§4397, 5374, 5406, 5410) and from that of *food* as truth marked by goodness (discussed in §§5293, 5340, 5342).   **5426**

And Joseph recognized his brothers means that this religious truth was visible to spiritual heavenliness in the latter's light. This can be seen from the symbolism of *recognizing* as perceiving and seeing, and therefore as something becoming visible; from the representation of *Joseph* as spiritual heavenliness (discussed before); and from the symbolism of *his brothers* as general religious truth (discussed above at §§5409, 5419). This being the symbolism of *Joseph recognized his brothers*—that general religious truth was visible to spiritual heavenliness—it follows that it was visible in the light bathing spiritual heavenliness and therefore in the light shed by spiritual heavenliness. In that light, which is truth from the Divine (§5417), one can look down to the earthly level and see absolutely every true concept there. The reverse is not possible, though, if there is not a middle ground, let alone a correspondence [between general religious truth and truth from the Divine], and through correspondence, union. The fact of the matter is plain from the ability of angels in the heavens, and therefore in heavenly light, to see each and every event in the world of spirits, the realm just beneath the heavens. Angels can also see everything happening in the underground realm and even in the hells. But the reverse is not so.   **5427**

[2] Moreover, the angels in a higher heaven can see everything that happens under them in the next lower heaven, but the reverse is not possible unless there is a middle ground. There are actually connecting spirits who provide contact back and forth. As a result, anyone lower down who lacks the middle ground and especially who lacks correspondence [with

heaven] sees nothing at all when looking at heaven's light. Everything there seems to be in total darkness, although the inhabitants of heaven actually live in the clearest daylight.

The point can be illustrated by this one experience: A big city with thousands upon thousands of exquisitely beautiful sights came into my view. I could see the whole scene because I saw what lay between it and me, but the spirits with me could not see even the smallest part, because for them there was nothing in between. I was told that spirits who lack correspondence [with heaven] are unable to detect anything at all, even if they are right there.

[3] The situation also resembles that of the inner self, or the human spirit, which is also called the soul. The inner self can see each and every thing that exists and happens in the outer self, but the reverse is not possible unless there is a correspondence and middle ground [between the outer and inner selves]. To an outer self that lacks correspondence, then, the inner self has no reality. In fact, when mention is made of the inner self, it seems so obscure that the outer self does not even want to turn its gaze in that direction. Either that, or the outer self sees the inner as a nonentity and nothing to believe in. When the outer self does have correspondence, though, then by means of the middle ground it sees what is going on in the inner self. The light belonging to the inner self flows through the middle ground into the light of the outer self—heavenly light flows into earthly light—and illuminates it, and the illumination makes the contents of the inner self visible. This yields understanding and wisdom in the outer, earthly self. However, if there is no middle ground, and especially if there is no correspondence, the inner self sees and perceives what is going on in the outer and to some extent even directs it, but not the reverse.

If the outer self is opposed enough to completely pervert or stamp out the inflow from the inner self, the inner self is deprived of the light it receives from heaven. Heaven is closed off to it, but contact with hell opens up to the outer self.

See the next section for more on this subject.

5428 *But they did not recognize him* means that truth from the Divine was not visible in earthly light unlit as yet by heavenly light, as the discussion just above shows. "Joseph recognized his brothers" means that general religious truth was visible to spiritual heavenliness in the latter's light. So it follows that *they did not recognize him* means that spiritual heavenliness, or truth from the Divine, was not visible to general religious truth in earthly light unlit as yet by heavenly light.

The way the matter stands can actually be seen from the remarks just above, but since it is a secret, let me illustrate it by examples.

Take heavenly glory. When people think about heavenly glory from earthly light that is unlit by heavenly light because they lack a middle ground—especially if they lack correspondence—they cannot help picturing it as resembling worldly glory. One instance in which this happens is when they read prophetic revelations, particularly those of John in the Book of Revelation, describing everything in heaven as magnificent. You can tell them that heaven's glory so vastly outstrips all the magnificence of the world that the two can hardly be compared. Yet this is not heavenly glory. No, heaven's glory consists in the divinity gleaming from every sight visible there and in a perception of what is divine. So it consists in wisdom. Such glory, however, belongs only to the inhabitants there who consider such magnificence worthless in comparison to wisdom and ascribe all wisdom to the Lord, not to themselves. You can say all this, but when people without any middle ground view that kind of heavenly glory from earthly light, especially if they have no correspondence, they do not acknowledge any of it.

[2] Take angelic power, too. When people think about angelic power from earthly light that is unlit by heavenly light because they lack a middle ground—especially if they lack correspondence—they cannot help picturing it as resembling the power of the world's most powerful people. This is particularly true if they think about the power of the archangels mentioned in the Word. Such people imagine that angels have thousands of women and men under them, at their command, and that superiority in heaven consists in this kind of command. You can tell them that angelic power exceeds all the power of the world's most powerful people. It is so strong that just one of the lesser angels can drive away tens of thousands of hellish spirits and thrust them down into their hells. That is why the Word calls them powers and also dominions. Yet the least of them is the greatest. In other words, those who believe, wish, and perceive that all power comes from the Lord and none from themselves are the most powerful. As a result, the mighty there utterly reject all self-generated might. You can say all this, but again, when people without any middle ground view it in an earthly light, especially if they have no correspondence, they do not acknowledge it.

[3] Take yet another example. When people without any middle ground regard freedom in an earthly way—especially if they lack correspondence—they cannot help equating it with self-guided thinking, self-will, and the opportunity to do as they think and wish without restraint. The earthly self wants to be extremely rich so that it can have anything it contemplates or wishes, and to be extremely powerful so it can *do* anything it contemplates or wishes. It believes it would then be at a pinnacle of freedom and true happiness. You can tell such people that true freedom, which is called heavenly freedom, is nothing like that. True freedom is having their will guided by the Lord rather than themselves, and their thinking guided by heaven rather than themselves, so [angels] are in abject sorrow and in pain if allowed to think or will for themselves. You can tell such people all this, but they do not acknowledge it.

These examples show to some extent what it means to say that truth from the Divine is not visible in earthly light unlit as yet by heavenly light, as symbolized by *Joseph's brothers did not recognize him.*

5429   Genesis 42:9–16. *And Joseph remembered the dreams that he had dreamed in regard to them and said to them, "You are spies; you have come to see the nakedness of the land." And they said to him, "No, my Lord, and your servants come to buy food. We are all of us sons of one man; we are upright. Your servants are not spies." And he said to them, "No, because you have come to see the nakedness of the land." And they said, "Your twelve servants are brothers, sons of one man in the land of Canaan, and here, the youngest is with our father today, and one does not exist." And Joseph said to them, "It is what I spoke to you, saying, 'You are spies.' In this you will be tested: As Pharaoh lives, if you go out from here and your youngest brother does not come here, . . . ! Send one of you, and let him take your brother, and you yourselves will be tied up, and your words will be tested, whether there is truth with you; and if not, as Pharaoh lives, . . . ! Because you are spies."*

And Joseph remembered the dreams that he had dreamed in regard to them means that spiritual heavenliness foresaw what would happen with general religious truth on the earthly plane. *And said to them* symbolizes a resulting perception. *You are spies* means that the sole purpose is financial gain. *You have come to see the nakedness of the land* means that they like nothing better than personally knowing that [such truth] is not true. *And they said to him, "No, my Lord, we are upright,"* means that in itself it is true. *And your servants come to buy food* means that it exists to be adopted by the earthly level, by means of goodness. *We are all sons of one man* means that this truth has a single origin. *We are upright* means that it is therefore true in itself. *Your servants are not spies* means that it is therefore not for the money. *And he said to them, "No, because you have come to see the nakedness of the land,"* means that they do not care whether it is true. *And they said, "Your twelve servants are brothers,"* means that all aspects of faith as a whole are accordingly united. *Sons of one man* means from a single origin. *In the land of Canaan* means in the church. *And here, the youngest is with our father today* means that there is also union with spiritual goodness. *And one does not exist* means that divine spirituality as the source [of union] is not visible. *And Joseph said to them* symbolizes a perception concerning this matter. *It is what I spoke to you* means that it is true, as I thought. *Saying, "You are spies,"* means that they do subscribe to the church's truth in order to become rich. *In this you will be tested* means that it will become clear whether this is the case. *As Pharaoh lives* symbolizes the certainty. *If you go out from here and your youngest brother does not come here, . . . !* means that truth cannot help being such in you unless united to spiritual goodness. *Send one of you, and let him take your brother* means as long as there is some connection with that kind of goodness. *And you yourselves will be tied up* means even if they are separate in all other respects. *And your words will be tested, whether there is truth with you* means that it will then come to light. *And if not, as Pharaoh lives, . . . ! Because you are spies* means otherwise it will be certain that the truth you have is only for financial gain.

And Joseph remembered the dreams that he had dreamed in regard to them means that spiritual heavenliness foresaw what would happen with general religious truth on the earthly plane, as the following shows: *Remembering* symbolizes presence, because whatever is being remembered stands present. For the idea that remembrance has to do with foresight, see §3966. *Joseph* represents spiritual heavenliness, as noted many times before. And *dreams* symbolize foresight, a prediction, and the outcome, as discussed at §§3698, 5091, 5092, 5104. Here they symbolize foresight of what would happen with general religious truth on the earthly plane. That is what Jacob's sons symbolize (§§5409, 5419), which is why the text says *that he had dreamed in regard to them.* **5430**

And said to them symbolizes a resulting perception. This can be seen from the symbolism of *saying* as a perception (discussed in §§1791, 1815, 1819, 1822, 1898, 1919, 2080, 2619, 2862, 3509). **5431**

You are spies means that the sole purpose is financial gain. This can be seen from the symbolism of *spies* as being for financial gain. That is exactly what spies mean in the inner sense, as the thread of the story **5432** shows. The inner meaning is talking about religious truth that is to be adopted by the earthly level and cannot be adopted except through an inflow from spiritual heavenliness, by way of a middle ground. The religious truth is Jacob's sons, or Joseph's brothers; the spiritual heavenliness is Joseph; and the middle ground is Benjamin.

The way this matter stands was already told in §5402. When we learn the church's religious truth (called doctrine) in the first stage of life, we grasp it and commit it to memory no differently than any other kind of knowledge. It keeps the form of knowledge until we start to look into it for ourselves, see whether it is true, and after seeing it is true, form an intent to act on it. This insight and intent turn it from items of information into rules for our life and eventually into life itself. In this way such truth enters our life and is adopted into it.

[2] When people reach adulthood and especially old age without looking into the religious truth called doctrine, seeing for themselves whether it is true, and then forming an intent to live by it, they do not retain it any differently than other kinds of knowledge. Such truth exists only in their earthly memory and therefore on their lips. When they speak it, they do so not from their inner self or from the heart but from their outer self with their lips. People in this state can never believe that the church's truth is true, no matter how firmly they view themselves as believers. They seem to themselves to believe its truth because they believe in other people and have proved others' ideas to their own satisfaction. To prove what we hear from others is very easy, whether true or false. All it takes is cleverness.

[3] Religious truths of this kind, or people who subscribe to religious truth in this way, are symbolized by spies coming to see the nakedness of the land. They believe their church's doctrines not from any desire for truth but from the desire to win high office or amass wealth. As a result they believe almost nothing for themselves. They usually deny it all at heart, viewing doctrine the way merchants view their wares. They view themselves as educated and wise if they can see personally that the doctrines are not true and yet persuade the common herd that they are. Most church leaders are like that, as one can tell quite plainly from experience with them in the other life. Wherever they go there, they carry the aura of their desires and resulting thoughts, and others pick up on the aura very clearly. Plain sensation tells everyone what kind of desire for truth and what kind of faith they had possessed. In the world this does not come out in the open, because people here do not have a spiritual perception

of such things. That being so, the leaders do not reveal their true nature, because they would be deprived of their affluence.

[4] You can see they are spies fairly clearly by reflecting that people like that are always looking for defects in anyone devoted to the truth that grows out of goodness. Such a person they seek to blame and condemn. Once they have proved the doctrines of their religion to themselves, whether they are among the so-called Papists, the Reformed, Quakers, Socinians, or Jews, are they anything but spies? They ridicule and condemn real truth, if they come across it, because they do not grasp the trueness of truth. They do not grasp it because they do not desire truth for its own sake (let alone for the sake of living by it) but for the sake of wealth.

When these people read the Word, they examine it closely, with the sole aim of confirming the teachings they know for the sake of financial gain. Many of them examine the Word to see the nakedness of the land— to see that the church's truth is not true but is merely useful for persuading others it is true, and this for financial gain.

[5] People who desire truth for its own sake, for the sake of life, and consequently for the sake of the Lord's kingdom do believe the church's doctrines, but they still examine the Word with no other aim than truth. That is the source of their faith and conscience. If anyone tells them they ought to cling to the doctrines of the church they were born into, they think, "If I had been born a Jew, a Socinian, a Quaker, a Christian pagan, or even outside the church, people in those groups would have told me the same. People everywhere say, 'Here's the church! Here's the church! Here's the truth, and nowhere else!' That being so, the Word should be examined with a devout prayer to the Lord for enlightenment." People like this do not pester anyone in the church or ever condemn others, knowing that everyone who is an individual church lives by her or his own faith anyway.

You have come to see the nakedness of the land means that they like nothing better than personally knowing that [such truth] is not true, as the following shows: *Coming to see* means itching to know something, so it means that they like nothing better than knowing. *Nakedness* means without truth, so it means that something is not true, as discussed below. And the *land* has its symbolism, so the *nakedness of the land* means no truth in the church. For the symbolism of the *land* as the church, see §§566, 662, 1066, 1262, 1733, 1850, 2117, 2118 at the end, 3355, 4447, 4535.

Nakedness symbolizes something stripped of truth, or without truth, because clothes in general symbolize truth, and each specific garment

5433

symbolizes a particular kind of truth; see §§2576, 3301, 4545, 4677, 4741, 4742, 4763, 5248, 5319. Nakedness, then, means being without truth, as the Scripture passages below will show.

[2] The situation in all this is plain from the discussion directly above in §5432: People who learn truth not for its own sake or for the sake of life but for the sake of the money cannot possibly help thinking privately that the church's truth is not true. This is because the desire for money is an earthbound desire, and the desire for truth is a spiritual desire. One or the other has to have dominion. No one can serve two masters. Where the one desire exists, then, the other does not; where the desire for truth exists, the desire for riches does not, and where the desire for riches exists, the desire for truth does not. As an inevitable consequence, if the desire for riches takes control, nothing is better than for truth not to be true. At the same time, nothing is better than for others to believe that truth *is* true.

If the inner self turns its gaze downward to the earth and makes that everything, it can never look up and make that anything. Earthly matters swallow up and smother everything. This is because heaven's angels cannot stay with us in earthbound things, so they withdraw, and spirits of hell, who cannot stay with us in heavenly things, then approach. The affairs of heaven are therefore worthless to us, and the affairs of earth are everything. When earthly affairs are everything to us, we believe ourselves better educated and wiser than anyone else for denying the church's truth to ourselves, telling ourselves in our heart that such truth is for simpletons.

We therefore have to be under the sway of either an earthly or a heavenly desire. We cannot be with heavenly angels and hellish spirits simultaneously, because we would then be hanging suspended between heaven and hell.

When we desire truth for the sake of truth, or for the sake of the Lord's kingdom (since that is where divine truth resides), and consequently for the sake of the Lord himself, we are among angels. We do not then despise financial means, since we need them for life in the world, but we do not make them our goal. Rather our goal is the use those means can serve, which we regard as an intermediate goal on the way to the final, heavenly goal. So by no means do we set our heart on wealth.

[3] The fact that nakedness symbolizes being without truth can also be seen from other places in the Word. In John, for instance:

> To the angel of the church of the Laodiceans write, "Because you say, 'I am rich and have been enriched, so that I have need of nothing'—since

you do not know that you are wretched and miserable and needy and blind and *naked, . . .*" (Revelation 3:17)

Being naked here stands for being destitute of truth. In the same author:

I advise you to buy from me gold purified by fire, [so that you will grow rich,] and white clothes, so that you will be dressed and the *shame of your nakedness* will not be exposed. (Revelation 3:18)

Buying gold stands for acquiring goodness and adopting it as one's own. "So that you will grow rich" means so as to enjoy heavenly and spiritual goodness. White clothes stand for spiritual truth. Shame over nakedness stands for being without goodness or truth. On the point that buying means acquiring and adopting as one's own, see §5374; that gold means heavenly and spiritual goodness, 1551, 1552; that clothes mean truth, 1073, 2576, 4545, 4763, 5248, 5319; and that white has to do with truth, because it comes from heaven's light, 3301, 3993, 4007, 5319. [4] In the same author:

Here, now, I come like a thief; fortunate are those who are watchful and keep their clothes, *to avoid walking naked.* (Revelation 16:15)

Those who keep their clothes stand for people who preserve the truth. "To avoid walking naked" means to avoid being without truth. In Matthew:

The king will say to those on the right, "*I was naked* and *you put a robe around me."* And to those on the left, "[I was] *naked, and you did not put a robe around me."* (Matthew 25:36, 43)

"Naked" stands for good people who acknowledge that there is nothing good or true in them (§4958). [5] In Isaiah:

Isn't this my fast: to break your bread for the one starving, and that you bring afflicted refugees into your house, *when you see the naked* and *cover them?* (Isaiah 58:7)

The meaning is the same. In Jeremiah:

Jerusalem sinned a sin; therefore she became like a menstruating woman. All who had honored her despised her, *because they saw her nakedness.* (Lamentations 1:8)

The nakedness stands for being without truth. In Ezekiel:

You came into [the time of] the most beautiful of ornaments; your breasts became firm, and your hair grew, yet you were *naked* and *bare.*

I spread my wing over you and *covered your nakedness.* You have not remembered the days of your youth, *when you were naked* and *bare.* (Ezekiel 16:7, 8, 22)

[6] This is about Jerusalem, which means the ancient church as it was when first established and as it later developed. At first it lacked truth, but then it was taught truth, which it rejected in the end. In the same author:

> If a righteous man who performs judgment and justice gives his bread to the starving and *covers the naked with a garment,* . . . (Ezekiel 18:7)

Covering the naked with a garment stands for teaching truth to people who long for it. In Hosea:

> . . . or else I will *strip her naked,* display her as on the day of her being born, make her like a wilderness, and cause her to be like a land of drought, and kill her with thirst. (Hosea 2:3)

Stripping someone naked stands for leaving someone without truth. In Nahum:

> I will show nations *your nakedness,* and monarchs your disgrace. (Nahum 3:5)

Showing nations someone's nakedness stands for making ugliness visible. All ugliness results from nontruth, and all beauty, from truth (§§4985, 5199).

5434   *And they said to him, "No, Lord, we are upright,"* means that in itself it is true, as the following shows: *Saying to him, "No, Lord,"* means that the purpose is not financial gain (as symbolized by Joseph's words "You are spies"; §5432), and they do *not* like nothing better than personally knowing it is not true (as symbolized by Joseph's words "You have come to see the nakedness of the land"; §5433). And *we are upright* means that in itself it is true. *Uprightness* symbolizes truth in an inner sense, here as in many other places in the Word.

This meaning—that in itself [general religious truth] is true—follows from the series of ideas. When people acquire religious truth for the sake of wealth, truth really is not true for them (as shown above in §5433) but can be true in itself. After all, Jacob's sons symbolize real religious truth in general.

"Upright" means truth in the abstract because in the inner meaning everything is detached from individuals; the concept of person turns into that of some attribute (see §§5225, 5287). The reason is that otherwise one's thoughts and therefore speech cannot help wandering off course, sliding from examination of the subject at hand into a discussion of individuals. Besides, there is no other way one's thoughts and therefore speech can become universal, embracing many considerations at once, let alone boundless indescribable ones, as happens with angels.

Nonetheless, the abstract idea still involves individuals—individuals with the attribute in question. That is why upright people symbolize truth.

And your servants come to buy food means that such truth exists to be adopted by the earthly level, by means of goodness, as the following shows: *Servants* symbolize what is lower and more earthbound, as discussed in §§2541, 3019, 3020, 5161, 5164, 5305. So they symbolize truth (§3409), since truth is subordinate to goodness. The Word refers to subordinate things as servants. Here, then, it refers that way to truth on the earthly plane in relation to spiritual heavenliness. *Buying* means being adopted as one's own, as discussed in §§4397, 5374, 5406, 5410. And *food* symbolizes heavenly and spiritual goodness, as discussed in §5147. It also symbolizes truth connected with goodness (§§5340, 5342), so here it symbolizes truth that is to be connected to the earthly level—and therefore adopted by it—through goodness. **5435**

[2] We never make truth our own except by means of goodness. When we use goodness to make it our own, though, truth turns into goodness, because it then acts in unison with goodness. Together the two make a single "body" whose soul is goodness. The truths permeating that goodness are like the spiritual fibers forming the body. As a result, these fibers also symbolize the inmost forms emanating from goodness, and the nerves themselves symbolize truths (§§4303, 5189 at the end).

We are all sons of one man means that this truth has a single origin. This can be seen from the symbolism of the *sons*—Jacob's sons—as truth in general (discussed many times before). *Of one man* means it has a single origin, as is self-evident. **5436**

We are upright means that it is therefore true in itself. This is established by the discussion just above in §5434 of the meaning of *we are upright* as being true in itself. **5437**

Your servants are not spies means that it is not for the money. This stands to reason from the meaning of *spies* as the idea that they subscribe to religious truth for the money (discussed above at §5432). Here it means they do not. **5438**

And he said to them, "No, because you have come to see the nakedness of the land," means that they do not care whether it is true. This can be **5439** seen from the symbolism of *coming to see the nakedness of the land* as the idea that they like nothing better than personally knowing it is not true (discussed at §5433). The meaning is similar here—that they do not care whether it is true.

5440   *And they said, "Your twelve servants are brothers,"* means that all aspects of faith as a whole are accordingly united, as the following shows: *Twelve* means all. When applied to Jacob's sons, as it is here, or to the tribes named for them, and when applied to the apostles, it symbolizes all aspects of faith taken together, as discussed at §§577, 2089, 2129, 2130, 2553, 3272, 3488, 3858, 3862, 3913, 3926, 3939, 4060. And *brothers* symbolize union through goodness. When true concepts are united through goodness, they take on a kind of brotherhood with each other.

If they seem to be united without goodness, they are not united. Falsity inspired by evil always enters and breaks them apart. This is because they have no single origin they stem from and no single goal to aim for. The beginning and end have to unite them if there is to be a union. The beginning has to be something good to stem from; the end has to be something good to aim for.

In addition, if truth is to be united, something good has to reign supreme throughout it. What reigns supreme throughout anything unites it.

For the meaning of a *brother* as a desire for or emotional response to goodness and therefore as goodness, see §§2360, 2524, 3303, 3459, 3803, 3815, 4121.

5441   *Sons of one man* means from a single origin. This can be seen from the discussion just above at §5436 where the same words occur.

5442   *In the land of Canaan* means in the church. This can be seen from the symbolism of the *land of Canaan* as the Lord's kingdom and the church (discussed at §§1413, 1437, 1607, 3038, 3481, 3686, 3705, 4447).

5443   *And here, the youngest is with our father today* means that there is also union with spiritual goodness. This can be seen from the representation of Benjamin, the *youngest,* as a uniting middle ground (discussed below) and from that of Jacob, now Israel, the *father* here, as spiritual goodness (discussed at §§3654, 4598).

For the idea that Benjamin means heavenly spirituality, which is a middle ground, see §§4592, 5411, 5413, 5419. To be specific, it is middle ground that the earthly level and its contents share with the spiritual heavenliness that is Joseph. Since Benjamin is a middle ground, and Israel is spiritual goodness, the clause *here, the youngest is with our father today* symbolizes union with spiritual goodness.

And one does not exist means that divine spirituality as the source [of
union] is not visible, as the following shows: Joseph—the *one*—represents
spiritual heavenliness, in other words divine spirituality, or truth from the
Divine, as discussed in §§3969, 4286, 4592, 4723, 4727, 4963, 5249, 5307,
5331, 5332, 5417. Divine spirituality initiates all union with earthly-level
truth, which is the reason for describing it as the source. And *does not
exist* means that it is not visible. It did exist but was not visible to them,
because there was no middle ground, no Benjamin. **5444**

And Joseph said to them symbolizes a perception concerning this
matter—that is, concerning what his brothers had said. This can be
seen from the symbolism of *saying* in scriptural narrative as a perception (discussed in §§1791, 1815, 1819, 1822, 1898, 1919, 2080, 2619, 3509). **5445**

It is what I spoke to you means that it is true, as I thought. This
can be seen from the symbolism of *speaking* as thinking (discussed in
§§2271, 2287, 2619). The fact that it means that the thing is true needs
no explanation. **5446**

Saying, "You are spies," means that they do subscribe to the church's
truth in order to become rich. This is established by the discussion in
§§5432, 5438 of the symbolism of *spies* as people who subscribe to the
church's truth solely to become rich. **5447**

In this you will be tested means that it will become clear whether this
is the case, as is self-evident. **5448**

As Pharaoh lives symbolizes the certainty. This can be seen from the
fact that *as Pharaoh lives* is a standard oath and so means that the thing
is certain. **5449**

Joseph knew they were not spies and had not come to see the nakedness of the land. Still, he swore it was so because the message of the inner
meaning was certain—that religious truth can have no other purpose than
material advantage in any of us, no matter who, if it has not been internalized by our inner self through goodness. When it *has* been internalized
by our inner self through goodness, we take goodness and truth itself as
our goal. This means that we take the church, the Lord's kingdom, and
the Lord himself as our goal. When we take these as our goal, we come
into as many financial resources as we need, in keeping with the Lord's
words in Matthew 6:33: "First seek God's kingdom and its justice and you
will gain all."

If you go out from here and your youngest brother does not come here, . . . !
means that truth cannot help being such in you unless united to spiritual goodness. Explaining this by the symbolism of the actual words would **5450**

not be very successful, but it is the meaning that wells from them. The *youngest brother* does mean union with spiritual goodness, after all; see §5443.

5451   *Send one [of] you, and let him take your brother* means as long as there is some connection with that kind of goodness, as the following shows: *Your brother,* the youngest, symbolizes union with spiritual goodness (as just above in §5450). And *sending one and taking him* means as long as there is some—that is, some connection. Skepticism is what is being displayed.

5452   *And you yourselves will be tied up* means even if they are still separate in all other respects. This can be seen from the symbolism of *being tied up* as being separated. One who is tied up and held is separated, specifically from the spiritual goodness that the father, Israel, symbolizes.

5453   *And your words will be tested, whether there is truth with you* means that it will then come to light. This can be seen from the meaning of the *testing of words* and of *whether there is truth* as certainty that it will all then come to light as declared by the brothers. The certainty relates to the statements they made and the inner content of those statements as discussed above at §§5434, 5435, 5436, 5437, 5438, 5439, 5440, 5441, 5442, 5443, 5444.

5454   *And if not, as Pharaoh lives, . . . ! Because you are spies* means otherwise it will be certain that the truth you have is only for financial gain. This can be seen from the symbolism of *as Pharaoh lives* as something certain (discussed at §5449) and from that of *spies* as subscribing to the church's truth for the sole purpose of financial gain (discussed at §§5432, 5438, 5447).

There is no need to explain this clause and the last few at any further length because I explained them in general earlier. What is more, they are the kinds of ideas that do not sink into the intellect very clearly. General concepts have to be present in the intellect first, before the kinds of particulars contained within the general points made above can enter as subconcepts. If the broad concepts are not welcomed first, the particulars cannot possibly gain entrance. In fact, they trigger boredom, because there is no interest in particulars where the broad concepts have not been received with affection first.

5455   *Genesis 42:17, 18, 19, 20. And he confined them to jail three days. And Joseph said to them on the third day, "Do this and you will live; I fear God. If you are upright, let one of your brothers be tied up in the house where you were jailed, and you yourselves go, take grain provisions for the famine of your houses. And your youngest brother you are to bring to me, and your words will be shown true, and you are not to die." And they did so.*

And he confined them to jail symbolizes separation from itself. *Three days* means to the full. *And Joseph said to them on the third day* symbolizes a perception by spiritual heavenliness about the truth separated from it, at the conclusion. *Do this and you will live; I fear God* means that this is how it has to be if that truth is to have life from the Divine. *If you are upright* means if it is true in itself. *Your brother will be tied up in the house where you were jailed* means that faith that belongs to the will has to be separated. *You yourselves go, take grain provisions for the famine of your houses* means that meanwhile they are free to see to their needs. *And your youngest brother you are to bring to me* means until the middle ground is present. *And your words will be shown true* means that what was declared concerning the truth will then be so. *And you are not to die* means that truth will therefore receive life. *And they did so* symbolizes the end of that state.

And he confined them to jail symbolizes separation from itself. This **5456** can be seen from the symbolism of putting or *confining someone in jail* as rejection and therefore separation (discussed at §§5083, 5101).

Three days means to the full. This can be seen from the meaning of **5457** *three days* as from start to finish and so to the full (discussed at §§2788, 4495). It is a new state that is being depicted now, and its whole duration is symbolized by the three days. "On the third day," which comes next, symbolizes an end to that state and something new resulting.

And Joseph said to them on the third day symbolizes a perception by **5458** spiritual heavenliness about the truth separated from it, at the conclusion, as the following shows: *Saying* symbolizes a perception, as discussed at §§1791, 1815, 1819, 1822, 1898, 1919, 2619, 3509. Jacob's sons represent the church's truth in general, as discussed before. At this point they symbolize that truth separated from spiritual heavenliness (§5456). *Joseph* represents spiritual heavenliness, as also discussed before. And *on the third day* symbolizes an ending, when something new begins, as discussed in §§5159, 5457, and therefore when there is a conclusion. Plainly, then, *Joseph said to them on the third day* symbolizes a perception by spiritual heavenliness about the truth separated from it, at the conclusion.

Do this and you will live; I fear God means that this is how it has to be **5459** if that truth is to have life from the Divine, as the following shows: *Do this* means that this is how it has to be. *You will live* symbolizes life present in that truth, the truth that Jacob's sons symbolize. And *I fear God* means that it comes from the Divine. Joseph represents the Lord in respect to truth from his divine side, which is the same as spiritual heavenliness. So on the highest level here, *I* symbolizes truth from the Lord's divine side, and *God* symbolizes the divinity itself within spiritual heavenliness, or the divinity within the truth. *Fearing* in the highest sense, when applied to the Lord, means love rather than fear. Moreover, fear of God throughout the Word symbolizes love for God. Love for God differs depending on the person in whom it exists. Such love becomes fear in people who engage in outward worship that lacks inward content. It becomes holy fear in people who engage in spiritual worship. But it becomes love containing holy awe in people who engage in heavenly worship. In the Lord, though, there was not fear but pure love. This shows that when the phrase *I fear God* describes the Lord, it symbolizes divine love and therefore the Divine.

5460   *If you are upright* means if it is true in itself. This can be seen from the discussion above in §§5434, 5437 of the symbolism of *being upright* as being true in itself.

5461   *One of your brothers will be tied up in the house where you were jailed* means that faith that belongs to the will has to be separated. This can be seen from the representation of Simeon, the *one brother* who was tied up (verse 24), as faith that belongs to the will (discussed in §§3869, 3870, 3871, 3872, 4497, 4502, 4503) and from the symbolism of being *tied up in the house [where you were] jailed* as being separated (discussed in §§5083, 5101, 5452, 5456).

Here is how the case stands: When faith that belongs to the will—a willingness to act on the truth taught by faith—is detached from people intent on religious truth, their connection with the Divine becomes so slight that it amounts to little more than acknowledgment. In people who have been reborn, you see, a divine inflow from the Lord acts on what is good in them and therefore on what is true. That is, it acts on their will and therefore on their intellect. In people devoted to faith's truth, then, the more they accept goodness from the Lord, the more the Lord forms a new will on their intellectual side (and it is indeed on their intellectual side; see §§927, 1023, 1043, 1044, 2256, 4328, 4493, 5113). He also flows into them more and more, creating in them a growing desire to do good, or to exercise charity toward their neighbor.

This shows what it means to say that faith that belongs to the will (represented by Simeon) has to be separated before the middle ground (Benjamin) comes into view.

5462   *You yourselves go, take grain provisions for the famine of your houses* means that meanwhile they are free to see to their needs, as the following shows: After the brothers were tied up and then one was held in their stead, *you yourselves go* means that meanwhile they are free. *Grain* *provisions* symbolize truth, as discussed at §§5276, 5280, 5292. *Famine* symbolizes a lack of knowledge, and desolation, as discussed at §§5360, 5376. And *your houses* symbolize the dwellings in which each individual's particular truth resides, or the earthly mind. For the meaning of a *house* as the earthly mind, see §§4973, 5023. For the idea that the truth represented by Jacob's sons belongs to the outer part of the church and is consequently located on the earthly plane, §§5403, 5415, 5428. All these meanings taken together show that *take grain provisions for the famine of your houses* means to see to the needs of themselves and their loved ones when desolate for lack of truth, as they currently are.

And your youngest brother you are to bring to me means until the middle ground is present. This can be seen from the representation of Benjamin as a middle ground, specifically between spiritual heavenliness and the earthly plane (discussed above at §§5411, 5443). **5463**

And your words will be shown true means that what was declared concerning the truth will then be so, as is self-evident. For what they declared about themselves and therefore about the church's truth, which they represent, see §§5434–5444 above. **5464**

Here is the situation: People who subscribe to the church's truth only for financial gain are just as skilled as others at declaring how matters stand with truth. For instance, they are capable of announcing that we never adopt truth as our own unless our inner self internalizes it. They are even capable of saying that we can internalize it only by means of goodness, and that until we do, truth has no life. Such people occasionally see these and other points as clearly as anyone—*more* clearly it sometimes seems—but only when they are actively discussing them with someone. [2] When talking to themselves and accordingly with their inner self—in other words, when thinking—people who subscribe to the church's truth only for profit see it all just the opposite. Although they see it just the opposite, however, and although they deny the truth at heart, they can still persuade others it is so. In fact, they can make the case that they themselves take truth in this way. A craving for wealth, high position, and the accompanying reputation makes them eagerly soak up any means of persuading others. And there are no means they drink in more eagerly than ideas that are basically true, since these ideas are secretly and inherently attractive.

We are all endowed with this ability to tell whether an idea is true, no matter what we are like, as long as we are not total idiots. The ability is given to us so that we can be reformed and regenerated through our intellectual side. When we head off in the wrong direction, though, and thoroughly reject the tenets of the church's faith, we no longer want to understand truth, even though we still can. We turn away from the truth as soon as we hear it.

5465   *And you are not to die* means that truth will therefore receive life— when truth is the way it was declared to be. This can be seen from the meaning of *you are not to die* as "you are to live" and therefore as the idea that the truth represented by the brothers will receive life.

5466   *And they did so* symbolizes the end of that state. This is established by the symbolism of *doing* or "it happened," which means the end of a previous state and involves the start of the next (discussed in §§4979, 4987, 4999, 5074).

There is no need to explain this passage any more fully, for the same reason I gave above at §5454. Still, it is important to know that it contains inexpressible secrets, and in the heavens these secrets shine from every word, even though not one of them is visible to people on earth. The awe we sometimes feel when we read the Word holds many of the secrets inside it, because all kinds of things that do not openly expose themselves to us lie hidden in the awe that moves us.

5467   Genesis 42:21, 22, 23, 24. *And they said, a man to his brother, "Without a doubt we ourselves are guilty over our brother, whose distress of soul we saw in his pleading to us, and we did not listen; therefore this distress has come to us." And Reuben answered them, saying, "Didn't I say to you, saying, 'Don't sin against the boy,' and you didn't pay attention? And his blood, too—here, it is being sought." And they did not know that Joseph was listening, because the interpreter was between them. And he turned from them and wept and returned to them and spoke to them and took Simeon from them and tied him up before their eyes.*

And they said, a man to his brother symbolizes a perception about the reason. *Without a doubt we ourselves are guilty over our brother* means that they are to blame because they disowned the inner dimension by not accepting what was good. *Whose distress of soul we saw* symbolizes the state of the inner plane in its goodness after it had been disowned. *In his pleading to us, and we did not listen* means that it was constantly appealing to them without ever being accepted. *And Reuben answered* symbolizes what was perceived nonetheless by a doctrinal, intellectual faith. *Didn't I say to you, saying,* symbolizes the degree of perception yielded. *Don't sin against the boy* means let there be no rift. *And you didn't pay attention* means no acceptance. *And his blood, too—here, it is being sought* symbolizes the resultant gnawing of conscience. *And they did not know that Joseph was listening* means that the earthly light shining on that truth makes it hard to believe that everything is visible by spiritual light. *Because the interpreter was between them* means that spiritual concepts are then taken in a completely different way. *And he turned from them* means pulling back somewhat. *And wept* symbolizes compassion. *And returned to them and spoke to them* symbolizes its inflow. *And took Simeon from them* symbolizes faith that belongs to the will. *And tied him up* means being separated. *Before their eyes* means perceptibly.

And they said, a man to his brother symbolizes a perception about the **5468** reason. This can be seen from the symbolism of *saying* in Scripture's narratives as a perception (discussed at §§1791, 1815, 1819, 1822, 1898, 1919, 2080, 2619, 3509) and from the meaning of a *man to his brother* as mutually (discussed at §4725).

They said, a man to his brother in this case symbolizes a perception about the reason (that is, the reason Joseph spoke harsh words, calling them spies, and held them in jail three days) because right after this they discuss the reason with each other. So the clause symbolizes a perception about the reason.

Without a doubt we ourselves are guilty over our brother means that **5469** they are to blame because they disowned the inner dimension by not accepting what was good. This can be seen from the symbolism of *being guilty* as being responsible and being to blame for rejecting what was good and true (discussed at §3400) and from the representation of Joseph, the *brother over whom* they were guilty, as the inner dimension they rejected or disowned. Joseph and Benjamin represent the inner dimension of religion, but Jacob's other ten sons represent its outer dimension. After all, Rachel, who gave birth to Joseph and Benjamin, means a desire for inner truth, and Leah means a desire for outer truth (§§3758, 3782, 3793, 3819). In this chapter Joseph represents spiritual heavenliness, or truth from the Divine, which is the inner dimension. Benjamin represents heavenly spirituality, which is the middle ground extending from spiritual heavenliness. Jacob's remaining ten sons represent truth known to the outer level of the church and therefore truth on the earthly plane, as noted many times before.

The chapter is also talking about the union of the church's inner part with its outer part—in general and in particular, since each individual has to be a church in particular in order to be part of the overall church. In the highest sense it is talking about the Lord and the way he united the inner and outer levels in his human nature in order to make his human nature divine.

5470 *When we saw his distress of soul* symbolizes the state of the inner plane in the interim after it had been disowned. This can be seen from the symbolism of *distress of soul* as the state of the inner plane when estranged from the outer.

To describe the state: The Lord continually flows into us with goodness, and within the goodness, truth. We either accept it or not. If we accept it, we are in a good position, but if not, we are in a bad position. If we feel a little uneasy when we do not accept the inflow, there is hope for our reformation, and this uneasiness is the "distress of soul." If we do not feel at all uneasy, the hope disappears. You see, we all have two spirits from hell with us and two angels from heaven. Because we are born with sins, we cannot possibly survive unless we have contact with hell on one side and heaven on the other. Our whole life depends on it. When we grow up, we start to take charge of our own affairs; that is, we seem to ourselves to rely on our own judgment in forming intentions and acting on them, and to rely on our own intellect in thinking and deciding about matters of faith. If we then resort to evil, the two spirits from hell come closer and the two angels from heaven move a little farther away. If we turn to goodness, though, the two angels from heaven come closer and the two spirits from hell move away.

[2] Consequently, if we resort to evil (which most people do as young adults) and feel somewhat uneasy in reflecting on the evil we have done, it is a sign that we will still accept the influence of angels from heaven in the future. It is also a sign that we will allow ourselves to be reformed. However, if we do not feel at all uneasy in reflecting on the evil we have done, it is a sign that we no longer want to accept the influence of angels from heaven. It is also a sign that we will not allow ourselves to be reformed from then on.

This passage, then, which deals with truth known to the outer part of the church as represented by Jacob's ten sons, mentions the distress of soul Joseph experienced when estranged from his brothers. Soon after, it also mentions that Reuben had warned them. The symbolism is that since this state came first, reformation would follow. Reformation is the union of the inner plane with the outer, which will be the subject later on [§§5505, 5506].

Consider that people who feel uneasy under those circumstances are inwardly acknowledging their evil. When the Lord recalls the acknowledgment to their mind, they confess and eventually repent.

In his pleading to us, and we did not listen means that it was constantly appealing to them without ever being accepted. This can be seen from the symbolism of *pleading* as making an appeal. When someone pleads not to be disowned, and the subject under discussion is an inflow of goodness from the Divine, it means an appeal for acceptance. Goodness, which flows in from the Lord, stands by at all times entreating us, but it is up to us to accept it. That is why a plea not to be disowned symbolizes a constant appeal.

It follows, then, that *not listening* means not being accepted.

The literal meaning involves a number of characters, such as Jacob's ten sons and Joseph, but the inner meaning is about qualities in a single individual. The truth known to the outer part of the church (or truth on the earthly plane) that Jacob's ten sons represent is truth in our outer self. The spiritual heavenliness represented by Joseph is truth from the Divine in our inner self.

It is the same elsewhere in the stories of the Word. The characters are there to symbolize different attributes, and the attributes themselves relate to a single individual in whom they exist.

5471

And Reuben answered them, saying, symbolizes what was perceived nonetheless by a doctrinal, intellectual faith, as the following shows: *Answering* or saying to his brothers symbolizes a perception. For the meaning of *saying* as a perception, see above at §5468. And *Reuben* represents a doctrinal, intellectual faith, or theological truth that enables us to achieve goodness in our lives, as discussed at §§3861, [3863,] 3866.

Since the text is dealing with goodness—or the divinity within goodness—and the way in which goodness appeals for acceptance, it mentions faith and the way faith teaches us to accept goodness. If we sense some uneasiness when we pull away from goodness, it is not because of an inner dictate we are born with but because of the faith we have imbibed ever since childhood. This is what is then dictating to us and making us uneasy. That is why Reuben, who represents such faith, speaks here.

I speak of a doctrinal, intellectual faith to distinguish it from a living, willing faith, which is represented by Simeon.

5472

Didn't I say to you, saying, symbolizes the degree of perception yielded. This can be seen from the symbolism of *saying* in the stories of the Word as a perception (discussed in §§1791, 1815, 1819, 1822, 1898, 1919, 2080, 2619, 3509). "Say" is used twice here and once just above, so the degree of perception is what is being symbolized.

5473

Don't sin against the boy means let there be no rift—no splitting of the outer plane from the inner, as the following shows: *Sinning* means

5474

creating a rift (as mentioned in §5229), since all sin drives a wedge; and Joseph, the *boy*, represents the inner plane (as above in §5469).

5475   *And you didn't pay attention* means no acceptance. This can be seen from the symbolism of listening or *paying attention* as obeying (discussed at §§2542, 3869, 4652–4660, 5017). Since it means obeying, it also means accepting (as above at §5471), because anyone who obeys the dictates of faith is receptive. In this case it means *no* acceptance, because the text says *you didn't pay attention.*

5476   *And his blood, too—here, it is being sought* symbolizes the resultant gnawing of conscience. This can be seen from the symbolism of *blood* as violence inflicted on goodness, that is, on neighborly love (discussed at §§374, 1005). When this violence or blood is *sought,* it creates deep uneasiness, which is called the gnawing of conscience—but only in people who have felt uneasy when they sin; see §5470.

5477   *And they did not know that Joseph was listening* means that the earthly light shining on that truth makes it hard to believe that everything is visible by spiritual light, as the following shows: Jacob's sons, the ones who *did not know,* represent truth known to the outer part of the church and therefore truth on the earthly level, as mentioned many times before. That is why the clause means that the earthly light shining on that truth hinders belief. And *Joseph* represents spiritual heavenliness, on which spiritual light shines. Spiritual light makes truth on the earthly level visible, and this is symbolized by *Joseph was listening. Listening* means both obeying and perceiving (§5017). The meaning is, then, that spiritual light made truth on the earthly plane visible but not the reverse.

[2] Here is how earthly and spiritual light work: Earthly light radiates from the world's sun, and spiritual light, from heaven's sun, which is the Lord. In regard to the religious truth we imbibe from childhood on, we grasp it all in terms of the kinds of objects and therefore images we see by worldly light. So we grasp absolutely all of it in an earthly way. As long as we live in the world, the ideas that make up our thoughts are all based on worldly phenomena. If these were taken from us, our thinking would die out completely.

People who have not been reborn have no idea whatever that spiritual light exists. They do not even know that in heaven there exists a light that has nothing in common with the world's light. Still less do they know that heaven's light is what illuminates images and objects seen in the world's light and gives us the ability to think, decide, and reflect. Spiritual light can do all this because it consists in wisdom itself radiating from the Lord. Wisdom presents itself to the eyes of the angels in heaven as light.

This light makes everything below—everything we acquire from earthly light—visible. The reverse does not happen, though, unless we have been reborn. Once we have been reborn, spiritual light illuminates heaven's features—features of goodness and truth—and makes them visible on the earthly plane, where we see them in a kind of representational mirror.

The Lord, then, who is light itself, obviously sees every single element of our thought and will and in fact of our entire nature. Absolutely nothing lies hidden from him.

[3] From this you can see what it means to say that the earthly light shining on that truth makes it hard to believe that everything is visible by spiritual light, as symbolized by *they did not know that Joseph was listening.*

Joseph's recognition of his brothers and their failure to recognize him (above in verse 8) involves a similar idea. The meaning there is that this religious truth was visible to spiritual heavenliness in the latter's light and that truth from the Divine was not visible in earthly light unlit as yet by heavenly light. Regarding these meanings, see §§5427, 5428.

Because the interpreter was between them means that spiritual concepts **5478** are then taken in a completely different way. This can be seen from the symbolism of an *interpreter between them* as the fact that spiritual concepts are taken in a different way. An interpreter translates one party's language into the other party's, presenting the one party's thoughts in a form the other party can understand. That is why an interpreter between them means that spiritual concepts are then taken in a completely different way. That is, they are taken in a completely different way by people with religious truth that has not yet been internalized by the inner self through goodness.

People who focus on goodness—in other words, people in whom religious truth has united with goodness—take that truth in a completely different way than people who do not focus on goodness. This seems puzzling, admittedly, but it is still true. People who focus on goodness take truth spiritually, because they are in spiritual light, but people who do not focus on goodness take it in an earthly way, because they are in earthly light. People who focus on goodness are always connecting truth with truth, but people who do not focus on goodness connect multitudinous mistakes and even falsities with truth. This is because truth reaches into heaven in people focused on goodness, but it does not reach into heaven in people not focused on goodness. Truth is therefore full in people focused on goodness but almost empty in people not focused on goodness. Neither the fullness nor the emptiness is visible to us as long as we are living in the world, but they are visible to angels.

If we knew how much of heaven was present in truth that has united with goodness, we would view faith in an entirely different way.

5479   *And he turned from them* means pulling back somewhat. This can be seen from the symbolism of *turning from them*, when it has to do with the inflow of goodness from the Divine, or the Lord, as pulling back somewhat. The Lord never turns away from anyone, but he adjusts the inflow of his goodness to the state of the person or angel. This adjustment is what I mean by pulling back.

5480   *And wept* symbolizes compassion. This can be seen from the symbolism of *weeping,* when ascribed to the Lord, whom Joseph is representing, as having compassion. Everyone knows that tears are a sign of grief and love, and they are consequently a sign of compassion, since compassion is love grieving. Divine love is therefore called compassion, because on its own the human race lives in hell. When we see this to be true of ourselves, we beg for compassion.

Since tears in an inner sense actually mean compassion, the Word sometimes describes Jehovah, or the Lord, as crying. In Isaiah, for instance:

> I will *weep* for the grapevine of Sibmah with the *weeping* of Jazer; I will *water you with my teardrop,* Heshbon and Elealeh. (Isaiah 16:9)

And in Jeremiah:

> "I know the rage of Moab," says Jehovah, "that he is not upright. Therefore over Moab I will *wail* and because of all Moab I will *cry out.* Over the *weeping* of Jazer I will *weep* because of you, grapevine of Sibmah." (Jeremiah 48:[30,] 31, 32)

Moab stands for people with earthly goodness who allow themselves to be led astray and who adulterate goodness once they have been led astray (§2468). Wailing, crying out, and weeping over Moab stands for feeling compassion and grief. The same is true in Luke:

> When Jesus drew near, looking at the city, he *wept over it.* (Luke 19:41)

The Jerusalem that Jesus wept over, or felt compassion for and grieved over, was not just the city Jerusalem but the church. In an inner sense it is referring to the church's final days, when there would no longer be any neighborly love or consequently any faith. As a result the Lord wept in compassion and grief. For the meaning of Jerusalem as the church, see §§2117, 3654.

And returned to them and spoke to them symbolizes its inflow. This **5481** can be seen from the symbolism of *returning to them and speaking to them,* after "turning from them," as an inflow. Spiritual heavenliness, or truth from the Divine, represented by Joseph, flows into truth on the earthly level. This is expressed in the literal story as returning to them and speaking to them. On the point that speaking also means flowing in, see §2951.

And took Simeon from them symbolizes faith that belongs to the will. **5482** This can be seen from the discussion in §§3869, 3870, 3871, 3872, 4497, 4502, 4503 of the representation of *Simeon* as faith that belongs to the will.

Faith that belongs to the will was separated from them because the middle ground, represented by Benjamin, was not yet present. Truth from the Divine, represented by Joseph, flows through the middle ground into the goodness belonging to faith and through this into the truth belonging to faith. To put the same thing another way, it flows into our intent to act on truth, and through this it flows into our understanding of truth. Or again, it flows into the love we have for our neighbor, and through this, into our faith. No other route for that inflow exists in a person who has been reborn, and no other route exists in angels.

[2] It is like the inflow of the sun into members [of the plant kingdom] on earth. When it brings them forth from seed and revitalizes them, it flows into them with warmth (at least during spring and summer) and at the same time with light. That is how it makes them grow. The sun makes nothing grow by light alone, as is evident from members [of the plant kingdom] during winter.

Spiritual warmth is the goodness that comes from love, and spiritual light is the truth that leads to faith. In members of the animal kingdom, spiritual warmth generates their vital heat, and spiritual light generates their resulting life.

And tied him up means being separated. This can be seen from the **5483** discussion in §§5083, 5101, 5452, 5456 of the symbolism of *tying up* as being separated.

Before their eyes means perceptibly. This can be seen from the symbol-**5484** ism of *eyes* as intellect and perception (discussed in §§2701, 4083, 4403–4421, 4523–4534).

5485　　Genesis 42:25, 26, 27, 28. *And Joseph commanded, and they filled their containers with grain, and [he said] to return their silver, each one's into his sack, and to give them provision for the way. And that is what he did with them. And [the brothers] lifted their grain provisions onto their donkeys and went from there. And one of them opened his sack to give fodder to his donkey in the inn and saw his silver, and here, it was in the mouth of his bag! And he said to his brothers, "My silver is returned, and also look—it is in my bag!" And their heart gave way, and they trembled, a man to his brother, saying, "What is this God has done to us?"*

And Joseph commanded symbolizes an inflow of spiritual heavenliness. *And they filled their containers with grain* means that knowledge received the gift of goodness based on truth. *And [he said] to return their silver* means without using any power of theirs. *Each one's into his sack* means wherever there was a container for it on the earthly level. *And to give them provision for the way* means that it also nourished the truth they had. *And that is what he did* symbolizes carrying it out. *And [the brothers] lifted [their] grain provisions onto their donkeys* symbolizes truth inserted into knowledge. *And went from there* symbolizes the life resulting. *And one of them opened his sack* symbolizes observation. *To give fodder to his donkey in the inn* means when they pondered knowledge existing on the outer earthly level. *And saw his silver* symbolizes a realization that it was apart from any power of their own. *And it was in the mouth of his bag* means that it had been given as a gift and laid on the threshold of the outer earthly level. *And he said to his brothers* symbolizes a general perception. *My silver is returned* means that they had not contributed. *And also look—it is in my bag!* means that it was on the outer earthly level. *And their heart gave way* symbolizes fear. *And they trembled, a man to his brother* symbolizes general terror. *Saying, "What is this God has done to us?"* means because of such great providence.

5486　　*And Joseph commanded* symbolizes an inflow of spiritual heavenliness, as the following shows: When spiritual heavenliness, or the inner plane in relation to the outer plane, is said to *command,* it symbolizes an inflow. The only way the inner plane commands is by inflow and then by creating the conditions for something useful. And *Joseph* represents spiritual heavenliness, as discussed many times before.

5487　　*And they filled their containers with grain* means that knowledge received the gift of goodness based on truth. This can be seen from the symbolism of *filling* as being given a gift (since it was free), from that of *containers* as forms of knowledge (discussed at §§3068, 3079), and from that of *grain* as goodness based on truth, or goodness-from-truth (discussed at §5295).

[He said] to return their silver means without using any power of theirs. **5488** This can be seen from the symbolism of buying with silver as acquiring something on one's own. *Returning silver,* then, means giving something freely, as a gift, without using any power of theirs. The same thing comes up in Isaiah:

> Everyone who is thirsty, come to the water, and *whoever does not have silver,* come, *buy* and eat! And come, *without silver* and without the price *buy* wine and milk! (Isaiah 55:1)

Each one's into his sack means wherever there was a container for it on **5489** the earthly level. This can be seen from the symbolism of a *sack* as a container (discussed below). It means on the earthly level because truth and knowledge on the earthly level are the focus here.

The *sack* here specifically symbolizes knowledge, because just as a sack is a container for grain, knowledge is a container for goodness—in this case, for goodness based on truth, as above in §5487.

Not many know that knowledge is a container for goodness, because few stop to think about such things, but here is how to see that it is: The knowledge entering our memory is always introduced into it by some desire. Knowledge that is not introduced by some desire does not stick but falls away. The reason it does is that desire holds life but knowledge does not, except through desire. Plainly, then, knowledge always comes with an element of desire, or ties to something we love. It therefore comes with some kind of goodness, because everything we love we call good, whether it really is good or we just think it is. What we know consequently enters a type of marriage with these kinds of goodness. As a result, when goodness of this kind is stimulated, the knowledge bound up with it is immediately stimulated as well. By the same token, when we recall something we know, the goodness bound up with it comes out. Everyone can experience this personally, if he or she wishes.

[2] In the unregenerate, therefore, who have rejected the idea of neighborly kindness, the knowledge constituting religious truth comes connected with the effects of self-love and love for worldly advantages and so with evil. Because they enjoy the evil, they call it good, and they prove it is good by misrepresenting it. When these two kinds of love reign supreme (and to the extent that they do), such knowledge comes out looking elegant.

In the regenerate, however, the knowledge constituting religious truth comes connected with the effects of love for their neighbor and love for God and so with genuine goodness. This goodness is restored to religious truth by the Lord in everyone who is being reborn. The consequence is that when the Lord inspires them with zeal for goodness, this truth then presents itself in its own proper pattern. When he inspires them with zeal for truth, this goodness is present, kindling the zeal.

This evidence shows that knowledge and truth act as a container for goodness.

5490 *And to give them provision for the way* means that it also nourished the truth they had. This can be seen from the symbolism of *giving provision* as nourishment, and from that of a *way* as truth (discussed in §§627, 2333). Here, on the *way* means while in that state, because being on the way symbolizes a state in which truth unites with goodness (§3123).

In David too provisions symbolize being nourished by truth and goodness:

> He rained manna on them for food, and the grain of the heavens he gave to them. A man ate the bread of the strong. *Provision* he sent them to the full. (Psalms 78:24, 25)

5491 *And that is what he did* symbolizes carrying it out, as is self-evident.

5492 *And [the brothers] lifted their grain provisions onto their donkeys* symbolizes truth inserted into knowledge. This can be seen from the symbolism of *grain provisions* as truth (discussed in §§5276, 5280, 5292, 5402) and from that of a *donkey* as knowledge (discussed in §2781). It follows, then, that *[the brothers] lifted their grain provisions onto their donkeys* means that truth was inserted into knowledge.

The idea that this is the symbolism of the clause seems strange to people who fix their thoughts on the literal story, particularly if they do not believe there can be another inner meaning than the one that shines directly from the literal meaning. They are bound to say to themselves, "How can lifting the grain provisions onto their donkeys mean truths inserted into knowledge?" I want them to know, though, that the Word's literal meaning crosses over into this kind of spiritual meaning when it passes from people to angels, or to heaven. In fact, it becomes an even more unfamiliar meaning when it reaches the inmost heaven, where each and every word of Scripture turns into some desire stemming from love or charity. The inner meaning serves as a foundation for this [inmost meaning].

[2] To people who base their conclusions on reason and who know something about the physical and spiritual realms it is evident that the Word's narratives melt away into another meaning when taken up to heaven. They can see that lifting grain provisions onto donkeys is purely physical, that there is nothing spiritual in it at all. They can also see that angels in heaven—that is, in the spiritual world—can take the words only in a spiritual way, and that they do so when they understand a word to mean what it corresponds to. This involves taking grain provisions to mean religious truth, and donkeys to mean knowledge on the earthly plane. (See §2781 for a demonstration of the idea that donkeys in the Word symbolize what is subservient and therefore symbolize knowledge, since knowledge is subservient to spiritual concepts and also to rational ones.)

This also clarifies what angelic thought and speech is like in relation to human thought and speech. Angelic thought and speech is spiritual, but human thought and speech is earthly. The angelic kind drops into the human kind when it comes down, and the human kind changes into the angelic kind when it goes up. If that did not happen, people would never have any contact with angels; the world would have no contact with heaven.

And went from there symbolizes the life resulting. This can be seen from the symbolism of *going* as living (discussed above at §§3335, 3690, 4882). The situation is similar with going, which in a spiritual sense means living, as with the meaning [of grain provisions lifted onto donkeys] given just above in §5492.

5493

And one of them opened his sack symbolizes observation. This can be seen from the symbolism of a *sack* as a container on the earthly level (discussed above at §5489), which had received the gift of goodness based on truth (§5487). *Opening* it means observing, as context shows, because the next clause, "to give fodder to his donkey in the inn," means when they pondered knowledge existing on the outer earthly level.

5494

To give fodder to his donkey in the inn means when they pondered knowledge existing on the outer earthly level, as the following shows: *Giving fodder to his donkey* means pondering knowledge. *Fodder* is the food donkeys feed on and consists of hay and straw, so it means all pondering of knowledge, since knowledge is what the pondering mind mainly feeds on. For the meaning of a *donkey* as knowledge, see just above at §5492. And an *inn* symbolizes the outer earthly level. The fact that the inn here symbolizes the outer earthly level cannot be confirmed by parallel passages

5495

elsewhere in the Word, only by the consideration that knowledge takes up residence in its inn, so to speak, when it is present in the outer earthly dimension. The earthly dimension has two parts, outer and inner; see §5118. When knowledge is present in the outer earthly dimension, it communicates directly with the outward bodily senses, lying down and resting on them. That is why the outer earthly level is an inn—that is, a place where knowledge rests or spends the night.

5496   *And saw his silver* symbolizes a realization that it was apart from any power of their own. This is established by the symbolism of *seeing* as understanding and perceiving (discussed in §§2150, 2325, 2807, 3764, 3863, 4403–4421, 4567, 4723, 5400) and by that of the returned *silver* as meaning without any power of theirs (discussed in §5488).

5497   *And it was in the mouth of his bag* means that it had been given as a gift and laid on the threshold of the outer earthly level. This can be seen from the symbolism of the *mouth of the bag* as the threshold of the outer earthly level. The idea that it had been laid there is implied. And the idea that it had been given as a gift follows from the previous explanation that it was apart from any power of their own.

Since the [mouth of] the bag was the front part of the sack, it simply symbolizes the front part of the container. So it symbolizes the outer earthly level, because that is also in front. For the meaning of a sack as a container, see §§5489, 5494.

I should define the outer and inner earthly levels again briefly, for the reader's information. Young people still in their adolescence cannot think on any more profound plane than the outer earthly level, because they form their thoughts from sense impressions. As they grow up and use what they learn from their senses to figure out the causes of things, they start thinking on an inner earthly level. They are then fashioning a certain amount of truth out of sense impressions, and this truth ventures beyond the senses, but it still remains within the earthly realm.

Once they mature into young adults, they might cultivate the ability to reason. If so, they are using the contents of the earthly plane to develop rational ideas, which are a still more elevated form of truth, abstracted from the contents of the inner earthly plane. The scholarly world refers to thoughts with these underpinnings as intuitive, immaterial ideas. Ideas based on knowledge belonging to both earthly planes are called material ideas, though, so far as they partake of the world and draw on the senses.

It is by our intellect, then, that we climb from earth toward heaven. Still, the intellect does not bring us into heaven unless we take in the goodness from the Lord that is constantly present and flowing in. If we take the goodness in, we also receive truth as a gift, since all truth lodges in goodness, and as we receive truth, we also receive the gift of understanding, which puts us in heaven.

And he said to his brothers symbolizes a general perception. This can be seen from the symbolism of *saying* in the narratives of the Word as a perception (mentioned many times before) and from that of *to his brothers* as a general one. Something said to everyone becomes general. **5498**

My silver is returned means that they had not contributed. This can be seen from the symbolism of *returning silver* as meaning without any power of theirs, or to say the same thing another way, without their contributing to it (discussed above at §§5488, 5496). **5499**

And also look—it is in my bag! means that it was on the outer earthly level. This can be seen from the symbolism of the *bag* as the outer earthly level (discussed above in §5497). **5500**

And their heart gave way symbolizes fear. This can be seen from the symbolism of a *heart's giving way* as fear. A heart's giving way means fear because in fear, one's heart pounds. **5501**

And they trembled, a man to his brother symbolizes general terror. This can be seen from the symbolism of *trembling* as terror and from that of a *man to his brother* as something general, as just above in §5498. **5502**

The text expresses fear twice here, by "their heart gave way" and "they trembled," because one term relates to the will, and the other, to the intellect. It is common for the Word (particularly the prophetic part) to express a single concept twice, changing only the words. Someone who does not know the mystery involved might suppose it to be empty repetition, but that is not the case. One expression relates to goodness; the other to truth. Since goodness has to do with the will and truth has to do with the intellect, one expression also relates to the will, and the other, to the intellect.

The reason for the pairing is that everything in the Word is holy, and holiness comes from the heavenly marriage, which is the marriage of goodness and truth. That is why the Word contains heaven, and consequently the Lord, who is the all-in-all of heaven. In fact the Lord *is* the Word. The Lord's dual name Jesus Christ embraces the same idea. "Jesus" means divine goodness, and "Christ" means divine truth; see §§3004,

3005, 3008, 3009. This also makes it plain that the Lord is present in every word of Scripture—so much so that he actually is the Word. (See §§683, 793, 801, 2516, 2712, 5138 for the idea that there is a marriage of goodness and truth—the heavenly marriage—in every detail of the Word.)

This evidence also leads to the plain conclusion that if we hope for heaven, we have to possess not only faith and its truth but also neighborly love and its kindness. Otherwise we have no heaven inside us.

5503 *What are these things God has done to us?* means because of such great providence. This can be seen from the symbolism of *God's doing* as providence. Nothing God does can be expressed by any other word than *providence*. This is because there is eternity and infinity in everything God, or the Lord, does, and the word *providence* carries that. The brothers were dumbfounded, so the clause means because of such great providence.

5504 Genesis 42:29, 30, 31, 32, 33, 34. *And they came to Jacob their father, to the land of Canaan, and told him everything that had happened to them, saying, "The man, the lord of the land, spoke harsh words with us and accused us of spying out the land. And we said to him, 'We are upright, we are not spies. We are twelve brothers, sons of our father. One does not exist, and the youngest today is with our father in the land of Canaan.' And the man, the lord of the land, said to us, 'In this I will know that you are upright: leave one of your brothers with me and take [food for] the famine of your houses and go. And bring your youngest brother to me and I will know that you are not spies, because you are upright. I will give you your brother, and you will travel the land on business.'"*

And they came symbolizes the next stage of reformation. *To Jacob their father* symbolizes goodness based on earthly truth. *To the land of Canaan* means which belongs to the church. *And told him everything that had happened to them* means reflecting, from the goodness based on that truth, on all that had been provided so far. *Saying* symbolizes a perception. *The man, the lord of the land,* symbolizes spiritual heavenliness ruling the earthly level. *Spoke harsh words with us* symbolizes a lack of connection with it because there was no correspondence. *And accused us of spying out the land* means that he had noticed an intention to use the church's truth for financial gain. *And we said to him, "We are upright, we are not spies,"* symbolizes a denial that their interest in religious truth was mercenary. *We are twelve brothers* symbolizes all truth taken together. *Sons of our father* means from a single origin. *One does not exist* means that divine spirituality as the source is not visible. *And the youngest today is with our father* means that this itself supplies a connection with spiritual goodness. *And the man, the lord of the land, said to us* symbolizes a perception about the spiritual heavenliness ruling the earthly plane. *In this I will know that you are upright* means if their interest in truth is not mercenary. *Leave one of your brothers with me* means his desire is for faith that belongs to the will to be separated from them. *And take [food for] the famine of your houses* means to look out for themselves in the meantime in that desolation. *And go* means so as to live. *And bring your youngest brother to me* means that if there is a middle ground, there is union. *And I will know that you are not spies* means that then there is no longer an intention to use truth for private gain. *Because you are upright* means that there is then correspondence. *I will give you your brother* means that truth will then turn into goodness. *And you will travel the land on business* means that truth will then proliferate in response to goodness and everything will turn out useful and profitable.

And they came symbolizes the next stage of reformation. This can be **5505** seen from the symbolism of *coming*—to "Jacob their father"—as the next stage of reformation. Jacob their father represents goodness-from-truth on the earthly level, and to *come* to it means to reform that far. You see, the inner meaning is talking about the way the religious truth represented by Jacob's sons was implanted on the earthly plane and afterward united with spiritual heavenliness. In other words, it is talking about the way truth in the [Lord's] outer self united with truth from his divine side in his inner self.

This shows that *they came* symbolizes the next stage of reformation here.

To Jacob their father symbolizes goodness based on earthly truth. This **5506** can be seen from the representation of *Jacob* as goodness based on earthly truth (discussed in §§3659, 3669, 3677, 3775, 4234, 4273, 4538) and from the symbolism of a *father* too as goodness (§3703). Coming to that goodness means reforming that far.

This goodness was later the means of creating a bond with the inner self (Joseph) once the middle ground (Benjamin) had been brought in.

To the land of Canaan means which belongs to the church. This can **5507** be seen from the symbolism of the *land of Canaan* as the church (discussed at §§3705, 4447). The truth-based goodness represented by Jacob is the goodness of the outer church, while the goodness represented by Israel is that of a relatively inward part of the church.

And told him everything that had happened to them means reflecting, **5508** from the goodness based on that truth, on all that had been provided so far, as the following shows: *Telling* means thinking and reflecting, as noted in §2862, because what is told to someone is thought about reflectively.

And *everything that had happened* symbolizes the results of providence, or what has been provided, as discussed below. The reflection came from truth-based goodness because the brothers were telling Jacob their father, who represents such goodness (§5506).

It was not the truth represented by Jacob's sons that produced the reflection, as the literal story implies. That is because all the reflecting and therefore all the thinking that a lower, outer level does comes from a higher, inner level, even though it appears to come from the outer, lower level. Since the truth-based goodness Jacob represents is inward, the clause symbolizes reflection from that kind of goodness.

[2] *Happenings* mean the results of providence (or what has been provided) because providence is responsible for all events or occurrences—otherwise known as coincidences—that are ascribed to chance, or luck. Divine providence works in this invisible, unfathomable way in order to allow us the freedom to ascribe events to either providence or chance. It would be dangerous for providence to act in a visible, fathomable way, because our eyes and minds might lead us to believe that events were providential, but afterward we might change our mind. So truth and falsity would unite in our inner self. The truth would be profaned, and profanation carries eternal damnation with it. People capable of it are therefore better off holding on to disbelief than developing faith at one point and then abandoning it. [3] That is what is meant in Isaiah:

> Tell this people, "Listen—listen!—but do not understand, and see—see!—and do not know." Make the heart of this people fat and make their ears heavy and smear their eyes, to prevent them from seeing with their eyes and hearing with their ears and understanding in their heart and *turning* and *being healed.* (Isaiah 6:9, 10; John 12:40)

This is also why miracles are not done nowadays. Like everything visible and comprehensible, they would compel us to believe, and compulsion robs us of freedom. Yet we reform and regenerate only when free. What is not implanted in freedom does not last. A seed is planted in freedom when we have a desire for what is good and true (§§1937, 1947, 2744, 2870–2893, 3145, 3146, 3158, 4031). [4] The great miracles Jacob's descendants witnessed were intended to force them to go through the motions of observing the statutes. That was enough for people whose religious activity was purely representational. They concentrated on superficialities detached from any inner depth, so their inner levels could not be reformed. They rejected any inner depth, so they were incapable of profaning truth (§§3398, 3399, 3479, 4680). People of that type were able to be compelled without danger of profaning something holy.

[5] Furthermore, the Lord's words to Thomas in John show that [even] today we ought to believe in things we cannot see:

> Because you have seen me, Thomas, you have believed; fortunate are those who do not see, and believe. (John 20:29)

The idea that circumstances otherwise ascribed to chance or luck are actually the result of divine providence is something the church does acknowledge but fails to believe. Who, on escaping some grave danger apparently by chance, does not acknowledge having been saved by God and thank him? Again, when someone is elevated to high position or comes into wealth, people call it a blessing from God. So the religious person acknowledges that happenstance is the result of providence and yet does not believe it.

More on this elsewhere, though, with the Lord's divine mercy [§§6493–6494, 7007, 8717, 9010].

Saying symbolizes a perception. This can be seen from the symbolism of *saying* in scriptural narrative as perceiving (noted many times before).

5509

The man, the lord of the land, symbolizes spiritual heavenliness ruling the earthly level, as the following shows: Joseph, who is the *man, the lord of the land,* represents spiritual heavenliness. A *man* relates to what is spiritual, and a *lord,* to what is heavenly, because in an inner sense a man means truth, and a lord means goodness. Truth from the Divine is what is called spiritual, and goodness from the Divine is what is called heavenly. And the *land*—the land of Egypt—symbolizes the earthly mind (discussed at §§5276, 5278, 5280, 5288, 5301). The fact that spiritual heavenliness, represented by Joseph, governed both earthly levels is contained in the inner meaning of the previous chapter. Joseph was appointed over the land of Egypt to represent that fact.

5510

[2] There are two ingredients on the earthly level: knowledge and religious truth. In regard to items of knowledge, the text has already described how spiritual heavenliness (or truth from the Divine) arranged them in order on the earthly level [§§5288, 5311, 5312, 5326, 5339]. As for religious truth, represented by the ten sons of Jacob, they form the current focus of discussion.

Items of knowledge have to be arranged in order there first, before religious truth, because truth needs to be grasped in terms of knowledge. Nothing can enter a person's intellect without the aid of concepts formed from the knowledge that person has acquired since childhood. We are completely unaware that every instance of religious truth (which people call the truth of faith) is founded on religious knowledge. We grasp it, remember it, and recall it from memory by means of concepts forged out of the things we know.

[3] It is not unusual for the quality of these concepts to be demonstrated vividly to any inhabitant of the other world who wishes it, because such concepts display themselves openly in heaven's light. It is also easy there to see what shadows or what rays of light filled the religious, doctrinal truth they had possessed. In some people such truth turns up among falsities; in some, among jokes; in some, among stumbling blocks to faith; in some, among sensory illusions; in some, among apparent truths; and so on. If the person had been devoted to goodness—in other words, had lived a life of neighborly love—then the goodness, like a flame from heaven, illuminates the truth. It also lends a beautiful glow to the sensory illusions that had surrounded the truth. When the Lord injects innocence, even illusions take on the appearance of truth.

5511   *Spoke harsh words with us* symbolizes a lack of connection with it because there was no correspondence. This can be seen from the symbolism of *speaking harsh words*—when attributed to the inner dimension, in relation to an outer dimension separated from it—as nonunion because of noncorrespondence (discussed above at §§5422, 5423). The outer dimension, if it does not correspond with the inner, sees everything that lies within or comes from within as harsh, because there is no union.

For instance, the inner dimension—or a person with depth—might say that we do not think on our own. Rather our thoughts come either from heaven (that is, through heaven from the Lord) or from hell. If we think something good, the thought comes through heaven from the Lord. If we think something evil, it comes from hell. This claim seems totally harsh to people set on having their own thoughts, who believe they would then be nonentities. Nonetheless it is perfectly true, and everyone in heaven lives in the awareness that it is so.

[2] Again, the inner dimension—or people with depth—might say that the joy angels feel comes from love for the Lord and charity for their neighbor. That is to say, it comes when they are actively doing what love and charity call for. Such activity holds joy and happiness so strong that it is utterly indescribable. This is inevitably harsh for people who feel joy only in self-love and materialism, not in love for their

neighbor, except when it benefits themselves. Nonetheless, heaven and heavenly joy take their start in us when self-interest ceases to figure in the services we perform.

[3] Take this for an example, too: The inner dimension might say that our soul is nothing but our inner self, and that our inner self appears exactly the same after death as a person in the world, with a similar face, body, capacity for sensation, and capacity for thought. Some people, though, have cherished the opinion that the soul is just mental activity and is therefore like a wisp of rarefied air, lacking shape, which will eventually be reclothed in a body. They are bound to consider these statements about the soul to be divorced from reality. Those who believe that the body is the whole person necessarily find it harsh to hear that the soul is the real person and that the body that is buried is good for nothing in the other life. This is the truth, as I know, because by the Lord's divine mercy I have been with those souls—not a few of them but many, not once but often—and have talked with them about it.

Likewise with countless other examples.

And accused us of spying out the land means that he had noticed an intention to use the church's truth for financial gain. This can be seen from the representation of Jacob's sons—*us*—as religious truth on the earthly level (discussed in §§5403, 5419, 5427, 5458) and from the symbolism of spies, or people *spying out the land,* as people who take to religious truth just for financial gain (discussed in §5432).

5512

And we said to him, "We are upright, we are not spies," symbolizes a denial that their interest in truth was mercenary, as the following shows: *Saying to him* means an answer, and here a denial. *We are upright* means that they subscribe to truth that is true in itself, as discussed in §§5434, 5437, 5460. And *spies* symbolizes people whose interest in religious truth is mercenary. In this case, then, the meaning is that it was *not* mercenary.

5513

We are twelve brothers symbolizes all truth taken together. This is established by the symbolism of *twelve* as everything. When it relates to Jacob's sons, as it does here, or to the twelve tribes named for them, or to the twelve apostles, it symbolizes all aspects of faith taken together. The symbolism is discussed in §§577, 2089, 2129, 2130, 2553, 3272, 3488, 3858, 3862, 3913, 3926, 3939, 4060.

5514

Sons of our father means from a single origin. This is established by the symbolism of *sons* as truths (discussed in §§489, 491, 533, 1147, 2623, 3373) and from that of a *father* as goodness (discussed in §§2803, 3703,

5515

3704). A *father's sons,* then, symbolize truths that come of goodness and therefore truths from a single origin. Besides, all truths come from unified goodness.

5516 *One does not exist* means that divine spirituality as the source is not visible. This can be seen from the remarks above at §5444, where the same words occur.

5517 *And the youngest today is with our father* means that this [divine spirituality, or spiritual heavenliness] itself supplies a connection with spiritual goodness. This can also be seen from the explanation above, at §5443, where the same words occur. The reason for saying that this itself supplies a connection is that the middle ground, represented by Benjamin, extends from spiritual heavenliness, which is Joseph.

5518 *And the man, the lord of the land, said to us* symbolizes a perception about the spiritual heavenliness ruling the earthly plane. This can be seen from the symbolism of *saying* in the narrative parts of the Word as perceiving (discussed many times before) and from that of the *man, the lord of the land,* as spiritual heavenliness ruling the earthly plane (discussed above in §5510).

5519 *In this I will know that you are upright* means if their interest in truth is not mercenary. This can be seen from the symbolism of *knowing* as wanting, which follows from context, and from the meaning of *that you are upright,* not spies, as having a nonmercenary interest in truth (dealt with at §§5432, 5512).

5520 *Leave one of your brothers with me* means his desire is for faith that belongs to the will to be separated. This can be seen from the representation of Simeon, the *one brother,* as faith that belongs to the will (discussed at §5482), and from the symbolism of *leaving* as being separated. The situation has already been explained [§5461].

5521 *And take [food for] the famine of your houses* means to look out for themselves in the meantime in that desolation. This can be seen from the remarks above in §5462, where the same words occur. It means in that desolation because a *famine* symbolizes desolation.

5522 *And go* means so as to live. This can be seen from the symbolism of *going* as living (discussed in §§3335, 3690, 4882, 5493).

5523 *And bring your youngest brother to me* means that if there is a middle ground, there is union. This can be seen from the representation of Benjamin, the *youngest brother,* as a middle ground (discussed at §§5411, 5413, 5443) and from the symbolism of *bringing him to me* as the resulting union. A middle ground enables the inner plane, represented by Joseph, to unite with outward qualities, represented by Jacob's sons, as shown above in §§5411, 5413, 5427, 5428.

And I will know that you are not spies means that then there is no lon- **5524** ger an intention to use truth for private gain. This is established by the symbolism of *spies* as people who take to religious truth for the sake of gain. Here it means that they no longer will, if there is union through a middle ground.

Because you are upright means that there is then correspondence. This **5525** can be seen from the symbolism of *you are upright* as their subscribing to truth. *Uprightness* means truth (§§5434, 5437), and since the point at which they subscribe to truth but not for mercenary reasons is when there is correspondence, *you are upright* also symbolizes that.

I will give you your brother means that truth will then turn into good- **5526** ness. This can be seen from the representation of Simeon, the *brother* he would *give to them,* as faith that belongs to the will (discussed in §5482), and from that of Jacob's ten sons, to whom Simeon would be given, as religious truth on the earthly plane (discussed in §§5403, 5419, 5427, 5428, 5512).

The reason *I will give you your brother* means that truth will then turn into goodness is that when faith exists in the will, truth turns into goodness. As soon as the truth belonging to faith (doctrinal truth) enters the will, it becomes the truth belonging to life, and truth in action. It is then called goodness and also becomes spiritual goodness, from which the Lord forms a new will in us.

The will turns truth into goodness because regarded in itself the will is nothing but love. Whatever we love, we will, and whatever we do not love we do not will. Moreover, everything we love or do with love seems good to us, because it delights us. So everything we will or do with a will is good.

And you will travel the land on business means that truth will then **5527** proliferate in response to goodness and everything will turn out useful and profitable. This can be seen from the symbolism of *doing business* as acquiring a knowledge of goodness and truth—which means acquiring religious truth—and sharing it (discussed at §4453). People who have this knowledge are called merchants (§2967). *Traveling the land* on busi- ness, then, means obtaining it wherever it exists. From this it follows that traveling the land on business also means the proliferation of truth in response to goodness. This is because the union of the outer self (Jacob's ten sons) with the inner self (Joseph) by means of the middle ground

(Benjamin)—the theme here—is the same as rebirth. When this union happens, or a person is reborn, goodness constantly causes truth to proliferate. After all, people with goodness have the ability to see specific truths that spring from a more general truth, over and over in a never-ending chain. The ability expands in the other world, where worldly and bodily concerns cast no shadow.

[2] Abundant experience has shown me that goodness carries this ability with it. There are spirits who had not been very clear-sighted when they lived as people in the world but had led a life of love for their neighbor, and I have seen them taken up into angelic communities. They then possessed the same understanding and wisdom as the angels there. In fact, as far as they could tell, they had that understanding and wisdom inside them. The goodness they possessed gave them the ability to receive every inflow from the angelic communities they were in.

This ability resides in goodness, so this kind of fruitfulness does too.

However, truth that proliferates in them in response to goodness does not remain truth. No, they commit it to life, where it becomes useful activity. Traveling the land on business, therefore, also means that everything will turn out useful and profitable.

5528   Genesis 42:35, 36, 37, 38. *And it happened that they were emptying their sacks, and here, each one had the packet of his silver in his sack! And they saw the packets of their silver, they and their father, and were afraid. And Jacob their father said to them, "You have bereaved me; Joseph does not exist, and Simeon does not exist, and Benjamin you are taking. On me will all these things be." And Reuben said to his father, saying, "My two sons you may put to death if I do not bring him to you; put him on my hands and I will return him to you." And he said, "My son will not go down with you all, because his brother is dead and he, he alone is left, and he may meet with harm on the way on which you will go, and you will make my white hair go down in sorrow to the grave."*

And it happened that they were emptying their sacks symbolizes use of the truth that exists on the earthly plane. *And here, each one had the packet of his silver* symbolizes sets of true ideas given for free. *In his sack* means in each one's container. *And they saw the packets of their silver* symbolizes a realization that it was so. *They and their father* means on the part of truth and of truth-based goodness on the earthly level. *And were afraid* symbolizes awe. *And Jacob their father said to them* symbolizes a perception they had from truth-based goodness. *You have bereaved me* means that there was accordingly no more church. *Joseph does not exist* means that there is no inner level. *And Simeon does not exist* means that there is also no faith that belongs to the will. *And Benjamin you are taking* means if the middle ground is also taken away. *On me will all [these] things be* means that this will destroy the substance of the church. *And Reuben said to his father* symbolizes traits of an intellectual faith, perceived by truth-based goodness. *Saying, "My two sons you may put to death,"* means that neither side of faith will survive. *If I do not bring him to you* means unless the middle ground is added on. *Put him on my hands* means as far as possible. *And I will bring him to you* means that it will be restored. *And he said, "My son will not go down with you all,"* means that it will not move down toward lower levels. *Because his brother is dead* means since the inner level is not present. *And he alone is left* means that he now takes the place of the inner dimension. *And he may meet with harm on the way on which you will go* means that in the sole company of truth on the earthly level, separated from the inner dimension, it would cease to exist. *And you will make my white hair go down* means that this is how the church will end. *In sorrow to the grave* means without hope of being revived.

And it happened that they were emptying their sacks symbolizes use of the truth on the earthly plane, as the following shows: *Emptying*—emptying the grain provisions they had carried down from Egypt—means making use of truth, since grain provisions symbolize truth (§§5276, 5280, 5292, 5402). And *sacks* symbolize containers on the earthly level (discussed in §§5489, 5494) and therefore the earthly level itself. About containers on the earthly level, see below at §5531.

5529

And here, each one had the packet of his silver symbolizes sets of true ideas given for free. This can be seen from the symbolism of a *packet,* or bundle, as a set (discussed below) and from that of *silver* as truth (discussed at §§1551, 2954). "Each one, in his sack" means that they were given for free.

5530

The reason a *packet* or bundle means a set is that truth is arranged and organized in a series in us. The truth that best matches the things we love goes in the middle. The truth that matches less well goes at the sides. Lastly the truth that does not match at all is relegated to the outermost edges. Outside the series lies anything that opposes what we love. The truth at the center is called a blood relative, because love creates a tie of blood. Truth at a greater distance is called a family connection. At the outer bounds, all relationship ends. Everything inside us is arranged in these serial sets, which are symbolized by bundles and packets.

[2] This makes it quite clear how matters stand with people immersed in love for themselves and worldly advantages, and with people immersed in love for God and their neighbor. In people who love themselves and worldly advantages, anything that favors this kind of love stands in the middle, and what is not very favorable stands on the edges. Anything that opposes it, such as anything that hints of love for God or for their neighbor, is thrown outdoors. That is the condition the hellish are in. As a result, they sometimes appear surrounded by a glow, but within the glow, where they themselves stand, is something dusky, monstrous, and ghastly.

Angels, though, have at their center a fiery brilliance given off by the goodness that goes with heavenly and spiritual love, and outside that a bright white glow all around. Anyone who looks this way is a likeness of the Lord. After all, when the Lord himself showed his divinity to Peter, James, and John, his face shone like the sun, and his clothes became like the light (Matthew 17:2). The fact that angels, who are [the Lord's] likenesses, appear in a fiery brilliance and consequently in white is plain from the angel who came down out of heaven and rolled the stone away from the opening of the [Lord's] tomb: "His appearance was like lightning, and his clothing white as snow" (Matthew 28:3).

5531　　*In his sack* means in each one's container. This is evident from the symbolism of a *sack* as a container (discussed at §§5489, 5494, 5529).

I need to say briefly what this container is. Our earthly level is divided into containers. Each container holds a general category, and arranged within it, subcategories (or relatively specific categories), and within these, individual items. Every general category of this kind, along with its subcategories and individual items, has its container—a place for it to exert itself, or alter its form and change its state.

In people who have been reborn, the number of these containers matches the number of general truths they know, and every container corresponds to some community in heaven. That is how [truth] is arranged in people dedicated to a loving goodness and consequently to religious truth.

These comments give some idea what "each one's container" means, when the phrase has to do with general truth on the earthly level, as represented by Jacob's ten sons.

5532　　*And they saw the packets of their silver* symbolizes a realization that it was so—that is, that sets of truth were given for free. This can be seen from the explanation just above at §5530.

5533　　*They and their father* means on the part of truth and of truth-based goodness on the earthly level. This can be seen from the representation of Jacob's sons—*they*—as truth on the earthly plane (discussed at §§5403, 5419, 5427, 5458, 5512) and from that of Jacob—*their father*—as truth-based goodness also on the earthly plane (discussed at §§3659, 3669, 3677, 3775, 4234, 4273, 4538).

What is a realization by truth and by truth-based goodness on the earthly level? Although it can be explained, the answer will not be comprehensible, except in the dimmest way. Spirits understand it as clear as day, though. To them it is one of the easier concepts. By the way, this shows to some extent what the difference is between the intelligence we have while living in the world and in its light, and the intelligence we have while living in heaven and in its light.

And were afraid symbolizes awe. This can be seen from the symbolism of *being afraid* when acts of divine providence occur, such as this free granting of truth (symbolized by "each one's packet of silver was in his sack"). The awe that then flows in also generates some fear along with holy reverence.

5534

And Jacob their father said to them symbolizes a perception they had from truth-based goodness. This is established by the symbolism of *saying* in the Word's narratives as a perception (mentioned many times before) and from the representation of *Jacob* as truth-based goodness (mentioned just above at §5533).

5535

You have bereaved me means that there was accordingly no more church, as the following shows: Jacob, who says this about himself, represents truth-based goodness, as discussed in §§3659, 3669, 3677, 3775, 4234, 4273, 4538, and because he does, he represents the church as well. The essential component of the church is goodness, so it is all the same whether you say truth-based goodness or the church. When goodness based on truth exists in a person, the church does too. For the meaning of Jacob as the church, see §§4286, 4520. Because Jacob represents the church, his sons represent religious truth (§§5403, 5419, 5427, 5458, 5512). And *bereaving* someone symbolizes robbing the church of its true ideas and good attributes. Here, for instance, it symbolizes robbing the church of the qualities represented by Joseph, Benjamin, and Simeon, who will be discussed next.

5536

[2] *Bereaving* someone means robbing the church of its truth because the church resembles a marriage. Its goodness is like a husband, and its truth, like a wife. The true ideas born of that marriage are like sons; the good attributes, like daughters; and so on. When bereavement is mentioned, then, it means that the church has been stripped of its truth and is therefore disappearing. The words *bereft* and *bereavement* are used

in this sense in various other places in the Word too. In Ezekiel, for instance:

> I will send famine on you, and the evil wild animal, and I will *leave you bereft*. (Ezekiel 5:17)

In the same author:

> When I make the evil wild animal pass through the land, and it *bereaves [the land]*, so that it becomes a desolate place, so that none is passing through, because of the wild animal, . . . (Ezekiel 14:15)

In Leviticus:

> I will send against you the wild animal of the field, which will *bereave you* and cut off your beasts and reduce you, so that your paths are devastated. (Leviticus 26:22)

[3] The famine here stands for a lack of knowledge about goodness and truth and, consequently, for desolation. The evil wild animal stands for falsity growing out of evil, and the land, for the church. Sending famine and the evil wild animal and bereaving the land stand for using the falsity that grows out of evil to destroy the church. They stand, then, for stripping the church bare of truth. In Jeremiah:

> I will winnow them with a winnowing fan in the gates of the land; I will *bereave* them; I will destroy my people. (Jeremiah 15:7)

Here again to bereave means to rob of truth. In the same author:

> Deliver their children to famine, and pour them out by the hand of the sword, *so that their wives become bereft and widowed*. (Jeremiah 18:21)

"So that their wives become bereft and widowed" stands for coming to be without truth or goodness. [4] In Hosea:

> Ephraim—like a bird will their glory fly away, abandoning birth and the womb and conception. For if they bring up their children, at that time I will *leave them bereft*, without one person. (Hosea 9:11, 12)

The same here. In Ezekiel:

> I will cause humankind—my people—to walk upon you, and they will inherit you, and you will become an inheritance to them *and not continue*

to bereave them anymore. This is what the Lord Jehovih has said: "Because they say to you, 'You are devouring humankind, and you have been *bereaving your peoples, . . .*'" (Ezekiel 36:12, 13)

Once more, to bereave means to rob of truth. [5] In Isaiah:

Now listen to this, pampered one, sitting securely, saying in your heart, "I am, and there is no other like me; I will not sit as a widow, *nor will I know bereavement.*" But these two things will come to you in an instant, on a single day: *bereavement* and widowhood. (Isaiah 47:8, 9)

This is about the daughter of Babylon and about Chaldea—in other words, about people with a pious surface and profane core who call themselves a church because of their outward piety. The bereavement and widowhood stand for a stripping away of truth and goodness. In the same author:

Lift your eyes all around and look: all are gathering; they are coming to you. *The children of your bereavements* will yet say in your ears, "The place is too narrow for me; withdraw from me so I can live here." But you will say in your heart, "Who bore these children for me, seeing that I am *bereft* and alone, an exile and distant? Who then has brought them up? As for me, I was left solitary; where were these?" (Isaiah 49:18, 20, 21)

This is about Zion, or a heavenly religion, and its fruitfulness after being devastated. The children of bereavements stand for true concepts stripped from that religion during its devastation, which were then restored and vastly increased.

Joseph does not exist means that there is no inner level. This can be seen from the representation of *Joseph* as spiritual heavenliness and therefore as religion's inner dimension (discussed at §5469). **5537**

And Simeon does not exist means that there is also no faith that belongs to the will. This can be seen from the representation of *Simeon* as faith that belongs to the will (discussed at §§3869, 3870, 3871, 3872, 4497, 4502, 4503, 5482). **5538**

And Benjamin you are taking means if the middle ground is also taken away. This can be seen from the representation of *Benjamin* as a middle ground (discussed at §§5411, 5413, 5443). **5539**

On me will all [these] things be means that this will destroy the substance of the church. This can be seen from the representation of Jacob, who says this of himself, as the church (discussed at §5536). When the **5540** church has no inner level (represented by Joseph) and no faith that belongs to the will (represented by Simeon), then if the uniting middle ground (represented by Benjamin) is taken away, the substance of the church has been destroyed. That is what is meant by *on me will all [these] things be.*

5541   *And Reuben said to his father* symbolizes traits of an intellectual faith, perceived by truth-based goodness, as the following shows: In Scripture narrative, *saying* means perceiving, as mentioned many times before. *Reuben* represents a doctrinal, intellectual faith, as discussed in §§3861, 3866, 5472, so he represents traits of that faith. And Jacob, the *father* whom Reuben addressed, represents truth-based goodness, as discussed in §§3659, 3669, 3677, 3775, 4234, 4273, 4538, 5533. This shows that *Reuben said to his father* symbolizes traits of an intellectual faith, perceived by truth-based goodness.

Reuben speaks here because the text is dealing with a religion in which a doctrinal, intellectual faith seems to play the leading role, teaching what needs to be done to prevent the substance of the church from being destroyed.

5542   *Saying, "My two sons you may put to death,"* means that neither side of faith will survive. This can be seen from the symbolism of Reuben's *two sons* as both sides of faith. Reuben represents a doctrinal, intellectual faith, and his sons mean the church's two doctrines: the doctrine about truth and the doctrine about goodness, or the doctrine about faith and the doctrine about charity. Neither of these sides of faith, or of the church, will survive unless the middle ground represented by Benjamin unites with it. That is what is meant by "my two sons you may put to death if I do not bring Benjamin to you." With these words Reuben confirms that it would be all over with the church if there were no middle ground.

Had the words not contained this inner meaning, Reuben would never have told his father to put his two sons to death if he did not bring Benjamin back. He would have been proposing to eradicate yet another clan, which violates all that is right and would therefore be heinous. But the inner meaning is offering a lesson, and that is why the statement is made.

5543   *If I do not bring him to you* means unless the middle ground is united with it. This can be seen from the representation of Benjamin—*he* whom Reuben would bring—as a middle ground (discussed at §§5411, 5413, 5443, 5539) and from the symbolism of *bringing* as being united.

Put him on my hands means as far as possible. This can be seen from | **5544**
the symbolism of a *hand* as power (discussed in §§878, 3387, 4931–4937,
5327, 5328). *Putting him on his hands* properly means entrusting [Benjamin]
to him, but the intellectual faith represented by Reuben has little trustwor-
thy power, because the truth that leads to faith takes its power from the
goodness that comes of charity (§3563). *Put him on my hands,* then, means
as far as possible.

And I will bring him to you means that it will be restored, as is self- | **5545**
evident.

And he said, "My son will not go down with you all," means that it | **5546**
will not move down toward lower levels. This is established by the symbolism of *going down* as a term used for going toward lower levels (discussed at §5406). Here it means down to truth in the form of knowledge
on the outer earthly level (§§5492, 5495, 5497, 5500), represented by
Jacob's sons.

Because his brother is dead means since the inner level is not present, as | **5547**
the following shows: Joseph, the *brother,* represents spiritual heavenliness,
or truth from the Divine, and consequently the inner level of the church
(discussed at §5469). And in this case *being dead* means not being present,
since Joseph was among the living but was not present.

And he alone is left means that he now takes the place of the inner | **5548**
dimension. This can be seen from the consideration that the inner dimension, or Joseph, was not present, and Benjamin alone of their mother's
children was left, so that it was as if he were now Joseph too.

Besides, both Joseph and Benjamin represent the inner dimension,
and Jacob's other ten sons represent the outer dimension (§5469).

And he may meet with harm on the way on which you will go means | **5549**
that in the sole company of truth on the earthly level, separated from the
inner dimension, it would cease to exist. This can be seen from the explanation above at §5413, where the same words occur.

And you will make my white hair go down means that this is how the | **5550**
church will end. This can be seen from the symbolism of *white hair,* when
the focus is on the church, as its end.

White hair symbolizes an end in Isaiah, too:

> Listen to me, house of Jacob, and all you survivors of the house of
> Israel, carried from the womb, borne from the uterus: *Even till old age* I
> am the same, and *till white hair* I myself will carry you. (Isaiah 46:3, 4)

The house of Jacob stands for the outer levels of the church, and the house of Israel, for its inner levels. "From the womb, from the uterus" means from its start. "To old age" and "till white hair" mean to its end. And in David:

> Those planted in Jehovah's house, in the courts of our God, will sprout. They will still be yielding produce *in [the time of] white hair.* (Psalms 92:13, 14)

"In [the time of] white hair" means at the end.

5551   *In sorrow to the grave* means without hope of being revived, as the following shows: This *sorrow* means without hope, because when there is no hope any longer, there is sorrow. And a *grave* symbolizes resurrection and rebirth, as discussed in §§2916, 2917, 3256, 4621, so it symbolizes revival—the revival of the church. If the church has no inner dimension (Joseph), no middle ground (Benjamin), and no faith that belongs to the will, or neighborly love (Simeon), there is no longer any hope of its revival.

[2] It does seem strange that a grave means revival, but what is actually strange is the way people think about graves. They do not detach graves from death or even from the corpse in a grave. Angels, on the other hand, cannot picture graves the way people do. The idea they have is totally different from a person's, because it is the idea of rising again, or being revived. When a person's body is committed to the grave, the person is revived in the other life, so angels' thoughts about graves involve not death but life and therefore revival.

Correspondence
with the Universal Human (Continued):
Correspondence of the Skin, Hair, and Bones

5552   HERE is how correspondence works: The parts of a person that have the most life correspond to the communities in the heavens that have the most life and therefore the greatest happiness. Examples of these communities are the ones to which our outer sense organs, our inner sense organs, and the parts devoted to our intellect and our will correspond.

The parts of a person that have less life correspond to the communities there that have less life. This includes the layers of skin that surround the entire body, and cartilage and bones, which support and sustain all parts of the body. It also includes hair, which grows out of the skin.

The communities to which the skin, cartilage, bones, and hair correspond need to be identified and described.

The communities to which the layers of skin correspond stand at **5553** the entrance to heaven. The inhabitants are given the ability to sense the character of spirits arriving at the first threshold, whom they either keep out or let in. These communities can therefore be called heaven's entrances or thresholds.

The communities that make up the body's outer coverings are numer- **5554** ous and differ from each other, from the face to the soles of the foot, because everything varies throughout the body. I have talked at length with the members of these communities.

In regard to their spiritual life, they had been the type of people who let others persuade them that a given idea was true. When they heard the idea proved from the literal meaning of the Word, they believed it implicitly and remained steadfast in their opinion. They also built a passable life on these ideas. However, they cannot interact easily with others whose disposition is unlike theirs, because once they have formed an opinion they stick to it tenaciously and do not let themselves be argued out of it.

Many from this planet are like that, because our world is given to superficialities and offers resistance to anything interior, as the skin does.

There are some who knew only the broad outlines of faith during **5555** bodily life. Perhaps they knew they were to love their neighbor and on the basis of this general principle helped the evil and the honest alike, without differentiation, saying that everyone was their neighbor. When [spirits] like this were alive in the world, they often allowed themselves to be led astray by charlatans, hypocrites, and frauds. The same thing happens to them in the other life, and they shrug off advice, because they stay on a sensory level and do not venture into reason.

These individuals also constitute the skin, but a less sensitive layer closer to the surface.

I spoke with the ones who constitute the skin over the skull. They differ a great deal from each other, just as our skin does in various spots, such as on different parts of the skull (the back of the head, the forehead, the temples), and on the face, chest, abdomen, groin, legs, arms, hands, and fingers.

5556   I also had the opportunity to learn who constitutes the outer layer of skin. This layer is the least sensitive of all the body's coverings, since it has smooth scales packed together, which are almost like thin cartilage. The communities that compose it consist of people who argue over every proposition, debating whether it is so or not so, without progressing any further. When I spoke with them, I was able to perceive that they had no idea what was true or not true. The more they argue, the less they grasp it. Yet they seem to themselves to be wiser than others, because they identify wisdom with the ability to reason cleverly. They are completely unaware that the chief trait of wisdom is to perceive without sophistic reasoning that a thing is true or is not true.

Many of them are people who developed this characteristic in the world as a result of the confusion that philosophy casts over goodness and truth. So they do not have much common sense.

5557   There are also spirits who act as mouthpieces for other spirits and barely understand what they themselves are saying. They have confessed as much. Still, they talk a lot. That is what becomes of people who during their physical life did nothing but babble, without giving any thought to what they were saying, and who loved to talk about everything.

I was told that there are hordes of them and that some groups relate to the membranes covering the body's inner organs. Others relate to layers of skin that exhibit little sensitivity. After all, these spirits are merely passive forces and do nothing on their own, only under others' power.

5558   There are spirits who, when they want to test an idea, state it outright, one member of the community after another. While talking, they watch to see whether it flows freely, without any spiritual resistance, because when the statement is not true, there is usually a sense of resistance from an inner level. If the spirits do not sense resistance, then, they assume the statement is true, without any other evidence.

Spirits of this kind constitute the glands in the skin, but they come in two types. Spirits of one type affirm an idea when they see the sort of easy flow just described. Since there is no resistance, they conclude that the idea is shaped to fit the heavenly form, that it consequently matches the truth, and therefore that it is reliable. Spirits of the other type brashly affirm that an idea is true even when they do not know so.

5559   The way the skin is woven together was shown to me by representations. With people in whom these outermost layers corresponded to something deeper, or whose physical matter was obedient to their spiritual side, the structure was a beautiful tapestry of coils woven together in quite a miraculous way, like a kind of lace that is utterly indescribable. They were blue.

Later there was a representation of forms with a still tighter weave, finer mesh, and more intricate pattern. That is how the skin looks in a regenerate person.

With the deceitful, though, these outermost layers look like jumbles of nothing but snakes. With someone who engages in sorcery, they look like disgusting entrails.

There are many communities of spirits to which cartilage and bones **5560** correspond, but they are the sort that have very little spiritual life in them, just as bones have very little life compared to the soft organs they surround. For instance, the skull and the bones of the head have little life in comparison with the two brains, the medulla oblongata, and the substances that support the senses. The same for the vertebrae and ribs in relation to the heart and lungs; and so on.

It was shown to me how little spiritual life exists in the spirits relating **5561** to the bones. They are mouthpieces for other spirits and have little notion themselves of what they are saying. They talk on anyway, since that is all they like to do.

This is the state spirits are reduced to when they had lived an evil life but still kept some remnant of goodness buried deep inside. This remnant creates the small share of spiritual life they receive after many decades of devastation. (For what a remnant is, see §§468, 530, 560, 561, 660, 1050, 1738, 1906, 2284, 5135, 5342, 5344.)

As just mentioned, they have little spiritual life. Spiritual life means the life that angels have in heaven. We are introduced to it in the world through the exercise of faith and charity. A desire for good that is done out of charity and for truth that leads to faith is itself spiritual life. Without it, human life is earthly, worldly, body-centered, and merely physical. This kind of life is not spiritual if there is no spiritual life within it, but rather is the kind of life animals generally have.

Spirits who emerge from devastation and perform the functions that **5562** bones perform do not have any distinct thoughts but rather generalized thoughts that are almost undefined. Their condition is like the one called absence of mind, as if they were not present in their body. They are slow, dull, stupid, and behind in everything. They are not necessarily agitated, though, because worries do not penetrate through to them but dissolve amid their general vagueness.

5563   Sometimes I feel pain in one part of my skull or another and sense some sort of lumps there, separate from the other bones, that cause the pain. From experience I have learned that they develop out of the falsities produced by cravings. Strange to say, general and particular kinds of falsity have specific places in the skull—as I also learned by much experience.

These lumps are hard spots, and in people who are reforming, they get broken up and softened, which is accomplished in various ways. The general means are lessons in what is good and true, an inflow of bitter truth (which hurts inwardly), and being actively torn apart (which hurts outwardly).

The very nature of the falsity produced by cravings is to create hard spots, because this falsity is contrary to truth. Truth follows the lead of heaven's form, so it flows spontaneously, freely, gently, and softly. Falsity inclines the other way, so it heads in an opposite direction, which stops up the fluidity of heaven's form and causes hardening.

As a result, spirits who had indulged in a murderous hatred, the revenge it inspires, and the consequent falsity possess severely hardened skulls. Some have skulls like ebony. Rays of light, or truth, never pierce these hardened skulls but always bounce off them.

5564   There are short spirits who thunder as they speak. One of them can sound like a whole battalion. Talking this way is instinctive to them. They come not from this planet but from another, which will be described when the inhabitants of various planets are discussed, with the Lord's divine mercy.

I was told that they relate to the scutiform cartilage at the front of the chest cavity that serves to support the ribs in front and also various muscles used in sound production.

5565   There are also spirits who relate to bones that are even harder, such as the teeth, but I have not been able to learn much about them. All I know is this: When spirits who have hardly any spiritual life remaining are presented to view in heaven's light, they do not appear with a face but only with teeth in lieu of a face. The face represents people's inner levels and therefore their spiritual and heavenly dimensions, or facets of faith and charity. Spirits who did not acquire any life on these levels during their physical life consequently look this way.

5566   Someone once came to me looking like a black cloud with erratically moving stars around it. When such stars appear in the other world, they symbolize falsity, while fixed stars symbolize truth. I perceived that it was a spirit who wanted to come close. When he did, he aroused fear, which is an ability possessed by certain spirits, especially robbers. From this I was able to conclude that he was a robber. While he was near me he tried as hard as he could to torment me by certain magic arts but without success. He stretched out a hand to exercise imaginary power, but that accomplished absolutely nothing.

Afterward I was shown what his face looked like. There was no face, but something pitch black instead. In it appeared a mouth gaping fiercely and hideously—a maw lined with a row of teeth. In short, he was like a rabid dog with its jaws open so wide that there was no face, only an open mouth.

One individual attached himself to my left side, but at the time I did not know where he was from or what he was like, and his actions were also obscure. He wanted to invade my mind more deeply but I refused. He imposed on me an aura of generalized thought that cannot be described. I do not remember ever having perceived so vague an atmosphere before. He was bound by no principles but was against everyone in general and was able to contradict and insult everyone in a skillful, clever manner, even though he did not know what was true. I marveled that anyone could be gifted enough to refute others cleverly without having any personal knowledge of truth to work from. **5567**

[2] Then he left, but he soon returned with an imaginary bottle in his hand and wanted to give me a drink from it. The liquid inside was a product of his fantasy, which robbed the people drinking it of their intellect. This was being represented because there had been people who clung to him in the world and he had deprived them of their ability to understand truth and goodness, although they clung to him anyway.

In heaven's light, he too did not appear to have a face but only teeth, because he had been able to laugh at others without knowing anything true himself.

I was told who he was. He had been among the famous when he was alive, and some people had known he was like this.

Several times I had with me those who gnash their teeth. They were from the hells of spirits who had not only led an evil life but also hardened their minds against anything divine and traced everything back to nature. They grind their teeth when they talk, which is horrible to listen to. **5568**

Just as the bones and skin layers have a correspondence, so does hair, which sprouts from roots in the skin. Everything that corresponds with the universal human exists in spirits and angels, since each spirit or angel reflects an image of the universal human. Angels consequently have hair, **5569** attractively and neatly arranged. Hair represents the earthly level of their life and the way it corresponds with their spiritual life.

On the point that hair symbolizes qualities associated with earthly life, see §3301; that cutting the hair means adapting earthly qualities to make them suitable and therefore appealing, see §5247.

5570   There are many—especially women—for whom beauty had been all-important, who did not think very deeply, and scarcely considered eternal life at all. Women are excused for being like this until they reach adulthood, when the burning passion that usually precedes marriage has died out. However, if they maintain the same attitude after they grow up, when they are capable of understanding differently, they develop a character that remains after death.

In the other world, spirits like this appear with long hair spread over their face, which they comb. They think that hair makes a person elegant. Combing one's hair symbolizes adapting earthly qualities to make them look appealing (§5247). That is how other spirits recognize their nature. Other spirits can tell by the color, length, and cascade of these spirits' hair what kind of outward life they had lived in the world.

5571   There are some who had believed that the material world was everything, who had proved the idea to themselves and therefore lived a carefree life, acknowledging no life after death and consequently no hell or heaven. Spirits like this are thoroughly earthbound, so when they appear in heaven's light, they do not seem to have a face. Instead they appear to have something bearded, hairy, and untrimmed. As mentioned above, the face represents the spiritual and heavenly qualities inside a person [§5565], while the hair represents earthly qualities [§§5569–5570].

5572   There are many in the Christian world today who attribute everything to nature and hardly anything to the Divine, but there are more of them in one nation than another. Let me relate a conversation I had with some from the nation where most of them live.

5573   Once there was a spirit above my head who was invisible but whose presence I could perceive from a stench of burnt horn or bone and a stink of [rotten] teeth. Later a great horde came upward from below, at my back, like a cloud, and these spirits too were invisible. They settled in above my head. I thought that they were invisible because they were subtle but was told that where the atmosphere is spiritual, they are invisible, and where it is earthly, they are visible. They are called the "earthly unseen."

The first thing I discovered about them was that they were trying with all their might, cunning, and skill to prevent any information about themselves from becoming public. For this purpose they had also learned how to rob others of their ideas and substitute different ideas that kept them from being exposed. They did this for quite a while. The experience enabled me to recognize that in bodily life they had been the kind of people who had not wanted anything they did or thought to come out in the open. They had presented themselves in look and words as something different from what they really were but nonetheless had not made the pretense in order to lie and deceive.

[2] I perceived that the ones who were present had been business-people during bodily life, but the kind who found their highest pleasure more in trade itself than in the money. Business had been their soul, so to speak. So I talked with them about commerce and was allowed to say that business dealings do not keep anyone from going to heaven, that in heaven there are rich people as well as poor. They objected, though. Their opinion had been that if they were saved they would have to give up businesses, donate all they owned to the poor, and make themselves miserable. "That is not the reality of the situation," I was allowed to answer. "You have fellow citizens who thought differently and are now in heaven because they were good Christians, even though they were rich. Some were among the very richest. What they adopted as their goal was the common good, and also love for their neighbor. They engaged in commerce only for the sake of their job in the world, and beyond that they did not set their heart on [riches]."

The reason the [invisible spirits] are down below is that they had been earthly through and through and therefore had not believed in life after death, hell, heaven, or even the spirit. They felt no twinge at heart over using every skill they possessed to deprive others of their goods, and could watch without pity as entire households were destroyed for their own enrichment. For that reason, they ridiculed anyone who spoke with them about spiritual life.

[3] The nature of the belief they had had in life after death, heaven, and hell was in fact demonstrated. We saw somebody taken up from left to right into heaven and were told that one who had recently died was being led directly up to heaven by some angels. We discussed the event, but even though the [invisible spirits] had also seen it happen, they maintained a very strong air of disbelief, which they spread out around them.

In fact, they wanted to persuade themselves and others that they had not seen what they had. Since they were so skeptical, I was allowed to say to them that if, while in the world, they had seen the resuscitation of someone lying dead in a coffin, their first reaction would have been disbelief, unless they had already seen a number of dead people revived. And if they had seen that, they would still have attributed it to natural causes. Later, after being left to their own thoughts for a while, they said that at first they would have believed it was a fraud. If they had been convinced it was not a fraud, they would have believed that the soul of the dead person was communicating secretly with the one performing the resuscitation. Finally they would have believed it to be some secret they did not understand, because nature is full of incomprehensible processes. They would never have been able to believe, then, that some force higher than nature had brought the event about. This revealed what their faith had been like. It had been such that they never could have been led to believe there was any life after death or hell or heaven. So they were purely earthly.

When spirits of this kind appear in heaven's light, they too appear without a face, and with a dense mass of hair in its place.

Genesis 43

1. And the famine was growing heavy in the land.

2. And it happened, as they finished eating the grain provisions that they had brought from Egypt, that their father said to them, "Go back; buy us a bit of food."

3. And Judah said to him, saying, "The man called sternly [on God] as witness against us, saying, 'You shall not see my face unless your brother is with you.'

4. If you are sending our brother with us, we will go down and buy you food.

5. And if you are not sending him, we will not go down, because the man said to us, 'You shall not see my face unless your brother is with you.'"

6. And Israel said, "Why did you wrong me, to tell the man whether you had yet another brother?"

7. And they said, "The man insistently asked as to us and as to our birth, saying, 'Is your father still alive? Do you have a brother?' and we told him according to the mouth of these words. Could we possibly have known that he would say, 'Bring your brother down?'"

8. And Judah said to Israel his father, "Send the youth with me and we will get up and go and live and not die, both we and you and our little children.

9. And I will be surety for him; from my hand you shall seek him. If I do not bring him to you and stand him before you, I will be sinning against you all my days.

10. Because if we had not delayed, we would have returned these two times now."

11. And Israel their father said to them, "If so, then do this: Take some of the songworthiness of the land in your containers and take an offering down to the man: a bit of resin and a bit of honey, wax and stacte, terebinth nuts and almonds.

12. And take double the silver in your hands. And the silver brought back in the mouth of your bags you shall return in your hand; maybe it was a mistake.

13. And take your brother and get up, go back to the man.

14. And God Shaddai grant you mercies before the man and send you your other brother and Benjamin. And I—however I am bereaved, I shall be bereaved."

15. And the men took this offering, and double the silver they took in their hand, and Benjamin, and got up and went down to Egypt and stood before Joseph.

16. And Joseph saw Benjamin with them and said to the one who was over his household, "Bring the men to the house, and slaughter abundantly and prepare [the meat], because the men will eat with me at noon."

17. And the man did as Joseph said, and the man brought the men to Joseph's house.

18. And the men were afraid because they had been brought to Joseph's house, and they said, "Over the matter of the silver taken back in our bags at first we are being brought. [They mean] to roll down on us and to throw themselves on us and to take us as slaves, and our donkeys."

19. And they went up to the man who was over Joseph's household and spoke to him in the doorway of the house.

20. And they said, "Upon my life, my lord; we did indeed come down at first to buy food.

21. And it happened when we came to the inn that we opened our bags, and here, each one's silver in the mouth of his bag—our silver in its weight! And we are returning it in our hand.

22. And other silver we have brought down in our hand to buy food; we do not know who put our silver in our bags."

23. And he said, "Peace to you; don't be afraid. Your God and the God of your father gave you a secret gift in your bags; your silver came to me." And he brought Simeon out to them.

24. And the man brought the men to Joseph's house and gave them water, and they washed their feet, and he gave fodder to their donkeys.

25. And they prepared the offering for the time of Joseph's coming at noon, because they had heard that they would be eating bread there.

26. And Joseph came home, and they brought him the offering that was in their hand, to the house, and bowed down to him to the earth.

27. And he asked them about their peace. And he said, "Does your old father, whom you mentioned, have peace? Is he still alive?"

28. And they said, "Your servant our father has peace; he is still alive," and bent and bowed.

29. And he raised his eyes and saw Benjamin his brother, the son of his mother, and said, "Is this your youngest brother, whom you mentioned to me?" And he said, "God show favor to you, my son."

30. And Joseph hurried, because his compassions were being stirred for his brother and he was seeking to weep, and he came to his private room and wept there.

31. And he washed his face and went out and controlled himself and said, "Set the bread."

32. And they set it for him by himself and for them by themselves and for the Egyptians eating with him by themselves, because the Egyptians cannot eat bread with the Hebrews, because it is abhorrent to the Egyptians.

33. And they were seated before him, the firstborn according to his status as firstborn, and the youngest according to his youth, and the men stared dumbfounded, each at his companion.

34. And he brought portions out from [before] his face for them and multiplied Benjamin's portion above the portions of them all by five measures. And they drank—and drank heavily—with him.

Summary

THIS continues to talk about the union of earthly-level truth known to the church (Jacob's ten sons) with spiritual heavenliness, or truth from the Divine (Joseph), through a middle ground (Benjamin). The inner meaning of the current chapter, though, deals with a general inflow that comes before the union.   **5574**

Inner Meaning

GENESIS 43:1, 2, 3, 4, 5. *And the famine was growing heavy in the land. And it happened, as they finished eating the grain provisions that they had brought from Egypt, that their father said to them, "Go back; buy us a*   **5575** *bit of food." And Judah said to him, saying, "The man called sternly [on God] as witness against us, saying, 'You shall not see my face unless your brother is with you.' If you are sending our brother with us, we will go down and buy you food. And if you are not sending him, we will not go down, because the man said to us, 'You shall not see my face unless your brother is with you.'"*

And the famine was growing heavy symbolizes desolation because of a pressing need for spiritual provisions. *In the land* means in the religious domain. *And it happened* symbolizes transition. *As they finished eating the grain provisions* means when they ran out of truth. *That they had brought from Egypt* means which had developed out of knowledge. *That their father said to them* symbolizes a perception from the church's point of view. *Go back; buy us a bit of food* means that in order to live they should acquire the goodness that comes from spiritual truth. *And Judah said to him* symbolizes goodness in the church. *Saying, "The man called sternly [on God] as witness against us,"* means that spirituality from within turned away from them. *Saying, "You shall not see my face,"* symbolizes an absence of compassion. *Unless your brother is with you* means unless you have a middle ground. *If you are sending our brother with us* means that if the church acts in such a way as to create a connection, there will be a middle ground. *We will go down and buy you food* means that goodness-from-truth will then be acquired there. *And if you are not sending him* means if not. *We will not go down* means that it cannot be acquired. *Because the man said to us* symbolizes a perception about spirituality. *You shall not see my face* symbolizes an absence of compassion. *Unless your brother is with you* means unless you have a middle ground.

5576   *And the famine was growing heavy* symbolizes desolation because of a pressing need for spiritual provisions. This can be seen from the symbolism of *famine* as a lack of knowledge about goodness and truth (discussed in §§3364, 5277, 5279, 5281, 5300) and consequent desolation (§§5360, 5376, 5415). Since desolation rises from a shortage of spiritual provisions and therefore a pressing need for them, famine also symbolizes such a need.

In the spiritual world, or heaven, famine is not a starvation for food, because angels do not feed on physical food, which is designed for the body that a person carries around in the world. Rather, it is a starvation for the kind of food that nourishes their minds. This food consists in understanding truth and being wise about goodness and is called spiritual food. Amazingly, such food nourishes angels, [2] as I have been able to tell from observing little children who died young. After they have been taught in heaven about truth (a matter of understanding) and goodness (a matter of wisdom), they no longer look like children but adults. The more they have grown in goodness and truth, the more adult they look.

I have been able to tell the same thing from the fact that angels have a constant desire for matters of understanding and wisdom. To the extent that evening falls for them—that is, a state in which matters of understanding and wisdom are lacking—they are relatively unhappy. Under those circumstances their greatest hunger and appetite is to see morning dawn anew on them and to return to a life of happiness, which is a life of understanding and wisdom.

[3] Anyone who reflects on it can see that understanding what is true and willing what is good is spiritual food. When we are enjoying physical food for the nourishment of our body, the food is more nourishing if we are in a cheerful frame of mind at the time and are discussing congenial ideas. This is a sign of the correspondence between spiritual food for the soul and physical food for the body. Further evidence is provided by people who long to steep their minds in what knowledge, understanding, and wisdom have to teach. When they are cut off from such information, they become depressed and anxious. They long like the starving to return to their spiritual food and to the nourishment of their soul.

[4] The Word too shows that spiritual food is what feeds the soul the way physical food feeds the body. In Moses, for instance:

> Humankind does not live by bread alone; rather *by every utterance of Jehovah's mouth does humankind live.* (Deuteronomy 8:3; Matthew 4:4)

The utterance of Jehovah's mouth means divine truth in general that issues from the Lord. It therefore means all of wisdom's truth, and specifically the Word, the container and source of what wisdom entails. And in John:

> Work, not for the *food* that perishes, *but for the food that lasts to eternal life,* which the Son of Humankind will give you. (John 6:27)

This food is plainly wisdom's truth, which issues from the Lord. [5] From such ideas you can also see what is meant by these words of the Lord's in the same chapter:

> My flesh is truly *food,* and my blood is truly drink. (John 6:55)

That is, the Lord's flesh is divine goodness (§3813), and his blood is divine truth (§4735). Since the Lord made his entire human nature divine, his flesh is consequently pure divine goodness, and his blood, divine truth. Obviously we are not supposed to understand the divine nature as containing something made of matter. Food in the highest sense, then, or food ascribed to the Lord, is the goodness that comes of his divine love for saving the human race. This food is also what is meant by the Lord's words in John:

> Jesus said to the disciples, "*I have food to eat* that you do not know of. *My food* is to do the will of him who sent me, and I will finish his work." (John 4:32, 34)

Doing the will of him who sent [Jesus] and finishing his work means saving the human race. The divine quality that brought the work about is divine love.

From these passages it is now evident what famine means in a spiritual sense.

5577   *In the land* means in the religious domain. This can be seen from the symbolism of the *land* in the Word as the church, and here, as the religious domain. Anything that symbolizes the church symbolizes the religious domain, because this is what constitutes the church.

The reason the land means the church when it is mentioned in the Word is that the land of Canaan was where the church had existed since earliest times. So when the Word mentions the land, it means the land of Canaan and consequently the church. When the land is mentioned, the inhabitants of the spiritual world concern themselves not with the idea of the land but with the idea of the nation there, and not with the idea of the nation but with the idea of that nation's character. So they think of the church when the land—meaning the land of Canaan—is mentioned.

This shows how deluded those people are who believe that on the day of the Last Judgment a new earth and new heaven will come into being, as prophesied in the Old Testament and by John in the New [Isaiah 65:17; 66:22; Revelation 21:1]. In those passages, though, the new earth actually means a new outer part of the church, and the new heaven actually means a new inner part. It also shows how deluded those people are who believe that where the Word mentions the whole earth it means anything besides the church. This in turn shows how weakly people grasp the Word if they do not imagine it contains any holier meaning than the one that shines from the literal sense alone.

The church was located in the land of Canaan since earliest times: §§3686, 4447, 4454, 4516, 4517, 5136. In the Word, the land symbolizes the church: §§662, 1066, 1068, 1262, 1413, 1607, 2928, 4447. The new heaven and new earth symbolize the inner and outer aspects of a new religion: §§1733, 1850, 2117, 2118 at the end, 3355 at the end, 4535.

And it happened symbolizes transition. This can be seen from the meaning of *it happened,* which involves a new stage (as noted in §§4979, 4987, 4999, 5074, 5466). In the original language, in ancient times, one thought was not separated from another by punctuation. The text was continuous, in imitation of heavenly language. What took the place of punctuation was "and," and also "it happened." That is why these expressions occur so often and why "it was" or "it happened" symbolizes transition. **5578**

As they finished eating the grain provisions means when they ran out of truth. This can be seen from the symbolism of *grain provisions* as truth (discussed at §§5276, 5280, 5292, 5402). Their running out of truth is meant by *they finished eating them.* **5579**

In the spiritual world the inhabitants fill up on truth and goodness, which is their food (§5576), but when it has served its purpose, they develop a pressing need again. It is like the use of physical food to nourish a person on earth; when the food has served its purpose, hunger returns. The starvation under discussion, which is a lack of spiritual provisions, is evening time in the spiritual world, or the shadow of its day, but half-light and morning then follow. So everything cycles there. The inhabitants come into this kind of evening, or spiritual famine, so as to develop an appetite and longing for truth and goodness, which nourish them better when they are hungry, as physical food does for a person who is famished.

These considerations show what is meant by a need for spiritual provisions when truth runs out.

That they had brought from Egypt means which had developed out of knowledge. This is established by the symbolism of *Egypt* as knowledge (discussed at §§1164, 1165, 1186, 1462). The idea that [the truth] had developed out of knowledge is symbolized by *they had brought them from there.* **5580**

In a positive sense, *Egypt* symbolizes things known to the church, items of knowledge that serve the church in its outward form (see §§4749, 4964, 4966). They introduce us to religious truth as does the entryway into a house, because they are what first greets our senses and consequently opens the way to deeper knowledge. As is recognized, the evidence of our outer senses is unlocked first, then the evidence of our inner senses, and finally the thoughts in our intellect. When these last have been unlocked, we see them reflected in the evidence of our senses, where they can be grasped.

The reason for this chain of events is that the thoughts in our intellect develop out of sensory information by being distilled from it. They are conclusions we draw, and when we have drawn them, they detach from the sensory information and soar aloft. What accomplishes this is an inflow of spiritual forces coming by way of heaven from the Lord.

These remarks show how it is that truth develops out of knowledge.

5581   *That their father said to them* symbolizes a perception from the church's point of view. This is established by the symbolism of *saying* in the Word's narratives as a perception (discussed many times before) and from the representation of Israel, the *father,* as the church. For the meaning of Israel as the inner spiritual church and of Jacob as the outer, see §§4286, 4292, 4570. The word *father* is used because a father in the Word also symbolizes the church, as does a mother. A mother symbolizes truth in the church, and a father symbolizes goodness in the church. This is because the church is a spiritual marriage that results from goodness as the church's father and truth as its mother.

5582   *Go back; buy us a bit of food* means that in order to live they should acquire the goodness that comes from spiritual truth. This can be seen from the symbolism of *buying* as acquiring and adopting (discussed in §§4397, 5374, 5406, 5410, 5426) and from that of *food* as the goodness that comes from truth (discussed in §§5340, 5342). Food here symbolizes the goodness that comes from spiritual truth, because the verses that follow talk about this kind of goodness. The idea that the goal was to live follows as a conclusion.

5583   *And Judah said to him* symbolizes goodness in the church. This can be seen from the representation of *Judah* as goodness in the church (discussed in §3654). The reason Judah speaks about Benjamin here, while Reuben spoke of him earlier (in verses 36, 37 of the previous chapter), is a secret that can become clear only from the inner meaning. Likewise the reason that when Reuben speaks of Benjamin, Jacob is called Jacob (Genesis 42:36), but here, where Judah speaks of Benjamin, Jacob is called Israel (verses 6, 8, 11). No one can deny that there is some significance to the fact, but what the significance is can never be seen from the literal, narrative meaning. The same is true in other passages that refer to Jacob now as Jacob, now as Israel (§4286). The secret involved will be explained later, by the Lord's divine mercy [§5595].

Judah speaks here because the current theme is the need to acquire the goodness that comes from spiritual truth (§5582). Accordingly, Judah, or goodness in the church, speaks with Israel, or the goodness that comes from spiritual truth, and serves as surety for Benjamin, the middle ground—since the middle ground is attached through goodness.

Saying, "The man called sternly [on God] as witness against us," means **5584** that spirituality from within turned away from them, as the following shows: *Sternly calling on as witness* means turning away, because the oath Joseph asked [God] to witness was that they would not see his face unless their brother was with them. This invocation is unfriendly, because not seeing his face symbolizes an absence of compassion, as will be explained just below. And Joseph represents divine spirituality, that is, truth from the Divine, as discussed at §3969. Because he is being called the *man,* he stands for something spiritual, or truth, flowing in from within.

Saying, "You shall not see my face," symbolizes an absence of compas- **5585** sion. This can be seen from the symbolism of a *face* when ascribed to a human being as the person's inner depths, or feelings and consequent thoughts (discussed at §§358, 1999, 2434, 3527, 3573, 4066, 4796, 4797, 5102). When ascribed to the Lord, though, it symbolizes mercy, or compassion, so *not seeing* his face means no mercy, or no compassion—Joseph in the highest sense here representing the Lord. Not that the Lord lacks compassion; after all, he is mercy itself. But when we have no middle ground to create a bond, it seems to us as though there is no compassion in the Lord. This is because we do not welcome goodness if we have no uniting middle ground, and when we do not welcome goodness, evil takes its place. If we then cry out to the Lord, we cry out at the urging of evil, on our own behalf, against everyone else. As a result we are not listened to, which looks like an absence of compassion.

[2] The meaning of Jehovah's or the Lord's face as mercy is clear in the Word. Strictly speaking, Jehovah's or the Lord's face means divine love itself, and since it means divine love, it means mercy, because mercy springs from love for the human race, established as we are in so much misery.

The identification of Jehovah's or the Lord's face with divine love can be seen from the appearance of the Lord's face when he was transfigured before Peter, James, and John—in other words, when he showed them his divinity. At that moment, *"his face shone like the sun"* (Matthew 17:2), the sun meaning divine love (see the proof in §§30–38, 1521, 1529, 1530, 1531, 2441, 2495, 3636, 3643, 4060, 4321 at the end, 4696). The Lord's divinity itself had never appeared in any face, only his divine humanity, and through his divine humanity or within it, his divine love, which in respect to the human race is divine mercy. Divine mercy within divine humanity is called the angel of the Lord's face in Isaiah:

> I will mention *Jehovah's mercies.* He repaid them according to *his mercies* and according to the abundance of *his mercies,* and he became a savior to them. And the *angel of his face* saved them *on account of his love* and on account of his compassion. (Isaiah 63:7, 8, 9)

He is being called an angel here because angels in the Word's inner meaning symbolize something about the Lord (§§1925, 2821, 4085). In this case the angel symbolizes his mercy, which is why it is called the angel of his face.

[3] The following passages also show that Jehovah's or the Lord's face means mercy, and also peace and goodness, since these are qualities of mercy. In [Moses'] blessing:

> *Jehovah make his face shine on you* and *have mercy on you. Jehovah lift his face toward you* and give you *peace.* (Numbers 6:25, 26)

Making his face shine means showing mercy, and lifting his face means giving peace, as is obvious. In David:

> May God *have mercy on us* and bless us; *may he make his face shine on us.* (Psalms 67:1)

Here too the face stand for mercy. In the same author:

> God, bring us back and *make your face shine,* so that we can be saved. (Psalms 80:3, 7, 19)

The meaning is similar. In the same author:

> Deliver me from the hand of my foes and my pursuers; *make your face shine on your servant.* (Psalms 31:15, 16; 119:134, 135)

In Daniel:

> Hear, our God, the prayer of your servant and his supplications *and make your face shine on the sanctuary,* which has been ruined. (Daniel 9:17)

Once again, making his face shine stands for showing mercy. [4] In David:

> Many are saying, "Who will cause us to see *goodness? Lift the light of your face on us."* (Psalms 4:6, 7)

Lifting the light of his face stands for giving something good, out of mercy. In Hosea:

> *Let them seek my face* when they have distress; let them seek me early. (Hosea 5:15)

In David:

> "*Seek my face*"; *your face, Jehovah, I seek.* (Psalms 27:8, 9)

In the same author:

> Seek Jehovah and his strength; *seek his face* constantly. (Psalms 105:4)

Seeking Jehovah's face stands for seeking his mercy. In the same author:

> As for me, in righteousness *I will see your face.* (Psalms 17:15)

And in Matthew;

> See that you do not despise any of these little ones. For I say to you that their angels in the heavens *always see the face of my Father,* who is in the heavens. (Matthew 18:10)

Seeing God's face stands for enjoying the peace and goodness that mercy supplies.

[5] Hiding his face and turning it away is the opposite and symbolizes not showing mercy, as in Isaiah:

> In the flood of my anger *I hid my face* from you for a moment, but with eternal *mercy* will I *have mercy* on you. (Isaiah 54:8)

A flood of anger stands for times of trial, and since at those times the Lord seems to show no mercy, the text says, "I hid my face from you for a moment." In Ezekiel:

> I will turn my face from them. (Ezekiel 7:22)

In David:

> How long, Jehovah, will you forget me forever? *How long will you hide your face from me?* (Psalms 13:1)

In the same author:

> *Do not hide your face from me;* do not rebuff your servant in anger. (Psalms 27:8, 9)

In the same author:

> Why, Jehovah, do you abandon my soul, do you *hide your face from me?*
> (Psalms 88:14)

In the same author:

> Hurry; answer me, Jehovah! My spirit has been consumed; *do not hide*
> *your face from me* so that I become like those going down into the pit.
> Make me hear *your mercy* in the morning. (Psalms 143:7, 8)

And in Moses:

> My anger will blaze against this people on that day, so that I abandon
> them and *hide my face from them,* so that they will be for consuming. *I*
> *will completely hide my face* on that day because of all the evil that they
> have done. (Deuteronomy 31:17, 18)

[6] The blazing of his anger stands for aversion (§5034), and hiding his
face stands for not having mercy. Jehovah—the Lord—is said to do these
things, although he never feels angry and never turns his face away or
hides it. The idea is expressed this way because of how it looks to a person
engaged in evil. People who take to evil turn away and hide the Lord's face
from themselves—in other words, distance themselves from his mercy.

The fact that the evil in us does this can also be seen from the Word.
In Micah, for instance:

> *Jehovah will hide his face from them* in that time, *as they have rendered*
> *their works evil.* (Micah 3:4)

In Ezekiel:

> Because they transgressed against me, therefore I have *hidden my face*
> *from them.* According to their uncleanness and according to their trans-
> gressions have I dealt with them, and I have *hidden my face from them.*
> (Ezekiel 39:23, 24)

And particularly in Isaiah:

> Your offenses are what cause a separation between you and your God;
> and *your sins hide his face from you.* (Isaiah 59:2)

These passages and many others disclose the inner meaning, which stands
out in various places for those who seek it to discover.

Unless your brother is with you means unless you have a middle ground. **5586**
This is established by the representation of Benjamin as a middle ground
(discussed at §§5411, 5413, 5443).

The middle ground that Benjamin represents is a middle ground
between the inner and outer selves, or the spiritual and earthly selves. It
consists in truth-from-goodness radiating out of truth from the Divine
(which is represented by Joseph). This truth-from-goodness is called
heavenly spirituality. On the point that Benjamin means heavenly spirituality, see §§3969, 4592.

Our inner and our outer dimensions are perfectly distinct from each
other—our inner dimension living in heaven's light, and our outer dimension in the world's light. Because they are so distinct, they cannot unite
except through a middle ground that partakes of both.

If you are sending our brother with us means that if the church acts **5587**
in such a way as to create a connection, there will be a middle ground,
as the following shows: Israel, the one *sending,* represents the church, as
discussed in §4286, so *if you are sending* means if the church acts in such
a way. And Benjamin, *their brother,* represents a middle ground, as discussed just above in §5586. Clearly, then, *if you are sending our brother
with us* means that if the church acts in such a way as to create a connection between its outer and inner parts, there will be a middle ground.

We will go down and buy you food means that goodness-from-truth **5588**
will then be acquired. This can be seen from the symbolism of *buying* as
acquiring and adopting, and from that of *food* as the goodness that comes
from truth—both meanings being mentioned above at §5582.

And if you are not sending him means if not—if the church does not **5589**
act in such a way as to create a connection. This is plain from the remarks
just above at §5587.

We will not go down means that it cannot be acquired, as the discus- **5590**
sion just above at §5588 shows.

Because the man said to us symbolizes a perception about spirituality. **5591**
This can be seen from the symbolism of the *man* as something spiritual
from within (discussed above at §5584) and from that of *saying* in the
Word's narrative as a perception (discussed many times before).

You shall not see my face symbolizes an absence of compassion, as **5592**
shown by the explanation above at §5585, where the same words occur.

Unless your brother is with you means unless you have a middle ground. **5593**
This can be seen from the discussion above in §§5586, 5587 concerning
Benjamin, the *brother,* showing that he is a middle ground.

5594   *Genesis 43:6, 7, 8, 9, 10. And Israel said, "Why did you wrong me, to tell the man whether you had yet another brother?" And they said, "The man insistently asked as to us and as to our birth, saying, 'Is your father still alive? Do you have a brother?' and we told him according to the mouth of these words. Could we possibly have known that he would say, 'Bring your brother down?'" And Judah said to Israel his father, "Send the youth with me and we will get up and go and live and not die, both we and you and our little children. I will be surety for him; from my hand you shall seek him. If I do not bring him to you and stand him before you, I will be sinning against you all my days. Because if we had not delayed, we would have returned these two times now."*

And Israel said, symbolizes a perception received from spiritual goodness. *Why did you wrong me, to tell the man whether [you had] yet another brother?* means that they would separate truth-from-goodness from him in order to unite it with something spiritual from within. *And they said, "The man insistently asked as to us,"* means that he perceived the contents of the earthly level clearly. *And as to our birth* means concerning the religious truth there. *Saying, "Is your father still alive?"* means and concerning the spiritual goodness that was its source. *Do you have a brother?* means concerning inner truth. *And we told him according to the mouth of these words* means that he perceived those things as agreeable. *Could we possibly have known that he would say, "Bring your brother down?"* means we did not believe he wanted truth-from-goodness united to him. *And Judah said to Israel his father* symbolizes a perception by the goodness belonging to the church about these matters. *Send the youth with me* means so that it could be connected to him. *And we will get up and go and live and not die* symbolizes spiritual life in its different degrees. *Both we* symbolizes the church's outer plane. *And you* symbolizes its inner plane. *And our little children* symbolizes what lay still deeper. *And I will be surety for him* means that it will be connected to him in the meanwhile. *From my hand you shall seek him* means that it will not be torn away, so far as this is within his power. *If I do not bring him to you and stand him before you* means unless it is entirely restored to the church. *I will be sinning against you all my days* means that the goodness belonging to the church will no longer exist. *Because if we had not delayed* symbolizes being stalled in a state of doubt. *We would have returned these two times now* means that there is outward and inward spiritual life.

5595   *And Israel said,* symbolizes a perception received from spiritual goodness. This can be seen from the symbolism of *saying* as perceiving (discussed before) and from the representation of *Israel* as spiritual goodness (discussed in §§3654, 4598). Since Israel means spiritual goodness, he also means the inner part of a spiritual religion (§§3305, 4286), because spiritual goodness is what makes a spiritual religion a religion.

Spiritual goodness is truth that has turned into goodness. Truth turns into goodness when we live by it, because it then passes into our will and from our will into our actions. In this way it becomes part of our life, and when truth becomes part of life it is no longer called truth but goodness. The will that changes truth into goodness is a new will existing in the intellectual side of our mind. This goodness is what is called spiritual goodness.

Spiritual goodness differs from heavenly goodness in that heavenly goodness is planted in our actual will side, as has been discussed many times before [§§1043, 2069, 2708, 2715, 2831].

[2] The reason Jacob is not being called Jacob, as he was in verse 36 of the previous chapter, but is being called Israel, is that this chapter is about goodness, while the previous chapter was about truth. For the same reason, the previous chapter quoted Reuben, who represents the church's doctrinal truth (§§3861, 3866, 4731, 4734, 4761, 5542), while the current chapter quotes Judah, who represents goodness in the church (§§3654, 5583). The reason goodness is now the subject is that this time a bond is created between the inner dimension (Joseph) and the outer (Jacob's ten sons) through a middle ground (Benjamin), and goodness is what creates the bond of inner with outer.

Why did you wrong me, to tell the man whether [you had] yet another brother? means that they would separate truth-from-goodness from him in order to unite it with something spiritual from within, as the following shows: *Wronging* him means causing a separation, because their separating Benjamin from him is what he is calling a wrong. *Telling* means giving another person something to think about and reflect on (§§2862, 5508) and therefore communicating something (§4856). Consequently, it also means creating union, because when the communication passes into the other person's will, it creates union. Notice that when Joseph heard that Benjamin was still alive and living with his father, he wanted Benjamin to come to him and then to stay behind with him, united with him, as a later part of the story shows. Joseph represents divine spirituality, and when he is referred to as the *man,* he represents something spiritual from within, as discussed at §5584. And Benjamin, the *other brother* they were telling about, represents truth that comes of goodness, as discussed in §5586.

5596

These remarks show that *Why did you wrong me, to tell the man whether [you had] yet another brother?* means that they would separate truth-from-goodness from him in order to unite it with something spiritual from within.

5597   *And they said, "The man insistently asked as to us,"* means that he perceived the contents of the earthly level clearly. This can be seen from the symbolism of *asking* as perceiving someone else's thoughts (discussed below) and from the representation of Jacob's ten sons, *us,* as religious [truths] on the earthly level (discussed at §§5403, 5419, 5427, 5458, 5512).

The reason *asking* means perceiving someone else's thoughts is that in heaven everyone's thinking is shared generally—so much so that no one needs to ask what another is thinking. That is why asking means perceiving another's thoughts. Circumstances on earth have as their inner meaning the equivalent circumstances in heaven.

5598   *And as to our birth* means concerning the religious truth there. This can be seen from the symbolism of *birth* as the birth of truth from goodness, or of faith from charity (discussed in §§1145, 1255, 4070, 4668).

This is what *birth* means in an inner sense because no other birth is meant in heaven than the kind called regeneration, which is brought about by religious truth and charitable goodness. This birth turns the children of humankind into children of the Lord, and they are the people described in John 1:13 as born of God.

All family relationships in heaven—all blood ties and more distant connections there—depend on the different varieties of goodness-from-truth and truth-from-goodness involved in the birth called regeneration. In heaven the variations are endless, but the Lord arranges them in a pattern that resembles clans, with their brothers, sisters, sons-in-law, daughters-in-law, grandsons, granddaughters, and so on. [2] Yet as a group they are arranged in such a form that they combine as one. They are like the varied parts of the human body, not one of which is exactly like another. In fact, not one part of a part is exactly like another. Nonetheless they are all arranged into such a form that they operate as a unit, and each area contributes directly or indirectly to making another area work. Considering that the human body has this kind of form, you can imagine what kind of form must exist in heaven, to which every part of the human body corresponds. Such a form must be complete and perfect.

5599   *Saying, "Is your father still alive?"* means and concerning the spiritual goodness that was its source. This is established by the representation of Israel, the *father,* as spiritual goodness (discussed at §§3654, 4598, 5595).

Religious truth descends from this goodness as if from its father (§5598), which is the reason for saying "that was its source."

Do you have a brother? means concerning inner truth. This can be **5600** seen from the representation of Benjamin as heavenly spirituality, that is, truth-from-goodness, or inner truth. (For the meaning of Benjamin as truth that contains what is good, or heavenly spirituality, see §§3969, 4592.) This inner truth is the same as the middle ground between truth from the Divine and truth on the earthly level.

And we told him according to the mouth of his words means that he per- **5601** ceived those things as agreeable, as the following shows: *Telling* means perceiving, as mentioned in §3608. In the spiritual world, or in heaven, the inhabitants do not need to tell anyone what they are thinking, because everyone's thinking is shared (§5597). So in a spiritual sense, telling means perceiving. And *according to the mouth of his words* means in an agreeable way, since those are the things he wanted to perceive.

Could we possibly have known that he would say, "Bring your brother **5602** *down?"* means we did not believe that truth-from-goodness would be united to him. This can be seen from the symbolism of *could we possibly know that he would say* as not believing, and from the representation of Benjamin, the *brother,* as truth-from-goodness (discussed just above at §5600). The union of this truth with [Joseph] is symbolized by [their brothers'] bringing him down, as is evident from the remarks above at §5596.

And Judah said to Israel his father symbolizes a perception by the good- **5603** ness belonging to the church about these matters. This can be seen from the symbolism in the Word's narrative of *saying* as perceiving (mentioned many times before), from the representation of *Judah* as goodness in the church (discussed above in §5583), and from the representation of *Israel* as the inner part of a spiritual religion (discussed in §§3305, 4286). Clearly, then, *Judah said to Israel his father* symbolizes a perception by the church from the goodness belonging to it.

Send the youth with me means so that it could be connected to him, **5604** or to goodness in the church, which Judah represents. This can be seen from the symbolism of *sending with him* as connecting to him and not to the others, since a later verse says, "I will be surety for him; from my hand you shall seek him"; and from the representation of Benjamin, the *youth,* as inner truth (mentioned just above at §5600). He is being called a youth because the Word refers to anything deep within as relatively youthful. The reason is that there is more innocence on an inner level than on an outer one, and innocence is symbolized by a child and also by a youth (§5236).

5605   *And we will get up and go and live and not die* symbolizes spiritual life in its different degrees, as the following shows: *Getting up* symbolizes elevation to higher or inner levels and consequently to the realm of spiritual life, as discussed at §§2401, 2785, 2912, 2927, 3171, 4103, 4881. *Going* means living, as discussed at §§3335, 3690, 4882, 5493, and since *and live* follows it, going symbolizes the start of spiritual life. *Living* symbolizes spiritual life, because no other kind of life is meant in the Word's inner sense. And *not dying* means not being damned any longer—in other words, being outside a state of damnation. No other kind of death is meant in the Word's inner sense than spiritual death, which is damnation. These comments show that *we will get up and go and live and not die* symbolizes life in its different degrees. That is, getting up symbolizes being introduced to life, going symbolizes the start of life, living symbolizes life itself, and not dying symbolizes being led away from that which lacks life.

[2] The notion that *going* in an inner sense means living seems strange to anyone who does not know anything about spiritual life, but it is like the use of "setting out" to mean the pattern of life and the way it develops (§§1293, 4375, 4554, 4585), and the use of "traveling" to mean being taught and living by the teachings (§§1463, 2025, 3672). I could say why it is that going, setting out, and traveling have this symbolism, but the reason is not one that can be easily accepted by people who do not know how matters stand with movement in the other world. Movement and progress there are nothing but changes in the state of one's life, because they result from such changes. On the outside, these changes look exactly like movement from one place to another, as I can confirm by many experiences in the other world. In spirit I have walked with and among the inhabitants there through their myriad neighborhoods, even though my body stayed in one place. I have also discussed with them how this can happen and learned that changes in the state of one's life are what cause movement from place to place in the spiritual world. [3] One piece of confirmation was the fact that spirits, through changes of state brought on them, can appear high up and then instantly down low, or far off to the west and then instantly in the east, and so on. To repeat, though, this cannot help sounding strange to people who know nothing about life in the spiritual world. After all, there is no space or time there but states of life instead. These states produce the completely realistic outward appearance of progress and motion. The appearance is as vivid and real as the

appearance of life itself, in that life appears to us as though it resides in us and is therefore our own, when in reality it flows in from the Lord, the source of all life. See §§2021, 2658, 2706, 2886, 2887, 2888, 3001, 3318, 3337, 3338, 3484, 3619, 3741, 3742, 3743, 4151, 4249, 4318, 4319, 4320, 4417, 4523, 4524, 4882.

Since going and moving symbolize living, the ancients had the saying "*in God we move,* live, and have our being." By moving they meant the outer aspect of life; by living they meant its inner aspect; and by being they meant the inmost core.

Both we symbolizes the church's outer plane. This can be seen from the discussion in §5469 of the representation of Jacob's ten sons, *we* here, as the church's outer plane. **5606**

And you symbolizes its inner plane. This can be seen from the representation of Israel, *you,* as the church's inner plane (discussed at §§4286, 4292, 4570). **5607**

And our little children symbolizes what lay still deeper. This can be seen from the symbolism of *little children* as something within (§5604). Inner depths are symbolized by children and youths because both of these symbolize innocence, and innocence is a very deep thing. **5608**

Here is the situation in the heavens: The third or inmost heaven consists of people with innocence. They are devoted to love for the Lord, and since the Lord is innocence itself, the inhabitants there have innocence because they have love for him. Although they are the wisest of anyone in heaven, to others they look like children. Because of this, and because children have innocence, children in the Word symbolize innocence.

[2] Since innocence is the inmost core of the heavens, everyone in the heavens has to have innocence inside. The situation resembles the relationship of things that follow in sequence, on one hand, to things that coexist, on the other; or the relationship between entities separated from each other on different levels, and the entities that emerge from them. Everything that emerges together on the same level rises out of things that follow one another in sequence. When the ones that coexist emerge from the ones that follow in sequence, they place themselves in the same order they were previously in when they were separated on different levels.

For illustration, take goal, means, and result, which follow in sequence and are separate from each other. When these three emerge on the same level, they place themselves in the same order, the goal being inmost, the means next, and the result last. This result is where they coexist. If the result does not contain the means, and if the means does not contain the goal, it is not a result. If you remove the means from the result, you destroy the result, and more so if you remove the goal from the means. The goal causes the means to be a means, and the means causes the result to be a result.

[3] The situation is the same in the spiritual world. Just as goal, means, and result are distinct from each other, so love for the Lord, charity for one's neighbor, and charitable acts are distinct from each other in the spiritual world. When the three meld into one, or coexist, the first has to be contained in the second, and the second in the third. Unless charitable deeds contain a willing or heartfelt charity inside them, they are not deeds of charity, and unless charity contains love for the Lord inside it, it is not charity. If you take away what is inside, then, the outside collapses, because the outside develops from and is sustained by its inner levels in order.

The case is the same with innocence, which is inseparable from love for the Lord. Unless innocence resides within charity, it is not charity, so unless charity containing innocence resides within charitable acts, they are not acts of charity. That is why everyone in the heavens has to have innocence inside. [4] This fact, and the symbolism of children as innocence, can be seen in Mark:

> Jesus said to the disciples, "Allow the *little children* to come to me and do not stop them, because these are the kind who make up the kingdom of God. Truly, I say to you: anyone who does not accept the kingdom of God like a *little child* will not enter it." So taking them up into the curve of his arms, he put a hand on them and blessed them. (Mark 10:14, 15, 16; Luke 18:15, 16, 17; Matthew 18:3)

The little children plainly symbolize innocence, because they possess innocence, and the innocent in heaven appear as children. No one can go to heaven without having some innocence (see §4797). [5] Besides, children let themselves be governed by angels who embody innocence. They are not yet self-directed, as are adults, who govern themselves from their own judgment by their own will. The Lord's words in Matthew show that children allow themselves to be ruled by these angels:

> See that you not despise any of *these little ones*. For I say to you that *their angels in the heavens* always see the face of my Father. (Matthew 18:10)

No one can see the face of God except from innocence.

[6] Children symbolize innocence in the following passages as well. In Matthew:

> Out of the mouth of *children* and *nursing babies* you have perfected praise. (Matthew 21:16; Psalms 8:2)

In the same author:

> You have hidden this from the wise and understanding and revealed these things to *children*. (Matthew 11:25; Luke 10:21)

The innocence symbolized by little children is wisdom itself, because real innocence resides in wisdom (§§2305, 2306, 4797). That is why it says, "Out of the mouth of children and nursing babies you have perfected praise," and that such things have been revealed to children. [7] In Isaiah:

> The heifer and bear will pasture; together their offspring will lie down, and a *nursing baby will play over the viper's hole*. (Isaiah 11:7, 8)

This is about the Lord's kingdom and specifically about the state of peace and innocence there. The nursing baby stands for innocence. Nothing bad can happen to people with innocence, which is symbolized by "a nursing baby will play over the viper's hole." Vipers mean the most deceitful people there are. The whole chapter talks quite openly about the Lord. In Joel:

> Blow a horn in Zion, gather the people, consecrate the assembly, collect the old, gather the *children* and those *sucking breasts*. (Joel 2:15, 16)

The old stand for the wise, the children and those sucking breasts for the innocent.

[8] In the following passages too children mean innocence, but in this case innocence that has been destroyed. In Jeremiah:

> Why are you doing great evil against your own souls, in cutting off from yourselves man and woman, *child* and *nursing baby* in the middle of Judah, to prevent me from leaving you a remnant? (Jeremiah 44:7)

In the same author:

> Lift your hands to him over the soul of *your children,* who faint from hunger at the head of all the streets. (Lamentations 2:19)

In Ezekiel:

> Cross through Jerusalem and strike—and do not let your eye spare any, and do not exercise compassion—old person, young man and young woman, and *child*. (Ezekiel 9:5, 6)

In Micah:

> The matrons of my people you banish, each from the house of her pleasures; *from her children* they take away my honor forever. (Micah 2:9)

[9] However, children's innocence is merely outward, not inward, and since it is not inward, it cannot be combined with any wisdom, while the innocence of angels, especially in the third heaven, is inward and is therefore combined with wisdom (§§2305, 2306, 3494, 4563, 4797). We also were created in such a way that in old age, when we turn childlike, we would unite wise innocence with the naive innocence we had in childhood and therefore pass into the other life as a true child.

5609   *And I will be surety for him* means that it will be connected to him in the meanwhile. This can be seen from the symbolism of *being surety for someone* as standing in for that person, which is clear from the next words and especially from the speech Judah makes to Joseph in the next chapter, Genesis 44:32, 33, about his promise. Since being surety [for Benjamin] means standing in for him, it also means his going along with [Judah], connected to him.

5610   *From my hand you shall seek him* means that it will not be torn away, so far as this is within his power, as the following shows: A *hand* symbolizes power, as discussed in §§878, 3387, 4931–4937, 5327, 5328, 5544. "So far as this is within his power" is meant because that is as far as one can go in being surety for another, or guaranteeing that other's appearance. (The inner meaning lays out what the reality is and describes its nature.) And *seeking him* from [Judah] means not being torn away, because a person who is sought from another has to be attached inseparably to that other.

5611   *If I do not bring him to you and stand him before you* means that it will be entirely restored to the church. This can be seen from the symbolism of *bringing someone to him and standing that person before him* as entirely restoring [the person], and from the representation of Israel, to whom [Benjamin] was to be restored, as the church (discussed in §§3305, 4286, 5595).

I will be sinning against you all my days means that the goodness belonging to the church will no longer exist, as the following shows: Judah, who says this about himself, represents goodness in the church, as mentioned in §§5583, 5603. *Sinning* symbolizes disconnection, as discussed in §§5229, 5474. It therefore means that a thing will not exist, since what is disconnected from us ceases to exist with us. And *all my days* means ever, and consequently no longer.

The text says this because the goodness belonging to the church cannot exist without a middle ground between the inner and outer levels, as represented by Benjamin. Both the goodness and the truth belonging to the church flow from an inner level through the middle ground into the outer level, so if it is important for the kind of goodness belonging to the church to exist, it is just as important for a middle ground to exist. That is why Judah serves as surety for Benjamin.

These words of Judah mean that the goodness belonging to the church cannot exist without a middle ground, and Reuben's words [in the previous chapter] mean the same thing about the truth belonging to the church (§5542).

Because if we had not delayed symbolizes being stalled in a state of doubt. This can be seen from the symbolism of *delaying* as a state of doubt. Just as going, advancing, traveling, and emigrating symbolize a state of life (§5605), delaying symbolizes a state of doubt. When our life is in a hesitant state, our outer plane is in a state of delay. Our body actually illustrates this. When our mind becomes mired in doubt, we stop walking and consider. The reason is that doubt leaves us stuck and wavering in regard to our state of life and consequently in regard to our physical progress, which is the outward effect of our state.

If we had not delayed, then, clearly symbolizes being stalled in a state of doubt.

We would have returned these two times now means that there is outward and inward spiritual life, as the following shows: Going symbolizes living, as noted above at §5605, so *returning* means living as a result [of going]. The brothers went to Egypt to acquire grain, and grain symbolizes goodness based on truth, which is the source of spiritual life. And *these two times* has to do with life, so it symbolizes outward and inward life. The grain the brothers received the first time symbolized outward life, or life on the earthly plane, because they had no middle ground (as discussed in the previous chapter). The grain they receive this time, though, symbolizes inward life, because now they came with Benjamin, the middle ground (as discussed in this chapter and the next). That is why *we would have returned these two times now* symbolizes outward and inward spiritual life.

[2] This symbolism must seem strange, especially to people who know nothing about the spiritual dimension. After all, it does not seem as though returning these two times has anything at all in common with spiritual life, as symbolized, but that really is the inner meaning of the words.

If you will believe it, the inner thinking of a person dedicated to goodness grasps this, because inner thinking is awake to the inner meaning, even if the person is deeply ignorant of the fact during bodily life. The inner or spiritual meaning accessible to inner thinking filters down into matter-based and sense-based ideas without the person's awareness. Such ideas partake of time and space and of worldly phenomena, so it does not appear as though inner thinking works this way. Our inner thoughts, you see, are like angels' thoughts, because our spirit keeps company with angels.

[3] After death it becomes clear that the thinking of a person dedicated to goodness accords with the inner meaning. When we enter heaven, we immediately catch on to the inner meaning, without any training, which would never happen if our inner thoughts were not aware of that meaning while we are in the world. We are inwardly aware of it because there is correspondence between spiritual qualities and earthly ones, and the correspondence is such that nothing exists, no matter how small, that does not have some counterpart. Therefore, since the inner, rational mind of a person with goodness is in the spiritual world, and the person's outer, earthly mind is in the physical world, the conclusion is inescapable that both minds think. The inner mind thinks spiritually, and the outer mind thinks in an earthly way. What is spiritual filters down into what is earthly and together they form a unit through correspondence.

[4] The inner mind of a person whose ideas are called intuitive and are said to be immaterial does not base its thinking on the words of any language and therefore not on physical forms. This is evident to anyone capable of reflecting on it, since it can take such a person over an hour to express the thought of a single moment. People like this think in comprehensive terms that embrace numerous individual concepts. Intuitive, immaterial ideas are spiritual and—when the Word is being read—identical with the inner meaning. Nonetheless the thinker might be unaware of this fact, for the reason given above: that these spiritual

ideas flow into the earthly plane and generate earthly ideas. Spiritual ideas are consequently so invisible that the uninformed believe there is no spiritual plane, unless it is like the earthly one. In fact, they believe their spirit thinks in exactly the same manner as their body speaks. That is how deep a shadow the earthly dimension casts on the spiritual.

Genesis 43:11, 12, 13, 14. *And Israel their father said to them, "If so,* **5615** *then do this: Take some of the songworthiness of the land in your containers and take an offering down to the man: a bit of resin and a bit of honey, wax and stacte, terebinth nuts and almonds. And take double the silver in your hands. And the silver brought back in the mouth of your bags you are to return in your hand; maybe it was a mistake. And take your brother and get up and go back to the man. And God Shaddai grant you mercies before the man and send you your other brother and Benjamin. And I—however I am bereaved, I shall be bereaved."*

And Israel their father said to them symbolizes a perception received from spiritual goodness. *If so, then do this* means if events have to play out that way, so be it. *Take some of the songworthiness of the land in your containers* symbolizes the church's most outstanding qualities, as contained in religious truth. *And take an offering down to the man* means in order to win favor. *A bit of resin and a bit of honey* symbolizes truth-from-goodness on the outer earthly plane, and the pleasure that goes with it. *Wax and stacte* symbolizes truth-from-goodness on the inner earthly plane. *Terebinth nuts and almonds* symbolizes a good life corresponding to these kinds of truth. *And take double the silver in your hands* symbolizes truth received in potential. *And the silver brought back in the mouth of your bags you are to return in your hand* means that they had best submit as fully as possible by using the truth given them for free on the outer earthly level. *Maybe it was a mistake* means to keep him from turning against them. *And take your brother* means that they would accordingly have faith-inspired goodness. *And get up, go back to the man* symbolizes life supplied by spiritual truth. *And God Shaddai* symbolizes being comforted after their ordeals. *Grant you mercies before the man* means for spiritual truth to welcome you graciously. *And send you your other brother* means for it to grant you the goodness associated with faith. *And Benjamin* means and inner truth. *And I—however I am bereaved, I shall be bereaved* means that the church will essentially be deprived of its truth until all this happens.

Israel their father said to them symbolizes a perception received from **5616** spiritual goodness. This is established by the symbolism of *saying* in the

Word's narratives as a perception, and by the representation of *Israel* as spiritual goodness, both of them dealt with above in §5595. Israel is called a *father* because the different types of truth represented by his sons come from spiritual goodness as their father.

5617   *If so, then do this* means if events have to play out that way, so be it, as is self-evident.

5618   *Take some of the songworthiness of the land in your containers* symbolizes the church's most outstanding qualities, as contained in religious truth. This can be seen from the symbolism of *songworthiness* as outstanding qualities (discussed below), from that of the *land* as the church (discussed above at §5577), and from that of *containers* as religious truth (discussed at §§3068, 3079, 3316, 3318).

The term *songworthiness* is used because the word in the original language comes from one that means singing. The songworthiness of the land, then, means its well-sung, highly praised products and therefore, in an inner sense, the most outstanding qualities.

5619   *And take an offering down to the man* means in order to win favor. This can be seen from the symbolism of *presenting an offering to the man*—Joseph, the "lord of the land"—as an effort to win favor.

In the representative church of the ancients, and therefore in that of the Jews, it had been customary for people approaching judges and (later on) monarchs and priests to give them some gift. It was even commanded. This was because the offerings people gave those figures represented the kinds of things in us that we ought to offer the Lord when we turn to him. They are the offerings we make freely and consequently from our very selves. What we do freely comes from the heart, and what comes from the heart comes from the will, and what comes from the will comes from love and desire, and what comes from love and desire is free and therefore belongs to our very self (§§1947, 2870–2893, 3158). From this supply we must give the Lord an offering when we approach him. That is the kind of offering that was being represented. Monarchs represented the Lord's divine truth (§§1672, 2015, 2069, 3009, 3670, 4581, 4966, 5044), and priests represented his divine goodness (§§1728, 2015 at the end, 3670).

These gifts or offerings were a means of introduction (see §4262), and the point of an introduction is to win favor.

5620   *A bit of resin and a bit of honey* symbolizes truth-from-goodness on the outer earthly plane, and the pleasure that goes with it. This can be seen from the symbolism of *resin* as truth-from-goodness, or truth that develops out of goodness (discussed in §4748). Resin has this symbolism because it is an example of an ointment and of a perfume. Perfumes symbolize attributes associated with the truth that develops out of goodness, especially when they are also ointments and therefore have an oily nature, because oil symbolizes what is good (§§886, 3728, 4582).

This resin was a perfume (see Genesis 37:25), so the same word in the original language also means balsam. These substances are obviously ointments, or solid oils. That is why resin symbolizes truth-from-goodness on the earthly level. In this case it is on the outer earthly level, because this item comes first and is linked with honey, which means pleasure on that level.

Honey means pleasure because it is sweet, and everything sweet in the physical world corresponds to something pleasant and delightful in the spiritual world. It is being described as "the pleasure that goes with it"— with the truth that develops out of goodness, on the outer earthly level— because all truth has its pleasure, especially when it is based on goodness. The pleasure comes from our desire for that truth and consequently from its usefulness.

[2] The meaning of *honey* as pleasure can be seen from other scriptural passages as well, as in Isaiah:

> The virgin will conceive and deliver a child. And she will call his name Immanuel [God with us]. He will eat butter and *honey*, in order to know to spurn what is evil and choose what is good. (Isaiah 7:14, 15)

This is about the Lord. The butter stands for something heavenly, and the honey for an outgrowth of what is heavenly. [3] In the same author:

> It will happen, on account of the abundance of milk [they] make, that he will eat butter. And butter and *honey* are what everyone who is left in the middle of the land will eat. (Isaiah 7:22)

This is about the Lord's kingdom. The milk stands for spiritual goodness, the butter for heavenly goodness, and the honey for what results from them: happiness, delight, and pleasure. [4] In Ezekiel:

> So you were adorned in gold and silver. And your clothes were fine linen and silk and embroidery. Flour and *honey* and oil you ate, so that you became very, very beautiful and succeeded to royalty. With flour, oil, and *honey* I fed you. But you have put it before [your idols] for a restful smell. (Ezekiel 16:13, 19)

This is about Jerusalem, which means a spiritual religion. The passage depicts the nature this religion had among the ancients and the nature it later developed. Its adornment in gold and silver means its adornment in heavenly and spiritual goodness and truth. Its clothes of fine linen, silk, and embroidery stand for truth on the rational plane and on both earthly planes. The flour stands for what is spiritual, the honey for its appeal, and the oil for its goodness. Anyone can see that the details symbolize the kinds of things that belong to heaven. [5] In the same author:

> Judah and the land of Israel were your dealers in minnith wheat and pannag, and *honey* and oil, and balsam. (Ezekiel 27:17)

This is about Tyre, which symbolizes a spiritual religion, as it was to begin with and as it later became, specifically in regard to its knowledge of goodness and truth (§1201). Here again honey stands for the delight and pleasure yielded by a desire to know and learn about heavenly and spiritual goodness and truth. [6] In Moses:

> He makes them ride onto the heights of the earth and feeds them with the produce of the fields; he makes them suck *honey from a crag,* and oil from a boulder of rock. (Deuteronomy 32:13)

This too is about the ancient spiritual church. Sucking honey from a crag stands for gaining pleasure from truth in the form of knowledge. [7] In David:

> I feed them from the fat of the wheat, and with *honey from the rock* I satisfy them. (Psalms 81:16)

Satisfying them with honey from the rock stands for satisfying people with pleasure from religious truth. [8] In Deuteronomy:

> Jehovah is bringing you to a good land; a land of rivers of water, springs, and gulfs issuing from the valley and from the mountain; a land of wheat and barley, and grapevine and fig, and pomegranate; a land of olive oil and *honey.* (Deuteronomy 8:7, 8)

This is about the land of Canaan, and in an inner sense, about the Lord's kingdom in the heavens. A land of olive oil and honey stands for spiritual goodness and its delight. [9] Of course the land of Canaan is also called a land flowing with *milk* and *honey* (Numbers 13:27; 14:7, 8; Deuteronomy 26:9, 15; 27:3; Jeremiah 11:5; 32:22; Ezekiel 20:6). As just mentioned, the land of Canaan in an inner sense means the Lord's kingdom. Its flowing with milk stands for an abundance of heavenly-spiritual qualities, and with honey, for a resulting abundance of happiness and pleasure. [10] In David:

> The judgments of Jehovah are truth; they are fair in their entirety, desirable above gold and above a large amount of pure gold, and *sweet above honey* and the *dripping of honeycombs*. (Psalms 19:9, 10)

The judgments of Jehovah stand for divine truth. "Sweet above honey and the dripping of honeycombs" stands for the pleasure afforded by what is good and the delight afforded by truth. In the same author:

> Sweet to my palate are your words; *above honey* to my mouth. (Psalms 119:103)

The same is true here.

[11] The manna that the descendants of Jacob used for bread in the wilderness is described this way in Moses:

> The manna was like coriander seed, white, and its taste like that of a *cake kneaded with honey.* (Exodus 16:31)

Manna symbolized divine truth, which comes down from the Lord through heaven, so it symbolized the Lord himself in his divine humanity, as he teaches in John 6:51, 58. The Lord's divine humanity is the source of all divine truth and indeed the subject of all divine truth. That being so, the pleasure and delight of manna is depicted by its taste, which was like that of a cake kneaded with honey. Taste means the pleasure of goodness and the appeal of truth; see §3502.

[12] John the Baptist represented the Lord as the Word—which is divine truth on the earth—as Elijah also had (§§2762, 5247 at the end). As a result, he was the Elijah who was to come ahead of the Lord (Malachi 4:5; Matthew 17:10, 11, 12; Mark 9:11, 12, 13; Luke 1:17). Accordingly there was symbolic meaning to his clothing and sustenance, which are described in Matthew:

> John had his clothing of camel's hair and a leather belt around his hips. His sustenance was locusts and *field honey.* (Matthew 3:4; Mark 1:6)

Clothing of camel's hair symbolized the Word and the earthly nature of the truth contained in the Word's literal meaning, which clothes its inner meaning. Both hair and camels symbolize what is earthly. And sustenance consisting of locusts and field honey symbolized the Word and the nature of the goodness contained in its literal meaning. Field honey symbolizes the pleasure of the literal meaning.

[13] In Ezekiel, honey depicts the pleasure to be found in divine truth's outer meaning:

> He said to me, "Son of humankind, feed your stomach and fill your belly with this scroll that I am giving you." And when I had eaten it, *in my mouth it was like honey for sweetness.* (Ezekiel 3:3)

And in John:

> The angel said to me, "Take the little book and eat it up. It will indeed make your stomach bitter, *but in your mouth it will be sweet like honey.*" So I took the little book from the angel's hand and ate it up, and *in my mouth* it was *like honey, sweet,* but when I had eaten it, my stomach turned bitter. Then he said to me, "It is necessary for you again to prophesy over many peoples and nations and tongues and monarchs." (Revelation 10:9, 10, 11)

The scroll in Ezekiel and the little book in John stand for divine truth. The fact that their flavor was sweet like honey means that divine truth is appealing on the outside. Divine truth, like the Word, is pleasant in its outward form, or literal meaning, because it allows itself to be explained and interpreted in anyone's favor. Not so the inner meaning, which is therefore symbolized by a bitter flavor, because it exposes our inner depths. The outer meaning gives pleasure because as just mentioned its statements can be explained in a biased way. It contains only general truth, and generalizations are open to interpretation until their nature is determined by particulars, whose nature has been determined by the smallest details. Another reason for the appeal of the outer meaning is that it is earthly and conceals something spiritual inside. What is more, it *has* to be appealing if we are to accept it—in other words, if we are to be enticed into it and not put off at the very threshold.

[14] The bees' honeycomb and roasted fish the Lord ate among the disciples after his resurrection also symbolized the Word's outer meaning. The fish symbolized the truth there, and the bees' honeycomb symbolized the delight to be had in it. Here is how Luke tells it:

> Jesus said, "Do you have something to eat here?" They gave him a piece of roasted fish and some bees' honeycomb, and taking it, he ate it in front of them. (Luke 24:41, 42, 43)

That being the symbolism, the Lord also says to them,

> These are the words that I spoke to you while I was still with you: that everything that has been written in the Law of Moses and the Prophets and the Psalms concerning me had to be fulfilled. (Luke 24:44)

It does not look as though this could have been the meaning, since the fact that the disciples had a piece of roasted fish and bees' honeycomb appears accidental; but it was providential. Not only this incident but all others in the Word were providential, down to the smallest circumstances of all. Because such things were being symbolized, the Lord talked about what was written concerning him in the Word. However, what was written about the Lord in the literal meaning of the Old Testament Word is meager. What the inner meaning holds is complete. That is what gives the Word its holiness. These are the ideas meant by the statement that everything that had been written in the Law of Moses and the Prophets and the Psalms concerning the Lord had to be fulfilled.

[15] From this discussion you can now see that honey symbolizes the pleasure afforded by goodness and truth, or by the desire for them, and that in particular it symbolizes outward pleasure, or pleasure on the outer earthly plane. This pleasure by its very nature comes from the world by way of the senses, so it has a great deal of worldly love in it. On that account, the use of honey in minhas was forbidden, as is said in Leviticus:

> No minha that you bring to Jehovah shall be made with yeast. For there shall be no yeast and *no honey* from which you would burn a fire offering to Jehovah. (Leviticus 2:11)

The honey stands for this outward pleasure. Because it contains some worldly love, it was equivalent to yeast, so it was forbidden. For the meaning of yeast, or leavened food, see §2342.

Wax and stacte symbolizes truth-from-goodness on the inner earthly plane. This can be seen from the symbolism of *wax*—aromatic wax, in this case—as the truth that comes of goodness (discussed below) and from that of *stacte* also as truth growing out of goodness (discussed at §4748). It is on the inner earthly plane because these perfumes are purer than resin and honey and are therefore named second. The Word lists items like this in order.

Wax here does not mean ordinary wax but aromatic wax, which is like a fragrant gum. This wax is meant by the term used in the original language, which also means perfume. It is evident, then, why this aromatic wax symbolizes truth that comes of goodness. On an inner level, all perfumes symbolize truth that comes of goodness, because they smell good. The connection can be seen from the fact that truth growing out of goodness triggers as wonderful a sensation in heaven as sweet fragrances do in the world. Consequently, when angels' perceptions turn into scents, which happens often, in the Lord's good pleasure, they smell like perfumes and flowers. That is why frankincense and other kinds of incense were made from substances with a pleasing odor and used for sacred purposes. It is also why perfumes were mixed into the anointing oil. Anyone who does not realize that such measures trace their origin to sensations in heaven is likely to think they were commanded merely to enhance people's outward worship, but then there would be nothing heavenly, nothing holy in the practice. As a result, this means of worship would have nothing divine in it.

See what has already been shown on this subject: Frankincense, other kinds of incense, and the scents in the anointing oil represented spiritual and heavenly qualities (§4748). Auras of faith and love turn into pleasing smells; and for this reason, pleasant, sweet, perfumelike smells symbolize the true ideas of faith that spring from a loving goodness (§§1514, 1517, 1518, 1519, 4628).

5622 *Terebinth nuts and almonds* symbolizes a good life corresponding to these kinds of truth, as the following shows: *Terebinth nuts* symbolize a good life corresponding to truth-from-goodness on the outer earthly plane (symbolized by the resin), as discussed below. And *almond* trees symbolize a good life corresponding to truth-from-goodness on the inner earthly plane (symbolized by the aromatic wax and stacte).

These nuts have such a symbolism because nuts are the fruit of a plant, and in the Word, fruits symbolize deeds. The fruit of useful trees symbolizes good deeds, which is to say a good life, since the useful aspect of goodness in life is good deeds.

Terebinth nuts symbolize a good life corresponding to truth-from-goodness on the outer earthly plane because they come from the lowlier tree [of the two], and comparatively superficial attributes are symbolized by lowlier objects. This is because what lies on the outside is inherently coarser than what lies on the inside, since it consists in a whole conglomeration of inner elements.

[2] *Almonds* symbolize a good life corresponding to truth-from-goodness on the inner earthly plane because the almond is the nobler

tree. The tree itself, on a spiritual level, symbolizes a perception of the inner truth that rises out of goodness. Its flower symbolizes this kind of truth, and its fruit symbolizes a good life stemming from it. That is the sense in which an almond is mentioned in Jeremiah:

> The word of Jehovah came, saying, "What do you see, Jeremiah?" and I said, "A *staff of almond* I see." Then Jehovah said to me, "You did a good job of seeing, because I am keeping watch over my word, to do it." (Jeremiah 1:11, 12)

The staff stands for power. The almond (tree) stands for a perception of inner truth, and since it is being associated with Jehovah, it stands for his watchfulness over that truth. His word stands for the truth.

[3] The almonds that flowered from Aaron's staff for the tribe of Levi also symbolize neighborly kindness, or goodness in life. Moses speaks of them this way:

> It happened the next day, when Moses entered the meeting tent, that look! Aaron's staff had budded for Levi's tribe and had put out a flower to bloom a bloom and bear *almonds.* (Numbers 17:8)

This was a sign that the tribe of Levi had been chosen for the priesthood because it symbolized neighborly love (§§3875, 3877, 4497, 4502, 4503), which is the essential element of a spiritual religion.

And take double the silver in your hands symbolizes truth received in potential, as the following shows: *Silver* symbolizes truth, as discussed at §§1551, 2954. *Double* symbolizes what comes next in sequence, as discussed at §1335—namely, the truth they had received for free, as a gift, and the truth they would again receive as a gift. And *hands* symbolize power, [or potential,] as discussed at §§878, 3387, 4931–4937, 5327, 5328.

5623

Truth in potential is truth capable of being accepted and therefore truth in proportion to that capability. The capacity or potential for accepting truth depends entirely on goodness, though. The Lord connects the capacity with goodness, because when he flows into us with goodness, he also flows in with that capacity. Truth received in potential, then, is truth in proportion to goodness.

A great deal of experience in the other world has shown me that the ability to accept truth depends on goodness. People with goodness there have the ability not only to perceive what is true but also to accept it, and their ability depends on the amount and nature of the goodness they have. People with evil, on the other hand, have no ability to accept truth.

This ability or inability results from pleasure and therefore from desire. People with goodness find pleasure in using truth to improve the goodness they have, because goodness takes its quality from truth. As a consequence they desire truth. People with evil, though, find pleasure in evil and in using falsity to justify it. As a consequence they desire falsity, and since they do, they loathe truth. That is why they have no ability to accept truth. They reject, smother, or corrupt it as soon as it reaches their ear or enters their thoughts.

What is more, everyone of sound mind has the ability to receive truth, but people who resort to evil extinguish the ability, while those who resort to goodness heighten it.

5624 *And the silver brought back in the mouth of your bags you are to return in your hand* means that they had best submit as fully as possible by using the truth given them for free on the outer earthly level, as the following shows: The *silver brought back* symbolizes truth given for free, as noted at §5530. *In the mouth of the bag* means on the threshold of the outer earthly level, as noted at §5497. And *in one's hand* means in one's power, as noted just above in §5623, so it means as much as possible. The fact that they had best submit by using that truth is symbolized by the request that they *return* the silver. In the spiritual world, to return truth to the Lord from whom one has received it for free means to submit oneself [to him] by using it. The brothers' conversation with the man who was over Joseph's household in verses 18–24, though, shows the manner in which they submitted themselves by using that truth.

5625 *Maybe it was a mistake* means to keep him from turning against them. This can be seen from the symbolism of a *mistake* as something adverse. The mistake they mean is the kind they would have committed if they had forgotten to hand over the silver and had therefore taken it home again, each in his sack. Joseph could have turned against them on that grounds, and they believed he had. After all, they were afraid because they had been brought to Joseph's house, and they said, "Over the matter of the silver taken back in our bags at first we are being brought. [They mean] to roll down on us and to throw themselves on us and to take us as slaves, and our donkeys" (verse 18).

Besides, sin symbolizes disconnection and opposition (§§5229, 5474), so a mistake, if there is sin in it, symbolizes the same thing on a smaller scale. That is the reason for saying "to keep him from turning against them."

5626 *And take your brother* means that they would accordingly have faith-inspired goodness. This can be seen from the representation of Simeon, the *brother* they were to *take,* as faith that belongs to the will (discussed at §§3869, 3870, 3871, 3872, 4497, 4502, 4503, 5482) and therefore as faith-inspired goodness. When the truth taught by faith passes over into the will, it becomes the goodness urged by faith, because it is passing over into a person's life, where it is regarded not as something to know but as something to do. As a result it alters its essential nature and becomes applied truth. So it is no longer called truth but goodness.

And get up, go back to the man symbolizes life supplied by spiritual truth, as the following shows: *Getting up* symbolizes elevation to inner levels and consequently to spiritual ones, as discussed in §§2401, 2785, 2912, 2927, 3171, 4103, 4881. *Going back* symbolizes the resulting life, as mentioned in §5614. And Joseph, when he is called the *man,* represents spiritual truth, as mentioned in §5584.

5627

And God Shaddai symbolizes being comforted after their ordeals. This can be seen from the symbolism of *Shaddai* as trials and being comforted after trials (discussed in §§1992, 4572). Here, then, it symbolizes being comforted after the ordeals they suffered in Egypt. The words that follow seamlessly after this—"grant you mercies before the man"—also show that it means comfort after their ordeals.

5628

The reason *Shaddai* symbolizes trials and comfort after trials is that the ancients designated the one God by various names according to what came from him, in all its variety. They believed trials were one of the things that came from him, so in trying times they referred to God as Shaddai. By that name they did not mean another god, only the one God in relation to hardships. When the ancient church went downhill, though, its people started to worship as many gods as there were names for the one God, and they added more of their own. The number of gods finally grew so large that each clan had its own, and the people of that clan made their god completely separate from any other god worshiped by others. [2] The family of Terah, to which Abraham belonged, worshiped Shaddai as its god (see §§1356, 1992, 2559, 3667), so not only Abraham but also Jacob recognized Shaddai as his god, and the same was true in the land of Canaan. The practice was tolerated in them, though, so that they would not be forced to give up their religious tradition—since no one is forced to give up what is sacred to her or him. Because the ancients used the name to mean Jehovah himself, or the Lord, whom they called Shaddai when they were undergoing crises, Jehovah (the Lord) took this name with Abraham (as is plain from Genesis 17:1) and with Jacob (Genesis 35:11).

Shaddai symbolizes consolation as well as trials because all spiritual challenges are followed by consolation. This I have had the opportunity of learning from experience in the other world. The inhabitants there suffer ordeals at the hands of evil spirits, who harass them, goad them into evil, and persuade them of falsity. Afterward, though, when the evil spirits have been removed, the sufferers are received by angels and are led into a state of solace by pleasures suited to their disposition.

5629   *Grant you mercies before the man* means for spiritual truth to welcome you graciously. This can be seen from the symbolism of *granting mercies* as welcoming graciously and from the representation of Joseph as spiritual truth, when he is being called the *man* (as above in §5627).

5630   *And send you your other brother* means for it to grant you the goodness associated with faith. This can be seen from the representation of Simeon, the *other brother*, as faith-inspired goodness (as above in §5626).

Sending means granting here because one speaks of sending a person but of granting the attribute symbolized by the person.

5631   *And Benjamin* means and inner truth. This is established by the discussion above in §5600 of the representation of *Benjamin* as inner truth.

5632   *And I—however I am bereaved, I shall be bereaved* means that the church will be deprived of its truth until all this happens. This can be seen from the representation of Israel—who says this about himself— as the church (discussed at §§3305, 4286) and from the symbolism of *being bereaved* as being deprived of truth known to the church (discussed at §5536).

Obviously that is how matters will stand until all the above happens. If there is no faith-inspired goodness, represented by Simeon (§5630), and no inner truth to serve as a middle ground, represented by Benjamin, the church has no truth—except for the kind that lies only on the lips rather than in the heart.

5633   Genesis 43:15, 16, 17. *And the men took this offering, and double the silver they took in their hand, and Benjamin, and got up and went down to Egypt and stood before Joseph. And Joseph saw Benjamin with them and said to the one who was over his household, "Bring the men to the house, and slaughter abundantly and prepare [the meat], because the men will eat with me at noon." And the man did as Joseph said and brought the men to Joseph's house.*

And the men took the offering means that truth had in it the where-withal to obtain favor. *And double the silver they took in their hand* means and truth received in potential. *And Benjamin* means and a middle ground. *And got up and went down to Egypt* symbolizes being promoted to acquiring life from the inner depths of knowledge. *And stood before Joseph* symbolizes the presence of spiritual heavenliness there. *And Joseph saw Benjamin with them* symbolizes a perception by spiritual heavenliness that truth had brought with it a spiritual middle ground. *And said to the one who was over his household* means to something in the outward part of the church. *Bring the men to the house* means that earthly-level truth should be introduced there. *And slaughter abundantly and prepare [the meat]* means through goodness on the outer earthly plane. *Because the men will eat with me at noon* means that union with them will be achieved, now that they have the middle ground with them. *And the man did as Joseph said* symbolizes execution of the plan. *And the man brought the men to Joseph's house* symbolizes being introduced for the first time into the goodness that comes of spiritual heavenliness.

And the men took this offering means that truth had in it the where- **5634** withal to obtain favor. This is established by the symbolism of *men* as truth (discussed at §3134) and by that of an *offering* given when approaching monarchs and priests as an effort to win favor (discussed at §5619).

And double the silver they took in their hand means and truth received **5635** in potential. This can be seen from the remarks above in §5623, where the same words occur. Review the same section to see what is meant by truth received in potential.

And Benjamin means and a middle ground. This can be seen from **5636** the discussion in §§5411, 5413, 5443 of the representation of *Benjamin* as a middle ground.

And got up and went down to Egypt symbolizes being promoted to **5637** acquiring life from the inner depths of knowledge, as the following shows: *Getting up* symbolizes elevation to the realm of spiritual life, as discussed in §§2401, 2785, 2912, 2927, 3171, 4103, 4881. *Going down* symbolizes the endeavor to acquire life. In this case, going down means the same thing as the earlier words "Send the youth with me and we will get up and go and live and not die" (verse 8), which symbolize spiritual life in its different degrees, as discussed in §5605. And *Egypt* symbolizes knowledge, as discussed in §§1164, 1165, 1186, 1462, 4749, 4964, 4966. Here it symbolizes the inner depths of knowledge because that is where the spiritual heavenliness represented by Joseph resides. For this reason the text directly afterward says, "And they stood before Joseph."

The inner depths of knowledge are spiritual concepts on the earthly level. Spiritual concepts exist on the earthly level when the items of knowledge there have been lit with heaven's light, and they are lit with heaven's light when we believe what the Word teaches, and we believe this when we devote ourselves to neighborly kindness. Under these circumstances, neighborly kindness serves as a flame that sheds light on true ideas and therefore on what we know. This is where true ideas and knowledge acquire their spiritual light.

This shows what is meant by the inner depths of knowledge.

5638   *And stood before Joseph* symbolizes the presence of spiritual heavenliness there. This can be seen from the symbolism of *standing before someone* as presence and from the representation of *Joseph* as spiritual heavenliness (discussed many times before). The presence of spiritual heavenliness on both earthly levels was represented by Joseph's being made lord over all Egypt. That is what is meant by the presence of spiritual heavenliness in the inner depths of knowledge, since knowledge exists on the earthly plane. Concerning the dominion of heavenliness over both earthly levels, see §§5316, 5324, 5326, 5327, 5328, 5333, 5337. The truth represented by Joseph's ten brothers is truth on the earthly plane.

5639   *And Joseph saw Benjamin with them* symbolizes a perception by spiritual heavenliness that truth had brought with it a spiritual middle ground, as the following shows: *Seeing* means understanding and perceiving, as discussed at §§2150, 2807, 3764, 4567, 4723, 5400. Jacob's ten sons, the ones *with whom* Joseph saw Benjamin, represent truth on the earthly plane, as discussed at §§5403, 5419, 5427, 5458, 5512. And *Benjamin* represents a middle ground, as discussed at §§5411, 5413, 5443. It is being called a spiritual middle ground because the truth represented by Jacob's ten sons was now to unite with truth from the Divine (Joseph) and that union requires a middle ground that is spiritual. As a consequence, at the point where this middle ground has been noticed, the text immediately goes on to say, "Joseph said to the man over his household, 'Bring the men to the house, and slaughter abundantly and prepare [the meat], because the men will eat with me at noon.'" These words mean that [truth] would be introduced and united because it had a middle ground with it.

[2] I need to go a little further in explaining what the spiritual dimension is in relation to the earthly one, because most people in the Christian

world do not know what spirituality is. In fact, when they hear the term they balk and say to themselves, "No one knows what 'spiritual' means."

In its essence, the spiritual dimension with us is a genuine desire for what is good and true for its own sake, not for selfish reasons, and a desire for what is just and fair for its own sake, not for selfish reasons. If these qualities give us a feeling of pleasure and delight, and especially if they leave us feeling fortunate and blessed, it is something spiritual in us. It does not come from the physical world but from the spiritual world, or heaven—that is, through heaven from the Lord.

This is the spiritual dimension, then, and when it reigns supreme in us, it affects and touches everything we think, will, and do. It gives a spiritual cast to our thoughts and the deeds of our will. Eventually, when we pass from the physical to the spiritual world, it causes thought, will, and deed to be spiritual in us.

In short, spirituality is a desire for charity and faith, or goodness and truth. It is also a pleasure and delight and more particularly a sense of good fortune and blessing from those qualities which is sensed deep within us and which makes us true Christians.

[3] Most people in the Christian world do not know what the spiritual plane is because they make faith rather than neighborly love the essential ingredient of religion. Even the few who are [not] obsessed with faith think little if at all about neighborly love or know what it is. Consequently, because there is no knowledge, there is also no awareness of the feeling. People who do not sense a feeling of love for others cannot possibly know what the spiritual plane is. This is especially true now, when hardly anyone has any neighborly love, because these are the church's final days.

It is important, though, to know that "spiritual" in its *broad* sense means a desire for both goodness and truth, which is why heaven is called the spiritual world and why the Word's inner meaning is called the spiritual sense. More strictly speaking, anything connected with a desire for goodness is called heavenly, while anything connected with a desire for truth is called spiritual.

And said to the one who was over his household means to something in the outward part of the church. This can be seen from the representation of *one who is over a household* as the outward part of the church, since one who is *in* a house is the inward part (discussed at §1795). Inner meaning has to do not with a person but with some subject matter (§§5225, 5287,

5640

5434), so one who is over a household symbolizes something in the outward part of the church.

5641   *Bring the men to the house* means that earthly-level truth should be introduced there. This can be seen from the symbolism of Jacob's sons as religious truth on the earthly plane (discussed in §§5403, 5419, 5427, 5458, 5512). *Bring them to the house* means that it should be introduced there.

5642   *And slaughter abundantly and prepare [the meat]* means through goodness on the outer earthly plane. This can be seen from the symbolism of *slaughtering*—which includes the animal slaughtered, such as an ox, young ox, goat, or other domesticated animal—as goodness on the earthly plane. An adult ox and a young ox symbolize goodness on the earthly plane (see §§2180, 2566, 2781, 2830), and here they symbolize goodness on the outer earthly plane, because [earthly truth] was being now initiated into union for the first time by means of that goodness. After all, "he brought the men to Joseph's house" symbolizes being initiated for the first time into the goodness that comes of spiritual heavenliness; see below at §5645. Since a young ox and an adult ox symbolized goodness on the earthly level, the whole process symbolized that kind of goodness. The one included the other.

5643   *Because the men will eat with me at noon* means that union with them will be achieved, now that they have the middle ground with them. This can be seen from the symbolism of *eating* as being communicated, united, and adopted (discussed in §§2187, 2343, 3168, 3513 at the end, 3596, 3832). Because they had the spiritual middle ground that was Benjamin with them (§5639), the verse says *at noon*. Noon symbolizes a state of light and therefore a spiritual state, which comes by way of a middle ground (§§1458, 3708).

5644   *And the man did as Joseph said* symbolizes execution of the plan, as is clear without explanation.

5645   *And the man brought the men to Joseph's house* symbolizes being introduced for the first time into the goodness that comes of spiritual heavenliness, as the following shows: *Bringing* symbolizes introduction, as above at §5641. Jacob's sons symbolize religious truth on the earthly level, as discussed at §§5403, 5419, 5427, 5428, 5512. A *house* symbolizes goodness, as discussed at §§3652, 3720, 4982, so it also symbolizes the church (§3720), since goodness makes the church a church. And *Joseph* represents spiritual heavenliness, as discussed many times before. *The man brought the men to Joseph's house,* then, plainly means that truth on the earthly level was introduced into the goodness that comes of spiritual heavenliness.

A first introduction is being symbolized because at this point they did not recognize Joseph but only ate with him. This symbolizes a general bond, and a general bond is a first introduction, in which truth flows in from the Divine in a general way without being recognized. When truth's inflow is perceived, a second bond forms, and this bond is symbolized by Joseph's revealing himself to his brothers, as told in the chapter after next, Genesis 45.

Genesis 43:18, 19, 20, 21, 22, 23. *And the men were afraid because they* **5646** *had been brought to Joseph's house, and they said, "Over the matter of the silver taken back in our bags at first we are being brought. [They mean] to roll down on us and to throw themselves on us and to take us as slaves, and our donkeys." And they went up to the man who was over Joseph's household and spoke to him in the doorway of the house. And they said, "Upon my life, my lord; we did indeed come down at first to buy food. And it happened when we came to the inn that we opened our bags, and here, each one's silver in the mouth of his bag—our silver in its weight! And we are returning it in our hand. And other silver we have brought down in our hand to buy food; we do not know who put our silver in our bags." And he said, "Peace to you; don't be afraid. Your God and the God of your father gave you a secret gift in your bags; your silver came to me." And he brought Simeon out to them.*

And the men were afraid symbolizes a recoiling. *Because they had been brought to Joseph's house* means that truth on the earthly level would be connected with the inner dimension and made subordinate to it. *And they said, "Over the matter of the silver taken back in our bags at first we are being brought,"* means that because truth given for free is appearing on the outer earthly plane, they would be put in a subordinate position. *[They mean] to roll down on us and to throw themselves on us* means that for this reason they would be subjected to absolute authority. *And to take us as slaves, and our donkeys* means to the point where nothing on either earthly plane has any consequence. *And they went up to the man who was over Joseph's household* symbolizes the church's doctrines. *And spoke to him in the doorway of the house* means turning to them for advice about entering. *And they said, "Upon my life, my lord,"* symbolizes testimony. *We did indeed come down at first to buy food* symbolizes an intent to acquire goodness on behalf of truth. *And it happened when we came to the inn that we opened our bags* symbolizes examination of the outer earthly level. *And here, each one's silver in the mouth of his bag* symbolizes an awareness that the truth had seemingly been given for free. *Our silver in its weight* symbolizes truth to match every individual's state. *And we are returning it in our hand* means that what had been given for free is being surrendered as much as possible. *And other silver we have brought down in our hand to buy food* means that the intent is to acquire goodness through truth from other sources. *We do not know who put our silver in our bags* symbolizes a lack of faith due to ignorance about the source of the truth on the outer earthly plane. *And he said, "Peace to you; don't be afraid,"* means all is well; they should not despair. *Your God and the God of your father* symbolizes the Lord's divine humanity. *Gave you a secret gift in your bags* means that it comes from him without any use of their prudence. *Your silver came to me* means that it will seem as though they acquired their own truth. *And he brought Simeon out to them* means that he connected the will with truth.

5647   *And the men were afraid* symbolizes a recoiling. This can be seen from the symbolism of *being afraid* here as a recoiling—a recoiling from union with the inner plane. Fear rises out of various causes, such as threats to one's life and the danger of financial loss or loss of rank and reputation. Then there is the fear of falling into some kind of slavery, losing one's freedom, and losing all pleasure in life along with it. That is the theme of the following verses. The men were afraid of any connection with the inner plane, which they feared would cost them their autonomy, and with their autonomy their freedom, and with their freedom all pleasure in life— since pleasure in life depends on freedom. That is why *the men were afraid* symbolizes a recoiling from the connection.

[2] Here at the outset a few words need to be said about this union, the union of the outer, earthly self with the inner, spiritual self. Our outer, earthly self is in control from the earliest stage of our life, and we do not know the inner, spiritual self exists. When we reform, therefore, and start to change from superficial, earthly people into deep, spiritual people, our earthly part at first rebels. This is because we learn that our earthly self needs to be yoked—in other words, that all our cravings have to be rooted out, along with any justifications. Left to its own devices, our earthly self thinks this will annihilate us, because it is fully convinced that the earthly dimension is everything. It has no idea whatever of the boundless, indescribable realities on the spiritual plane. When the earthly self thinks this way, it recoils and refuses to be subordinated to what is spiritual. That is what is symbolized here by fear.

5648   *Because they had been brought to Joseph's house* means that truth on the earthly level would be connected with the inner dimension and made subordinate to it. This can be seen from the symbolism of *being brought* *to Joseph's house* as being united with the inner dimension and made subordinate to it. *Joseph,* you see, represents the inner dimension, because he represents truth from the Divine, or spiritual heavenliness, as discussed in §§5307, 5331, 5332, 5417, 5469. A *house* symbolizes both our inner and our outer part (§§3128, 3538, 4973, 5023). This time it symbolizes the inner part, because it is said to be Joseph's house. And *being brought* to the inner dimension means being connected, and because it means being connected, it means being made subordinate. The reason is that the earthly level becomes subordinate to the inner level when connected to it, because the controlling power that used to belong to the earthly self then passes to the spiritual self. This controlling power will be discussed below, by the Lord's divine mercy.

[2] I need to explain briefly about inner meaning. The Word's inner meaning is mainly for the inhabitants of the other world. When they are present with someone on earth who is reading the Word, they perceive what is read according to its inner meaning, not its outer meaning. They do not understand any human words, only the meaning of the words, which they understand in terms of their own spiritual thoughts rather than people's earthly thoughts. The earthly meaning that the person takes from the reading instantly changes into this kind of spiritual meaning. It is like a person who turns what others are saying in their language into his or her own different language, which happens quickly. In the same way, the earthly meaning, couched in human thought, turns into a spiritual meaning. Spiritual language or speech is the angels' language, while earthly language is ours. The sudden transformation of one "language" into the other is due to the correspondence of everything in the physical world with something in the spiritual.

[3] Now since the Word's inner meaning is mainly for the spiritual world's inhabitants, the inner meaning here takes up the types of subjects that they benefit from, that they delight and revel in. The deeper such subjects are, the further beyond our grasp they are. We delight and revel only in worldly and bodily pleasures and therefore consider the spiritual subjects of the inner meaning worthless and tiresome. Look to see within yourself whether you do not grow sick and tired of the inner-level contents of the next few verses, even though they are the most delightful subjects possible for angelic communities. As you reflect you will be able to tell the difference between human and angelic pleasures. You will also be able to tell where angels pinpoint wisdom and where people do. Angels identify wisdom with ideas that we hold cheap and loathe. We identify

wisdom with ideas in which angels have no interest, and many of us identify it with ideas that angels reject and avoid.

5649   *And they said, "Over the matter of the silver taken back in our bags we are being brought,"* means that because truth given for free is appearing on the outer earthly plane, they would be put in a subordinate position. This can be seen from the symbolism of *silver taken back* as truth given for free (discussed at §§5530, 5624), from that of a *bag* as the threshold of the outer earthly plane (discussed at §5497), and from that of *being brought* as being connected and made subordinate (discussed just above at §5648).

[2] Here is the situation: [The truths meant by the brothers] perceived that truth in the form of knowledge had been given for free on the outer earthly plane and that they were therefore being invited to unite with the inner plane and accordingly to place themselves under its control. As mentioned just above [§5647], they felt that this would rob them of their freedom and consequently of all pleasure in life.

Human beings have absolutely no idea that this is so—that there can be any perception that truth in the form of knowledge is given for free, and given on the earthly plane, whether outer or inner. This is because we have no perception of it ourselves. We know nothing at all about what is given to us for free, let alone what is stored away in our outer and inner earthly planes. The overarching reason we do not perceive it is that worldly and earthly concerns matter to us and heavenly and spiritual concerns do not. As a result, we do not believe in any inflow from the Lord through heaven, so we never think of ourselves as receiving gifts. The reality, though, is that whenever we draw truth as a rational conclusion based on some information, thinking we have done so by our own power, it is actually a gift we have received. Still less are we able to perceive whether this truth has been deposited in our outer or our inner earthly level. That is because we do not realize that our earthly level is twofold, consisting in an outer part that edges up to the physical senses and an inner part that pulls away from them to turn in rationality's direction. [3] Since we are ignorant on both scores, we can have no perception of either. We have to know about a thing before we can perceive it.

Angelic communities have clear and accurate knowledge and perception on both scores. They can tell not only what is given them for free but also where it is located, as the following experience demonstrates: When spirits enter an angelic community (which they can do if they are governed by goodness), they also come into all the knowledge and understanding that community possesses, although they had not had access to it before. While there, they have no idea they had not already acquired the knowledge and understanding on their own, but when they stop to reflect, they can tell it is being given to them for free by the Lord through the angelic community. They also know from the angelic community just where they are, whether on the outer or inner earthly level, because some angelic communities are on the outer and some on the inner. However, their earthly level is not like ours. It is a spiritual earthly level, which became spiritual through union with the spiritual level and subordination to it.

[4] These remarks show that the circumstances mentioned in the inner meaning here actually occur as such in the other world; the inhabitants there can tell what is given to them for free and where it is stored. People on earth today know nothing about it, but in ancient times, people in the church did have the information, taught them by their arts and sciences and their doctrines. They were people with depth, but ever since those days humankind has gradually grown shallower, until today people are centered in their bodies and therefore on the outermost surface. A mark of the situation is the fact that people today do not know what the spiritual dimension is or what inward depths are and do not believe these exist. In fact, they have wandered so far from their inner depths into the utter superficiality of the body that they do not even believe in life after death, heaven, or hell. In moving from inner planes all the way to this outermost surface, they have become so stupid in spiritual matters that they consider human life equivalent to animal life and believe we will die the way animals do. Amazingly, the educated subscribe more strongly to this belief than the uneducated, and anyone who believes otherwise is considered a simpleton.

[They mean] to roll down on us and to throw themselves on us means **5650** that for this reason they would be subjected to absolute authority. This can be seen from the symbolism of *rolling down on someone* as blaming that person, and from the symbolism of *throwing oneself on someone* as subjecting that person to authority. The authority is absolute in this case because the text adds, "to take us as slaves, and our donkeys."

Here is the situation: Before our earthly self unites with our spiritual self, or our outer self with our inner, we are left to consider whether we want to banish the cravings that rise out of self-love and materialism and the ideas we use to defend them, and to yield control to the spiritual, inner self. We are left to consider this so that we can freely choose what we want. When our earthly self ponders the question without our spiritual self, we reject the idea. We love our compulsions because we love ourselves and worldly advantages. As a result we fret, thinking that if our cravings were banished, we would no longer have any life, since we consider our earthly, outer self to be our all-in-all. Or else we imagine that we will never be able to do anything on our own again and that everything we think, will, and do is going to flow in from heaven, so that we will no longer be our own masters. When our earthly self is left alone in this frame of mind, it recoils and resists.

However, when a bit of light flows from the Lord through heaven into our earthly side, we begin to think differently. We realize it is better for our spiritual self to take control, because then we can think what is good and will what is good and go to heaven, but not if our earthly self is to have control. We consider that all angels in the whole of heaven follow this course and feel indescribable joy as a consequence. Under these circumstances we fight our earthly self and eventually wish to become subject to our spiritual self. That is the position we are placed in when we are being reborn, so that we can freely turn whichever direction we want. The more we freely turn in the latter direction, the more we regenerate.

These two trains of thought are what the inner meaning is talking about.

5651   *And to take us as slaves, and our donkeys* means to the point where nothing on either earthly plane has any consequence, as the following shows: Jacob's ten sons, who say this about themselves, represent truth on the earthly plane, as discussed in §§5403, 5419, 5427, 5458, 5512. *Slaves* symbolize things of lesser importance (§§2541, [2567]), and in this case what is of no consequence, as discussed below. And *donkeys* symbolize the contents of the earthly plane, which is to say knowledge, as mentioned in §5492. Here they symbolize knowledge on the outer earthly level, because the truth symbolized by Jacob's sons is on the inner earthly level.

[2] A word about the inconsequentiality of everything on either earthly plane: If we are to become spiritual, our earthly level has to be effaced. That is, it has to become completely incapable of anything on its own. To the extent that the earthly level is capable of anything on its own, the spiritual level is impotent.

From childhood on, our earthly level has absorbed nothing but the urges of self-centered and materialistic desires and therefore urges opposing neighborly love. These evils make it impossible for goodness from the Lord to flow into us through our inner self, because whatever flows in turns into evil on the earthly level. The earthly plane is the platform on which that inflow comes to rest, so unless the earthly plane—or the evil and falsity that have formed it—grows insignificant, goodness from the Lord can never flow in through heaven. It has nowhere to settle and dissolves. It cannot linger amid evil and falsity. That is why the inner plane closes up to the extent that the earthly plane fails to become a nonentity.

The church knows this fact from the teaching that we have to shed the old self in order to put on the new. [3] Rebirth is actually subduing what is earthly and letting what is spiritual gain the upper hand, and earthly elements are subdued when they are reduced to correspondence. When the earthly level has been reduced to correspondence, it no longer rebels but does as it is ordered, and follows at the nod of the spiritual level. It is almost the same as when physical action follows at the nod of the will, or when our words and facial expression follow along with the inflow of our thoughts. Clearly, then, the will of our earthly plane has to lose all value in order for us to become spiritual.

[4] Keep in mind that the old, earthly self must become inconsequential, formed as it is of evil and falsity. And when it becomes nothing to us, we receive the gift of a new earthly part, which is called a spiritual earthly part. It is called spiritual because the spiritual dimension is what acts through it and becomes perceptible through it, as a cause does through its effect. People know that the cause is the all-in-all of the effect. When the new earthly part thinks, wills, and brings about an effect, then, it is simply representing the spiritual part. When this happens, we receive goodness from the Lord; and when we receive goodness, we are granted truth; and when we are granted truth, we are perfected in understanding and wisdom; and when we are perfected in understanding and wisdom, we are blessed with happiness forever.

And they went up to the man who was over Joseph's household symbolizes the church's doctrines, as the following shows: The *man over Joseph's household* symbolizes something in the outward part of the church, as discussed above at §5640, so he symbolizes doctrine, since it is the church's. What is more, a *man* symbolizes truth and therefore doctrine (§3134), and a *household* symbolizes the church (§1795). Since *Joseph* means what is inward (§5469), *Joseph's household* means the inward part of the church. Doctrine from the Word is what is over this household, serving and assisting it. **5652**

And spoke to him in the doorway of the house means turning to them for advice about entering, as the following shows: *Speaking to him*—to the **5653**

man over Joseph's household—means turning to them—the doctrines—
for advice. And the *doorway of the house* symbolizes entry, as discussed in
§§2356, 2385. In this case it is entry from the earthly, outer self into the spiritual, inner self, which is this chapter's subject.

Because this is the symbolism, the original language actually just says
"the doorway of the house" rather than "*in* the doorway of the house."

5654   *And they said, "Upon my life, my lord,"* symbolizes testimony. This can
be seen from the phrase itself, which testifies to the truth of what they
are about to say concerning the silver discovered in the mouth of each
one's sack.

5655   *We did indeed come down at first to buy food* symbolizes an intent to
acquire goodness on behalf of truth. This can be seen from the symbolism
of *coming down* as an intent, because when someone goes down some-
where, or heads off in a particular direction, it is with intent. Here the
intent was to acquire goodness on behalf of truth, as symbolized by *to buy
food. Buying* means acquiring and adopting (§§4397, 5374, 5406, 5414,
5426), and *food* symbolizes goodness that comes of truth (§§5340, 5342).
Here it symbolizes goodness intended for the truth represented by Jacob's
sons, who are making the statement about themselves.

5656   *And it happened when we came to the inn that we opened our bags* symbolizes examination of the outer earthly level, as the following shows:
An *inn* symbolizes the outer earthly level in general (discussed at §5495).
Opening symbolizes examination, since when someone opens something,
the point is to examine it. And a *bag* symbolizes the outer earthly level in
particular (discussed at §5497).

5657   *And here, each one's silver in the mouth of his bag* symbolizes an awareness that the truth had seemingly been given for free. This can be seen
from the discussion in §§5530, 5624 of the symbolism of "each one's silver
in his sack" as truth given for free. Likewise with *each one's silver in the
mouth of his bag,* except that this means that the truth given for free was
laid on the threshold of the outer earthly level. The *mouth of a bag* symbolizes the threshold of the outer earthly level (§5497).

It means *seemingly* given for free because they are in doubt about
whether they want to form a bond with the inner plane and become
inconsequential, and people in doubt look askance even at truth that
supports their viewpoint.

5658   *His silver in its weight* symbolizes truth to match every individual's
state. This can be seen from the symbolism of *silver* as truth (discussed at
§§1551, 2954) and from that of *weight* as the state of goodness in a thing

(discussed at §3104). Truth to match every individual's state, then, means truth to match the goodness each is capable of receiving.

Many passages in the Word bring up weights and measures, but in an inner sense they do not mean weights and measures. No, weights symbolize the state of goodness in a thing, and measures symbolize the state of truth in a thing. Likewise for weight and extension as qualities. Weight in the physical world corresponds to goodness in the spiritual world, and extension, to truth. The reason is that in heaven, from which correspondences come, neither weight nor extension exists, because space does not exist. It does look as though objects with weight and extension exist among spirits, but the objects are appearances resulting from states of goodness and truth in a higher heaven.

[2] The symbolism of *silver* as truth was very well known in ancient times. That is why ancient people divided time—starting with the world's earliest days and finishing with its end—into the Golden Age, the Silver Age, the Bronze Age, and the Iron Age. They also added an age of clay. The Golden Age was their name for a time of innocence and perfection, when everyone did what was good out of goodness and what was just out of justice. The Silver Age was what they called a time when there was no longer innocence, although there was a kind of perfection that consisted not in doing good at the urging of goodness but in acting on truth at the urging of truth. The Bronze Age and the Iron Age is what they labeled times that were even less exalted.

[3] They gave the eras these names by way not of metaphor but of correspondence. The ancients knew that silver corresponded to truth and gold to goodness, and they knew it from communication with spirits and angels. When the inhabitants of a higher heaven discuss goodness, something gold appears down among the inhabitants of the first or outermost heaven below them. When they discuss truth, something silver appears there. Sometimes the manifestation is such that not only the walls of the rooms where they live but even the air itself sparkles with gold and silver. Among angels of the first or outermost heaven devoted to goodness because it is good, there also appear tables, lampstands, and many other objects of gold. Among those devoted to truth because it is true, there appear similar objects of silver.

But who today knows that correspondence was the reason the ancients called the ages golden and silver? In fact, who today knows anything about correspondence? People who do not know—especially if they consider it both a pleasure and a mark of wisdom to debate whether there is such a thing or not—cannot even begin to learn about the innumerable corresponding relationships that exist.

5659   *And we are returning it in our hand* means that what had been given for free is being surrendered as much as possible. This can be seen from the fact that in this case *returning* symbolizes submitting and that *in our hand* means as much as possible, both of which were dealt with above in §5624. The fact that it was what had been given for free is symbolized by the silver in the mouth of the bags that they were to return (§5657).

5660   *And other silver we have brought down in our hand* means that the intent is to acquire goodness through truth from other sources, as the following shows: *Silver* symbolizes truth, as noted just above at §5658, and because it does, *other silver* symbolizes other truth and therefore truth from other sources. There is no truth that is genuine except from the Lord, who gives it away for free, so there is no real truth from other sources. And *bringing down* symbolizes an intent to acquire—to acquire the truth-based goodness symbolized by the grain they were to buy.

According to the literal meaning of the story, the other silver would also have gone to Joseph, to buy food from him, so there would not have been another source. The inner meaning, though, does not reside in the literal, narrative meaning, which it does not care about, but in the actual idea being discussed. That idea is that if they were going to be put in the subordinate position of slaves just because a measure of truth had been given for free on the outer earthly level, they would go elsewhere to acquire goodness through truth. That is also the sequence in the inner meaning, because directly afterward the text says, "We do not know who put the silver in our bags," which means that they did not believe, because they did not know the source of the truth on the outer earthly plane.

[2] The same thing happens in the other life among spirits being initiated into goodness through truth, and especially into the reality that everything good and true flows in from the Lord. When they realize that everything they think and will flows in, that they cannot think or will anything on their own, they fight back as hard as they can. They believe that if this were true, they would have no life of their own and would therefore lose all their pleasure, which they equate with selfhood. Moreover, they believe, if they could not do what is good on their own or think what is true on their own, they would have to throw up their hands, doing and thinking nothing on their own but merely waiting for inspiration. Such thinking is permitted to them, even if it leads them to the verge of deciding they do not want to accept goodness or truth

from that source, only from another that does not bereave them of their autonomy this way. Sometimes they are also allowed to inquire where to find it. Later, though, when they find it nowhere, the ones who are being reborn come back and freely choose to be led by the Lord in their willing and thinking. Then they are informed that they will receive a heavenly selfhood like the one angels have, and along with it, bliss and happiness forever.

[3] About heavenly selfhood: It rises out of a new will given us by the Lord and differs from human selfhood in that we no longer focus on ourselves in everything we do and in everything we learn and teach. Instead we focus on our neighbor, the public, the church, the Lord's kingdom, and consequently the Lord himself. The purposes of our life are what change. Purposes aimed low, on worldly advantage and ourselves, are moved aside and replaced with purposes aimed high. The goals of our life are nothing short of our life itself, because they are our very will and the very things we love. What we love we will, and take as our purpose.

People with the gift of heavenly selfhood also have serenity and peace. They trust in the Lord, believe that nothing evil can touch them, and know that perverse desires will not plague them. Furthermore, people with heavenly selfhood are in true freedom. Freedom is to be led by the Lord, since anyone led by the Lord is led in goodness, from goodness, to goodness. People with heavenly selfhood, then, clearly have bliss and happiness, because there is nothing to bother them. They have no self-love and therefore no hostility, hatred, or vengefulness. They have no love for worldly advantages and therefore no deceitfulness, fear, or disquiet.

5661 *We do not know who put the silver in our bags* symbolizes a lack of faith due to ignorance about the source of the truth on the outer earthly plane, as the following shows: *Not knowing* in a spiritual sense means not believing, or a lack of faith. *Who put* symbolizes ignorance about the source. *Silver* symbolizes truth, as discussed in §5658. And a *bag* symbolizes the outer earthly plane, as discussed in §5497.

5662 *And he said, "Peace to you; don't be afraid,"* means all is well; they should not despair. This can be seen from the symbolism of *peace* as being well (discussed below) and from that of *don't be afraid* as reassurance that they should not despair. The inner meaning is dealing with a change of state. They were no longer using their own power to acquire truth, and through truth, goodness, but were receiving them as a gift from the Lord. Imagining that this would mean a loss of autonomy and accordingly of freedom and consequently of all pleasure in life, they were in despair, as is plain from what comes earlier [§5647]. That is why *don't be afraid* means that they should not despair. Fear rises out of various causes (§5647), so it has various meanings.

[2] *Peace* means being well because it is very deep and therefore reigns supreme throughout the whole of heaven. Peace in heaven is like springtime on earth or like dawn, which achieve their effect not by our detecting various changes but by a widespread loveliness that touches everything we perceive. The individual objects themselves, not just our perception of them, are permeated by an appealing quality.

Hardly anyone today knows what peace means where the Word mentions it, as in the benediction "Jehovah lift his face on you and *give you peace*" (Numbers 6:26) and elsewhere. Almost everyone believes that peace is safety from one's enemies and tranquillity at home and among one's companions—but that is not the peace meant. What is meant is a peace that vastly transcends it. What is meant is the heavenly peace described just above. No one can receive the gift of this peace without being led by the Lord and living in the Lord, that is, in heaven, where the Lord is the all-in-all. Heavenly peace flows in when cravings born of self-love and materialism have been removed, because these cravings are what banish peace. They infest our inner depths and eventually cause us to find disquiet restful and hostilities peaceful, because they cause us to find pleasure in evil. As long as we involve ourselves in these banes, we cannot possibly know what peace is. In fact, as long as we do, we believe the other type of peace to be worthless. If anyone tells us we will not arrive at a sense of peace till the pleasures of self-love and materialism have been removed, we laugh, because we identify peace as pleasure in evil, which is actually the opposite of peace.

[3] Since peace is like this—since it is central to all happiness and blessing and therefore reigns supreme everywhere in everything—the ancients used the words "Peace to you" as a stock phrase meaning "Be well." They would also ask, "Do you have peace?" when they meant, "Are you well?"

See earlier remarks on peace, and supporting evidence: Peace in the heavens is like springtime and dawn on earth: 1726, 2780. In the highest sense, peace means the Lord, and in a representative sense it means his kingdom; it is the Lord's divine nature affecting us with goodness from within: 3780, 4681. All disquiet results from evil and falsity, while peace results from goodness and truth: 3170.

5663   *Your God and the God of your father* symbolizes the Lord's divine humanity. This can be seen from the fact that wherever the Word mentions God or Jehovah, it means the Lord and no other (§§1343, 1736, 2921, 3035).

When it says *your God and the God of your father,* which is the God of Israel or Jacob and the God of his sons, it means the Lord's divine humanity, and specifically the earthly divinity of it (§§3305, 4286, 4570). Israel represented the Lord's inner earthly level, and Jacob, the Lord's outer earthly level. His sons represented the truth on the Lord's earthly level.

[2] The Jewish religion did not know that God and Jehovah in the Word meant the Lord, and the Christian religion today does not know it. The Christian church does not know it because Christianity has split the Godhead into three persons. However, the ancient church, which came after the Flood, and more particularly the earliest church, which came before the Flood, understood Jehovah and God to be nobody but the Lord and in fact the Lord in his divine humanity. They knew about the divinity itself in the Lord, which he calls his Father, but they could not think about it. They could think only about his divine humanity. So they could not unite with any other divinity, because union comes about through thought in the intellect and through desire in the will and consequently through faith and love. When one thinks about divinity itself, one's thoughts fall on a kind of boundless universe and dissolve. No union results. The case is different when one thinks about divinity itself in the form of divine humanity. And the ancients knew they could not be saved unless they formed a bond with the Divine. [3] Divine humanity was therefore what the ancient churches worshiped.

Jehovah also revealed himself in his divine humanity among the ancients. His divine humanity was his divinity itself as it existed in heaven, because heaven constitutes a single human being called the universal human (discussed at the ends of the chapters leading up to here). This divinity in heaven is nothing other than divinity itself, but in the form of a divine person in heaven. This humanity is what the Lord took on and made divine in himself. He united it with divinity itself, just as it always had been united. From eternity, it was one. These things he did because the human race could not have been saved otherwise. It was no longer enough for his divinity itself to be able to flow into people's minds through heaven and thus through the divine humanity there. That is why divinity itself wanted to unite divine humanity with itself in a tangible way, through a human nature assumed in the world. Both are the Lord.

Gave you a secret gift in your bags means that it comes from him without out any use of their prudence. This can be seen from the symbolism of a *secret gift* as truth and goodness given by the Lord without the person's knowledge, and from that of the silver taken back in the sacks, or *in bags,* which means without using any power of theirs (discussed in §§5488, 5496, 5499). This shows that *he gave you a secret gift in your bags* means that truth and goodness on the earthly plane come from him—the Lord in his divine humanity—without any use of their power. Since it means without any use of their power, it also means without any use of their prudence. I speak of prudence because it corresponds to providence, and what comes of divine providence does not come of human prudence.

5664b   *Your silver came to me* means that it will seem as though they acquired their own truth. This is established by the symbolism of *silver* as truth (discussed in §§1551, 2954). The fact that their silver *came to him* means that they had done the buying and acquiring for themselves. Buying means acquiring (§5655). That is why *your silver came to me* symbolizes truth acquired by them. Religious truth is never acquired by anyone, though, but is instilled and given by the Lord, even though it appears to be acquired. That is the reason for saying it will *seem* as though they acquired their own truth.

[2] The church knows that truth is instilled and given by the Lord, because it has the teaching that faith comes from God rather than from us. Not only the trust belonging to faith comes from him, then, but also the truth belonging to it. Even so, it looks as though we acquire such truth. We are deeply unaware that it comes to us, because we do not perceive the inflow. The reason we do not perceive it is that our inner reaches are closed off, which leaves us unable to come into perceptible contact with spirits and angels. When our inner reaches are closed off, we cannot know anything at all of spiritual inflow.

[3] Bear in mind, though, that it is one thing to know religious truth and another to believe it. People who merely know religious truth file it in their memory the same way they file information from any other branch of knowledge. This type of religious truth can be acquired without out spiritual inflow, but it has no life. Look at the fact that an evil person no matter how bad can learn religious truth as easily as an honest, godly person. In evil people, though, as just mentioned, the truth is lifeless. When they bring it back out, they put every point to work for their own glory or enrichment. It is self-love and materialism that inspire them and create a semblance of life, but that life is the kind in hell, which is called spiritual death. As a result, they produce truth from their memory, not from their heart, when they bring it back out.

People who believe the truth that constitutes faith, on the other hand, produce it from their heart when they produce it with their lips. In them, religious truth takes root by sending its root down into their outer memory and growing inward or upward from there like a fruit tree. Like a tree it decks itself with leaves and eventually flowers for the purpose of bearing fruit.

[4] Likewise with these believers. They too have no other intention for religious truth than to put it to use in the exercise of neighborly love, which is the way they bear fruit. This truth is what we cannot acquire for ourselves in even the smallest way. Instead, the Lord gives it to us for free, every moment of our life, and believe it or not, in immeasurable quantities every moment. We are so designed, though, as to lack an awareness that it is flowing in. If we could tell it was, we would rebel, as mentioned above [§§5647, 5660]. We would believe it would mean giving up our autonomy, and with our autonomy our freedom, and with our freedom our pleasure, becoming a nothing in the process. Because of this, things are set up so that we have no idea we are not acquiring it for ourselves. That is what is meant, then, by the statement that it will *seem* as though they acquired their own truth.

In addition, we have to do good as if on our own and think what is true as if on our own in order to be given heavenly selfhood and heavenly freedom; but when we reflect, we must acknowledge that it all comes from the Lord. See §§2882, 2883, 2891.

And he brought Simeon out to them means that he connected the will with truth, as the following shows: *Simeon* represents faith that belongs to the will, or the will to act on faith's truth, as discussed at §§3869, 3870, 3871, 3872, 4497, 4502, 4503, 5482. And Jacob's sons—the ones *to whom* the man brought Simeon out—represent earthly-level truth known to the church, as discussed at §§5403, 5419, 5427, 5458, 5512. Clearly, then, *he brought Simeon out to them* means that he connected the will with truth. **5665**

Genesis 43:24, 25, 26, 27, 28. *And the man brought the men to Joseph's house and gave them water, and they washed their feet, and he gave fodder to their donkeys. And they prepared the offering for the time of Joseph's coming at noon, because they had heard that they would be eating bread there. And Joseph came home, and they brought him the offering that was in their hand, to the house, and bowed down to him to the earth. And he asked them about their peace. And he said, "Does your old father, whom you mentioned, have peace? Is he still alive?" And they said, "Your servant our father has peace; he is still alive," and bent and bowed.* **5666**

And the man brought the men to Joseph's house symbolizes initiation into a bond with the inner level. *And gave them water* symbolizes a general inflow of truth from the inner level. *And they washed their feet* symbolizes a consequent purification of the earthly level. *And he gave fodder to their donkeys* symbolizes instruction about goodness. *And they prepared the offering* means ingratiating oneself. *For the time of Joseph's coming at noon* means until the inner dimension was present with its light. *Because they had heard that they would be eating bread there* symbolizes a realization that goodness would unite with truth. *And Joseph came home* symbolizes the presence of the inner plane. *And they brought him the offering that was in their hand* symbolizes ingratiating oneself as much as possible. *And bowed down to the earth* symbolizes humility. *And he asked them about their peace* symbolizes a perception that all is well. *And he said, "Does your old father, whom you mentioned, have peace?"* means even for spiritual goodness. *Is he still alive?* means that it has life. *And they said, "Your servant our father has peace,"* symbolizes a perception received from there by the earthly level that all is well with the goodness that is its source. *He is still alive* means and that it has life. *And bent and bowed* symbolizes outward and inward humility.

5667   *And the man brought the men to Joseph's house* symbolizes initiation into a bond with the inner level. This can be seen from the symbolism of *bringing the men to Joseph's house* as connecting truth on the earthly level with the inner level (discussed above at §5648). The reason it means initiation into a bond is clear from subsequent events: that they ate there, and that Joseph did not reveal himself to them at that point. This symbolizes a general inflow, which is the subject of the next clause and is the same as initiation.

5668   *And gave them water* symbolizes a general inflow of truth from the inner level. This is established by the symbolism of *water* as truth (§§2702, 3058, 3424, 4976), and indeed as truth in general. *Giving* water, then, symbolizes a general inflow of truth. It means an inflow from the inner level because the setting was Joseph's house (§5667).

A general inflow of truth is enlightenment that creates an ability to perceive and understand truth. The enlightenment comes from heaven's light, which comes from the Lord, and that light is nothing but divine truth (§§2776, 3138, 3167, 3195, 3222, 3339, 3485, 3636, 3643, 3993, 4302, 4413, 4415, 5400).

5669   *And they washed their feet* symbolizes a consequent purification of the earthly level. This can be seen from the discussion in §3147 of the symbolism of *washing feet* as purification of the earthly level.

And he gave fodder to their donkeys symbolizes instruction about good- **5670**
ness. This can be seen from the symbolism of *giving fodder* as teaching
about goodness, since *fodder* symbolizes the goodness that goes with truth
in the form of knowledge (§3114), and *giving* fodder, or feeding an animal,
means teaching about that kind of goodness. On the point that feeding or
grazing an animal means teaching, see §5201. *Donkeys* symbolize knowledge (§5492). *Giving fodder to donkeys,* then, plainly symbolizes instruction
about the goodness associated with knowledge. The goodness associated
with knowledge is a pleasure in knowing truth. Truth in the form of knowledge is the most general sort of truth, which is visible in the earthly light
known as the light of the world. If we are to see this truth, and see that it is
true, there must be a general inflow from within (§5668). That is, we must
be enlightened with heaven's light.

And they prepared the offering means ingratiating oneself. This can be **5671**
seen from the symbolism of an *offering* as a way of winning favor (§5619).
Preparing an offering consequently means ingratiating oneself.

For the time of Joseph's coming at noon means until the inner dimen- **5672**
sion was present with its light. This can be seen from the symbolism of *for
the time of his coming* as when it was present, from the representation of
Joseph as the inner dimension (mentioned at §5648), and from the symbolism of *noon,* [or the south,] as a state of light (discussed at §§1458,
3195, 3708).

Noon means a state of light because the times of day, such as morning,
afternoon, and evening, correspond to different kinds of enlightenment
in the other life. Different kinds of enlightenment are different forms of
understanding and wisdom, because heaven's light contains understanding
and wisdom. Changes in enlightenment there resemble morning, afternoon, and evening on earth. A state of evening shadow is created not by
the sun there, or the Lord, who is always shining, but by angels' sense of
self. When they are let into their selfhood, they enter a shadowy evening
state, and as they are lifted from their own selfhood into a heavenly selfhood, they enter a state of light. This shows why noon corresponds to a
state of light.

Because they had heard that they would be eating bread there symbolizes **5673**
a realization that goodness would unite with truth. This is established by
the symbolism of *hearing* as a perception (discussed at §5017), from that
of *eating* as being adopted and united (discussed at §§2187, 3168, 3513 at
the end, 3596, 3832, 5643), and from that of *bread* as a loving goodness

(discussed at §§2165, 2177, 2187, 3464, 3478, 3735, 3813, 4211, 4217, 4735, 4976).

5674 *And Joseph came home* symbolizes the presence of the inner plane. This is established by the symbolism of *coming home* as being present, or as presence (as above in §5672), and from the representation of *Joseph* as the inner dimension (mentioned at §5648).

5675 *And they brought him the offering that was in their hand, to the house,* symbolizes ingratiating oneself as much as possible. This can be seen from the symbolism of an *offering,* which was habitually given to monarchs and priests, as winning favor and therefore as ingratiating oneself (mentioned just above at §5671) and from the symbolism of *that was in their hand,* which means as much as possible (also mentioned above, at §§5624, 5659).

5676 *And bowed down to the earth* symbolizes humility. This can be seen from the symbolism of *bowing down to the earth* as being humble (discussed at §2153; see also below at §5682).

5677 *And he asked them about their peace* symbolizes a perception that all is well. This can be seen from the symbolism of *asking* as perceiving someone else's thoughts (discussed at §5597) and from that of *peace* as being well (discussed at §5662).

5678 *And he said, "Does your old father, whom you mentioned, have peace?"* means even for spiritual goodness. This can be seen from the symbolism of *peace* as being well (as above in §5677) and from the representation of Israel, the *father,* as spiritual goodness (discussed in §§3654, 4286, 4598).

5679 *Is he still alive?* means that it has life. This is established by the symbolism of *being alive* as spiritual life (discussed in §5407).

5680 *And they said, "Your servant our father has peace,"* symbolizes a perception received from there by the earthly level that all is well for the goodness that is its source. This can be seen from the symbolism of *saying* as perceiving (discussed in §§1898, 1919, 2080, 2619, 2862, 3395, 3509), from that of *peace* as being well (discussed in §§5662, 5677), and from the representation of Israel as spiritual goodness (mentioned just above at §5678). This goodness is being called a *father* because it is the fatherlike source of the true ideas and good desires on the earthly level represented by Israel's ten sons. Since they represent true ideas and good desires on the earthly level, they also symbolize that level itself. The earthly level is the container, the truth and goodness there are the contents, and they form a unit. This discussion now shows that *They said, "Your servant* *our father has peace,"* symbolizes a perception received from there by the earthly level that all is well for the goodness that is its source.

I am saying a perception received *from there*—from the inner dimension represented by Joseph (§5648)—because all perception by the earthly level comes from the spiritual level. Since it comes from the spiritual level, it comes from the inner level, or rather from the Lord by way of the inner level. The earthly level never has any perception or even any energy for thought or feeling except that which comes from the spiritual level. On its own, everything in the earthly dimension is dead, but it comes alive with the inflow of the spiritual world—that is, with an inflow from the Lord through the spiritual world. Everything in the spiritual world is alive with light from the Lord, because that light contains wisdom and understanding.

The fact that these words symbolize a perception on the earthly level received *from there,* or from the inner level, also follows from earlier remarks in §5677.

He is still alive means and that it has life. This can be seen from the citation just above at §5679. Compare the remarks at §5407.

5681

And bent and bowed symbolizes outward and inward humility. This can be seen from the symbolism of *bending* as outward humility and from that of *bowing* as inward humility. Bending is a less extreme form of bowing, so it means outward humility, and bowing is more extreme, so it means inward humility.

5682

What is more, bending means the humility of truth, that is, of people devoted to truth, and therefore of spiritual people. Bowing means the humility of goodness, that is, of people devoted to goodness, and therefore of heavenly people. From this standpoint as well bending means outward humility, and bowing, inward, because people devoted to goodness have more depth than those devoted to truth.

For the most part, the explanations for the contents of the inner meaning in this set of verses have provided only the symbolism of the words, the reason being that the content has been explained before.

Genesis 43:29, 30, 31, 32, 33, 34. *And he raised his eyes and saw Benjamin his brother, the son of his mother, and said, "Is this your youngest brother, whom you mentioned to me?" And he said, "God show favor to you, my son." And Joseph hurried, because his compassions were being stirred for his brother and he was seeking to weep, and he came to his private room and wept there. And he washed his face and went out and controlled himself and said, "Set*

5683

the bread." And they set it for him by himself and for them by themselves and for the Egyptians eating with him by themselves, because the Egyptians cannot eat bread with the Hebrews, because it is abhorrent to the Egyptians. And they were seated before him, the firstborn according to his status as firstborn, the youngest according to his youth, and the men stared dumbfounded, each at his companion. And he brought portions out from [before] his face for them and multiplied Benjamin's portion above the portions of them all by five measures. And they drank—and drank heavily—with him.

And he raised his eyes symbolizes reflection. *And saw Benjamin* symbolizes an awareness of the middle ground. *His brother, the son of his mother,* symbolizes an inner dimension born of the earthly level, which functions as its mother. *And said,* symbolizes a perception. *Is this your youngest brother, whom you mentioned to me?* means a child born after all the others, as they knew. *And he said, "God show favor to you, my son,"* means that divinity also existed with heavenly spirituality, or the middle ground, because this emanates from spiritual heavenliness, which is truth from the Divine. *And Joseph hurried* means from his inmost core. *Because his compassions were being stirred* symbolizes mercy rising out of love. *For his brother* means toward the inner dimension born from itself. *And he was seeking to weep* means an effect of the mercy generated by love. *And he came to his private room and wept there* means internally, not visibly. *And he washed his face* means that he managed the situation this way. *And went out* means by moving off. *And controlled himself* means by hiding. *And said, "Set the bread,"* symbolizes a perception of union with truth on the earthly level through the middle ground. *And they set it for him by himself and for them by themselves* symbolizes the outward appearance that the inner dimension was separated from them. *And for the Egyptians eating with him by themselves* symbolizes the separation of knowledge that is inverted. *Because the Egyptians cannot eat bread with the Hebrews* means that they could never unite with the church's truth and goodness. *Because it is abhorrent to the Egyptians* means they are opposites. *And they were seated before him* means that they were arranged in order by his presence. *The firstborn according to his status as firstborn, and the youngest according to his youth* means according to the order truth follows when subordinate to goodness. *And the men stared dumbfounded, each at his companion,* symbolizes a change of state for each in relation to the others. *And he brought portions out from [before] his face for them* symbolizes different kinds of goodness applied to everyone individually out of mercy. *And multiplied Benjamin's portion above the portions of them all* symbolizes goodness for the middle ground beyond the goodness applied to truth on the earthly level. *By five measures* means greatly increased. *And they drank* means applying truth under the supervision of goodness. *And drank heavily* means in large quantities.

And he raised his eyes symbolizes reflection. This can be seen from the symbolism of *raising one's eyes* as thinking and focusing (discussed in §§2789, 2829, 4339) and noticing (§4086), and therefore as reflecting. To reflect is to focus one's intellectual vision and to notice first whether a thing is so and afterward *that* it is so.   **5684**

And saw Benjamin symbolizes an awareness of the middle ground. This can be seen from the symbolism of seeing as understanding and sensing (discussed in §§2150, 2325, 3764, 3863, 4403–4421, 4567, 4723, 5400) and from the representation of *Benjamin* as a middle ground (discussed at §§5411, 5413, 5443, 5639).   **5685**

His brother, the son of his mother, symbolizes an inner dimension born of the earthly level, which functions as its mother. This can be seen from the representation of Benjamin, the *brother,* and the *son of his mother,* as the inner dimension (discussed at §5469). Because it is a middle ground, it springs from the spiritual heavenliness that is Joseph as its father and from the earthly plane as its mother. It has to draw on both if it is to serve as a middle ground. That is what is meant, then, by an inner dimension born of the earthly level, which functions as its mother. The spiritual heavenliness that is Joseph had likewise sprung from the earthly dimension as its mother but from divinity as its father. That is why Benjamin is called his brother, the son of his mother—as Benjamin actually was by birth. Soon after, Joseph also calls him son. The Lord, who is meant by Joseph in the highest sense here, calls each of us his sister or brother, but if we show any neighborly kindness from him, he also calls us his mother's son or daughter. In that case, though, his mother means the church.   **5686**

And said, symbolizes a perception. This can be seen from the symbolism of *saying* in the stories of the Word as a perception (discussed many times before). Saying means perceiving because heaven's inhabitants, unlike the world's, pick up on the actual thoughts that underlie speech. That is why perceiving in a spiritual sense is talking or saying in a literal sense, or (to put it another way) in the earthly sense.   **5687**

Is this your youngest brother, whom you mentioned to me? means a child born after all the others, as they of course knew. This can be seen from the meaning of a *youngest brother* as one born after all the others   **5688** (discussed below) and from that of *whom you mentioned to me* as the fact that it was perceived by them. Mentioning, [or saying,] symbolizes something perceived (see just above at §5687), so it symbolizes something known.

Benjamin is being called *their youngest brother*—born after all the others, or youngest by birth—as he actually was, because the same holds true in a spiritual sense for the middle ground that Benjamin represents. The middle ground in us is born after all the others because when we are born spiritually (that is, reborn), the Lord first regenerates our rational level, which is our inner humanity, and then our earthly level (§§3286, 3288, 3321, 3493, 4612). The middle ground has to draw something both from a spiritual rationality, a rationality made new, and from the earthly level, and it cannot draw anything from the earthly level until this too is made new. As a consequence, the middle ground can be born only after the earthly level is reborn and indeed to the extent that it is reborn.

[2] Everything the Word says about Jacob's children happened the way it did in providence because the Word would be written about them and their descendants. It would contain the heavenly qualities (and in its highest sense the divine qualities) that they represented in their actions. Benjamin, being the last born, would therefore represent a middle ground between the inner and outer levels, or between the spiritual heavenliness the Lord had in the world and the earthly level he also had, which he would make divine.

[3] In its highest sense, everything said about Joseph and his brothers represents the glorification of the Lord's human nature. That is, it represents the way he made the humanity in himself divine. The reason for the representation is to render the Word utterly holy in its inmost sense. Another reason is for every detail to contain the kind of knowledge that could be incorporated into angels' wisdom. As is recognized, angelic wisdom so far transcends human understanding that we can grasp almost none of it. It is also a real joy to angels that the Word in every detail is about the Lord, because they live in the Lord. Besides, the glorification of the Lord's humanity is a model for our rebirth. Our rebirth, then, is also presented in the Word's inner meaning wherever the Lord's glorification is dealt with. Human rebirth with its countless secrets is also incorporated into angels' wisdom, and it brings them joy when the information is put to use in human reformation.

5689   *And he said, "God show favor to you, my son,"* means that divinity also existed with heavenly spirituality, or the middle ground, because this emanates from spiritual heavenliness, which is truth from the Divine. This can be seen from the symbolism of *God's showing favor,* when the spiritual heavenliness that is Joseph addresses the words to the heavenly spirituality that is Benjamin and calls him his *son.* The symbolism is that divinity also existed with heavenly spirituality, or the middle ground, because this emanates from spiritual heavenliness, which is truth from the Divine. For the meaning of Benjamin as heavenly spirituality, see §§3969, 4592; and as a middle ground, see §§5411, 5413, 5443, 5639.

[2] In the highest sense, as just mentioned, the Lord's inner human nature consisted in spiritual heavenliness, which was truth from the Divine, or the layer directly clothing divinity itself in the Lord. Heavenly spirituality, which is the middle ground, emanated from this. The conclusion follows, then, that divinity also existed with heavenly spirituality. What emanates from something draws its essence from that thing. However, it gets clothed in elements that serve to communicate it and therefore serve to make it useful in a lower sphere. The enveloping layers are drawn from elements in the lower sphere, to enable the inner plane from which it emanates to act in the lower sphere through the kinds of elements that exist there.

[3] What contributes the essence is like a father, because the essence is the soul. What clothes it is like a mother, because the layer clothing it is the body of that soul. That was the reason for saying earlier that the middle ground has to draw on both if it is to be a middle ground—on the inner level, which functions as its father, and on the outer level, which functions as its mother [§§5686, 5688].

And Joseph hurried means from his inmost core. This can be seen from the symbolism of *hurrying* in this case as something that bursts out from deep within. After all, the verse goes on to say, "because his compassions were being stirred," which symbolizes mercy rising out of love. When this mercy surges up, it surges from one's inmost core, at a glance, or at the first stirring of one's thoughts. That is why hurrying actually means from his inmost core.   **5690**

Because his compassions were being stirred symbolizes mercy rising out of love. This can be seen from the symbolism of the *stirring of compassions* as mercy rising out of love. It is described as mercy because Benjamin had not yet recognized Joseph. It is described as rising out of love because it emanated as a middle ground from him.   **5691**

The word being used for compassions in the original language means a very deep and tender love.

5692 *For his brother* means toward the inner dimension born from itself. This can be seen from the representation of Benjamin, the *brother,* as a middle ground and therefore as an inner dimension (discussed at §5469). It emanates as a middle ground and inner dimension from the spiritual heavenliness that is Joseph, which is the reason for saying "toward the inner dimension born *from itself.*"

The Lord, who is Joseph in the highest sense here, speaks of anyone who receives any divine quality from him—anyone who takes up neighborly kindness, for instance—as his brother or sister and also his child.

5693 *And he was seeking to weep* means an effect of the mercy generated by love. This can be seen from the discussion in §§3801, 5480 of the symbolism of *tears* as an effect of the mercy generated by love.

5694 *And he came to his private room and wept there* means internally, not visibly. This can be seen from the symbolism of *coming to one's private room* as internally, so that a thing is not visible.

It had been customary for the ancients to speak of entering one's room and shutting the door when they meant doing something unseen. The turn of phrase grew out of symbols in the ancient church. By a house, in a spiritual sense, they meant a person (§3128), and by chambers and rooms they meant a person's inner reaches. Going to one's room, or entering it, therefore meant internally, so that the thing was not visible.

Because entering one's room was symbolic, the Word uses the phrase in several places. In Isaiah, for instance:

> Go, my people; *enter your private rooms* and *shut your door after you.* Hide yourself as for a bit of a moment, until the anger passes. (Isaiah 26:20)

Entering one's private rooms obviously does not mean entering one's private rooms but keeping oneself hidden, keeping to oneself. [2] In Ezekiel:

> He said to me, "Have you seen, son of humankind, what the elders of the house of Israel are doing in the dark, a man in the *chambers devoted to his idol?* Because they are saying, 'Jehovah is not seeing us.'" (Ezekiel 8:12)

Doing something "in the dark, a man in the chambers devoted to his idol" means internally, in one's thoughts. Their inner depths of thought and feeling were represented to the prophet by inner rooms and were called the chambers of one's idol. [3] In Moses:

> Outside, the sword—and *from the inner rooms*, terror—will bereave both the young man and the young woman, the nursing baby along with the man of old age. (Deuteronomy 32:25)

The sword stands for the devastation of truth and for punishment for falsity (§2799). "From the inner rooms, terror" stands for a person's inner depths. Again it is plain that the rooms here do not mean rooms. [4] In David:

> . . . who waters the mountains *from his chambers*. (Psalms 104:13)

In a spiritual sense, watering the mountains means blessing people who love the Lord and their neighbor. A mountain means the heavenly quality of love; see §§795, 1430, 4210. "From his chambers" means from the inner depths of heaven. In Luke:

> Whatever you said in the dark will be heard in the light. And what you spoke in the ear *in the private rooms* will be proclaimed on the roofs. (Luke 12:3)

Here too private rooms stand for a person's inner depths—what the person had thought, had intended, and had endeavored to do. In Matthew:

> When you pray, *enter into your private room,* and *shutting your door,* pray in secret. (Matthew 6:6)

Entering into one's private room and praying stands for doing so out of sight. The saying is based on representation.

And he washed his face means that he managed the situation this way. **5695** This can be seen from the symbolism of *washing his face* here as managing the situation to prevent it from showing. Joseph was washing his face to keep his tears from showing, so that is how he was managing things. By the Lord's divine mercy, this matter will be explained later [§5696]. Here I need to say something about the correspondence of the face with inner levels.

The face is a surface representing what lies inside. It was designed to display our inner realm in a kind of representational mirror and to show others what our attitude toward them is, so that when we talk we might reveal our sentiments both in our words and in our face. That is the kind of face the earliest people had, and they were from a heavenly church. Angels all have this same kind of face, because they have no wish to hide what they are thinking from others. They never think of their neighbor in any way but a good one and never harbor a secret thought of wishing their neighbor well for selfish reasons.

Hellish types, though, as long as they do not appear in heaven's light, have a face that does not correspond to their inner reaches. This is because during bodily life they used their face to signal charity toward their neighbor, merely for the sake of prestige and wealth, yet never wished their neighbor well, except to the extent that their neighbor showed them favoritism. That is why the arrangement of their features is at odds with their interiors. In fact, some have antagonism, hatred, vengefulness, and a lust to kill inside, while their face is composed to gleam with love for their neighbor.

These comments show how big a gap there is today between people's inner core and outer surface. That is why such techniques are found everywhere.

5696 *And went out* means by moving off. This can be seen from the symbolism of *going out* as moving off, since one who moves off goes out or withdraws from another.

The situation in the inner meaning is this: Joseph in the highest sense represents the Lord. Israel's ten sons represent truth and goodness on the earthly level in people being reborn. Benjamin represents a middle ground. The Lord has mercy born of love for the middle ground, because it is the means by which everything lower is reborn, but his love and mercy do not show until union has been brought about through the middle ground. He manages the situation so as to keep love and mercy from showing because if they were visible, regeneration could not take place.

The Lord manages the situation through a moving off and hiding. It is not that he ever removes or hides his mercy but that when people who are being reborn are let into their evils, he appears distant and hidden to them. Evil is what gets in the way and makes this happen. To offer a comparison, it is like dark clouds that seem to remove and hide the sun by putting themselves in between; that is the type of hiding and removal that is meant.

5697 *And controlled himself* means hiding. This can be seen from the symbolism of *controlling himself* as hiding, because people who control themselves hide what they have inwardly aimed at. For an explanation of this kind of hiding, see just above at §5696.

And said, "Set the bread," symbolizes a perception of union with truth **5698**
on the earthly level through the middle ground. This can be seen from
the symbolism of *saying* as a perception (mentioned many times before)
and from that of *setting the bread* as union with truth on the earthly level
through the middle ground. Setting bread means the meal itself, and
dinners together and banquets symbolize union—specifically, being initiated into union (§§3596, 3832, 5161). The fact that it is union with truth
on the earthly plane through the middle ground follows from context.
Benjamin means the middle ground, and Jacob's ten sons mean truth on
the earthly plane, as shown before. The middle ground had made union
possible, now that Joseph had seen Benjamin, so he ordered them to eat
with him: "And Joseph saw Benjamin with them and said to the one
who was over his household, 'Bring the men to the house, and slaughter
abundantly and prepare [the meat], because the men will eat with me at
noon'" (verse 16).

And they set it for him by himself and for them by themselves symbol- **5699**
izes the outward appearance that the inner dimension was separated from
them. This can be seen from the symbolism of *setting it for him by himself and for them by themselves* as separation. Since Joseph represents the
inner dimension, and Israel's ten sons the outer dimension (§5469), these
words symbolize the separation of the inner from the outer dimension.
The separation is only apparent, though, because he gave them food from
his own table, sending them each portions.

And for the Egyptians eating with him by themselves symbolizes the **5700**
separation of knowledge that is inverted. This can be seen from the representation of *Egyptians* here as knowledge that is inverted, which is discussed below, and from the symbolism of *eating with him, by themselves,*
as separation (as just above in §5699).

The *Egyptians eating with him* means Egyptians eating at Joseph's house.
Obviously they were not eating *with* Joseph, since they were eating by
themselves.

In a positive sense, Egypt or *Egyptians* symbolize the knowledge belonging to the church (see §§1462, 4749, 4964, 4966), but in a negative sense
they symbolize knowledge that is inverted and therefore knowledge that
opposes the church's truth (§§1164, 1165, 1186). The Word speaks of Egypt
in this sense in many passages.

Egypt symbolizes knowledge of this type because of what happened
to the knowledge of the ancient church. What was known to the people
of the ancient church represented and symbolized heavenly and spiritual

attributes, and those people cultivated the knowledge more assiduously than others did. The Egyptians turned this knowledge—the knowledge belonging to the representative church—into magic, totally inverting it.

[2] Knowledge is said to be inverted when people exploit the heavenly plan in order to do evil. The heavenly plan is to do good to everyone. When people turn this plan on its head, they eventually come to deny what is divine, what belongs to heaven, and consequently what belongs to neighborly love and faith. People who develop such a character know how to use knowledge to reason sharply and skillfully, because they reason from sensory evidence. To reason from sensory evidence is to reason from shallow factors, or from bodily and worldly considerations, which monopolize one's senses and instincts. Unless light from heaven shines on those factors and realigns them in a completely different pattern, we are left in the dark on heavenly matters. The darkness is so deep that not only do we fail utterly to grasp heavenly ideas, we entirely deny and eventually reject them. Then, so far as we are free to do so, we blaspheme them.

When knowledge is in its proper order, it is arranged by the Lord in the form of heaven, but when it is inverted, it is arranged in the form of hell. The grossest falsities then lie in the middle, and supporting falsities flank them, but truth lies beyond the perimeter. Because it does, it cannot make contact with heaven, where truth reigns supreme. The inner levels of people like this are therefore shut off, since our inner levels make heaven accessible to us.

5701 *Because the Egyptians cannot eat bread with the Hebrews* means that they could never unite with the church's truth and goodness, as the following shows: The *Egyptians* represent people who are inverted, or dedicated to evil and falsity, as discussed just above in §5700. *Eating bread* means uniting, as also discussed above, in §5698. And the *Hebrews* represent people who are in true order, or dedicated to the church's truth and goodness. The land of the Hebrews symbolizes the church (see §§5136, 5236) because the Hebrew church was a second ancient church (§§1238, 1241, 1343).

The text says "eat bread" and (above) "set the bread" because *bread* means all food in general (§2165), so it means a meal. The reason bread means all food and the meal itself is that in a spiritual sense bread is heavenly love. Heavenly love contains everything that goodness and truth embrace and therefore everything that spiritual food embraces. For the meaning of bread as heavenly love, see §§276, 680, 2165, 2177, 2187, 3464, 3478, 3735, 4211, 4217, 4735, 4976.

Because it is abhorrent to the Egyptians means they are opposites, as the following shows: The *Egyptians* represent people who are inverted (§5700), and the Hebrews, with whom *it was abhorrent to the Egyptians* to eat, represent people who are in true order (§5701). So they represent qualities opposed to each other. The opposition gives rise to loathing and in the end to abhorrence.

5702

Regarding this abhorrence: It needs to be known that people who are inverted—that is, who live for evil and the resulting falsity—loathe the church's goodness and truth. They finally come to loathe it to such an extent that when they hear about it, and especially about the inner levels of it, they abhor it so much that they become almost nauseated and sick to their stomach. This was told and shown to me when I wondered why the Christian world does not accept these inner contents of the Word. Spirits from the Christian world appeared, and when forced to listen to the Word's inner message, they were seized with such nausea that they said they felt almost as if they needed to throw up. I was told that the Christian world is like this nearly everywhere today. The reason it is like this is that it does not desire truth for the sake of truth. Still less does goodness within it prompt it to desire goodness. The fact that Christians base some of what they think and say on the Word or on their doctrines is due to habit reaching back to childhood and to established custom. It is therefore superficial behavior without any inner significance.

[2] Everything in the Hebrew religion—which was later established among Jacob's descendants—was abhorrent to Egyptians. This is evident not only from their refusal even to eat with the Hebrews but also because the sacrifices the Hebrew church considered its main form of worship were abhorrent to them. This is plain in Moses:

Pharaoh said, "Go; sacrifice in the land." But Moses said, "It is not advisable to do so, because we will be *sacrificing what the Egyptians abhor to Jehovah our God.* Look, if we *sacrifice what the Egyptians find abhorrent* in their eyes, will they not stone us?" (Exodus 8:25, 26)

The shepherding of smaller livestock and the shepherds themselves were also abhorrent to Egyptians, as is plain in Moses:

Every shepherd of the flock is abhorrent to Egyptians. (Genesis 46:34)

Everything in that religion, then, was abhorrent to Egyptians. Why? Egyptians too had originally been among the people who constituted the representative ancient church (§§1238, 2385). Later on, though, they rejected the God of the ancient church—Jehovah, or the Lord—and served idols, particularly calves. Moreover, they took the representation and symbolism of heavenly and spiritual attributes known to the ancient church, which they had learned when part of that church, and turned it into magic. So they were inverted, and every facet of religion was consequently abhorrent to them.

5703 *And they were seated before him* means that they were arranged in order by his presence, as the following shows: *Being seated* means being arranged in order. The brothers were placed in order by Joseph, as the next few phrases show, because they were dumbfounded that he seated the firstborn according to his status as firstborn, and the youngest according to his youth. And *before him* means by his presence.

Here is the situation: In the highest sense Joseph represents the Lord, and Israel's sons represent goodness and truth on the earthly level. When the Lord is present, his very presence arranges everything in order. The Lord is order itself, so where he is present, there is order, and where there is order, he is present.

What follows next describes true order, in which truth is arranged in proper order under the control of goodness.

5704 *The firstborn according to his status as firstborn, and the youngest according to his youth* means according to the order truth follows when subordinate to goodness. This can be seen from the symbolism of being seated *according to one's status as firstborn* and *according to one's youth* as according to the order truth follows when subordinate to goodness. Israel's sons represent the church's truth in its proper arrangement; see the explanation at Genesis 29 and 30 [§§3759, 3858–3882, 3902, 3904–3969]. Being seated in their birth order, then, means in truth's order. However, the church's truth, which Israel's sons represent, achieves order only through Christian goodness, or the goodness associated with charity for one's neighbor and love for the Lord. What is good contains the Lord, you see, and consequently contains heaven, so it contains life and therefore a living, driving force. Truth lacking in goodness contains none of this force.

Goodness rearranges truth to resemble itself, as is obvious from any kind of love. This includes love for oneself and worldly advantages, or the love of revenge, hatred, and similar evils. People with these kinds of love call evil good, because they enjoy it. This so-called goodness of theirs lines up falsity (which is their "truth") to favor itself. In the long run it arranges all the falsity they call truth into such a well-organized pattern that it becomes conviction. The pattern, though, is like the pattern in hell.

On the other hand, the pattern truth follows when subordinate to the goodness belonging to a heavenly sort of love is like the pattern in the heavens. As a result, a person in whom this pattern exists, or a regenerate person, is called a miniature heaven and actually is a heaven in its smallest form, because such a person's inner levels correspond to the heavens.

[2] The pattern in the heavens makes it clear that goodness is what arranges truth in order. All the communities there are arranged according to truth under the control of goodness from the Lord. The Lord is nothing but divine goodness. Divine truth is not in the Lord but radiates from him. All communities in the heavens are arranged according to this divine truth under the control of divine goodness.

The fact that the Lord is nothing but divine goodness, and that divine truth is not in him but radiates from him, can be illustrated by comparison with the world's sun. The sun is nothing but fire. Light is not in it but radiates from it. In addition, recipients of light in the world, such as plants, are also marshaled into order by the warmth radiating from the sun's fire, which is contained in its light. This is evident in spring and summer.

Since the earthly universe is a theater representing the Lord's kingdom, this universal law also represents his kingdom. The sun represents the Lord. Its fire represents his divine love. The warmth from it represents goodness that comes from him, and the light represents the truth belonging to faith. Furthermore, because of this representation, in the Word's spiritual sense the sun means the Lord (§§1053, 1521, 1529, 1530, 1531, 3636, 3643, 4321 at the end, 5097, 5377) and fire means love (§§934, 4906, 5071, 5215). The sun's fire is therefore divine love, representationally speaking, and the warmth it gives off is goodness given off by divine love. Light is truth; see §§2776, 3138, 3190, 3195, 3222, 3339, 3636, 3643, 3862, 3993, 4302, 4409, 4413, 4415, 4526, 5219, 5400.

And the men stared dumbfounded, each at his companion, symbolizes a change of state for each in relation to the others, as the following shows: *Staring dumbfounded* symbolizes an unlooked-for, sudden change in the state of one's thinking. Because such a change makes a person stare dumbfounded, that is what is symbolized in an inner sense. And *each at his companion* means for each in relation to the others. **5705**

The topic under discussion is the pattern imposed on truth by the presence of the inner dimension when truth is subordinate to goodness (§§5703, 5704). Since the pattern is a new one, each truth undergoes a change of state in relation to the others, and this is symbolized by *the men stared dumbfounded, each at his companion.*

5706   *And he brought portions out from [before] his face for them* symbolizes different kinds of goodness applied to everyone individually out of mercy, as the following shows: *Portions*—portions of food—symbolize different kinds of goodness, because all foods symbolize goodness, and drink of every type symbolizes truth. Their being applied to everyone individually can be seen from what follows and is symbolized by *brought out for them.* And a *face,* when attributed to the Lord, whom Joseph is representing, symbolizes mercy, as discussed at §§222, 223, 5585.

5707   *And multiplied Benjamin's portion above the portions of them all* symbolizes goodness for the middle ground beyond the goodness applied to truth on the earthly level, as the following shows: *Portions* symbolize goodness, as was said just above in §5706. *Benjamin* represents the middle ground, as discussed in §§5411, 5413, 5427, 5428, 5443, 5586, 5612. And Jacob's ten sons, *above whose portions he multiplied Benjamin's portion,* represent truth on the earthly level, as discussed in §§5403, 5419, 5427, 5458, 5512. From this you can see that *he multiplied Benjamin's portion above the portions of them all* symbolizes goodness for the middle ground beyond the goodness applied to truth on the earthly level.

[2] The middle ground received goodness beyond the goodness applied to truth on the earthly level because the middle ground is more inward, and what is within abounds in goodness more than what is outward does.

Few know that an inner plane abounds in goodness and truth more than outer planes do, because few if any so far have recognized that the inner dimension is distinct from the outer one. The two are so distinct that they can be split apart, and when they are split, the inner plane lives and the outer plane dies. As long as they are united, though, the outer plane lives off the inner. If this had been recognized, it could then have been known what inner levels are like in relation to outer ones. The inner dimension contains thousands of elements that look like a single whole in the outer dimension, because the inner dimension is in a purer realm, and the outer dimension in a coarser one. Anything in a purer realm has a greater capacity than anything in a coarser realm for taking in thousands of distinct elements.

That is why people who have lived a good life and go to heaven after death can receive millions of times as much understanding, wisdom, and happiness as they could while living in the world. In heaven they are in a purer realm and in their inner depths. They have shed the coarser elements of the body.

This discussion now shows what is meant by goodness for the middle ground beyond the goodness applied to truth on the earthly level, as symbolized by *he multiplied Benjamin's portion above the portions of them all.*

By five measures means that it increased greatly. This can be seen from the symbolism of *five* as much (discussed below) and from that of *measures* as a state of truth marked by goodness (discussed at §3104).

5708

As for *five,* it is a number that symbolizes either a little or some or much. Its symbolism stems from its relationship to the number it rises out of (§5291). When it rises out of ten, it involves the same meaning as ten but to a lesser degree, being half of ten. Just as multiplied numbers have the same symbolism as their factors (§§5291, 5335), divided numbers have the same symbolism as their products. So five has the same symbolism as ten, twenty, one hundred, one thousand, and so on. Ten symbolizes fullness (see §§3107, 4638). Five measures were given to Benjamin above the rest of his brothers because of the symbolism in the inner meaning—since he could not be given ten measures. That would have been far too much.

The ancients knew what certain numbers symbolized because the information had been handed down from the earliest church. As a consequence they used those numbers when dealing with the kind of idea the numbers served to symbolize. That is why five is used here. They applied many other numbers in other situations, such as three to symbolize something complete from beginning to end, seven to symbolize something holy, and twelve to symbolize everything taken together.

And they drank means applying truth under the supervision of goodness. This can be seen from the symbolism of *drinking* as the communication and adoption of truth (discussed in §§3168, 3772, 4017, 4018) and therefore as the application of it. "Under the supervision of goodness" is meant because whenever truth is applied, it is applied under the supervision of goodness. See above, §5704.

5709

And drank heavily means in large quantities. This can be seen from the symbolism of *drinking* as applying truth under the supervision of goodness (discussed just above in §5709). *Drinking heavily,* then, means in large quantities.

5710

The explanation of this chapter's contents shows that it is about initiation into union of the earthly plane with spiritual heavenliness. The next chapter is about a first bond, a first bond being represented by Joseph's revealing himself to his brothers. A second bond is represented by his going to meet his father and brothers and bring them into Egypt [Genesis 46:29–47:11].

Correspondence (Continued): How Diseases Correspond with the Spiritual World

5711 SINCE I am going to be dealing with the correspondence of disease, the reader needs to know that all human disease also has a correspondence with the spiritual world. Nothing will exist anywhere in the physical world that lacks correspondence with the spiritual world. Such an entity would have no cause to emerge from and therefore to be sustained by. Effects are all that exist in the physical world. The causes of those effects exist in the spiritual world, and the causes of the causes (which are purposes) exist in an inward heaven.

Moreover, an effect cannot last unless the cause is constantly present in it. When the cause stops, the effect stops. Regarded in itself, an effect is simply a cause, but a cause clothed in an outward layer enabling it to do its work in a lower realm. [2] And just as an effect has this relationship to its cause, the cause has a similar relationship to its purpose. Unless a cause springs from its own cause, which is the purpose, it is not a cause. A cause without a purpose is a cause completely out of order, and where there is no order, nothing happens.

From this discussion you can now see that an effect viewed in itself is its cause, a cause viewed in itself is its purpose, and a good purpose exists in heaven, where it emanates from the Lord. So an effect is not an effect unless it contains a cause constantly present in it, and a cause is not a cause unless it contains a purpose constantly present in it. A purpose is not a good purpose unless it contains something divine emanating from the Lord.

You can also see that just as absolutely everything in the world sprang from the Divine, everything continues to be sustained by the Divine.

These remarks are to show that even disease has a correspondence **5712** with the spiritual world. Disease does not correspond with heaven, the universal human, but with people on the opposite side, in the hells. (The spiritual world in its broadest sense means both heaven and hell. When we die, we pass from the physical into the spiritual world.)

The reason disease corresponds with the hellish is that it corresponds to cravings and passions in the lower mind, which are also its origins. The general origins of illness are excess, overindulgence of various kinds, pleasures that are purely physical, and also envy, hatred, vengefulness, lust, and so on. These things destroy our inner reaches, and when our inner reaches have been destroyed, our outer level suffers, dragging us into disease and then death. The church knows that evil (or sin) causes human death, so it also causes sickness, since sickness is connected with death.

These points show that disease also has a correspondence with the spiritual world, but with unclean elements there. Sickness is inherently unclean, because it wells up out of what is unclean, as mentioned just above.

All hellish spirits bring on illness (with differences) because all the **5713** hells crave evil and are obsessed with it. They therefore work against influences from heaven and have the opposite effect on us. Heaven, the universal human, keeps everything connected and safe from harm. Hell, being opposed, destroys everything and rends it apart. If hellish spirits latch on, then, they trigger illness and eventually death.

However, hellish spirits are not permitted to flow right into the solid parts of the body, or the parts composing a person's organs, viscera, and limbs, just into a person's corrupt desires and distorted ideas. Only when we fall sick do they act on the unclean substances connected with disease. To repeat, nothing ever occurs in us unless its cause actually exists in the spiritual world. If our earthly plane were detached from our spiritual plane, it would be detached from everything that brings it into being and therefore from any life force.

Nonetheless, this does not prevent the possibility of physical cure. The means of healing coincide with the Lord's providence.

Much experience has taught me that this is the case, so many times and for so long a time that not a shred of doubt remains. Evil spirits from these kinds of places have often latched onto me for long periods, causing pain and also illness, depending on where they were present. I was shown where they were located and what they were like and was told where they came from.

5714   There was a man who had been extremely adulterous during bodily life and had found his highest pleasure in committing adultery with large numbers of women. Once he was done, he immediately rejected them and turned his back on them. He held to this course into old age. He was devoted to sensual pleasures, and refused to help anyone or perform any service unless doing so benefited him and especially his adulteries.

He was with me for several days, visible under my feet. While the aura of his life was being communicated to me, it inflicted pain on my periostea and nerves wherever it went, such as the toes of my left foot. When he himself was allowed to come forward, he caused pain to the parts where he was, especially to the periostea in my lower abdomen, to the periostea of my chest under the diaphragm, and inside my teeth.

When his aura was active, it also created a very heavy feeling in my stomach.

5715   I saw a large, square tunnel that slanted downward, stretching deep below. At the bottom appeared a round hole that lay open at that moment but soon closed. From it wafted warm, unwholesome air collected from various hells, which rose out of compulsions of various kinds, such as pride, lust, adultery, hatred, vengefulness, feuds, and fighting. These produced the warm air in the hells that was wafting out. When it acted on my body, it would immediately make me feel sick, as if I had a burning fever, but the moment the warmth stopped affecting me, the symptoms stopped.

When we develop an illness brought on by our lifestyle, an unclean aura corresponding to the illness takes hold at once and stays with us as a means of fueling the fire.

In order for me to learn for sure that this was so, spirits from many hells would join me and communicate the atmosphere exhaling from their hells. When they were allowed to act on the solid parts of my body, I would be gripped with a corresponding feeling of heaviness, pain, and sickness, which would instantly stop when the spirits were banished. This happened a thousand times, to avoid leaving any room for doubt.

5716   There are other spirits not far from there who pour in unclean chills, of the kind that accompany a fever, as I was also granted to learn by experience. The same spirits create mental disturbances, too, and cause fainting.

The spirits from that place are extremely malevolent.

5717   There are some spirits who not only relate to the stickiest substances in the brain, which are its waste products, but also know how to contaminate them with a kind of poison.

When spirits of this type arrive, they rush inside the skull and from there straight into the spinal cord. People who have not been given access to their own inner reaches cannot feel it, but I was repeatedly granted a clear sensation of their invasion. I could also tell what they were attempting, which was to kill me, though they failed, since the Lord was protecting me. They wished to rob me of all intellectual ability. I sensed their maneuvering very plainly and also the pain it caused, although this soon stopped.

Afterward I talked with them, and they were forced to tell where they came from. They said they live in dark woods, where they do not dare inflict any harm on their companions, because their companions would then be allowed to abuse them viciously. This holds them in check. They look ugly, have faces like wild animals, and are hairy.

[2] I was told they are the type of spirits that once killed off whole armies, as we read in the Word. They stormed the compartments of each warrior's brain, terrifying them all and driving them so crazy that they slaughtered each other. Nowadays spirits like this are kept shut up in their hell and are not released.

They also relate to fatal tumors of the head inside the skull.

I mentioned that they rush inside the skull and from there straight into the spinal cord, but it needs to be realized that the spirits themselves only appear to rush in. They move outside the body along a path that corresponds to those spaces in the body, and the movement is sensed as an internal invasion. Correspondence creates the sensation. Because of the correspondence, their activity is easily transferred into the person on whom it is focused.

Spirits of a certain kind want to be in control and to be the only ones ruling everyone else. For that purpose they arouse enmity, hatred, and conflict among others. I saw the fighting that results and in amazement asked who they were. I was told that they are the type of spirits who stir up this sort of trouble because they aim to wield supreme and solitary power, in accord with the maxim *divide and conquer*.

5718

I also had an opportunity to speak with them, and they immediately said they were in charge of everyone. "You are out of your minds if you resort to that kind of approach to bring you power," I was allowed to answer. They spoke with me from above, not too far over my forehead, and spoke fluently, since they had been very eloquent in bodily life.

I learned that they are the type who relate to thick phlegm in the brain, which they drain of life and make sluggish by their presence. This causes blockages—the origin of many diseases—and dull wits.

[2] They were devoid of conscience, I observed, and for them human prudence and wisdom consisted in arousing enmity, hatred, and infighting among others in order to gain the upper hand.

I was permitted to ask them whether they knew they were now in the other world, where they would live forever. "Do you know there are spiritual laws here that flatly forbid that kind of behavior?" I asked. "When you were in the world, you could be considered and accepted as the wise among fools, but you are lunatics among the wise." This displeased them.

"You ought to know that heaven consists in mutual love," I went on, "or the love one person has for another. That is why heaven is orderly and why so many myriads are governed as one. But it is the opposite with you. You inspire others to plot nothing but acts of hatred, revenge, and cruelty against their comrades."

"We can't be anything but ourselves," they answered.

"That tells you that our life awaits each of us," I was allowed to respond.

5719 There are spirits who scorn and ridicule the literal text of the Word, and especially the contents of its deeper sense, and therefore any teachings based on the Word as well, and who have no love for their neighbor, only for themselves. They relate to blood disorders that pervade all the veins and arteries and contaminate the whole supply. In an effort to keep them from inflicting anything of the kind on people by their presence, they are quarantined in their hell. They make contact only with spirits of their own kind, since these plunge themselves into the fumes and aura of that hell.

5720 Once I had with me some hypocrites—spirits who talked reverently on divine subjects, discussed the public and their neighbor with love and affection, spoke up for justice and fairness, yet in their hearts felt contempt for it all and even laughed at it. When they were allowed to flow into the parts of my body to which they corresponded in a negative sense, they wracked my teeth with pain. When they drew their closest, the pain grew so intense it was unbearable; the farther off they moved, the more the pain abated. The demonstration was repeated over and over to prevent any lingering doubt in my mind.

Among them was a man I had known during his bodily life, so I spoke with him. In this case too, the closer he was, the more my teeth and gums hurt. When he rose up toward the left, the pain spread into my upper left jaw and the bone in my left temple, reaching to my cheekbones.

5721 The most insolent of all are the ones who seemed more righteous than others during life in the world and were also high-ranking. Both of these qualities lent them authority and weight. Yet they did not believe in anything and lived a life of nothing but self-love. They burned with hidden hatred and with revenge against anyone who failed to cater to them or worship them and particularly against anyone who opposed them in any way. If they detected a minor flaw in an opponent, they made a huge evil out of it and slandered the person, even if that person had been one of the best citizens.

[2] In the other life, spirits like this talk the way they had in the world—with authority, weight, and apparent righteousness—so that many consider them more credible than others. They are terribly malicious, though. When they fasten on to us, they generate tremendous pain in the form of world-weariness, which they are constantly inflicting on us and intensifying until it becomes completely insufferable. The feeling is so debilitating to our mind and therefore our body that we can hardly get out of bed. This was shown to me by the fact that just such a weakness overtook me when they were nearby, but the farther away they moved, the less weakness there was.

[3] They have many techniques they use for filling us with weariness and consequent weakness. Their main method is to spread criticism and slander among themselves and their friends and to inject us with the general atmosphere of their slanders.

When they sit in their private rooms reasoning about divine worship, faith, and eternal life, they totally reject it all, and preen themselves on being unusually wise for doing so.

In the other life they want to be known as devils—as long as they are allowed to rule the hells and to use this power (as they believe) for undermining the Divine.

They are filthy to the core, because they have more self-love than others and therefore display more hatred, vengefulness, and cruelty toward anyone who does not worship them.

[4] Severe punishment is inflicted on them, I heard, until they stop misleading others by appearing to be upright. Once they have been deprived of the appearance, they take a different tone. Later they are cast out from the world of spirits, off to the left, where they are thrown deep into hell. This hell is on the left, not too far away.

There are others who were quite vile during physical life. Their vile behavior is best left unmentioned. By their presence with and inflow into the solid parts of the body, they trigger disgust for life, and such languor in one's limbs and joints that one cannot get out of bed.

5722

They are very stubborn. Punishment does not stop them the way it stops other devils. They show up near the head, apparently lying down there. When they are driven away, they do not leave suddenly but slowly, gradually tumbling down to the nether regions. When they reach the bottom, they undergo such painful torture that they cannot help giving up their harassment of others.

They enjoy doing evil so much that nothing gives them more pleasure.

5723   There were some spirits with me who produced such leaden heaviness in my stomach that it seemed to me I could barely survive. The weight was so heavy it would have knocked others unconscious. The spirits were taken away, though, and the attack instantly ended. I was told that these spirits are ones who had not been dedicated to accomplishing anything during physical life, not even at home, but only to enjoying themselves. They had lived lazy, idle lives, without a care for anyone else, and had scoffed at faith. In short, they had been animals, not humans. The aura of such spirits enfeebles the limbs and joints of sick people.

5724   There are sticky substances in the brain that have a volatile, lively element mixed in with them. These sticky substances, purged from the blood, are discharged between the meninges first and then between the fibers. Some of them empty into the large ventricles in the brain and continue on from there.

Spirits who relate by correspondence to the sticky substances that have something volatile and lively in them appear almost directly above the middle of the head, not too far away. They are the types who raise moral objections and inject them into matters having nothing to do with morality, out of a habit they developed in bodily life. So they burden the conscience of ordinary people. They do not know what really ought to stir the conscience, since no matter what happens, they assume conscience applies.

[2] These spirits create a palpable anxiety in the part of the abdomen under the region of the diaphragm. They are also present in times of trial, instilling an anxiousness that is sometimes unbearable. The ones corresponding to a sticky phlegm that is less lively then bog our thoughts down in those worries.

I struck up a conversation with them in order to learn what they were like. They kept trying to burden my conscience in various ways—which had been their central pleasure in life. I was able to observe that they could not listen to reason and that they had no broad overview of matters from which to see particulars.

I had the opportunity to learn from experience what a flood or deluge is in a spiritual sense. There are two kinds: a flood of corrupt desires and a flood of false ideas. Corrupt desires flood the volitional side of the mind, and this flood takes place in the right side of the brain. False ideas flood the intellectual side of the mind, and this flood affects the left side of the brain.

5725

When people who had lived good lives are let back into their self-absorption and therefore into the environment created by their own self-life, a kind of flood seems to occur. While immersed in the flood, they seethe, rage, think turbulent thoughts, and experience fierce cravings—in one way when the flood inundates the left side of their brain, where falsity resides, and in another when it inundates the right side, where evil resides.

[2] In contrast, when they are being held in the environment created by the life they had received from the Lord through rebirth, they stand entirely outside any such flood, under a clear, sunny sky, so to speak, in a cheerful, happy place. So they are far from seething, rage, turbulence, cravings, and so on. This situation is morning or springtime for spirits. The other is their evening or fall.

I was allowed to perceive that I was standing outside the flood for a fairly long time, and during that time I saw that other spirits were inside it. Later on, though, I myself was submerged, and I then experienced something like a flood. People undergoing times of trial have the same experience.

This episode taught me what a flood symbolizes in the Word. It symbolizes the fact that the last descendants of the earliest people, who had come from the Lord's heavenly church, were totally flooded with evil and falsity and died out as a result.

Death comes from sin and nowhere else, and sin is everything opposing the divine plan. Because of this, evil closes off the very smallest vessels, which are completely invisible and which combine to make the next larger vessels, also invisible. The very smallest, completely invisible vessels extend from our inner reaches. The closure introduces the first and deepest blockage and the first and deepest defect into the blood. As the defect accumulates, it causes sickness and eventually death.

5726

If humankind had lived a life of goodness, our inner depths would lie open to heaven and through heaven to the Lord. Our tiniest, invisible vessels would stay open too (if I might refer to the slender traces of our first rudiments as little vessels, on account of the correspondence), with the result that we would be free of sickness. We would slow down only at the last stages of old age, until we finally became little children again, but wise children. Then, when our body could no longer serve our inner self, or spirit, we would pass without illness from our earthly body into the kind of body angels have. So we would pass directly from the world into heaven.

5727   Here ends the discussion of correspondence. With the Lord's divine mercy, the ends of later chapters will discuss the spirits and angels with us, spiritual inflow and the soul's interaction with the body, and the inhabitants of other planets.

Genesis 44

1. And he commanded the one who was over his household, saying, "Fill the men's bags with food, as much as they can carry, and put each one's silver in the mouth of his bag.

2. And my cup, the silver cup, you are to put in the mouth of the youngest's bag, and the silver of his grain." And he did according to Joseph's word that he spoke.

3. Morning shone, and the men were sent off, they and their donkeys.

4. They went out of the city—they had not gone far—and Joseph said to the one who was over his household, "Get up; follow after the men, and you are to overtake them and say to them, 'Why are you repaying evil for good?

5. Isn't this what my lord drinks from? And he assuredly does divination with it. What you've done, you have done wrongly.'"

6. And he overtook them and spoke these words to them.

7. And they said to him, "Why does my lord speak according to these words? Far be it from your servants to do according to this word!

8. Look: the silver that we found in the mouth of our bags we brought back to you from the land of Canaan; and how are we going to steal silver or gold from the house of your lord?

9. The one of your servants with whom it is found, let him die, and we also will become slaves to my lord."

10. And he said, "Even now according to your words, so be it: the one with whom it is found will be a slave to me, and you yourselves will be guiltless."

11. And they hurried, and they each brought their bag down to the ground, and they each opened their bag.

12. And he searched; he started with the oldest, and he finished with the youngest, and the cup was found in Benjamin's bag.

13. And they ripped their clothes, and each loaded his donkey, and they returned to the city.

14. And Judah and his brothers went in to Joseph's house, and he—he was still there, and they fell before him to the earth.

15. And Joseph said to them, "What is this deed you have done? Did you not know that a man like me surely does divination?"

16. And Judah said, "What shall we say to my lord; what shall we speak, and how are we going to be excused? God has found out the wickedness of your servants. Here, now, we are slaves to my lord, both we and the one in whose hand the cup was found."

17. And he said, "Far be it from me to do this! The man in whose hand the cup was found, he will be a slave to me, and you yourselves go up in peace to your father."

18. And Judah drew close to him and said, "By my life, my lord; please let your servant speak a word in my lord's ears, and may your anger not burn against your servant, because like Pharaoh, like you.

19. My lord asked his servants, saying, 'Do you have a father or brother?'

20. And we said to my lord, 'We have an old father, and the son of his old age, the youngest, and his brother is dead, and he alone is left to his mother, and his father loves him.'

21. And you said to your servants, 'Bring him down to me and let me lay my eye on him.'

22. And we said to my lord, 'The youth cannot leave his father, and should he leave his father, [his father] will die.'

23. And you said to your servants, 'If your youngest brother does not come down with you, you will not see my face again.'

24. And it happened when we went up to your servant my father and told him the words of my lord

25. that our father said, 'Go back; buy us a little food.'

26. And we said, 'We cannot go down. If our youngest brother is with us, we will go down, because we cannot see the man's face and our youngest brother not be with us.'

27. And your servant my father said to us, 'You know that my wife bore me two.

28. And one went out from me, and I said, "Surely he has been mauled"; and I have not seen him up till now.

29. And you are taking this one also from my presence, and should harm happen to him, you will make my white hair go down in evil to the grave.'

30. And now as I come to your servant my father, and the youth is not with us—and [the father's] soul is bound up in [the youth's] soul—

31. it will happen, as he sees that the youth is not there, that he will die, and your servants will make the white hair of your servant our father go down in sorrow to the grave.

32. Because your servant served as surety for the youth with my father, saying, 'If I do not bring him back to you, I will be sinning against my father all my days.'

33. And now let your servant please stay in place of the youth as a slave to my lord, and let the youth go up with his brothers.

34. Because how am I going to go up to my father and the youth not be with me? Maybe I will see the evil that will find my father."

Summary

THE inner meaning of this chapter discusses the middle ground between the [Lord's] inner, heavenly self and his outer, earthly self. It starts by saying that his inner, heavenly self filled the middle ground with spiritual truth from itself. The middle ground is Benjamin. The spiritual truth with him is Joseph's silver cup. The inner, heavenly self is Joseph. The outer, earthly self is Jacob's ten sons. **5728**

Then it discusses trials for the outer, earthly self, which continued until [the brothers] willingly surrendered to the inner, heavenly self. The trials are depicted by the accusation against them, and by the fact that they went back to Joseph without hope. Willing surrender is depicted by the offer they all made to become slaves and the offer Judah made to become a slave in their stead. The union of the outer self with the inner does not happen without trials and voluntary surrender. **5729**

The representative meaning on a narrative level is about Jacob's descendants. It says that they were rejected but stubbornly insisted on filling a representative role. Their being rejected is meant by Joseph's wish to send them away and keep only Benjamin. The fact that they stubbornly insisted is meant by the things contained in their confession and plea. **5730**

Inner Meaning

GENESIS 44:1, 2. And he commanded the one who was over his household, saying, "Fill the men's bags with food, as much as they can carry, and put each one's silver in the mouth of his bag. And my cup, the silver cup, **5731**

*you are to put in the mouth of the youngest's bag, and the silver of his grain."
And he did according to Joseph's word that he spoke.*

And he commanded the one who was over his household, saying, symbolizes an inflow from himself. *Fill the men's bags with food* means of goodness-from-truth into the earthly level. *As much as they can carry* means enough. *And put each one's silver in the mouth of his bag* means [and] of truth on the outer earthly level, yet again. *And my cup, the silver cup, you are to put in the mouth of the youngest's bag* symbolizes inner truth given to the middle ground. *And the silver of his grain* symbolizes truth-from-goodness. *And he did according to Joseph's word that he spoke* means that it was done.

5732   *And he commanded the one who was over his household, saying,* symbolizes an inflow from himself, as the following shows: *Commanding* symbolizes an inflow, as discussed in §5486. And *who was over his household* means who would communicate. Of course the inflow comes from himself, that is, from the inner heavenliness represented by Joseph.

Commanding symbolizes an inflow because heaven's inhabitants do not command or order anyone but communicate their thinking, and the other person voluntarily acts on the thought. To communicate one's thoughts, while wanting the other person to feel the need for something specific to happen, is inflow. On the part of the person receiving the message, it is perception, so commanding also symbolizes perception (§§3661, 3682).

[2] In heaven they not only think but also talk to each other. They talk about matters of wisdom, but their words contain no hint of command over another. No one wants to be master and to regard others as slaves. No, everyone wants to help and to serve others.

This shows what form of government exists in the heavens. The Lord describes it in Matthew:

> It shall not be this way among you, but anyone among you who wants to become great has to be your attendant. And anyone who wants to be first will have to be your slave. (Matthew 20:26, 27)

And in the same author:

> The one who is greatest of you must be your attendant. Any who lift themselves up will be humbled, and any who humble themselves will be lifted up. (Matthew 23:11, 12)

That is how people act when they sincerely love their neighbor, or at least find pleasure and bliss in doing good to others for reasons that are not selfish—that is, when they have charity for their neighbor.

Fill the men's bags with food means of goodness-from-truth into the earthly level. This can be seen from the symbolism of a *bag* as the outer earthly level (discussed at §5497) and from that of *food* as goodness-from-truth (discussed at §§5340, 5342, 5410, 5426, 5487, 5582, 5588, 5655). Plainly, then, "He commanded the one who was over his household, 'Fill the men's bags with food,'" symbolizes an inflow from himself of goodness-from-truth into the earthly level.

5733

Since the terms *goodness-from-truth* and *truth-from-goodness* come up often, I need to distinguish them. Anyone who does not know what a heavenly religion is in relation to a spiritual one can never see the difference. Truth-from-goodness characterizes a heavenly religion, and goodness-from-truth a spiritual one. In the people of a heavenly religion, goodness was planted in the will part of their mind, which is the proper seat for goodness. This goodness, or rather the Lord working through this goodness, gave them a perception of truth. That is how truth-from-goodness was acquired by them. In the people of a spiritual religion, though, goodness is planted in the intellectual part through truth, since all truth belongs to the intellectual side. Through truth they are led to goodness, since acting on truth is their form of goodness. That is how goodness-from-truth is acquired by them. In this I am speaking strictly, but people in a spiritual religion can also be credited with truth-from-goodness, although strictly speaking it is not accurate. More on this subject elsewhere [§§3969, 4592, 5307, 5586, 5600, 6440].

As much as they can carry means enough, as is evident without explanation.

5734

And put each one's silver in the mouth of his bag means and of truth on the outer earthly level, yet again. This can be seen from the symbolism of *silver* as truth (discussed at §§1551, 2954, 5658) and from that of the *mouth of a bag* as the threshold of the outer earthly level (discussed at §5497). For a definition of the outer and inner earthly levels, see §§4570, 5118, 5126, 5497, 5649. It means truth yet again because silver had also been laid in the mouth of their bags earlier, in a previous chapter, Genesis 42:25, 27, 28, 35.

5735

And my cup, the silver cup, you shall put in the mouth of the youngest's bag symbolizes inner truth given to the middle ground, as the following

5736

shows: A *silver cup* symbolizes religious truth growing out of charitable goodness, as discussed in §5120, and since it is called *my cup*, or Joseph's, it symbolizes inner truth. Because Benjamin represents a middle ground, including the truth there, he represents inner truth (§§5600, 5631) and therefore *spiritual* truth (§5639). The *mouth of a bag*, when the bag is said to belong to Benjamin as the middle ground, symbolizes the place where the earthly level attaches. A middle ground communicates with the outer surface and inner core in order to be a middle ground (§§5411, 5413, 5586), and the outer surface here is the earthly plane. And Benjamin, the *youngest*, represents a middle ground, as discussed in §§5411, 5413, 5443, 5688.

This shows what is symbolized by Joseph's putting his silver cup in Benjamin's bag.

5737   *And the silver of his grain* symbolizes truth-from-goodness. This can be seen from the symbolism of *silver* as truth (discussed at §§1551, 2954, 5658) and from that of *grain* as goodness (discussed at §§5295, 5410). Inner, spiritual truth, which radiates from the inner heavenliness that Joseph stands for, is truth-from-goodness. For what this kind of truth is, see §5733 just above.

5738   *And he did according to Joseph's word that he spoke* means that it was done, as is evident without explanation.

5739   Genesis 44:3, 4, 5. *Morning shone, and the men were sent off, they and their donkeys. They went out of the city—they had not gone far—and Joseph said to the one who was over his household, "Get up; follow after the men, and you are to overtake them and say to them, 'Why are you repaying evil for good? Isn't this what my lord drinks from? And he assuredly does divination with it. What you've done, you have done wrongly.'"*

Morning shone symbolizes a state of enlightenment then. *And the men were sent off, they and their donkeys,* means that the outer earthly self with its truth and its knowledge is partially put aside. *They went out of the city—they had not gone far* symbolizes how much it is put aside. *And Joseph said to the one who was over his household* symbolizes a perception and inflow, yet again. *Get up; follow after the men* symbolizes the necessity of connecting them to itself now. *And you are to overtake them* symbolizes an indirect connection. *And say to them, "Why are you repaying evil for good?"* means why the turning away? *Isn't this what my lord drinks from?* means that they have with them inner truth received from what is heavenly. *And he assuredly does divination with it* means that the heavenly element, under the power of the divinity behind it, sees into mysteries.

What you've done, you have done wrongly means that to claim it for one's own violates divine law.

Morning shone symbolizes a state of enlightenment then. This can be **5740** seen from the symbolism of *morning* and *shining* as a state of enlightenment. In the highest sense, morning means the Lord (see §§2405, 2780), so when the text says *morning shone*, it symbolizes a state of enlightenment, because the Lord is the source of all enlightenment. "Getting up in the morning" also means a state of enlightenment (see §§3458, 3723).

And the men were sent off, they and their donkeys, means that the outer **5741** earthly self with its truth and its knowledge is partially put aside, as the following shows: Jacob's sons, the *men,* represent religious truth on the earthly plane, as discussed in §§5403, 5419, 5427, 5458, 5512. Consequently they represent the outer earthly self (§5680). *Donkeys* symbolize knowledge, as discussed in §5492. And *being sent off* but "not going far" symbolizes being partially put aside—which is done to the outer earthly self. It stands to reason, then, that "the men were sent off, they and their donkeys—they had not gone far" means that the outer earthly self with its truth and its knowledge is partially put aside, some distance away from the inner heavenliness represented by Joseph.

[2] About the symbolism of *donkeys:* They symbolize one thing in situations where they were used for transportation, since judges, monarchs, and royal offspring rode male and female donkeys and also mules. Under those circumstances donkeys symbolized truth and goodness on the rational plane and on the earthly plane; see §2781. That was why the Lord, when he entered Jerusalem as a judge and king, rode a jenny with her foal [Matthew 21:1–10; Mark 11:1–11; Luke 19:29–44; John 12:12–15]; it was a sign of a judge and of a monarch.

Donkeys symbolized something else, though, when they served as beasts of burden, as they did here. They then symbolized knowledge. That is exactly how knowledge serves. People who ask themselves what constitutes our inner depths without venturing beyond memorized information imagine that we consist entirely of knowledge. They do not realize that knowledge resides on our lowest level and is mostly something that gets buried when our body dies (§§2475, 2476, 2477, 2479, 2480). However, what items of knowledge hold within them remains, and that is truth and goodness, along with a desire for truth and goodness. In the evil, falsity and evil remain, along with a desire for them. Knowledge in effect provides a body for these traits. As long as we are alive in the world, we store these traits—either truth and goodness or falsity and evil—within knowledge, because knowledge is a container. Since items of knowledge contain and therefore "carry" what lies inside, they are symbolized by donkeys, which serve as beasts of burden.

5742   *They went out of the city—they had not gone far* symbolizes how much it is put aside, as can be seen from the preceding remarks.

5743   *And Joseph said to the one who was over his household* symbolizes a perception and inflow, yet again. This is established by the symbolism of *saying* in the Word's narratives as perceiving (discussed many times before). Because it means perception in relation to the person who hears the message and takes it in, it symbolizes inflow in relation to the person who delivers it, since these activities answer to each other.

"He commanded the one who was over his household" means an inflow from himself; see above at §5732.

5744   *Get up and follow after the men* symbolizes the necessity of connecting them to itself now. This can be seen from the symbolism of *following after the men* and overtaking them as forming a connection. *Following* them is intending to form a connection, and overtaking them is forming the connection.

The rest of this chapter is about the return of Jacob's sons. The next is about Joseph's unmasking, which symbolizes the union between spiritual heavenliness and truth on the earthly plane. So following after the men plainly symbolizes the necessity of connecting them to itself now.

5745   *And you are to overtake them* symbolizes an indirect connection. This can be seen from the symbolism of *overtaking them*—done by the one who was over Joseph's household—as an indirect connection.

5746   *And say to them, "Why are you repaying evil for good?"* means why the turning away? This can be seen from the symbolism of *repaying evil for good* as turning away. Evil is nothing but a turning away from goodness, because people immersed in evil spurn goodness, and specifically spiritual goodness, which is the goodness that comes of neighborly love and faith.

Those in the other life who live for evil illustrate clearly that evil is a turning away. In heaven's light they appear with their feet up and head down (§3641), or completely inverted and therefore the wrong way around.

5747   *Isn't this what my lord drinks from?* means that they have with them inner truth received from what is heavenly. This can be seen from the symbolism of the cup, meant by *what my lord drinks from,* as inner truth (mentioned at §5736), and from the representation of Joseph, *my lord,* as spiritual heavenliness (discussed at §§5307, 5331, 5332). Here he represents heavenliness by itself, because the passage is talking about inner truth, which is the spiritual element and radiates from the Lord. Its reception is symbolized by the cup's being laid in the mouth of Benjamin's bag at Joseph's command.

[2] The men are charged with having taken the cup. The reason for the charge, despite the fact that the cup was planted there, is evident from the inner meaning, which is this: When the Lord gives us truth, we receive it at first as if it were not a gift. Before rebirth, we imagine that we acquire truth for ourselves, and as long as we are thinking this way, we are committing spiritual theft. To claim goodness and truth as our own and attribute them to our own righteousness and merit is to steal from the Lord; see §§2609, 4174, 5135.

Joseph acted as he did to represent this fact, but there is more: The men were accused of theft in order to bring about union. Until we have been reborn, we cannot help believing [that we acquire truth and goodness on our own]. We do say with our lips on the basis of doctrine that all the truth that constitutes faith and all the goodness that constitutes neighborly love comes from the Lord, but we do not believe it until faith has taken root in goodness. Then for the first time we acknowledge it with our heart. [3] Saying so because the church teaches it is entirely different from saying so because we believe it. Lots of people are capable of acknowledging this from doctrine, even people who are not committed to goodness. To them, doctrine is merely a matter of knowledge. The only people who can acknowledge it with faith are those committed to spiritual goodness, or to charity toward their neighbor.

Here is further evidence that the men were accused of theft in order to bring about union: It allowed Joseph to bring them back and make them spend some time thinking about what had happened. Then he revealed himself to them, or united with them.

And he assuredly does divination with it means that the heavenly element, under the power of the divinity behind it, sees into mysteries. This is clear from the symbolism of *doing divination* as seeing into mysteries. The reason this happens from divinity is that spiritual heavenliness, represented by Joseph, is truth from the Divine, or truth that contains divinity; see §5417.

5748

What you've done, you have done wrongly means that to claim it for one's own violates divine law. This can be seen from the symbolism of theft, meant by the *wrong they had done* as claiming for one's own what belongs to the Lord—that is, claiming the truth symbolized by Joseph's silver cup (discussed at §5747). Clearly this violates divine law; see §2609.

5749

The reason we should not claim for ourselves what comes from the Lord, and therefore not truth or goodness, is that we can then be awake to the true situation. The more awake we are to the truth, the more we enjoy the light that shines on angels in heaven, and the more we enjoy that light, the more understanding and wisdom we have, and the more understanding and wisdom we have, the more happiness we have. That is why we ought to acknowledge with heartfelt belief that nothing true or good comes from us but that it all comes from the Lord; and we ought to acknowledge it because it is so.

5750 [Genesis 44:6, 7, 8, 9, 10.] *And he overtook them and spoke these words to them. And they said to him, "Why does my lord speak according to these words? Far be it from your servants to do according to this word! Look: the silver that we found in the mouth of our bags we brought back to you from the land of Canaan; and how are we going to steal silver or gold from the house of your lord? The one of your servants with whom it is found, let him die, and we also will become slaves to my lord." And he said, "Even now according to your words, so be it: the one with whom it is found will be a slave to me, and you yourselves will be guiltless."*

And he overtook them symbolizes an indirect connection. *And spoke these words to them* symbolizes an inflow of this concept. *And they said to him* symbolizes an awareness. *Why does my lord speak according to these words?* means pondering why such a thing is flowing in. *Far be it from your servants to do according to this word* means as it is not intentional. *Look: the silver that we found in the mouth of our bags* means since truth was granted for free. *We brought [back] to you from the land of Canaan* means that they submitted it [to the Lord] from religious principle. *And how are we going to steal silver or gold from the house of your lord?* means why then would we claim truth and goodness from divine heavenliness for ourselves? *The one of your servants with whom it is found, let him die* means that anyone who does such a thing is damned. *And we also will become slaves to my lord* means that they will be permanently grouped together, without the freedom of self-rule. *And he said, "Even now according to your words,"* means yes, it would only be right. *So be it* symbolizes a milder sentence. *The one with whom it is found will be my slave* means that the one who has it will permanently lack self-directed freedom. *And you yourselves will be guiltless* means that the rest will be in charge of themselves because they do not share the guilt.

5751 *And he overtook them* symbolizes an indirect connection, as above in §5745.

And spoke these words to them symbolizes an inflow of this concept. **5752**
This can be seen from the symbolism of *speaking* as flowing in (discussed in §§2951, 3037, 5481) and from that of *words* as concepts. *Word* is even the term for a concept in the original language.

And they said to him symbolizes an awareness. This is established by **5753**
the symbolism of *saying* in the narrative parts of the Word as a perception.

Why does my lord speak according to these words? means pondering why **5754**
such a thing is flowing in. This can be seen from the symbolism of *speaking* as flowing in, and from that of *according to these words* as that concept, or that type of thing (mentioned just above at §5752). *Why?*—a word used to ask oneself a question—involves pondering.

Far be it from your servants to do according to this word means as it **5755**
is not intentional. That is, they do not intend to claim truth as their own. This is established by the symbolism of *doing* as intending, since all deeds involve intent. The deed itself is earthly; the intent is its spiritual origin. That it is *not*—not intentional—is symbolized by *far be it from your servants.*

Look: the silver that we found in the mouth of our bags means since truth **5756**
was granted for free, as the following shows: *Silver* symbolizes truth, as discussed in §§1551, 2954, 5658. *We found* means granted for free, because the silver for each one's grain had been repaid to them and had therefore been given for free; see §§5530, 5624. And the *mouth of the bags* symbolizes the threshold of the outer earthly level, as discussed in §5497.

We brought back to you from the land of Canaan means that they sub- **5757**
mitted it [to the Lord] from religious principle. This can be seen from the symbolism of *bringing back* as submitting (discussed in §5624) and from that of the *land of Canaan* as religious principle. The land of Canaan symbolizes a range of things, because what it symbolizes enfolds many other things. It symbolizes the Lord's kingdom and it symbolizes the church, so it also symbolizes someone in the church, because such a person *is* a church. Since it symbolizes these things, it also symbolizes what is heavenly in the church (the goodness that comes from love) and what is spiritual in the church (the truth that leads to faith). And so on. Here, then, it symbolizes religious principle, which is part of the church. After all, we have it from religious principle in the church that we are not to claim truth and goodness as our own.

This discussion shows why one word sometimes has a range of symbolisms. When a word embraces many ideas together, it also symbolizes everything it embraces, depending on the context of the inner meaning.

The land of Canaan means the Lord's kingdom; see §§1413, 1437, 1607, 3038, 3481, 3705. It also means the church; §§3686, 3705, 4447. From these meanings stem all the rest of its symbolisms.

5758   *And how are we going to steal silver or gold from the house of your lord?* means why then would we claim truth and goodness from divine heavenliness for ourselves? This is established by the symbolism of *stealing* in a spiritual sense as claiming for oneself what belongs to the Lord (discussed above at §5749), from that of *silver* as truth (discussed at §§1551, 2954, 5658), and from that of *gold* as goodness (discussed at §§113, 1551, 1552, 5658).

The whole chapter is about spiritual theft, which is to claim goodness and truth from the Lord as one's own. This is such an important issue that after death we cannot be let into heaven until we acknowledge in our heart that no goodness or truth comes from us, only from the Lord, and that anything from us is pure evil. After death we have many experiences showing that this is so. Angels in heaven plainly perceive that everything good and true comes from the Lord, that the Lord keeps us from evil and anchors us in goodness and therefore in truth, and that he does so with a mighty power.

[2] I too have been allowed to perceive this manifestly for many years now. I have also seen that the more I am left to myself and my own devices, the more I am flooded with evil; and the more the Lord withholds me from myself and the desire to govern myself, the more I am lifted out of evil into goodness.

To claim truth and goodness as one's own, then, violates the universal rule in heaven. It also contradicts the acknowledgment that all salvation comes of mercy, which is to say that on our own we live in hell but the Lord in his mercy pulls us out. What is more, unless we acknowledge that nothing but evil comes from us and that everything good comes from the Lord, we cannot have humility. So we cannot accept the Lord's mercy, because his mercy acts on us only in humility, or acts only on a humble heart. Besides, we otherwise take credit for our deeds as a matter of merit and eventually of righteousness. To claim truth and goodness from the Lord as our own is to be self-righteous. Many evils bubble up from this spring, because we then focus on ourselves in each thing we do for our neighbor, and when we do that, we love ourselves more than all others, whom we despise, if not out loud, at least in our heart.

5759   *The one of your servants with whom it is found, let him die* means that anyone who does such a thing is damned. This can be seen from the symbolism of *dying* as being damned, because spiritual death is nothing but damnation.

People who claim the Lord's truth and goodness as their own cannot be in heaven but are outside heaven, as the remarks in §5758 just above show, and anyone outside heaven is damned. This law is a law of judgment based on truth, though. When judgment is based at the same time on goodness, those who do what is true and good and attribute it to themselves out of simple ignorance are not damned. Instead, they are set free in the other life by a certain kind of purging.

Besides, we all ought to do what is true and good as if on our own but still believe it comes from the Lord; see §§2882, 2883, 2891. If we do, then when we mature, and our understanding and faith grow, we shed the illusion. Eventually we acknowledge at heart that all our effort to do what is good and think what is true has come from the Lord and continues to do so.

For the same reason, the man sent by Joseph actually confirms the judgment (that the brother with whom the cup was found would die) but then rejects it right afterward. He says, "Even now according to your words, so be it: the one with whom it is found will be a slave to me, and you yourselves will be guiltless"—symbolizing a milder sentence.

The case is different with people who act this way not out of simple ignorance but from principles they have solidified by their beliefs and their life. Still, since they accomplish good, the Lord in his mercy preserves in them a bit of simple ignorance.

And we also will become slaves to my lord means that they will be permanently grouped together, without the freedom of self-rule. This can be seen from the symbolism of *we also* as being grouped together, and from the symbolism of *becoming slaves* as being without the freedom of self-rule. People who are slaves lack self-directed freedom, because they are at the call of their owner's self-rule and freedom.

What it is to lack the freedom of self-rule will be told later, with the Lord's divine mercy [§§5763, 5773, 5786].

And he said, "Even now according to your words," means yes, it would only be right, as the explanations just above in §§5758, 5759 show. *Even now according to your words* means that it would only be right—right for one who acts this way to die—but a milder sentence now follows.

So be it symbolizes a milder sentence. This can be seen from the next clauses, which dictate the milder sentence.

5760

5761

5762

5763   *The one with whom it is found will be my slave* means that the one who has it will permanently lack self-directed freedom. This is established by the symbolism of a *slave* as being without self-directed freedom, as above at §5760.

Here is the situation: Joseph's silver cup, planted on Benjamin at Joseph's orders, symbolizes inner truth (§§5736, 5747). Anyone with access to inner truth knows that everything true and good comes from the Lord and that all freedom derived from ourselves and our sense of autonomy is hellish. When we do or think anything out of self-directed freedom, all we do and think is evil. This makes us the Devil's servant, because everything evil flows in from hell. We find pleasure in that kind of freedom because it harmonizes with the evil we live in and were born with. This self-directed freedom has to be stripped away and replaced with heavenly freedom, which is to will what is good and therefore do good, and to desire what is true and therefore think truth. When we receive this freedom, we are the Lord's servant, and then we enjoy real freedom. We are not subject to our previous servitude, which seemed to be freedom.

This now is what being permanently without self-directed freedom means. For what freedom is and where it comes from, see §§2870–2893. For being led by the Lord as real freedom, see §2890.

5764   *And you yourselves will be guiltless* means that the rest will be in charge of themselves because they do not share the guilt. This can be seen from the symbolism of *guiltless* people, compared to a slave, as being in charge of themselves. Naturally it is because they do not share the guilt.

Non-Christians once had a custom that when one person sinned, they would extend the guilt to others connected with the person and even punish a whole household for the crime of one member. Such a law grew out of hell, where all the members of a group plot evil together. The communities of hell are set up in such a way that the members work against goodness together, as one. This keeps them connected with one another, even though each member nurses a lethal hatred against the next. They have the oneness and friendship of thieves. Since companions in hell plot evil together, then, they are all punished for carrying it out.

To do the same thing in the world, though, is diametrically opposed to the divine plan. In the world, good people team up with evil ones because no one knows what the next person is like inside and usually no one cares. The divine law for people on earth is therefore that we

each pay the penalty for our own wickedness. Here is what Moses says
about it:

> Parents shall not die on account of their children, and children shall not
> die on account of their parents. They shall each be killed in their own
> sin. (Deuteronomy 24:16)

And in Ezekiel:

> The soul that has sinned, that soul shall die, nor shall a parent carry the
> wickedness of the child. The uprightness of the upright person shall be
> on that person, and the godlessness of the godless person shall be on
> that person. (Ezekiel 18:20)

These comments show what was going on here, where Jacob's sons
said, "The one of your servants with whom it is found, he shall die, and
we also will become slaves to my lord," but the man sent by Joseph altered
the judgment and said, "The one with whom it is found will be my slave,
and you yourselves will be guiltless." Likewise further on, where Judah
says to Joseph, "Here, now, we are slaves to my lord, both we and the one
in whose hand the cup was found," and Joseph says, "Far be it from me
to do this! The man in whose hand the cup was found, he will be a slave
to me, and you yourselves go up in peace to your father" (verses 16, 17).

Genesis 44:11, 12. *And they hurried, and they each brought their bag* **5765**
down to the ground, and they each opened their bag. And he searched; he
started with the oldest, and he finished with the youngest, and the cup was
found in Benjamin's bag.

And they hurried symbolizes impatience. *And they each brought their*
bag down to the ground means that they referred the contents of the earthly
level to the senses. *And they each opened their bag* means so as to make the
matter clear to themselves. *And he searched* symbolizes exploration. *He*
started with the oldest, and he finished with the youngest symbolizes the
order. *And the cup was found in Benjamin's bag* means that inner truth,
received from what is heavenly, exists with the middle ground.

And they hurried symbolizes impatience. This can be seen from the **5766**
symbolism of *hurrying*, when people are eager to prove their innocence,
as impatience.

And they each brought their bag down to the ground means that they **5767**
referred the contents of the earthly level to the senses, as the following
shows: Anticipating the next few words as it does, *bringing down* means

referring. A *bag* symbolizes the outer earthly level, as discussed at §5497. And when the text says they brought something down to the *ground,* it symbolizes the last and lowest level. So it symbolizes the sensory level, because this is the last and lowest. After all, the senses are positioned on the threshold to the surrounding, outside world.

To refer something to the senses is to demonstrate positively that it is so, because the question is then reduced to sensory evidence.

5768   *And they each opened their bag* means so as to make the matter clear to themselves. This can be seen from the symbolism of *opening a bag* as opening up what lies on the earthly plane and therefore as making the matter clear.

5769   *And he searched* symbolizes exploration, as is self-evident.

5770   *He started with the oldest, [and] he finished with the youngest* symbolizes the order, as the remarks at §5704 show.

5771   *And the cup was found in Benjamin's bag* means that inner truth, received from what is heavenly, exists with the middle ground. This can be seen from the symbolism of the *cup* as inner truth (discussed in §5736) and from the representation of *Benjamin* as a middle ground (discussed in §§5411, 5413, 5443). The fact that this truth, received from what is heavenly, exists with the middle ground is symbolized by the cup's being placed in Benjamin's bag on Joseph's orders.

Previous discussions give further details on all these concepts.

5772   Genesis 44:13, 14, 15, 16, 17. *And they ripped their clothes, and each loaded his donkey, and they returned to the city. And Judah and his brothers went in to Joseph's house, and he—he was still there, and they fell before him to the earth. And Joseph said to them, "What is this deed you have done? Did you not know that a man like me surely does divination?" And Judah said, "What shall we say to my lord; what shall we speak, and how are we going to be excused? God has found out the wickedness of your servants. Here, now, we are slaves to my lord, both we and the one in whose hand the cup was found." And he said, "Far be it from me to do this! The man in whose hand the cup was found, he will be a slave to me, and you yourselves go up in peace to your father."*

And they ripped their clothes symbolizes mourning. *And each loaded his donkey, and they returned to the city* means that truth was drawn back from the sensory realm to the realm of knowledge. *And Judah and his brothers went in* symbolizes goodness in the church and the truth that goes with it. *To Joseph's house* symbolizes communication with the inner dimension. *And he—he was still there* symbolizes foresight. *And they fell before him to the earth* symbolizes humility. *And Joseph said to them* symbolizes a perception they then had. *What is this deed you have done?* means that to claim what is not one's own as one's own is terribly wrong. *Did you not know that a man like me surely does divination?* means that it cannot be concealed from one who sees what is to come and what is hidden. *And Judah said,* symbolizes a perception granted to goodness on the earthly plane belonging to the church. *What shall we say to my lord; what shall we speak?* symbolizes ambivalence. *And how are we going to be excused?* means that we are guilty. *God has found out the wickedness of your servants* symbolizes a confession. *Here, now, we are slaves to my lord* means that we will be permanently deprived of self-directed freedom. *Both we* means not only those who are grouped together. *And the one in whose hand the cup was found* means but also the one who has inner truth, received from divine heavenliness. *And he said, "Far be it from me to do this!"* means that this will never happen. *The man in whose hand the cup was found* means but the one who has inner truth, received from the Divine. *He will be a slave to me* means this person will be permanently subordinate. *And you yourselves go up in peace to your father* means that those who are grouped together and lack inner truth will return to their former condition.

And they ripped their clothes symbolizes mourning. This can be seen from the symbolism of *ripping one's clothes* as mourning over lost truth (discussed at §4763), and in this case, over self-determined truth. They could no longer claim this truth as their own because they offered to become slaves, in the presence of both the one who was over Joseph's household (verse 9) and Joseph himself (verse 16). The symbolism of the offer is that they would be without the freedom of self-rule and therefore without truth as determined by themselves.

A word about grief over self-determined truth, as symbolized by their ripping their clothes and offering to become slaves: You need to know that something switches in people who are being reborn. Truth leads them to goodness, and afterward goodness leads them to truth. When the switch is occurring, or the state is changing and becoming the reverse of what it was, grief arises, because they are then subjected to trial. Through times of trial, what comes of self-rule is undermined and weakened, and goodness is instilled. Along with goodness comes a new will, and along with a new will, new freedom, and therefore new self-rule.

This is represented by the return of Joseph's brothers to Joseph without hope, their offer to become slaves to him, their fairly long suspense in that state, and the fact that Joseph did not reveal himself until after the time of trial. Once a trial has reached its end, the Lord shines down with comfort.

5774   *And each loaded his donkey, and they returned to the city* means that truth was drawn back from the sensory realm to the realm of knowledge, as the following shows: A *donkey* symbolizes knowledge, as discussed at §5492. *Loading* one means drawing it back from the senses because bringing their bag down to the ground means referring the contents of the earthly level to the senses (§5767). "Loading" here means lifting the bag back off the ground. A *city* symbolizes doctrinal truth, as discussed at §§402, 2449, 2943, 3216.

[2] I should explain briefly what it is to draw truth back from the sensory realm to the realm of knowledge. Sensory information is one thing, knowledge is another, and truth is another. They come one after the other, because knowledge develops out of sense impressions, and truth develops out of knowledge. Impressions entering through our senses are stored in our memory, and we draw knowledge as a conclusion from them, or else we perceive in them the knowledge we are learning. From knowledge we draw truth as a conclusion, or we perceive in it the truth we are learning. That is how we move forward from our youth as we grow up. When we are young, we use sense impressions as a basis for thought and comprehension. When we grow older, we use knowledge as a basis for thought and comprehension; and still later we use truth. This is the path to acquiring the power of judgment, which we grow into as we mature. [3] This shows that sensory information, knowledge, and truth are distinct from each other. They actually remain distinct, too—so much so that we move from one to the other. Sometimes we contemplate sensory information, which happens when our thoughts do not venture beyond what meets our senses. Sometimes we contemplate what we know, which happens when we raise ourselves out of sense impressions and think more deeply. Sometimes we contemplate truth, drawn as a conclusion from knowledge, which happens when we think still more deeply. Any who reflect on the situation can see it for themselves.

We can also lower truth to the realm of knowledge and see truth within knowledge, and we can lower knowledge to the sensory realm and contemplate knowledge within sensory evidence. We can do the reverse as well.

These considerations now show what is meant by referring the contents of the earthly level to the senses and drawing truth back from the sensory realm to the realm of knowledge.

And Judah and his brothers went in symbolizes goodness in the church and the truth that goes with it. This can be seen from the representation of *Judah* as goodness in the church (discussed in §§5583, 5603) and from that of *his brothers* as truth on the earthly plane.

5775

Why was it Judah who went in and spoke with Joseph rather than Reuben, the firstborn, or one of the others? It is because Judah was the main one to represent goodness, and what communicates with heavenliness from the Divine is goodness, not truth. Truth has no communication with the Divine except through goodness. That is why only Judah spoke.

To Joseph's house symbolizes communication with the inner dimension. This can be seen from the symbolism of going into a *house* as communication, and from the representation of *Joseph* as the inner dimension (discussed in §5469).

5776

Entering a house stands for communication because a house symbolizes a person her- or himself (§§3128, 5023) and therefore what makes the person, which is that individual's mind, with the truth and goodness in it (§§3538, 4973, 5023). When the text speaks of entering a house, then, it means entering the person's mind, so it means having communication.

And he—he was still there symbolizes foresight. This stands to reason from Joseph's foreseeing that they would be back and his staying home on that account. His purpose was to reveal himself to Benjamin and therefore to the others—or, in an inner sense, for truth on the earthly plane to unite with divine heavenliness.

5777

Foresight is mentioned because the highest meaning is about the Lord, who is meant by Joseph on that level.

And they fell before him to the earth symbolizes humility, as is self-evident.

5778

And Joseph said to them symbolizes a perception they then had. This can be seen from the symbolism of *saying* as a perception. It means a perception *they* had because the one saying something is Joseph, who represents the inner dimension, and all perception comes from the inner dimension, or rather from the Lord through that dimension. There is no other source for perception or even for sensation. It seems as though sensation and perception as well flow in from outside us, but that is an illusion. The inner plane is what senses things through the outer plane. The senses located in our body are simply tools or instruments serving our inner self, enabling it to sense what exists in the world. The inner

5779

dimension therefore flows into the outer dimension in order to gather sensations, with the aim of gleaning perception from the sensations and being perfected. The reverse is not so.

5780   *What is this deed you have done?* means that to claim what is not one's own as one's own is terribly wrong. This can be seen from the symbolism of the theft they were charged with as usurpation of the Lord's truth and goodness. This is the *deed* meant in an inner sense. For how bad it is, see §§5749, 5758 above.

5781   *Did you not know that a man like me surely does divination?* means that it cannot be concealed from one who sees what is to come and what is hidden. This is established by the symbolism of *doing divination* as seeing into mysteries under the power of the divinity behind him (discussed at §5748) and also into the future, because it applies to the Lord, who is meant by Joseph in the highest sense. The fact that it cannot be concealed is plain from the words themselves.

5782   *And Judah said,* symbolizes a perception granted to goodness on the earthly plane belonging to the church, as the following shows: In the Word's narrative, *saying* symbolizes a perception, as noted many times. The perception is something granted because all perception comes from the inner dimension. That is, it flows in from the Lord through the inner dimension (§5779). And *Judah* represents goodness belonging to the church, as discussed in §§5583, 5603, 5775.

Concerning Judah's representation, keep in mind that in the highest sense he represents the Lord and his divine love, and in an inner sense the Lord's heavenly kingdom; see §§3654, 3881. So he represents the heavenly quality of love there. In the current passage, then, he represents the church's loving goodness on the earthly plane, because he is currently among men who represent the contents of the earthly plane, which needs to be united with the inner plane.

5783   *What shall we say to my lord; what shall we speak?* symbolizes ambivalence. This can be seen from the emotion behind the words, which is ambivalence.

5784   *And how are we going to be excused?* means that we are guilty. This can be seen from the symbolism of *how are we going to be excused?*—that is, that they cannot be excused—as the fact that they are guilty. Anyone who cannot be excused is guilty. It is obvious that they considered themselves guilty, since they offered themselves as slaves to Joseph.

5785   *God has found out the wickedness of your servants* symbolizes a confession. The confession is that they behaved wickedly in selling Joseph, and in an inner sense, that they disowned truth and goodness, separating themselves from the inner plane. This is evident without explanation.

Here, now, we are slaves to my lord means that we will be permanently deprived of self-directed freedom. This can be seen from the symbolism of *slaves* as being without the freedom of self-rule—a symbolism discussed in §§5760, 5763. These same sections also discussed what it is to lack the freedom of self-rule, but since the subject is extremely important, it bears repeating.

We have an outer and an inner self. Our outer self is the one through which our inner self acts, because our outer self is simply the tool or instrument of our inner self. This being so, our outer self must be wholly under the command and control of our inner self. When it is, heaven acts through our inner self on our outer self and adapts it to heavenly kinds of pursuits.

[2] The opposite happens when our outer self is not under control but *in* control, and it is in control when we take as our aim the pleasures of our body and our senses. Our outer self is particularly in control when we make the concerns of self-love and materialism rather than the concerns of heaven our aim. To take them as our aim is to love the one and not the other. After all, when we make self-centered and materialistic concerns our goal, we no longer believe any inner self exists. We stop believing we have anything in us that will live on when our body dies. Because our inner dimension lacks dominance, it merely serves the outer dimension, enabling our outer mind to think and reason against what is good and true. The inflow of the inner dimension is not then visible in any other form. That is why people like this have utter contempt for heavenly values and even loathe them.

These considerations make it plain that the outer self, which is identical with the earthly self, ought to be totally subject to the inner, spiritual self and consequently to be without the freedom of self-rule.

[3] The freedom of self-rule consists in yielding to all kinds of sensual pleasure, despising others in comparison with ourselves, and making them our slaves. If not that, it consists in persecuting them, hating them, delighting in their misfortune (especially when we ourselves inflict it, through zeal or deceit), and wishing for their death. Such are the effects of self-directed freedom. This shows what we are like when we have such freedom: we are devils in human form.

When we give up this freedom, we receive heavenly freedom from the Lord. People with self-directed freedom have not the least idea what heavenly freedom is. They imagine that if robbed of self-centered freedom,

5786

they would have no remaining life. The reality, though, is that life actually starts then, and with it comes genuine pleasure, bliss, and happiness, accompanied by wisdom—because heavenly freedom is from the Lord.

5787 *Both we* means not only those who are grouped together. This can be seen from the symbolism of *both we*, [or "we also,"] as being grouped together (as above in §5760).

5788 *And the one in whose hand the cup was found* means but also the one who has inner truth, received from divine heavenliness. This can be seen from the symbolism of *in whose hand* as the one who has, from that of the *cup* as inner truth (discussed at §5736), and from the representation of Joseph as divine heavenliness.

5789 *And he said, "Far be it from me to do this!"* means that this will never happen, as is plain without explanation.

5790 *The man in whose hand the cup was found* means the one who has inner truth, received from the Divine. This can be seen from the remarks just above in §5788.

5791 *He will be a slave to me* means this person will be permanently subordinate. This can be seen from the symbolism of a *slave* as being permanently without the freedom of self-rule (discussed just above at §5786) and therefore permanently subordinate.

5792 *And you yourselves go up in peace to your father* means that those who are grouped together and lack inner truth will return to their former condition, as the following shows: Jacob's ten sons represent the group among which the cup—that is, the inner truth symbolized by the cup (§§5736, 5788, 5790)—was not found. And *going up in peace to your father* means returning to a former condition. When the inner dimension (Joseph) does not accept them, their former condition awaits them.

5793 Genesis 44:18–31. *And Judah drew close to him and said, "By my life, my lord; please let your servant speak a word in my lord's ears, and may your anger not burn against your servant, because like Pharaoh, like you. My lord asked his servants, saying, 'Do you have a father or brother?' And we said to my lord, 'We have an old father, and the son of his old age, the youngest, and his brother is dead, and he alone is left to his mother, and his father loves him.' And you said to your servants, 'Bring him down to me and let me lay my eye on him.' And we said to my lord, 'The youth cannot leave his father, and should he leave his father, [his father] will die.' And you said to your servants, 'If your youngest brother does not come down with you, you will not see my face again.' And it happened when we went up to your servant my father and told him the words of my lord that our father said, 'Go back; buy us a little food.' And we said, 'We cannot go down. If our youngest brother is with* *us, we will go down, because we cannot see the man's face and [our] youngest brother not be with us.' And your servant my father said to us, 'You know that my wife bore me two. And one went out from me, and I said, "Surely he has been mauled"; and I have not seen him up till now. And you are taking this one also from my presence, and should harm happen to him, you will make my white hair go down in evil to the grave.' And now as I come to your servant my father, and the youth is not with us—and [the father's] soul is bound up in [the youth's] soul—it will happen, as he sees that the youth is not there, that he will die, and your servants will make the white hair of your servant our father go down in sorrow to the grave."*

And Judah drew close to him symbolizes communication of the outer self with the inner through goodness. *And said,* symbolizes a perception. *By my life, my lord* symbolizes a plea. *Please let your servant speak a word in my lord's ears* means to be received and heard out. *And may your anger not burn against your servant* means for him not to turn away. *Because like Pharaoh, like you,* means that he has ruling power over the earthly level. *My lord asked his servants, saying,* symbolizes a perception of their thinking. *Do you have a father or brother?* means that they have goodness as a source and truth as a means. *And we said to my lord* symbolizes an answering perception. *We have an old father* means that they have spiritual goodness as their source. *And the son of his old age, the youngest,* symbolizes truth from it, which is new. *And his brother is dead* means that there is no inner goodness. *And he alone is left to his mother* means that the church has only this truth. *And his father loves him* means that it has a bond with spiritual goodness that is on the earthly level. *And you said to your servants* symbolizes a perception granted. *Bring him down to me* means that this new truth will be subordinate to inner goodness. *And let me lay my eye on him* symbolizes the inflow at that time of truth based on goodness. *And we said to my lord* symbolizes an answering perception. *The youth cannot leave his father* means that this truth cannot be separated from spiritual goodness. *And should he leave his father, [his father] will die* means that if it were separated, the church would perish. *And you said to your servants* symbolizes a perception on this point. *If your youngest brother does not come down with you* means if it does not submit to inner goodness. *You will not see my face again* means that there will then be no mercy and no bond with truth on the earthly plane. *And it happened when we went up to your servant my father* symbolizes being raised to the level of spiritual goodness. *And told him the words of my lord* symbolizes a knowledge of the matter. *That our father said,* symbolizes a perception received from spiritual goodness. *Go back; buy us a little food* means that goodness based on truth needs to be adopted. *And we said, "We cannot go down,"* symbolizes an objection. *If our youngest brother is with us, we will go down* means unless the uniting middle ground is present. *Because we cannot see the man's face* means because there is no mercy and no bond. *And our youngest brother not be with us* means except through the middle ground. *And your servant my father said to us* symbolizes a perception received from spiritual goodness. *You know that my wife bore me two* means that if there is spiritual goodness in the church, there will be inner goodness and truth. *And one went out from me* symbolizes the apparent departure of inner goodness. *And I said, "Surely he has been mauled,"* symbolizes a sense that it had been destroyed by evil and falsity. *And I have not seen him up till now* means because it had vanished. *And you are taking this one also from my presence* means if the new truth also leaves. *And should harm happen to him* means from evil and falsity. *You will make my white hair go down in evil to the grave* means that spiritual goodness and therefore the core of the church will perish. *And now as I come to your servant my father* symbolizes goodness in the church, corresponding to spiritual goodness in the inner part of the church. *And the youth is not with us* means if the new truth is not present. *And [the father's] soul is bound up in [the youth's] soul* means since there is a tight bond. *It will happen, as he sees that the youth is not there, that he will die* means that spiritual goodness will perish. *And your servants will make the white hair of your servant our father go down in sorrow to the grave* means that it will be all over for the church.

5794   *And Judah drew close to him* symbolizes communication of the outer self with the inner through goodness. This can be seen from the symbolism of *drawing close* to speak with someone as communication, and from the representation of *Judah* as goodness on the earthly level belonging to the church (discussed in §5782). It is the outer self communicating with the inner because Judah represents goodness belonging to the church as it exists in the earthly, outer self, while Joseph represents goodness in the inner self.

The reason it takes place through goodness is that communication is possible only through goodness, not through truth, unless there is goodness in the truth.

5795   *And said,* symbolizes a perception. This can be seen from the often discussed symbolism of *saying* as a perception.

5796   *By my life, my lord* symbolizes a plea, as the next several verses show.

5797   *Please let your servant speak a word in my lord's ears* means (a plea) to be received and heard out, as the following shows: *Speaking a word* symbolizes an inflow, as mentioned in §§2951, 5481, and therefore reception on the other person's part (§5743). And *ears* symbolize obedience, as discussed in §§4551, 4653. Here they symbolize a kindly hearing or audience, since a common man is speaking to a higher-up. Clearly, then, *Please let your servant speak a word in my lord's ears* symbolizes a plea to be received and heard out.

And may your anger not burn against your servant means for him not to turn away. This is established by the symbolism of *anger* as a turning away, [or aversion,] (discussed at §5034). Angry people turn away, because their thoughts do not agree with the other person's but conflict, while the mood lasts.

5798

The meaning of *anger* as aversion is plain in many Scripture passages, especially those that describe Jehovah, or the Lord, as having anger and wrath, which symbolize aversion. It is not that Jehovah, or the Lord, ever turns away, but that we ourselves do, and when we turn away it looks to us as though the Lord does, because we are not heard. The Word speaks this way in keeping with the appearance.

Since anger means aversion, it also means antipathy against goodness and truth on the part of people who avert themselves. On the part of people who do not avert themselves, it does not mean antipathy but rather disgust, due to an aversion for evil and falsity.

[2] Section 3614 demonstrated that anger means *antipathy*. The following passages show that it also means *aversion* and that it means *punishment* for attacking what is good and true. In Isaiah:

> Doom to those decreeing wicked decrees! They will fall under the prisoner and under the slain. In all this, though, *his anger will not turn back.* Doom to Assyria, the *rod of my anger!* Against a hypocritical nation I will send him, and against a *people of wrath* I will order him. He thinks what is not right, and his heart contemplates what is not right. (Isaiah 10:1, 4, 5, 6, 7)

The anger and wrath stand for aversion and antipathy on the part of human beings. When we are punished and not heard in times of aversion and antipathy, it looks like anger. Because it is on our part, the text says, "Doom to those decreeing wicked decrees! He thinks what is not right, and his heart contemplates what is not right." [3] In the same author:

> Jehovah [comes] with the implements of his anger to destroy all the earth. Look—Jehovah *comes, cruel, with outrage, wrath,* and *anger,* to make the earth a wasteland so that its sinners he can destroy from it. "I

will shake heaven, and the earth will shake out of its place, *in the out-rage of Jehovah Sabaoth* and *on the day when his anger blazes up.*" (Isaiah 13:5, 9, 13)

Heaven and earth stand for the church. Its devastation and ruin (since it had turned away from truth and goodness) is depicted in Jehovah's outrage, anger, and wrath. The reality is just the opposite, though. When we take to evil, we feel outrage, anger, and wrath and set ourselves against goodness and truth. The punishment, which grows out of the evil, is ascribed to Jehovah because of the appearance. Other passages scattered through the Word refer to the church's final days and its ruin as the day of Jehovah's anger. [4] In the same author:

> Jehovah has broken the staff of the ungodly, the rod of rulers; *you will strike the peoples in fury, with a blow that is not curable,* as you rule the nations *with anger.* (Isaiah 14:5, 6)

Likewise in this passage. The case resembles that of criminals punished by the law who blame the monarch or judge rather than themselves for the miseries of their punishment. In the same author:

> Because Jacob and Israel have not been willing to walk in Jehovah's ways and have not listened to his law, he has *poured out onto them the wrath of anger* and the violence of war. (Isaiah 42:24, 25)

In Jeremiah:

> I myself will fight against you with an outstretched hand and a strong arm and *in anger* and *in wrath* and *in great rage. May my fury not go forth like fire* and *burn* and *be unquenched* because of the wickedness of your deeds! (Jeremiah 21:5, 12)

The fury, anger, and great rage actually mean the miseries that are the punishment for aversion and antipathy toward goodness and truth. [5] By divine law, all evil carries a penalty with it, and surprisingly, the evil and its penalty are inseparable in the other life. As soon as a hellish spirit acts more wickedly than usual, disciplinarian spirits show up and punish the spirit, but without being detected. Turning away is obviously what brings on the miseries of the punishment, since the text says "because of the wickedness of your deeds." In David:

> He sent against them the *wrath of his anger,* his *outrage,* and *fury,* and anguish, and a delegation of evil angels. He straightened out a path *for his anger;* he did not withhold their soul from death. (Psalms 78:49, 50)

See also Isaiah 30:27, 30; 34:2; 54:8; 57:17; 63:3, 6; 66:15; Jeremiah 4:8; 7:20; 15:14; 33:5; Ezekiel 5:13, 17; Deuteronomy 9:8, 19, 20; 29:20, 21, 23, 24; Revelation 14:9, 10; 15:7. In these places too, wrath, anger, outrage, and fury stand for aversion, antipathy, and consequent punishment.

[6] Why is the punishment for aversion and antipathy blamed on Jehovah, or the Lord, and described as anger, wrath, and fury in him? The people of the nation descended from Jacob had to be held to their role representing a religion—a purely superficial role—and they could be held to it only through fear and terror of Jehovah. They needed to believe he would do them harm if roused to anger and wrath. When people are intent on outward acts devoid of inward content, that is the only way they can be led to fulfill the outward requirements, because they have no inward sense of obligation. Besides, simple-thinking people inside the church are inevitably led by appearances to think that God becomes angry when someone does wrong.

Still, anyone who reflects can see that Jehovah, or the Lord, harbors no anger, much less fury, because he is mercy itself and goodness itself and is infinitely beyond wishing ill to anyone. People with charity for their neighbor do not do anyone harm, and angels in heaven never do either. How could the Lord himself do such things?

[7] Here is how matters stand in the other world: When the Lord reduces heaven and its communities into order (which happens constantly, because of new arrivals), he gives them bliss and happiness, which flows into the opposing communities. (In the other world, all the communities of heaven have communities opposing them in hell, which creates a balance.) When the opposing communities sense a change due to heaven's presence, they grow angry, blaze up, and erupt into evil. Then they incur the miseries of punishment. In addition, when evil spirits or demons approach heaven's light, they start to suffer distress and torment (§§4225, 4226). This they blame on heaven and consequently on the Lord, although the torment is actually self-inflicted. Evil feels tortured when it goes near goodness. These comments show that nothing but goodness comes from the Lord and that all evil comes from those people themselves who turn away, put up opposition, and attack.

From this secret piece of information, you can see how the matter stands.

Because like Pharaoh, like you, means that he has ruling power over the earthly level. This can be seen from the representation of *Pharaoh* as the earthly level in general (mentioned at §5160) and from that of Joseph as the inner dimension (discussed before). The inner dimension's ruling power over the earthly level is represented by Joseph's being set in charge over all the land of Egypt and over Pharaoh's whole household (Genesis 41:40, 41).

5800   *My lord asked his servants, saying,* symbolizes a perception of their thinking. This can be seen from the symbolism of *asking* as perceiving someone else's thoughts (discussed at §5597). Asking has this symbolism because in the spiritual world, or heaven, no one needs to ask what another is thinking on subjects that touch that other's heart, since one person perceives the thoughts rising out of the other's emotions. What is more, the inner plane that Joseph represents does not ask questions of the outer plane that Jacob's sons represent, because the outer plane receives everything it has from the inner. This too shows that asking symbolizes the perception of thoughts.

In addition, it occasionally happens in the Word that Jehovah asks a person a question, even though he knows absolutely everything the person is thinking. This happens because we human beings are fully convinced that our thoughts are visible to no one, dwelling inside us as they do. It is due to this appearance and humankind's belief in it that the questions are asked.

5801   *Do you have a father or brother?* means that they have goodness as a source and truth as a means, as the following shows: Israel, the *father,* represents spiritual goodness, or the goodness that grows out of truth (discussed at §§3654, 4598). He represents goodness *as a source* because truth on the earthly plane comes from spiritual goodness. And Benjamin, the *brother,* represents truth. He represents truth *as a means* because it is through this that religious truth on the earthly level, represented by Jacob's sons, unites with spiritual goodness, represented by Israel. Because the union depends on truth as a means, the text repeatedly describes how Benjamin's father loved Benjamin, who represents such truth, and how neither Judah nor the others could go back to their father unless Benjamin was with them. For a discussion of such truth, see below at §5835.

5802   *And we said to my lord* symbolizes an answering perception. This can be seen from the symbolism of *saying* as a perception (discussed frequently). Obviously it is an answering perception.

5803   *We have an old father* means that they have spiritual goodness as their source. This is established by the representation of Israel, the *father,* as spiritual goodness as a source (discussed just above at §5801).

In regard to Israel's representation, see §§4286, 4292, 4570. To be explicit, he represents a spiritual religion and specifically its inner level, which is the goodness that grows out of truth, or spiritual goodness on the earthly plane. For a definition of spiritual goodness, or the goodness that grows out of truth, see §§5526, 5733.

And the son of his old age, the youngest, symbolizes truth from it, which **5804** is new, as the following shows: Benjamin, the *youngest son,* represents truth, as noted above in §5801. Besides, a *son* symbolizes truth; see §§489, 491, 1147, 2623, 3373. And *old age* symbolizes new life, as discussed in §§3492, 4620, 4676. This shows that the *son of his old age, the youngest,* symbolizes truth that is new.

Here is the situation: When we are being reborn and becoming spiritual, at first we are led by truth to goodness. We do not know what spiritual goodness is—in other words, what Christian virtue is—except through truth, or teachings from the Word. That is how we are introduced to goodness. Later, when we have been introduced, we are no longer led through truth to goodness but through goodness to truth. Not only do we see the truth we already knew, now from a standpoint of goodness; we also produce new truth out of goodness, truth that we did not and could not know before. Goodness carries with it a desire for truth. It feeds on truth, so to speak, because it is perfected by truth. This new truth is vastly different from the truth we knew before, because the truth we knew before had little life, while the truth we now accept receives life from goodness.

[2] When we have arrived at goodness through truth, we become Israel. The truth that we afterward receive from goodness, or rather from the Lord through goodness, is new truth, which is represented by Benjamin—as long as he was with his father. By means of this truth, goodness reproduces on the earthly level and brings forth unlimited quantities of truth containing goodness. That is how the earthly level is reborn. In its fruitfulness it comes at first to resemble a tree with good fruit and gradually a garden.

This shows what is meant by new truth from spiritual goodness.

And his brother is dead means that there is no inner goodness, as the **5805** following shows: Joseph represents spiritual heavenliness, as discussed in §§4592, 4963, 5249, 5307, 5331, 5332, so he represents inner goodness, which is the same as spiritual heavenliness. And *being dead* means no longer existing, as discussed at §494.

The difference between the representation of Joseph as inner goodness and of Israel as spiritual goodness is this: Joseph is inner goodness on the rational plane, and Israel is inner goodness on the earthly plane; see

§4286. The difference is like that between heavenly goodness, or the goodness found in a heavenly religion, and spiritual goodness, or the goodness found in a spiritual religion. Earlier sections have discussed these two kinds of goodness many times [§§4448, 4980, 5113, 5595, 5733].

Inner heavenly goodness is what is being said not to exist there, and it is the goodness symbolized by *his brother is dead.*

5806   *And he alone is left to his mother* means that the church has only this truth. This can be seen from the representation of Benjamin, the one *alone left,* as new truth (discussed just above at §5804) and from the symbolism of a *mother* as the church (discussed at §§289, 2691, 2717, 5581).

Here is the situation with the idea that this truth, represented by Benjamin and described above in §5804, is the only truth in the church: This truth is truth derived from the spiritual goodness that is Israel and is represented by Benjamin when he is with his father. (When he is with Joseph, he represents a still deeper kind of truth.) This truth represented by Benjamin when he is with his father—called new truth—is the only truth we act on in order to become an individual church, because it contains living energy imparted by goodness. That is, a person with religious truth based on goodness is an individual church, but a person with religious truth who lacks charitable goodness is not. In this latter person, truth is dead, even if it is the exact same truth.

From this you can see what it means to say that the church has only this truth.

5807   *And his father loves him* means that it has a bond with spiritual goodness that is on the earthly level, as the following shows: *Love* symbolizes a bond, as discussed below. Israel, the one who *loves him,* represents spiritual goodness on the earthly level, as discussed in §§4286, 4598. And Benjamin, *him* whom his father loves, represents new truth, as discussed above in §§5804, 5806. The bond between this kind of truth and that kind of goodness is what *his father loves him* symbolizes.

This truth cannot help uniting with that goodness because it grows out of that goodness. The two have the kind of bond that exists between parent and child. It is also the kind of bond that exists between the mental activities of willing and understanding. All goodness belongs to the capacity for will, and all truth to the capacity for understanding. When the will intends what is good, goodness is instilled in the intellect, where it takes form, in accord with the nature of the goodness. The form it takes is truth. Since that is how the new truth is born, there obviously must be a bond.

[2] Regarding love as a bond, keep in mind that love is a spiritual bond, because it is a union of minds, or of two people's thoughts and intentions. This makes it plain that love viewed in itself is purely spiritual, and that its earthly aspect is the pleasure of fellowship and close connection.

In its essence, love is harmony resulting from changes of state and from variations in the forms or substances of which the human mind consists. If the harmony follows a heavenly pattern, it is a heavenly type of love. Clearly, then, love cannot trace its origin to any other source than divine love itself from the Lord. So love is divinity flowing into the forms and managing them in such a way that their changes of state and variations follow heaven's harmony.

[3] The opposite kinds of love—love for ourselves and worldly advantages—do not unite but divide. They appear to unite, but that is because we consider others to be in unison with us as long as they act in unison with us when it comes to material advantages, acquiring rank, taking revenge on our opponents, and persecuting them. As soon as the other person stops catering to us, there is a rift.

Not so with heavenly love, which is totally averse to helping anyone for selfish reasons. Heavenly love does good for the sake of the goodness in another, which that other receives from the Lord, and consequently for the sake of the Lord himself, the source of what is good.

And you said to your servants symbolizes a perception granted. This **5808** can be seen from the symbolism of *saying* in the Word's narratives as a perception, and since the words were said *to them*, it means a perception granted.

Bring him down to me means that this new truth will be subordi- **5809** nate to inner goodness. This can be seen from the symbolism of *bringing down*, because going to an inner dimension to unite with it means surrendering to it. Everything lower or outer has to be completely under the command and control of what is higher or inner if union is to take place. The meaning can also be seen from the representation of Benjamin, the one they were to bring down, as new truth (discussed above at §§5804, 5806) and from the representation of Joseph, the one he was to go down to, as inner goodness (discussed before [§5805]).

And let me lay my eye on him symbolizes the inflow at that time of truth **5810** based on goodness. This can be seen from the symbolism of *laying an eye on someone* as communicating religious truth. The *eye* corresponds to the sight of the intellect and to religious truth; see §§4403–4421, 4523–4534.

Since laying an eye on someone means communicating, it also means an inflow. The inner goodness that Joseph represents communicates with the truth that is Benjamin only by an inflow into it, because this truth is on a lower level.

5811   *And we said to my lord* symbolizes an answering perception, as above in §5802.

5812   *The youth cannot leave his father* means that this truth cannot be separated from spiritual goodness. This is established by the symbolism of *leaving* as separating, from the representation of Israel as spiritual goodness on the earthly level (discussed in §§4286, 4598, 5807), and from the representation of Benjamin as new truth (discussed in §§5804, 5806). This truth is called a *youth* because it is born last. It cannot be born until we have been reborn. Once reborn, we take new life through this new truth united with goodness. As a result, this truth is also symbolized by "the son of his old age, the youngest" (§5804).

5813   *And should he leave his father, [his father] will die* means that if it were separated, the church would perish. This is established by the symbolism of *leaving* as separating (as just above in §5812) and from that of *dying* as no longer existing (discussed in §494), and therefore as perishing.

This truth united to spiritual goodness makes the church (§5806), so if it were separated from that goodness, the church would perish. Besides, Israel, the *father,* represents the church (§4286), but not without this truth.

5814   *And you said to your servants* symbolizes a perception on this point, as above in §5808.

5815   *If your youngest brother does not come down with you* means if it does not submit to inner goodness. This can be seen from the remarks above in §5809.

5816   *You will not see my face again* means that there will then be no mercy and no bond with truth on the earthly plane. This can be seen from the symbolism of a *face,* when associated with the Lord, as mercy (discussed in §§222, 223, 5585), so that *not seeing his face* means that there is no mercy (§§5585, 5592). When there is no mercy, there is no bond, either, because there is no love, which is a spiritual bond. Divine love is called mercy in relation to the human race, established as we are in so much misery. The reason it means no bond with truth on the earthly plane is that Jacob's sons, to whom these words are addressed, represent that truth (§§5403, 5419, 5427, 5458, 5512).

[2] Here is why there would be no mercy and no bond with truth on the earthly level unless the truth represented by Benjamin submitted to

the inner goodness that is Joseph: The truth that causes a person to be a church is truth based on goodness. When we are governed by goodness, then from the standpoint of goodness we see truth and perceive it and therefore believe it to be true; but we never do this if we are not governed by goodness. Goodness is like a tiny flame that illuminates and enlightens us and causes us to see, perceive, and believe what is true. A desire for truth-from-goodness turns our inner eyes in that direction, away from worldly and bodily concerns, which impose darkness. That kind of truth is what Benjamin represents here. Truth based on goodness is the only truth in the church (see §5806)—that is, the only truth that causes us to be a church ourselves. However, such truth has to be fully subordinate to the inner goodness represented by Joseph. The Lord flows in through inner goodness, giving life to the truth below, including this truth, which is truth growing out of spiritual goodness on the earthly level (represented by Israel, §§4286, 4598).

[3] From these considerations it is also evident that truth based on goodness provides the means of union with lower kinds of truth. After all, unless this kind of truth submitted to inner goodness, enabling goodness to flow into it, there would be no acceptance of the mercy that is constantly flowing in from the Lord through inner goodness. There would be no acceptance because there would be no middle ground. And if there were no acceptance of mercy, there would be no union either.

That is the symbolism of the statement "If your youngest brother does not come down with you, you will not see my face again."

And it happened when we went up to your servant my father symbolizes being raised to the level of spiritual goodness. This can be seen from the symbolism of *going up* as being raised (dealt with below) and from the representation of Israel, the *father,* as spiritual goodness on the earthly level (discussed in §§4286, 4598).

The raising symbolized by *going up* is an elevation to more inward levels, such as the elevation here from truth on the earthly plane (represented by Jacob's ten sons) to spiritual goodness on the earthly plane (represented by Israel). The earthly plane has an outer and an inner part (§§5497, 5649). The inner earthly plane holds the spiritual goodness that is Israel, and the outer earthly plane holds the religious truths that are the sons of Jacob. Going up to their father, then, symbolizes being raised to the level of spiritual goodness.

And told him the words of my lord symbolizes a knowledge of the matter, as is evident without explanation.

5817

5818

5819   *That our father said,* symbolizes a perception received from spiritual goodness. This is established by the symbolism of *saying* in the Word's narrative parts as a perception (discussed many times) and from the representation of Israel, the *father,* as spiritual goodness (discussed at §§3654, 4286, 4598).

5820   *Go back; buy us a little food* means that goodness based on truth needs to be adopted. This is established by the symbolism of *buying* as adopting (mentioned at §§4397, 5406, 5410, 5426) and from that of *food* as truth-based goodness (mentioned at §§5410, 5426, 5487, 5582, 5588, 5655).

Spiritual food is all goodness in general, but in particular it is goodness acquired by means of truth. In other words, it is truth in our will and our actions. This truth turns into goodness by being willed and acted on and is called goodness-from-truth. Unless truth turns into goodness in this way, it is of no use to us in the other life. When we arrive in the other life, it dissolves, because it does not match our will and consequently does not suit our pleasure, or what we love. Some people learn religious truth in the world simply to know and teach it, with an eye to rank and wealth, not in order to will and do it and thereby turn it into goodness. Even if this had earned them a lofty reputation as scholars in the world, in the other life the truth they knew is taken from them and they are left to their will, that is, to their life. They then remain the kind of people they had been in their lifetime. Surprisingly, they now turn against all religious truth and deny it to themselves, however much they had formerly confirmed it.

To adopt truth-based goodness, as symbolized by *buy us a little food,* therefore means turning truth into goodness by willing and doing it—in other words, by living it.

5821   *And we said, "We cannot go down,"* symbolizes an objection, as is self-evident.

5822   *If our youngest brother is with us, we will go down* means unless the uniting middle ground is present. This can be seen from the representation of Benjamin, the *youngest brother,* as a uniting middle ground (discussed at §§5411, 5413, 5443, 5639, 5688).

Let me explain Benjamin's dual representation as a middle ground between spiritual heavenliness, or inner goodness (Joseph), and truth on the earthly plane (Jacob's ten sons) and as new truth (above at §§5804, 5806, 5809): If a middle ground is to be a middle ground, it has to partake of both inner and outer dimensions. Otherwise it is not a uniting middle ground. The middle ground that Benjamin represents partakes of the outer, earthly level by virtue of being new truth on that level. The new truth he represents exists on the earthly level because it grows out of spiritual goodness on the earthly level, represented by his father when he is named Israel (§§5686, 5689). The same middle ground partakes of the inner level represented by Joseph by receiving its inflow. So it partakes of both. That is why Benjamin represents a uniting middle ground and new truth as well—new truth when with his father, and a uniting middle ground when with Joseph.

This is a secret that cannot be explained more clearly. It cannot be understood except by people who think of humans as having an inner and an outer part, each distinct from the other, and who also have a desire for knowing what is true. Heaven's light illuminates these people's intellectual side to see what others do not—including this secret.

Because we cannot see the man's face means because there is no mercy | **5823** and no bond. This can be seen from the treatment above at §5816, where the same words occur.

And our youngest brother not be with us means [except] through the | **5824** middle ground. This is established by the representation of Benjamin as a middle ground (dealt with just above in §5822).

And your servant our father said to us symbolizes a perception received | **5825** from spiritual goodness. This is established by the symbolism of *saying* as a perception (discussed frequently) and from the representation of Israel, the *father,* as spiritual goodness on the earthly level (discussed at §§3654, 4598, 5801, 5803, 5807).

You know that my wife bore me two means that if there is spiritual | **5826** goodness in the church, there will be inner goodness and truth, as the following shows: Israel, who is referring to himself, represents spiritual goodness on the earthly level, as noted just above at §5825. Rachel, the *wife who had borne him two,* represents the desire for inner truth, as discussed in §§3758, 3782, 3793, 3819. And Joseph and Benjamin, the *two* she had borne, represent inner goodness and truth—Joseph inner goodness, and Benjamin inner truth.

[2] As for the idea that there will be inner goodness and truth if there is spiritual goodness in the church: The spiritual goodness that Israel represents is truth-based goodness, or truth in our will and our actions. This truth, or goodness-from-truth, causes the church to exist in a person. When truth has been planted in the will—and one can tell it has been by the fact that one is drawn to truth for the sake of living by it—then inner goodness and truth exist.

When we are immersed in this goodness and truth, we have the Lord's kingdom in us. We are therefore an individual church, and together with others like us, we constitute the church in general. For the church to be a church, then, there obviously has to be spiritual goodness, or truth-based goodness. There can never be truth alone, and today it is truth alone that gives the church its name and distinguishes one religion from another. Think about it: Is truth anything if it does not have life as its goal? What are doctrines without that goal? By the same token, what are the Ten Commandments without a life according to them? If someone knows them and fully understands their meaning but lives contrary to them, what good do these commandments do? Surely they do no good, and for some people they are damning. The same holds true for religious teachings taken from the Word, which are the commandments of a Christian life, since they are spiritual laws. They too are no use unless they become part of life. Consider privately whether there is anything inside you that really is anything, besides what has become part of your actual life. Consider whether human life that truly is life exists anywhere but in the will.

[3] This, then, is the reason the Lord said in the Old Testament and confirmed in the New that all the Law and all the Prophets are founded on love for God and love for one's neighbor. As a result they are founded on life itself, not on faith apart from life and therefore not on faith alone and consequently not on trust, because trust is not possible without charity for one's neighbor. If trust appears to be present in evil people during life crises or when death is at the door, it is either artificial or deceitful, because in the other life they do not display a bit of that trust, no matter how ardently they had seemed to proclaim it on their deathbed. Whether you call it trust or reliance, faith accomplishes nothing in the evil, as the Lord himself teaches in John:

> As many as did accept him, to them he gave the power to be God's children, to those believing in his name, who had their birth not from blood or from the will of the flesh or from a man's will but from God. (John 1:12, 13)

[4] Those who have their birth from blood stand for people who inflict violence on charity (§§374, 1005) and for people who profane truth (§4735). Those who have their birth from the will of the flesh stand for people caught up in the evils resulting from self-love and materialism (§3813). Those who have their birth from a man's will stand for people with a convinced belief in falsities. (A man symbolizes truth, and in

a negative sense, falsity.) Those who have their birth from God stand for people who have been regenerated by the Lord and therefore have goodness. They are the ones who accept the Lord, they are the ones who believe in his name, and they are the ones to whom he gives the power to be God's children. The others are not. This shows quite plainly what faith alone contributes to salvation.

[5] Furthermore, if we are to be reborn and become an individual church, we have to be introduced to goodness through truth, and this happens when truth becomes truth in our will and our actions. This kind of truth is goodness and is called truth-based goodness. It is constantly bringing forth new truth, because when it makes this change it starts to become fruitful for the first time. The truth then brought forth or produced is the thing called inner truth, and the goodness out of which it grows is called inner goodness. Nothing becomes inner until it has been planted in the will. Our capacity for willing is the inmost thing in us. As long as goodness and truth stand outside our will, restricted to our intellect, they stand outside us, because our intellect is outside and our will is within.

And one went out from me symbolizes the apparent departure of inner **5827** goodness. This is clear from the symbolism of *going out* or leaving as a departure and from the representation of Joseph as inner goodness (mentioned above). Clearly the departure was merely apparent, because Joseph was still alive.

Here is the situation: Everything said about Joseph, from beginning to end, in order, represents the glorification of the Lord's human side. On a lower level of meaning, then, it represents a person's rebirth, which is an image or model of the Lord's glorification (§§3138, 3212, 3296, 3490, 4402, 5688). Regarding a person's rebirth: In the first stage, when we are being introduced to goodness through truth, truth is easy to see, because it dwells in the world's light, not far from the physical senses. Goodness is not easy to see, though, because it dwells in heaven's light, far from the physical senses, since it dwells inside, in our spirit. That is why the truth of which faith consists is easy to see but goodness is not, even though it is always present, flowing in and giving life to truth. Otherwise we could never be reborn. Once this stage ends, goodness reveals itself. It reveals itself as love for our neighbor and a desire for truth for the sake of living by it.

These are the realities represented by Joseph and the fact that he was taken away and was not visible to his father but eventually revealed himself to him. That is also what is meant by the apparent departure of inner goodness, symbolized by *one went out from me.*

5828   *And I said, "Surely he has been mauled,"* symbolizes a sense that it had been destroyed by evil and falsity. This can be seen from the symbolism of *saying* as a perception (discussed often) and from that of *being mauled* as being destroyed by evil and falsity. The destruction is that of the inner goodness represented by Joseph (§5805).

This is the symbolism of mauling because the only kind of mauling that happens in the spiritual world is the mauling of goodness by evil and falsity. It is the same as with death and everything surrounding death, which in a spiritual sense does not mean physical death but spiritual death, or damnation. There is no other kind of death in the spiritual world. Mauling in a spiritual sense likewise does not mean the kind of mauling wild animals do but the tearing apart of goodness by evil and falsity. Additionally, in a spiritual sense, animals that maul symbolize evil cravings and the falsities they give rise to, and in the other life, these are represented by wild animals.

[2] Goodness, which is constantly flowing into us from the Lord, is destroyed only by evil and the resulting falsity, and by falsity and the resulting evil. As soon as the flow of goodness through the inner self reaches the outer, earthly self, it is met by evil and falsity, which maul and obliterate it in various ways as wild animals would. This blocks off and stops up the flow of goodness through the inner self and therefore closes the inner mind, which is the channel for the flow. It lets through only enough spiritual force to enable the earthly self to reason and talk, but only in earthly, bodily, and worldly terms at that, and only in opposition to goodness and truth, or else in accord with them as a sham or a lie.

[3] It is a universal law that inflow adapts to outflow. If the outflow stops, the inflow stops. Goodness and truth from the Lord flow in through the inner self and have to flow out through the outer self. That means they have to flow out into a person's life, which means into the exercise of neighborly love. When they do flow out, the inflow from heaven—or rather from the Lord through heaven—is steady. On the other hand there may be no outflow. The outer, earthly self may put up the resistance of evil and falsity, which maul and obliterate the inflowing goodness. If so, the above-mentioned universal law inevitably leads the inflow to adapt to the outflow, and the inflow of goodness consequently withdraws, shutting off its inner channel. This closure causes so much stupidity in spiritual

matters that the person does not know anything about eternal life and does not want to know. People like this go crazy in the end. They pit falsity against truth, calling falsity truth, and truth falsity. They pit evil against goodness, deeming evil good and goodness evil. So they tear goodness to shreds.

[4] The Word in various places mentions torn flesh, which in its proper meaning symbolizes something destroyed by the falsity that comes of evil. Anything destroyed by evil, though, is called a carcass. When torn flesh is mentioned by itself, it means both; the one symbolism involves the other. It is different when the two terms are used together, because they are then distinguished.

Since torn flesh in a spiritual sense symbolized something destroyed by the falsity that comes of evil, the representative religion had a ban on eating torn flesh. Such a thing would never have been forbidden had this spiritual evil not been meant by it in heaven. Otherwise, what harm would there have been in eating flesh torn by a wild animal?

[5] Here is what Moses says about not eating what is torn:

> The fat of a *carcass* and the fat of *torn flesh* shall be for every use, as long as you absolutely do not eat it. (Leviticus 7:24)

In the same author:

> *Carcass* and *torn flesh* they shall not eat, or they will be defiled with it; I am Jehovah. (Leviticus 22:8)

In the same author:

> Men of holiness you shall be to me. Therefore you shall not eat *flesh torn in the field;* you shall throw it to the dogs. (Exodus 22:31)

In Ezekiel:

> "Oh, Lord Jehovih!" says the prophet. "Look: My soul has not been defiled, and a *carcass* and *torn flesh* I have not eaten from my youth up to now, so that *abominable flesh* has not come into my mouth." (Ezekiel 4:14)

These passages show that eating torn flesh was an abomination, not because it was torn but because it symbolized the mauling of goodness by falsities rising out of evil; while a carcass symbolized the death of goodness at the hand of evil.

[6] The mauling of goodness by falsity and evil is also meant in an inner sense in the following places in David:

> The likeness of the ungodly is as a lion—they long to *maul*—and as a young lion that sits in its hiding places. (Psalms 17:12)

In another place:

> They opened their mouth against me as *a lion mauling* and roaring. (Psalms 22:13)

And in yet another place:

> May they not seize my soul like a lion, *mauling* but no one rescuing! (Psalms 7:2)

The lion stands for people who devastate the church.

Earlier in Joseph's story, too, when his brothers sold him, dipped his coat in blood, and sent it to his father, his father said, "My son's coat. A *bad wild animal* ate him up; *Joseph has surely been mauled*" (Genesis 37:33). See that spot, §4777, for the idea that being mauled means being dispersed by the falsity that rises out of evil.

5829   *And I have not seen him up till now* means because it had vanished, as is self-evident.

5830   *And you are taking this one also from my presence* means if the new truth also leaves, as the following shows: Benjamin, the subject of these words, represents new truth, as discussed in §§5804, 5806, 5809, 5822. And *taking him from my presence* symbolizes removal from spiritual goodness and therefore departure. New truth grows out of spiritual goodness (Israel), so if it leaves, spiritual goodness is at an end. Goodness takes its quality from truth, and truth takes its very existence from goodness, and this brings both to life simultaneously.

5831   *And should harm happen to him* means from evil and falsity. This can be seen from the symbolism of *harm's happening to someone* as being hurt by evil and falsity. No other harm is meant in a spiritual sense, because in the spiritual world, all harm comes from there—from evil and falsity.

5832   *You will make my white hair go down in evil to the grave* means that spiritual goodness and therefore the core of the church will perish, as the following shows: Israel represents spiritual goodness (as noted in §§5807, 5812, 5813, 5817, 5819, 5825) and the inner core of a spiritual religion (§4286). *White hair* symbolizes the end of the church. And *going down in evil to the grave* means perishing (as noted in §4785). Going down in goodness to the grave and rising again means being reborn (§§2916, 2917, 5551), so going down in evil to the grave means the opposite: perishing.

To expand on the idea that the core of the church will perish if the truth represented by Benjamin is lost: Goodness needs to have its truth in order to be goodness, and truth needs to have its goodness in order to be truth. Goodness without truth is not good, and truth without goodness is not true. They combine in a marriage, which is called the heavenly marriage. If one leaves, then, the other perishes, and a mauling by evil and falsity can part them.

And now as I come to your servant my father symbolizes goodness in the church, corresponding to spiritual goodness in the inner part of the church. This can be seen from the representation of Judah, who is talking about himself, as goodness in the church (mentioned at §§5583, 5603, 5782) and from that of Israel, *his father,* as spiritual goodness (mentioned at §§5807, 5812, 5813, 5817, 5819, 5825). **5833**

The goodness that Judah represents in the church is goodness in the outer part of the church, but the spiritual goodness that Israel represents is goodness in the inner part of the church (§4286). Every church that is the Lord's has an inner and an outer part, and the attributes of the outer part correspond to those of the inner part. So the goodness that is Judah in the church corresponds to the spiritual goodness that is Israel.

And the youth is not with us means if the new truth is not present. This is established by the representation of Benjamin, the *youth,* as new truth (discussed at §§5804, 5806, 5822). **5834**

And [the father's] soul is bound up in [the youth's] soul means since there is a tight bond. This can be seen from the symbolism of a *soul* as life. *The one's soul is bound up in the other's soul* therefore means that the life of one lies within the life of the other and consequently that there is a tight bond. The bond is between spiritual goodness (Israel) and the truth growing out of that goodness (Benjamin). **5835**

Here is how matters stand with the fact that there is as tight a bond between goodness and its truth as the soul of one bound up in the soul of another: The human mind—the actual person, where a person's life resides—has two faculties, one devoted to the truth composing faith and the other devoted to the goodness composing neighborly love. The faculty devoted to the truth composing faith is called the intellect, and the one devoted to the goodness composing neighborly love is called the will. If a person is to be a person, these two faculties have to make a single whole.

[2] In modern times, though, the two faculties are utterly separate, as demonstrated by the fact that we can understand that something is true and yet can fail to will it. We can understand that all the contents of the Ten Commandments are true and that to some extent so are the contents of doctrines drawn from the Word. In fact, we can confirm them in our intellect or by preaching about them. But we still wish otherwise, and from wishing, act otherwise, which shows that the two faculties are separate in us.

They should not be separate, however, as can be seen from the fact that understanding truth would lift us up toward heaven, while willing evil would drag us down toward hell. We would then hang suspended between the two. Even so, our will, in which our real, actual life consists, would pull us downward and we would inevitably wind up in hell. To prevent this, the two faculties need to be united, which is accomplished through regeneration by the Lord, which in turn is accomplished through the planting of faith's truth in charity's goodness. Through faith's truth we then receive the gift of a new intellect, and through charity's goodness we then receive the gift of a new will. As a result we have two faculties constituting one mind.

5836   *It will happen, as he sees that the youth is not there, that he will die* means that spiritual goodness will perish—if the truth that is Benjamin leaves, that is. This is established by the representation of Israel as spiritual goodness (discussed before) and by the symbolism of *dying* as ceasing to be what it is (discussed in §494) and therefore as perishing. For the idea that goodness would perish if the truth connected with it left, see above at §§5830, 5832.

5837   *And your servants will make the white hair of your servant our father go down in sorrow to the grave* means that it will be all over for the church. This is established by the explanation above at §5832, where similar words appear.

Israel (the *father*) means the church here because the spiritual goodness he represents constitutes the church in a person—so much so that it is the same whether you say spiritual goodness or the church. They cannot be separated. That is why Israel in the Word (especially in its prophetic parts) means a spiritual religion.

5838   Genesis 44:32, 33, 34. *"Because your servant served as surety for the youth with [my] father, saying, 'If I do not bring him back to you, I will be sinning against my father all my days.' And now let your servant please stay in place of the youth as a slave to my lord, and let the youth go up with his*

*brothers. Because how am I going to go up to my father and the youth not be
with me? Maybe I will see the evil that will find my father."*

Because your servant served as surety for the youth with my father, saying,
symbolizes a connection with [Judah]. *If I do not bring him back to you*
means unless it is united with spiritual goodness. *I will be sinning against
my father all my days* symbolizes a turning away, with the result that there
is no goodness in the church. *And now let your servant please stay in place
of the youth as a slave to my lord* symbolizes surrender. *And let the youth go
up with his brothers* means in order for inner truth to unite with spiritual
goodness. *Because how am I going to go up to my father and the youth not
be with me?* symbolizes spiritual goodness on the earthly level, without
inner truth. *Maybe I will see the evil that will find my father* symbolizes an
awareness that it will perish.

Because your servant served as surety for the youth with my father, say- **5839**
ing, symbolizes a connection. This can be seen from the symbolism of
being surety as connecting something to oneself (as before, at §5609).
During a time when the truth that Benjamin represents is not really with
the spiritual goodness that his *father* represents, it can accompany the
goodness that exists in the outward part of the church, which Judah represents. This latter goodness and spiritual goodness act in unison through
correspondence.

If I do not bring him back to you means unless it is united with spiri- **5840**
tual goodness. This can be seen from the symbolism of *bringing back*
as reuniting and from the representation of Israel as spiritual goodness
(mentioned many times before).

I will be sinning against my father all my days symbolizes a turning **5841**
away, with the result that there is no goodness in the church. This can be
seen from the symbolism of *sinning* as disconnection (noted at §§5229,
5474) and therefore as a turning away. If goodness in the outward part
of the church (represented by Judah) turns its back on goodness in the
inward part (represented by Israel), there ceases to be any goodness at all
in the church. The connection itself brings into existence the goodness
from which the church springs.

Here is the situation with the two kinds of goodness, in the inward
and outward parts of the church: Goodness in the inward part of the
church, or inner goodness, flows in and produces goodness in the outward part of the church, or outer goodness. This being so, inner goodness
raises the outer goodness up to its own level, leading outer goodness to
focus on inner goodness and through inner goodness to look up toward

the Lord. That is what happens when they are united. If there is disconnection, on the other hand, outer goodness turns its back and looks downward, which destroys it.

This is the turning away symbolized by *I will be sinning against my father all my days.*

5842   *And now let your servant please stay in place of the youth as a slave to my lord* symbolizes surrender. This can be seen from the consideration that offering oneself as a slave in place of another means depriving oneself of the freedom of self-rule and surrendering to another absolutely.

These words symbolize the surrender of the earthly, outer self to the inner. When goodness in the outer self surrenders, you see, the truth there does too, because truth belongs to goodness.

5843   *And let the youth go up with his brothers* means in order for inner truth to unite with spiritual goodness, as the following shows: Benjamin represents new truth, as discussed in §§5804, 5806, 5809, 5822, and therefore inner truth. And *going up with his brothers* means being reunited with his father, that is, with the spiritual goodness that Israel represents. The inner truth that Benjamin represents here is new truth, because new truth is more inward than the truth below it. Truth that develops out of goodness is inner truth, and that is what new truth is, because it develops out of the spiritual goodness that is Israel.

Charitable goodness rising out of the will and therefore out of desire is inner goodness, or goodness in the inward part of the church. Charitable goodness rising out of obedience rather than desire, and out of doctrine rather than the will, is outer goodness, or goodness in the outward part of the church. The same can also be said of the truth resulting from each kind of goodness.

5844   *Because how am I going to go up to my father and the youth not be with me?* symbolizes spiritual goodness on the earthly level, without inner truth. This can be seen from the representation of Israel, the *father,* as spiritual goodness on the earthly level (discussed before) and from the representation of Benjamin, the *youth,* as inner truth (discussed just above at §5843).

5845   *Maybe I will see the evil that will find my father* symbolizes an awareness that it will perish. This is established by the symbolism of *seeing* as understanding (discussed in §§2807, 3863, 4403–4421) and therefore as perceiving (§§3764, 4567, 5400). The fact that it will perish is symbolized by the *evil that will find him.* The meaning resembles that of "making his white hair go down in evil to the grave" (§5832), and of the father's dying if he did not see Benjamin with his brothers (§5836). This is the *evil* that is symbolized.

For the fact that the spiritual goodness that is Israel will perish if the truth that is Benjamin leaves it, see above at §5832.

The Angels and Spirits with Us

THE overarching rule for the spiritual world's *inflow* into us is that we cannot think or will anything on our own; everything flows in. Goodness and truth come from the Lord through heaven and therefore through the angels with us. Evil and falsity come from hell and therefore through the evil spirits with us. These flow into our thought and our will.   **5846**

I know that this is true, although it cannot help boggling the mind, since it is contrary to appearances. Actual experience, however, must determine how the matter stands.

People, spirits, and angels absolutely do not have life on their own, so they cannot think or will on their own either, since to think and to will is our life. (The kind of life that consists in talking and doing is derived from it.) There is only one life force, and that is the Lord's. It flows into all of us, but we receive it in different ways, depending on the nature we have given our own soul by the way we live. Goodness and truth consequently turn into evil and falsity in evil people, but good people receive goodness as goodness, and truth as truth.   **5847**

A comparison can be drawn with light, which flows from the sun into physical objects, where it is modified. The form of the component parts changes the light in various ways, turning it into either gloomy or cheerful colors.

The whole time we are living in the world, we are shaping the most refined substances of our inward parts, so that we can be said to be forming our soul, or our character. This form determines how we receive the Lord's life, which is the life of his love for the entire human race.

For the idea that there is only one life force and that people, spirits, and angels merely receive life, see §§1954, 2021, 2706, 2886–2889, 2893,

3001, 3318, 3337, 3338, 3484, 3741, 3742, 3743, 4151, 4249, 4318, 4319, 4320, 4417, 4524, 4882.

5848   In order that the Lord's life can flow in and be received in exactly the way prescribed for us, we always have angels and spirits with us—angels from heaven and spirits from hell. I have been told that we each have two spirits and two angels.

The reason there are spirits from hell is that of ourselves we are always absorbed in evil, because we are always absorbed in the pleasures of self-love and materialism. To the extent that we are absorbed in evil, or in those pleasures, angels from heaven cannot be present with us.

5849   The two spirits connected to us put us in contact with hell, and the two angels put us in contact with heaven. If we were not in touch with heaven and hell, we could not live for even a second. Deprived of the two kinds of communication, we would fall down as dead as a log, because we would then be deprived of connection with the original source of existence—the Lord.

This too was once demonstrated to me by experience. The spirits with me backed off a little, and as they did, I started to feel as though I were dying. I really would have died, too, if they had not been sent back to me.

However, I know that few believe they have any companion spirit or even that there are such things as spirits. The main reason for their skepticism is that there is no faith today because there is no neighborly love. So people do not believe in hell or heaven, and accordingly they do not believe in life after death. A second reason is that they do not see spirits with their eyes. "If I saw them I'd believe in them," they say. "What I see exists, but if I can't see something, I don't know whether it exists." Yet they realize—or are capable of realizing—that human vision is too dull and crude to see the most superficial phenomena of the physical world even when these are comparatively obvious. The optical devices that render such things visible prove it to be so. How then could the human eye see beyond the more refined levels of nature to where spirits and angels exist? We can see these beings only with the eye of our inner self, which is adapted to seeing such sights. The eye of our inner self, though, is not open to us as long as we are in the world, for many reasons.

This evidence now shows how wide a gap there is between modern faith and the faith of ancient times, which was that we each had our own angel with us.

Here is the situation: There is a *general inflow* and a *particular inflow*   **5850**
from the Lord through the spiritual world into recipients of that inflow in
the physical world. The general inflow affects recipients that follow the code
ordained for them; the particular inflow affects recipients that do not.

Animals of every kind live by the code ordained by their nature, so
general inflow is what affects them. Their adherence to that code can be
seen in the fact that they are born with everything they need. They need
no instruction in order to assume their role.

We human beings, on the other hand, do not live by the code ordained
for us or by any individual law of that code, so particular inflow is what
affects us. That is, we have with us angels and spirits through whom the
inflow occurs. If we did not, we would hurl ourselves into every kind of
wickedness and quickly plunge headlong into the deepest hell. The spirits
and angels bring us under the Lord's control and guidance.

If we followed the code we were created to live by, we would love our
neighbor as ourselves and in fact more than ourselves. That is what angels
do. Instead we love only ourselves and the world. We hate our fellow
human beings except to the extent that they encourage our domineering
ways and give us worldly blessings. Since our lives go directly against the
heavenly pattern, then, the Lord governs us through individual spirits
and angels.

The same spirits do not stay with us permanently. Rather, they change   **5851**
as we change in regard to the state of our desires, or of our passions and
goals. Earlier spirits leave and new ones take their place.

The spirits with us are ones that resemble us, generally. If we are
greedy, we have greedy spirits with us. If we are arrogant, we have arrogant spirits. If we are vengeful, we have vengeful spirits. If we are underhanded, we have underhanded ones. We invite spirits from hell in accord
with our life.

The hells are divided up very precisely along the lines of evil desire
in all its different varieties, so a person in whom evil is active never lacks
like-minded spirits to call on and connect with.

Although the evil spirits we have with us are from the hells, they are   **5852**
not actually in hell while they are with us but are removed from it. The
place they then inhabit is midway between hell and heaven and is called
the world of spirits. I have mentioned this place many times before.

The realm called the world of spirits is inhabited by good spirits too,
who also keep us company. We enter that world immediately upon death,

and after spending time there, we are sent off to the underground region, or let down into hell, or taken up into heaven, depending on the way we have lived. The world of spirits forms the upper boundary of the hells— which either close off or open up there in the Lord's good pleasure—and the lower boundary of heaven. Consequently it creates a gap separating heaven from hell. This shows what the world of spirits is.

When the evil spirits with us are in that world, they are not suffering any hellish torment. No, they are enjoying the pleasures of self-love and materialism and all the indulgences we ourselves are enjoying, because they are sharing all our thoughts and feelings. When they are sent back to their hell, though, they return to their previous condition.

5853   The spirits who come to us enter into the entire contents of our memory, including every bit of knowledge we possess. They make it all their own (so thoroughly that they have no idea it is *not* theirs). This is an advantage spirits have over people on earth. As a result, they think whatever we think, and intend whatever we intend. The reverse is also true; whatever they think, we think, and whatever they intend, we intend. Spirits and people act as one because of their common bond.

Each party considers itself the home and origin of the thoughts and intents; the spirits do, and the people do. This is not the case, however.

5854   The Lord provides that spirits influence our thoughts and wishes but that angels influence our ultimate goals, and through our goals, the consequences that result. Angels also flow through good spirits into the good deeds we do and the religious truth we believe, using these to lead us away from evil and falsity as much as possible. Their influence is silent, and imperceptible to us, but even though it is secret, it works.

Angels' main role is to turn aside evil aims and inspire good ones; to the extent they cannot do this, they withdraw and exert a relatively distant, remote influence. Evil spirits then move in. You see, angels cannot be present in evil aims, or in self-love and materialism, but they remain present at a distance.

[2] The Lord, working through angels, *could* lead us to good aims by his almighty power, but to do so would be to rob us of life, because our life is composed of passions directly opposed to good aims. It is therefore an unbreakable law of God that we are to be free, and that the seeds of goodness and truth, or of neighborly love and faith, are to be planted in the soil of our freedom, never in the soil of coercion. What is accepted under pressure does not last; it vanishes. To force something on us is not to infuse it into our will, because it is someone else's will that we are being

obliged to carry out. When we regain our own will, then, or our freedom, we root it out. The Lord consequently governs us by means of our freedom and withholds us as much as he can from the freedom of thinking and intending evil. If the Lord did not withhold us, we would constantly plunge headlong into the lowest hell.

[3] As just mentioned, the Lord, working through angels, could lead us to good aims by his almighty power. Even if evil spirits surrounded us by the millions, they could be driven off instantly, and by a single angel. But we would then encounter such fierce pain and such awful hell that we could never endure it. We would have our life ripped from us in the most wretched way. After all, our life consists of cravings and delusions opposed to what is good and true. If this life were not sustained by evil spirits and were not gradually being put right, it would be reduced to almost nothing. We would not survive a split second. What is lodged within us, pure and simple, is self-love, love of gain, and a love of the resulting prestige—in other words, whatever opposes the ordained plan. If we were not reduced to compliance with that plan in a temperate, gradual way, by the redirection of our freedom, we would die at once.

Until the opportunity to talk with spirits opened up to me, I held the **5855** opinion that no spirit or angel but only God could possibly know and perceive my thoughts, since they were inside me. Afterward, though, I once happened to notice that a certain spirit did know what I was thinking, because he said a few words about it to me and gave a sign indicating he was present. I was dumbfounded, mainly at his knowing my thoughts.

This showed me how much difficulty people have believing that a spirit could ever know what they were thinking. In reality, though, spirits know not only the thoughts we ourselves are aware of but also thoughts and feelings we are unaware of, in exquisite detail. In fact, they know things we never could know in bodily life. This I have learned from many years of constant experience.

Communities make contact with each other by sending spirits out **5856** to speak on their behalf. These spirits are called *agents*. On the occasions when a community would join me, I could not tell it was there until its inhabitants sent me a spirit. The instant they sent a spirit, a channel of communication opened. This is quite an ordinary event in the other life and happens often.

Clearly, then, the purpose of the spirits and angels with us is to provide contact with communities in hell and in heaven.

5857   Several times I talked with some spirits about an ability in which they far excel people on earth, and that is the ability to adopt all the contents of a person's memory as soon as they reach the person. Even if the spirits previously knew nothing about the academic disciplines, about languages, or about the subjects the person had been taught and trained in from childhood to old age, they still take possession of it all in a moment. With the erudite they are therefore erudite; with the clever they are clever; with the wise they are wise.

The spirits I was talking to swelled with pride over these observations, because they were not good spirits, so I was allowed to add that with the ignorant they are ignorant, with the stupid they are stupid, and with crazy fools they are crazy fools. They adopt everything inside the person they are with, so they also adopt all the person's errors, delusions, and falsities. Accordingly, they adopt all the person's insanities and follies.

They cannot approach babies, because babies do not yet have anything in their memory for the spirits to adopt. A baby's companions are therefore good spirits and angels.

5858   A great deal of experience has taught me that when spirits use the memory of a person on earth, they imagine that everything they think and say is theirs and is inside them. If you tell them that is not the case, they fume. Such is the sensory illusion that controls them.

To convince them it was not true, I asked, "How do you know how to speak my native language, even though you knew absolutely nothing about it during your bodily life? And how do you know the other languages I know, not one of which you knew on your own? Do you think these things are yours?" I read Hebrew to them, too. They understood it as well as I did (even the children among them) and no better. "And everything I know about the arts and sciences, you know," I said. This convinced them that when they join a person they come into possession of all the person's knowledge and that they are mistaken in considering it their own.

They do have their own knowledge, but they are not allowed to draw on it [when they are with us], because they are to use what is ours in helping us. There are many other reasons as well, which are discussed in §§2476, 2477, 2479. In addition, extreme confusion would result if spirits flowed into us with their own memory (§2478).

5859   Some spirits came climbing up to me saying they had been with me from the start, since they did not know any better. Because I proved the opposite to them, though, they eventually admitted they had just arrived.

They said they could not have known any better, since they had immediately adopted the entire contents of my memory. This also demonstrated that the moment spirits arrive they adopt all our knowledge as their own. Even when a crowd of spirits is present, they all adopt the knowledge individually and all imagine individually that it is theirs. People develop this ability immediately after death.

This is another reason why good spirits, when they go to a community in heaven, appropriate as their own all the wisdom shared by everyone in that community. Such is the common bond there. They share in the wisdom even if during physical life they had been totally ignorant on the kinds of topics that community discusses—as long as they had lived a life of charitable goodness in the world. It is inherent in such goodness to make all wisdom its own; the tendency is intrinsic to goodness itself. As a result, such spirits understand spontaneously (so to speak) what had been incomprehensible and even ineffable to them during bodily life.

The spirits with us also adopt our false convictions, whatever those may be, as has been borne out for me by much experience. They adopt our delusions not only on public and private issues but also on spiritual questions of faith. Plainly, then, when spirits are with people who subscribe to heresies, to fallacies and delusions regarding religious truth, and to outright falsities, the spirits have the same bad thinking and do not waver from it a hair's breadth. The purpose is to leave people in freedom and prevent a spirit's own ideas from causing them trouble. **5860**

All this evidence shows several things: While we are living in the world we are in company with other spirits in regard to our inner depths and therefore in regard to our own spirit. We are so tightly linked to them that we cannot think or will anything unless we do so in unison with them. This puts our inner reaches in touch with the spiritual world. And it is the only way the Lord can lead us. **5861**

When people enter the other life, they take with them an inability to believe any spirit had ever been with them, let alone a spirit from hell. If they wish, then, they are shown the community of spirits in whose company they had been—the community whose messenger spirits had been present with them. After first going through several other necessary stages, they eventually return to that same community, because it is at one with the kind of love that came to reign supreme in them.

Several times I have observed as [newcomers] were shown their communities.

5862   The spirits with us do not know they are with us; only angels from the Lord know. This is because they are connected to our soul, or spirit, not to our body. Thoughts expressed in bodily speech, and wishes expressed in bodily deeds, flow into action in an orderly way by means of general inflow, and correspondence with the universal human governs the process. The spirits with us, then, have no part in the process. They do not talk through our tongue; that would be possession. Neither do they see anything in the world through our eyes or hear anything in the world through our ears.

Not so with me. The Lord has opened my inner levels to let me see sights in the other world, so spirits have realized that I am a person still living in the body. They have been granted the ability to see worldly sights through my eyes and to hear the people around me talking with me.

5863   If evil spirits could tell they were with us and distinct from us, and if they could influence our bodily activity, they would try to destroy us a thousand ways, because they hate us with a deadly hatred. Since they *have* seen that I am a person still living in the body, they have kept up a continual attempt to destroy not just my body but more especially my soul. After all, destroying a person or a spirit is life's highest pleasure for everyone in hell. The Lord has constantly protected me, though.

This shows how dangerous it is to be in direct contact with spirits if you do not have a goodness that comes of faith.

5864   Some evil spirits heard that spirits are present with a person, so they decided to find the particular spirits who were with a given person. They searched a long time but without success. What they had in mind was to destroy [the person and the spirits]. Just as heaven's pleasure and bliss is to help people and contribute to their eternal welfare, so it is hell's pleasure in turn to hurt people and promote their eternal ruin. They are therefore on opposite sides.

5865   There was a spirit—not an evil one—who was allowed to cross over to a certain person and talk with me from there. When the spirit reached the person, he said the person looked to him like something black and inanimate, like a black lump devoid of life. It was the person's physical life that the spirit was being allowed to observe.

I was told that when one is permitted to observe the physical life of a person committed to the goodness called for by faith, it does not look black but has the appearance and color of wood.

Another experience taught me the same thing. A certain evil spirit was put into a physical state by thinking thoughts that were based on the physical senses and therefore on his outer memory. He too then looked to me like a lifeless black lump. When he was restored, he said he thought he had been alive in his body.

Aside from these experiences, spirits are not allowed to look at people's bodily plane. A person's bodily plane exists in the world and its light. When spirits look at objects of worldly light, those objects look like mere black spots.

There is more on the angels and spirits with us at the end of the next chapter [§§5976–5993].

5866

[CONTINUED IN VOLUME 9]

Biographical Note

EMANUEL SWEDENBORG (1688–1772) was born Emanuel Swedberg (or Svedberg) in Stockholm, Sweden, on January 29, 1688 (Julian calendar). He was the third of the nine children of Jesper Swedberg (1653–1735) and Sara Behm (1666–1696). At the age of eight he lost his mother. After the death of his only older brother ten days later, he became the oldest living son. In 1697 his father married Sara Bergia (1666–1720), who developed great affection for Emanuel and left him a significant inheritance. His father, a Lutheran clergyman, later became a celebrated and controversial bishop, whose diocese included the Swedish churches in Pennsylvania and in London, England.

After studying at the University of Uppsala (1699–1709), Emanuel journeyed to England, the Netherlands, France, and Germany (1710–1715) to study and work with leading scientists in western Europe. Upon his return he apprenticed as an engineer under the brilliant Swedish inventor Christopher Polhem (1661–1751). He gained favor with Sweden's King Charles XII (1682–1718), who gave him a salaried position as an overseer of Sweden's mining industry (1716–1747). Although Emanuel was engaged, he never married.

After the death of Charles XII, Emanuel was ennobled by Queen Ulrika Eleonora (1688–1741), and his last name was changed to Swedenborg (or Svedenborg). This change in status gave him a seat in the Swedish House of Nobles, where he remained an active participant in the Swedish government throughout his life.

A member of the Royal Swedish Academy of Sciences, he devoted himself to studies that culminated in a number of publications, most notably a comprehensive three-volume work on natural philosophy and metallurgy (1734) that brought him recognition across Europe as a scientist. After 1734 he redirected his research and publishing to a study of anatomy in search of the interface between the soul and body, making several significant discoveries in physiology.

From 1743 to 1745 he entered a transitional phase that resulted in a shift of his main focus from science to theology. Throughout the rest of his life he maintained that this shift was brought about by Jesus Christ, who appeared to him, called him to a new mission, and opened his perception to a permanent dual consciousness of this life and the life after death.

He devoted the last decades of his life to studying Scripture and publishing eighteen theological titles that draw on the Bible, reasoning, and his own spiritual experiences. These works present a Christian theology with unique perspectives on the nature of God, the spiritual world, the Bible, the human mind, and the path to salvation.

Swedenborg died in London on March 29, 1772 (Gregorian calendar), at the age of eighty-four.